D0046497

MANAGING A FEDERAL AGENCY

Louis K. Bragaw is professor of management at the Hartford
Graduate Center of Rensselaer Polytechnic Institute. President of the
Eastern Academy of Management in 1979, he is coauthor of several
books, including *The Challenge of Deepwater Terminals*. Dr. Bragaw
was head of the department of economics and management at the
United States Coast Guard Academy from 1969 to 1980.

MANAGING A FEDERAL AGENCY

THE HIDDEN STIMULUS

LOUIS K. BRAGAW

The Johns Hopkins University Press
Baltimore and London

The Johns Hopkins University Press, Baltimore, Maryland 21218
The Johns Hopkins Press Ltd., London

Library of Congress Cataloging in Publication Data
Bragaw, Louis K
  Managing a Federal agency.
  Bibliography: p. 285
  Includes index.
  1. United States. Coast Guard—Management.   I. Title.
HJ6645.B67   353.0074   79-27702
ISBN 0-8018-2265-3

*For Kathy, Lou, Steve, and Joe
and for Mary*

CONTENTS

FIGURES

TABLES

PREFACE

This book describes the process of managing one federal agency—the United States Coast Guard. The audience for the book is broad; it may include both private and public decision-makers who are interested in improving the performance of federal agencies by understanding better how general management theory applies to the public sector; educators interested in generic applications of general management theory; and students of private and public management alike. The audience also includes those interested in the policies of the federal government toward the marine industry and the marine environment and in how the Coast Guard has been involved with these policies since 1790.

In the federal agency chosen as a sample, we find at work a hidden stimulus for efficiency, effectiveness, and even innovation. In weak form, this hidden stimulus is the threat of a budget cut; in stronger form it is the threat of a loss of one or more programs; and in severe form, there may be the threat of an outright liquidation of the agency. Though this stimulus is a basic and even a negative force, it has had significant effect on the behavior of the agency studied. The judicious application of this hidden stimulus in the public sector can improve the general management processes of federal agencies.

The sample agency—the United States Coast Guard is examined from three perspectives: how, historically, it has evolved a strategy and a structure; how, organizationally, it has developed a planning and a resource allocation process; and how, managerially, it has responded to the challenges of the external environment.

The book begins by developing six categorical charges often leveled against government agencies and posing three research questions designed to delineate the problems involved in agency management. The most serious charge is that government agencies lack the stimulus for effectiveness, efficiency, and innovation that is provided in the private sector by the market mechanism and by competition. This charge is predicated on the popular belief that the public sector has no parallel to the market mechanism and to competition. The final charge leads to the three research questions, which explore whether some analogous stimulus to innovation exists in the public sector, and examines possible responses to such a stimulus.

To respond to the categorical charges and to answer the research questions, the book looks at the management process as conducted within the modern Coast Guard structure, focusing on how resource allocation processes interact with several levels of internal structure and with the external environment that surrounds the structure.

The book then examines how the Coast Guard has dealt with certain challenges from the external environment, looking specifically at loran, a long-range radio-navigation system, and at the Marine Environmental Protection program. The hidden stimulus proves to be a hierarchy of threats ranging from budget cuts to program losses to extinction as an identifiable organization—a distinctive public-sector analogue to the supposed private-sector stimulus of the market mechanism and competition that has brought about proactive and often innovative behavior by the Coast Guard. Because similar responses occur in the two sectors, there is great potential for transferring general management techniques between them. But to understand the hidden stimulus and use it to stimulate the desired behavior in the federal organization one must understand and use the three-branch form of the American government and the institutions that have grown up around it.

The ubiquitous presence of the hidden stimulus in the case of this federal agency has helped the Coast Guard avoid many of the pitfalls and problems often associated with general management of a federal agency. The mechanism through which this stimulus works is in itself a fundamental difference between public and private management.

Some studies of differences between public and private management focus on superficial variations such as the civil service system versus a private personnel system, or the public planning and budgeting system versus a private planning and budgeting system. Though this book discusses these areas of difference, it goes beyond and attempts to identify a fundamental theory of difference between public and private management. Although the general management responses of federal agencies are similar to general management responses of large organizations in the private sector, the hypothesis that the stimulus to efficient performance is quite different in the two sectors has profound implications for effective management in the public sector.

This theory of difference in stimulus-response patterns has wide potential application for all who deal with and attempt to understand the behavior of large public organizations. The importance of this subject has received wide recognition—as evidenced by the problems of our cities, the spreading popularity of "Proposition 13" politics, and the growing concern over the sheer size of the federal government—to say nothing of the size and effectiveness of the federal budget and the inflationary economy it has helped spawn. This book deals with these applications as they apply to one federal agency, the United States Coast Guard. The importance of better applications of general management theory in the public sector, however, can only become even more widely recognized in the years ahead as the nation deals with the dilemmas of inflation and government spending. One key to a better economy will involve an integrated strategy designed to restore economic growth without inflation. Effective use of monetary and fiscal policy will help. I believe the president and Congress will find political acceptance for the hidden stimulus as an important part of this strategy.

ACKNOWLEDGMENTS

Appreciation is due many individuals and organizations whose contributions made this book possible. The list of thank yous is long because ideas for the project span not only my academic career of the last ten years but my years as a Coast Guard officer as well.

The plan for the research was born in concept in May 1973 in a discussion with Professor James P. Baughman of Harvard University. We examined ways to relate the business policy and planning literature to the process of strategic management in a federal agency. The ideas developed during that discussion were expanded and tested in the spring of 1974 in a seminar at the United States Coast Guard Academy. The possibility for a book took further shape in discussions in the summer of 1974 with Captains James S. Gracey and John D. Costello and Rear Admiral Edward D. Scheiderer, then chief of staff of the Coast Guard.

A cadet sent to Washington on a summer project told one of these officers that a Coast Guard professor taught cadets the Coast Guard budget was the outcome of a top admiral presenting a "shopping list" written on the back of an envelope to his favorite congressman, and taught them the Coast Guard would not "fight" for a proper budget. The officer, in charge of budget preparation, asked me if I was interested in writing about the budget process and dispelling these myths. He also asked me to develop a model that would accurately forecast Coast Guard budget requirements. The resulting model became known as "Coast Guard Limited" and was very successful in illustrating the capital needs of the Coast Guard.

In the summer of 1975, fresh from this research at Coast Guard Headquarters and another year of teaching at the Coast Guard Academy, I was appointed a Lilly Endowment Fellow at Yale University. There Professor A. Bartlett Giamatti, Douglas T. Yates, and John M. Blum encouraged my research. In the winter of 1976 Coast Guard Headquarters approved a sabbatical leave and Rear Admiral

Robert Scarborough, the new chief of staff, approved the writing of the book and promised "appropriate staffs will be encouraged to assist" me in my work. I received a visiting appointment at the Harvard Business School for the spring semester of 1977 set aside for sabbatical leave. There Professors James P. Baughman and Alfred D. Chandler, Jr., generously offered valuable advice, guidance, and encouragement. Upon my return to the Coast Guard Academy, Rear Admiral Malcolm E. Clark had become superintendent and encouraged me to continue my research and writing.

Many associated with the Coast Guard gave of their time for interviews and freely provided comments. I am particularly grateful to W. Michael Benkert, Loren E. Brunner, John D. Costello, Lawrence M. Harding, Robert D. Johnson, Joseph A. McDonough, William B. Mohin, Alfred C. Richmond, and William F. Roland. Donald A. Naples, John B. Smythe, and Alvin J. Temin provided background information and also commented on the entire manuscript.

Of particular help to me were the staffs of the Sterling Memorial Library, Yale University; the Baker Library, Harvard University Graduate School of Business Administration; and the United States Coast Guard Academy Library, particularly librarians Robert Dixon and Edna Jones.

The feeling many fine teachers had left with me made me work harder for the cadets and officers who were my students and who in turn provided help that was indispensable in producing this book. Many more could be named but let me list three: Bruce A. Drahos, Daniel J. Elliott, and Richard J. Losea. Faculty colleagues at the Coast Guard Academy such as David N. Arnold, Paul F. Foye, James R. Kelly, Rodney M. Leis, Phillip B. Moberg, J. David Spade, William A. Stowe, Richard E. Ruhe, and Jimmie D. Woods were also very encouraging and helpful at different stages of the research and writing.

Faculty colleagues gained over ten years were also supportive of this research. They include: William R. Allen of the University of Rhode Island, James P. Baughman of Harvard University, David S. Brown of George Washington University, John Ellison of the Industrial College of the Armed Forces, Joel D. Goldhar of the National Research Council, Don Hellriegel of Texas A & M University, Henry S. Marcus of Massachusetts Institute of Technology, William Naumes of Clark University, Robert A. Pitts of the Pennsylvania State University, Gary C. Raffaele of the University of Texas, Daniel D. Roman of George Washington University, Robert L. Taylor of the Air Force Academy, Israel Unterman of San Diego State University, and Max S. Wortman of Virginia Polytechnic and State University. Several colleagues at The Hartford Graduate Center, including Homer D. Babbidge, Jr., Allen F. Chapman, and William J. Luddy, Jr., are also sources of constant support, encouragement, and good fun.

Of all these helpful colleagues, three deserve further comment for their suggestions and encouragement on the manuscript and the tasks that came up along the way. Bill Allen's and Jim Wood's insights as humans, scholars, and friends mean a great deal to me. Phil Moberg's friendship and skillful insights are deeply appreciated.

At the Johns Hopkins University Press editorial director Anders Richter was very helpful at several important points in the development of the manuscript, as were editors Mary Lou Kenney and Alice Swayne.

At the Coast Guard Academy Edythbelle Vail was a dedicated professional secretary for over twenty years and I am proud to have been associated with her for the ten years she was secretary in the Department of Economics and Management. I thank her for her editing, support, and especially for her good cheer.

My wife, Kathy Bragaw, and sons, Lou, Steve, and Joe, encouraged me to continue on the project, although it meant not being together on many weekends and vacations. I thank them for their patience.

If my acknowledgments appear as a preface to a story or a trackline for a voyage, they are. As the voyage ends, you will understand how happy I am to accept full responsibility for the facts and opinions presented and go ashore. As you sample the waters I have sailed, you can also guess I may sail these waters again.

ABBREVIATIONS

ABC	Alliance, bargain, and compromise
AC&I	Acquisition, construction, and improvement budget, or capital budget
AIMS	American Institute of Merchant Shipping
BMIN	Bureau of Marine Inspection and Navigation
BTU	British thermal unit
CBU	Budget Division, Coast Guard headquarters
CCR	Coastal confluence region
CCZ	Coastal confluence zone
CEQ	Council on Environmental Quality
CNO	Chief of naval operations
COTP	Captain of the Port
CPA	Program Division, Coast Guard headquarters
CPE	Plans Evaluation Division, Coast Guard headquarters
Cytac	An experimental radio-navigation system developed during World War II
Decca	A radio-navigation system developed in England during World War II
DOD	Department of Defense
DOT	Department of Transportation
EECEN	Coast Guard Electronics Engineering Center
EPA	Environmental Protection Agency
FWPCA	Federal Water Pollution Control Act
GAO	General Accounting Office
G-CBU	See CBU (the letter G is a DOT symbol meaning Coast Guard)
G-CPA	See CPA
G-CPE	See CPE
Gee	A radio-navigation system developed in England during World War II
ICAO	International Civil Aviation Organization
IMCO	Inter-Governmental Maritime Consultative Organization
IRAC	Interagency Radio Advisory Committee
ITT	International Telephone and Telegraph

LOOP	Louisiana Offshore Oil Port
Loran-A	A radio-navigation system developed during the 1940s
Loran-B	A experimental radio-navigation system
Loran-C	A radio-navigation system developed during the 1950s
LRV	Long range view
M	Staff symbol for the Office of Marine Safety at Coast Guard headquarters
MBD	Million barrels per day
MEP	Marine Environmental Protection
MIO	Marine Inspection Office
MIT	Massachusetts Institute of Technology
MSO	Marine Safety Office
NDRC	National Defense Research Committee
NEPA	National Environmental Policy Act
NPC	National Petroleum Council
OCMI	Officer in charge of marine inspection
OCS	Outer continental shelf
OMB	Office of Management and Budget
Omega	A postwar radio-navigation system
OPEC	Organization of Petroleum Exporting Countries
OPSTAGE	Operating stage, present year, budget
OST	Office of the Secretary of Transportation
OTP	Office of Telecommunications Policy
PAD	Petroleum Administration for Defense district
PICAO	Provisional International Civil Aviation Organization
PIRS	Polluting Incident Reporting System
PPBS	Planning, programming, budgeting system
Quad	A quadrillion BTUs
R&D	Research and development
RAF	Royal Air Force
RCA	Radio Corporation of America
RCP	Resource change proposal
RIHANS	River and Harbor Aids to Navigation System
TAPS	Trans-Alaska-Pipeline System
UNCTAD	United Nations Conference for Trade and Development
VLCC	Very large crude carrier
VTS	Vessel Traffic System and, later, Vessel Traffic Service
W	Staff symbol for the Office of Marine Environment and Systems at Coast Guard headquarters
WEP	Environmental Protection Division, Coast Guard headquarters
XRCP	Resource change proposal for zero-base budgets
ZBB	Zero-base budgeting

MANAGEMENT THEORY

1 AGENCY MANAGEMENT: THE GOVERNMENT'S BUSINESS

A RATIONALE
FOR THE BOOK

Critics often contend that federal agencies are not as active in anticipating national needs as the public and public leaders want them to be. Stereotypes abound to further this all-too-popular image. To the extent that the stereotypes are true, the process of managing a federal agency is a national problem. Agency management should be, after all, both the business of the government and the concern of the public.

I will examine this problem by concentrating on the process of managing one federal agency. Although it admittedly uses a small sample, this technique has the advantage of allowing an in-depth analysis of that agency. Light shed by a longitudinal examination of one agency's anticipation of national needs in its area of competence should also illuminate the stimulus for effective management in the public sector at large—if indeed there is any—which would be a valuable contribution to general management theory. Whether such a stimulus were found to be similar in nature to the stimulus in the private sector—competition and the market mechanism*—or different, it would be meaningful to a general theory of difference between public and private management. Such contributions could also help identify potential for transferring management technique from the private sector to the public.

General management is by definition the management of a total enterprise or an autonomous subunit of an enterprise.† Because the general managers of

---

*Discussions of the role of competition and the market mechanism in the private sector date back two centuries to Adam Smith. More than a hundred years later Alfred Marshall helped make this role sacred. Its importance has been debated recently, however, by J. K. Galbraith in *The New Industrial State* (Boston: Houghton Mifflin, 1967), and in his *Economics and the Public Purpose* (Boston: Houghton Mifflin, 1973). Bruce Scott disagrees with Galbraith in "The Industrial State: Old Myths and New Realities," *Harvard Business Review* 51, no. 2 (1973): 133–48.
†See, for example, the discussion of general management by Kenneth R. Andrews, *The Concept of Corporate Strategy* (Homewood, Ill.: Dow Jones–Irwin, 1971), pp. 1–26, or Edmund P. Learned, C.

federal agencies are responsible for the performance of their agencies, they are the target of several categorical charges against public organizations. These charges are broad and serious, and they should be considered at the outset. Investigating their validity may also contribute to a theory of difference between public and private management.

The categorical charges take on at least six dimensions.* First, government organizations are said to be good at adding new programs but poor at cutting them back or dropping them. In other words, they are considered good initiators but poor liquidators. Second, as they grow larger and more mature, government organizations are said to replace the client-centered human services characteristic of their early years with more impersonal technology, systems, and procedures. As they become more aggregative and less personal, public agencies can lose the human reality of the people they were formed to serve.

Third, government organizations with regulatory functions are said to be co-opted over time by the very publics they were created to regulate. With only a single demand for their services and the same single source of support, the regulatory agency gradually shifts to a captive rather than a supervisory role. Fourth, as they grow, government organizations are said to become increasingly centralized in Washington, resulting in a lack of flexibility and responsiveness in the field where they deliver their services.

Fifth, government organizations and their general managers are said to contrive dubious threats to the nation that they claim their weaker programs can relieve or even answer if such programs are strengthened rather than cut back or eliminated. By this very contrivance to justify retaining or expanding programs, federal managers lose credibility with the public. Even the suggestion of this charge inflames opponents of public bureaucracy. Finally, and probably most serious of all, government organizations are said to lack the stimulus to effectiveness, efficiency, and innovation that is provided in the private sector by the market mechanism and by competition. This charge is predicated on the belief that the public sector has no parallel to the market mechanism and competition. If this final charge is true, general managers in federal agencies have no motivation to search for real efficiency and effectiveness, or for real innovation, and their agencies are doomed to decreasing productivity.

The breadth and seriousness of these charges have led scholars and prac-

---

Roland Christensen, Kenneth R. Andrews, and William D. Guth, *Business Policy* (Homewood, Ill.: Richard D. Irwin, 1965).

*For a discussion of the general workings of a large bureaucracy, see Anthony Downs, *Inside Bureaucracy* (Boston: Little, Brown, 1967); Francis E. Rourke, *Bureaucracy, Politics, and Public Policy,* 2d ed. (Boston: Little, Brown, 1976); or Harold Seidman, *Politics, Position, and Power,* 2d ed. (New York: Oxford University Press, 1975).

Many of the elements of the six categorical charges against public organizations are also discussed in William A. Niskanen, Jr., *Bureaucracy and Representative Government* (Chicago: Aldine, Atherton, 1971). Niskanen delineates bureaucratic, market, and political alternatives for the behavior of public organizations. This area will be discussed in the final two chapters of this book.

titioners alike to conclude that the parallels between public and private management require closer scrutiny.* They generally agree that this scrutiny should not
take the viewpoint of management as viewed by either schools of business or
public administration *alone,* but should try to view management "as a generic
process, with universal implications and with application in any institutional
setting—whether a private firm or a public agency."[1] This view is becoming
more prevalent in the literature of general management, and management schools
have even been formed with this as a principal justification. I will employ the
same justification to examine the process of managing a federal agency; but at the
same time I will attempt to construct a general theory of how public management
and private management differ.

THE COAST GUARD: A SAMPLE OF
ONE

This book presents a detailed case study of one federal agency, with certain
theoretical implications. The agency selected is the United States Coast Guard, a
federal organization that delivers services directly to the public. A general management approach often used for analyzing large multidivision, multitechnology
firms in the private sector will be adapted and applied to an analysis of the Coast
Guard.[2] Parts 2 and 3 will both record a selective history of the Coast Guard and
analyze its evolving of strategy and structure, its developing of the management
process, and its ways of dealing with the threats and opportunities presented by
the external environment. The story that unfolds will show how this federal
agency is managed.

The story focuses on the emerging Coast Guard structure and on two large
Coast Guard programs—radio-navigation aids and marine environmental protection. It does not, however, dwell on the historical evolution of the Coast Guard,
which occurred through incremental changes in strategy and structure that many
will find intriguing.

As a federal agency, the Coast Guard is neither enormous nor small. Its size
and scale—in terms of human, physical, and political resources—are ideal for
study. As the Coast Guard prepares to deal with the challenges of the 1980s, it
has nearly forty-five thousand employees, and its capital-asset base has a replacement value of over five billion dollars. In 1976 its capital and expense
budget exceeded one billion dollars for the first time. The strategic profile of the
Coast Guard is discussed explicitly in chapter 3. The Coast Guard, however, has

---

*Michael Murray summarized these viewpoints in an essay comparing public and private manage-
ment. Murray examined existing practices in general terms and asked, "Are public and private
management comparable?" He then called for a more extensive examination of the similarities and
differences between the two sectors. See Michael A. Murray, "Comparing Public and Private
Management: An Exploratory Essay," *Public Administration Review* 35, no. 4 (1975): 364–71.

developed important approaches to general management that make it a far more interesting subject for research than would be warranted by its human and physical resources alone. The Coast Guard calls these approaches the *dual-role strategy* and the *multimission concept.* *

The Coast Guard has undergone great changes while growing from the "Revenue Marine" of 1790 to the "Coast Guard" of 1915 to its current role as manager of a portfolio of roles and missions for the 1980s. The Coast Guard is a military organization and a branch of the armed forces of the United States as well as a federal agency. Except for the action against the Barbary pirates, it has served in every war or extended military operation since the Revolution. Within the United States government the organizational character of the Coast Guard is unique, however, in that it is more than a military organization. No other federal agency is like it in either structure or roles.

The dual-role strategy of the Coast Guard commits it to work with the navy during war or national emergency and to serve as the principal federal agency of the United States enforcing maritime law, ensuring marine safety, and facilitating marine transport in time of peace. The multimission concept involves sharing resources across many roles and missions. It permits the Coast Guard to use many of the same human and physical resources to carry out a wide array of different programs at the same time.

In its nearly two-hundred-year history as a federal agency, the Coast Guard has been greatly influenced by external economic, social, political, and technological events. The climate produced by these events, combined with limited internal resources and the efforts of Coast Guard leadership, have created many examples of the opportunities and threats that face management in a federal agency. Table 1 presents a simple chronology of important organizational changes within the Coast Guard.

Appendix 1 presents an expanded list of the dates and the nature of many of the important events that challenged the Coast Guard. By examining this more detailed chronology one can see that, as the years passed, the Coast Guard faced an increasingly complex environment. The rate of change has accelerated since 1967, when the Coast Guard left the Treasury Department and became part of the then-new Department of Transportation.

Recent examples of such changes are numerous. In 1969 the National Environmental Policy Act was passed. The Federal Water Pollution Control Act and the Ports and Waterways Safety Act that followed have also had profound effects. These acts reflected national needs that were ultimately met, through the public policy process, by new Coast Guard programs. In fact, the Federal Water Pollution Control Act and the Ports and Waterways Safety Act added a whole new area—marine environmental protection—to the Coast Guard's respon-

---

*Both approaches developed incrementally. In fact, the evolution of the dual-role strategy and the multimission concept can be traced to the nineteenth century, as can the name Coast Guard, which was first used officially in 1915.

TABLE 1
Important Organizational Events in the Evolution of the Coast Guard, 1790–1980

Year	Event
1790	Act of Congress creates the Revenue Marine as a part of the Treasury Department.
1915	Act of Congress adds the existing Life Saving Service to the Revenue Cutter Service, the name assumed by the Revenue Marine. The act names the expanded organization the Coast Guard and places the military officer who heads the Revenue Cutter Service at its head.
1939	Coast Guard acquires the U.S. Lighthouse Service.
1942	Coast Guard acquires the Bureau of Marine Inspection and Navigation from the Commerce Department—Transfer made permanent in 1946.
1967	Act of Congress moves the Coast Guard from the Treasury Department to the Transportation Department.

sibilities. The Coast Guard's roles in protecting the marine environment from the hazards of commerce and at the same time protecting marine commerce from the hazards of the environment provide an interesting example of how a federal agency may effectively answer national needs.* These two programs show the multimission concept in action, for both use many of the same human and physical resources.

Other examples are available. In the early 1970s national interests turned to a two-hundred-mile offshore fishing limit. This expanse seaward from the United States is larger than the historic Louisiana Purchase. The Coast Guard became involved nationally and internationally with many facets of this problem. Creating the National Navigation Plan called for expansion of the Coast Guard Loran-C navigation system, a service with applications to all modes of transport. Another public concern that provides an opportunity or a threat, depending on the outcome, came with the development of the National Ocean Policy, where the federal government must deal in an area in which myriad complex and sensitive issues surround the oceans and marine commerce.†

---

*Protecting marine commerce from the hazards of the environment is a responsibility that dates from the 1790s. The program expanded in size through increases in marine commerce as the nation grew, and in scope through the acquisition of the Life Saving Service in 1915, the Lighthouse Service in 1939, and the Bureau of Marine Inspection and Navigation in 1946. The National Environmental Policy Act, combined with increasing public concerns for the quality of the marine environment, caused the Coast Guard to create an Office of Marine Environment and Systems in 1971. The Marine Environmental Protection program emerged as a Coast Guard response to new environmental and technological threats to United States shorelines in the 1970s.

†The development of the Loran-C navigation system is the subject of chapters 5, 6, and 7. The issues involved in the "two-hundred-mile fishing limit" or in the broader area of national ocean policy will not be discussed in detail, except for the case study in Appendix 2. The interested reader might consult Robert E. Osgood, Ann L. Hollick, Charles S. Pearson, and James C. Orr, *Toward a National Ocean Policy: 1980 and Beyond* (Washington, D.C.: Government Printing Office, 1975). For another view see Edward Wenk, Jr., *The Politics of the Ocean* (Seattle: University of Washington Press, 1972), or Claiborne Pell, with Harold Leland Goodwin, *Challenge of the Seven Seas* (New York: William Morrow, 1966).

A PLAN FOR THE BOOK

Of the many research designs that could be applied to the process of managing a federal agency, three seem particularly appropriate for probing the six categorical charges presented earlier. Each of these approaches lets us examine the agency from a separate vantage point.

The first approach would examine the *role of management process* as conducted within the structure. Part 2 does this by examining the process of planning and resource allocation. Chapter 3 examines the planning process empirically, specifically the relationship of the structure to its environment. Chapter 4 examines resource allocation, covering both internal and external processes. We shall see how these two processes interact with several levels of internal structure and with the environment that surrounds the structure.

The second approach would examine *case studies* of challenges presented by the external environment. Part 3 explores examples of how the Coast Guard structure has dealt with specific opportunities and threats over extended periods. Chapters 5, 6, and 7 deal with loran, a long-range navigation system initially developed during World War II. Loran might not have become a Coast Guard program had it not been for the acquisition of the Lighthouse Service by the Coast Guard in 1939. Chapters 8, 9, and 10 deal with the Marine Environmental Protection program. MEP might not have become a Coast Guard program had it not been for the acquisition of the Bureau of Marine Inspection and Navigation in 1946.

These two empirical approaches can be taken a step further by a third case study provided in Appendix 2, which deals with the Enforcement of Laws and Treaties program, particularly as it applies to the formulation and implementation of policies for a two-hundred-mile offshore fishing zone. There I shall introduce the actors, the Coast Guard structure, and the set of issues, then open the case for discussion and analysis.

The third approach would examine *how this federal agency historically managed* both its external and its internal environments. This administrative history method would let us trace the dual-role strategy, the multimission concept, and the development of the human, physical, and political resources of the Coast Guard from 1790 to their place within its modern structure. Periods of internal diversification, external acquisition, war, still more diversification, and, finally, management of a portfolio of roles and missions could all be examined.

Each approach has its advantages; the research design for this book, however, incorporates only the first and second approaches, although some material based on the third approach is presented at the beginning of chapter 3 as background to the empirical material that follows.

I selected the Coast Guard for detailed study because it is a specialized federal agency of moderate size and therefore easier to describe than some larger agencies. Also, I had access to many untapped papers and documents concerning its development and was able to interview numerous Coast Guard staff members. I also was permitted to observe and describe Coast Guard management sessions.

A research net of coarse design cast over a single agency, however, may allow a bigger catch than a finer net cast over a sample of many agencies. Indeed, the broad nature of the six categorical charges almost demands a longitudinal study of empirical material covering a long time span. How else could the process of managing one federal agency be meaningfully analyzed?

THREE RESEARCH QUESTIONS

Armed with a rationale, a sample agency, and a plan for the book, we can also develop a theoretical approach. Possibly the most basic question is how a federal agency responds to its leadership, its environment, and the demands of the public. Here the verb "respond" implies both a *proactive* and a *reactive* posture. In fact, the concept of proactivity will be basic as we look at the performance of this federal agency in dealing with its environment.* A second question should surely ask how the internal structure of the agency anticipates and defines the national need and how the individual actors adapt and innovate—or, for that matter, survive. Possibly both questions can be distilled into one. Can an agency—the Coast Guard—be proactive and at the same time satisfy externally defined national needs?

The six categorical charges against public organizations provide excellent material for developing more specific research questions that probe basic theoretical relationships. For example, the sixth charge stated that public organizations are said to lack the stimulus for effectiveness, efficiency, and innovation that the market mechanism and competition provide in the private sector. This charge clearly implies that there is no public-sector analogue to the market mechanism and to competition.

This charge invites us to search for the basic stimulus for managing a federal agency. Indeed, is there in theory any such basic stimulus? Can variants of the market mechanism and competition be found in the public sector that stimulate the search for effectiveness, efficiency, and innovation and thereby increase productivity?

Consider the private sector. If one uses concepts of competition and innovation as cause and effect, or *stimulus* and *response,* one can construct a simple but interesting model of private sector behavior.† This model is presented in figure

---

*For this research *proactivity* is defined as active behavior, as opposed to reactive behavior. *Proactive* behavior is initiated before a stimulus for the behavior is immediately obvious. For an organization, proactive behavior is directed at influencing the environment in ways that are advantageous to the organization. It includes anticipating and seizing environmental opportunities and anticipating and mitigating environmental threats.

†One may think of this *stimulus-response* model as the simple one-dimensional model of cause and effect often utilized in the social sciences. The model may be envisioned for an enterprise functioning

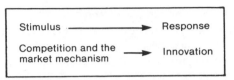

FIG. 1. A stimulus-response model for
general management in the private sector.

1. In this model, competition and the market mechanism are the stimuli that bring about a response of innovation and innovative behavior in the firm.*

Turning to the public sector, what is the stimulus—the analogue to competition and to the market mechanism? Who are the competitors? Can any process in the public sector be identified and described as such an analogue? What is the stimulus for proactive and, indeed, innovative behavior in the public sector? Are there any impediments or barriers to the action of whatever that stimulus is?

Obviously the last two questions are sides of the same coin—both probe the nature of the stimulus for innovation in the public sector. The unidentified stimulus—the analogue of competition and the market mechanism—is the missing element in the comparison drawn between the two sectors in figure 2. But to answer these two questions and identify the possible stimulus for public-sector management, one must go beyond merely counting the times a sample agency was proactive and innovative. The questions require a theory of innovation and productivity for the public sector that explains the stimulus for this behavior and analyzes how the behavior differs from that observed in the private sector.

Such a theory would illuminate the basic differences between public and

---

within an environment and in even larger contexts. Arnold Toynbee provides an example when he views whole civilizations as functioning within environments and responding to stimuli. Toynbee points out that the effectiveness of the stimulus is often in direct proportion to the degree of difficulty it brings. When discussing the cyclical growth and disintegration of civilization, Toynbee states: "Growth takes place whenever a challenge evokes a successful response that in turn evokes a further and different challenge." See Arnold J. Toynbee, with D. C. Somervell, *A Study of History,* abridgment of vols. 7–10 (New York: Oxford University Press, 1957), p. 274.

*Joseph Schmookler provides a precise definition of *innovation* that uses the test of market acceptance to apprise the enterprise of the positive value of the innovation. "When an enterprise produces a good or service or uses an input that is new to it, it makes a . . . change. The first enterprise to make a given . . . change is an innovator. Its action is innovation." See Joseph Schmookler, *Invention and Economic Growth* (Cambridge: Harvard University Press, 1966), p. 1.

In market theory, the need to compete is the stimulus for innovation. Innovation, then, is the response to this stimulus, but it is well ahead of the particular environmental opportunity or threat with which the innovation deals. In this theory a strategy of innovation is termed a push, rather than a pull.

For this research the term innovative is intended as a fuller, more positive adjective than the term proactive. Although proactive implies initiative, it is still a neutral term in that it also implies that the initiative could eventually bring about either constructive or destructive consequences. For example, the behavior of Japan at Pearl Harbor might be termed proactive, whereas the behavior of Japan in emerging as an economic giant in the 1960s might be termed innovative.

private management. It would have to deal with the absence of the market mechanism and the possible presence of some definable analogue. The literature of private management clearly describes how general management within a firm competes for survival by relying on a well-defined set of strategic options or responses to chart the future and alter both course and speed with changing times. The literature of public management, on the other hand, describes how the general managers of federal agencies rely on similar responses in relating to the president and the executive branch, the Congress and its committee structure, and the public and special interest groups. In both cases, however, the theories describe responses. The basic question remains: What is the stimulus, the driving force, in the public sector that brings about this response?

In comparing public and private management, one could examine the stimulus and the response in both sectors for similarities and differences. I propose to probe these similarities and differences by three research questions:

1. Is there a mechanism analogous to the market that stimulates innovation in the public sector?
2. If there is, what is the set of strategic options, or feasible responses, available in the public situation?
3. Given the existence of the stimulus, and given the set of feasible responses, what is the potential for transferring technique from the private situation to the public situation?

Using the stimulus-response model of figures 1 and 2, we can rephrase these questions in even simpler terms. Is there a stimulus in the public sector analogous to the stimulus in the private sector? Is there an analogous set of responses? If so, to what degree are the analogies tenable in both stimulus and response? These questions can be distilled into one basic question: To what degree is the stimulus-response model a valid analogy?

Finding answers to these three research questions will help us to identify important similarities and differences between public and private management and to probe the six categorical charges against public organizations as well. To answer these questions, I will explore both the evolutionary and the recent experiences of the sample federal agency—the Coast Guard.

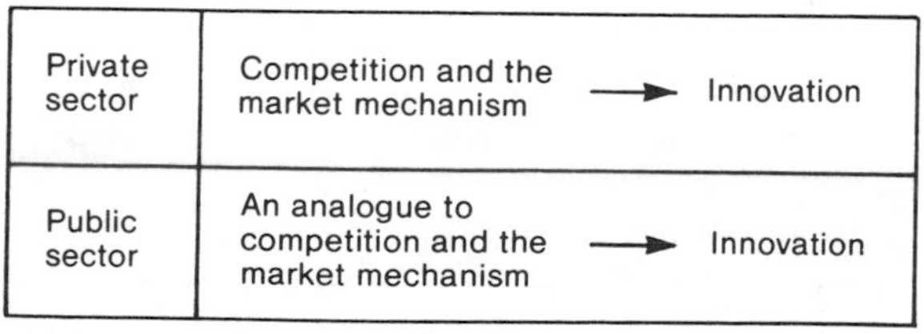

Private sector	Competition and the market mechanism ⟶	Innovation
Public sector	An analogue to competition and the market mechanism ⟶	Innovation

FIG. 2. A comparison of stimulus-response models between the private and public sectors.

ANSWERING THE RESEARCH
QUESTIONS

Although the basic purpose of this book is to examine the process of managing one federal agency, the three research questions stated above do have interesting theoretical implications. To answer these questions based on the detailed empirical study of the Coast Guard, one would have to examine the agency's planning, policy-making, and resource allocation processes. One could then deduce, rather than construct by induction, certain management principles for federal agencies—to the extent that this is possible from the case of one agency.

Planning, policy-making, and resource allocation are the keys to the formulation and implementation of agency programs and are the vehicles for responding to changing national needs and mandates. The budget process is the key to power-brokering and to the agency's relationships with the president, the Congress, the public, and the interest groups. Budget items tell the result of the general management processes; they are policy statements. A public budget is in fact an annual "go-around" as distinguished from a multiyear capital budget in the private sector. Budget processes represent a central difference between general management processes in the public and private sectors.[3]

A definition of public management is now in order. Many definitions go into the dichotomy of policy-maker and policy-administrator, or of politics and administration, dating from the writings of Thomas Paine and later Woodrow Wilson and Frank Goodnow.[4] These definitions, depending on their perspective, have often formed a basis for the political science or the public administration view. The three research questions and the six categorical charges, however, apply to the functions of both the policy-maker *and* the policy-administrator and the processes by which each manages.

The procedural or operational definition of public management offered in Steiss's *Public Budgeting and Management* is appropriate to the general management processes in the Coast Guard.[5] This definition is stated in terms of four broad procedures or tasks:

1. Establishing the overall strategic goals and objectives and selecting the objectives of a particular public enterprise.
2. Determining the requirements for meeting these objectives and establishing the necessary operations or activities to carry out the strategic plan, including selecting the best sequence for performing these operations (the operations plan).
3. Determining the available resources (men, money, machines, materials, and time) needed for the public program as a whole, and judiciously allocating these resources according to the operations plan (the operations schedule).

4. Controlling the entire process from point of decision or commitment to completion by reacting to deviations between predicted and actual progress in order to ensure that the public program is kept to its schedule.[6]

The planning, policy-making, and resource allocation processes of the Coast Guard fit within this broad definition of public management. Annual budgets are, after all, written statements of the output of these processes. As is stated in the fourth part of this definition, however, there can be, and often are, deviations in public budgets. Studying these deviations may help us probe the categorical charges and at the same time answer the research questions.

The research questions, of course, can be explored through various formats. One way would be to examine decision-making.[7] But the research design chosen earlier focuses on "policy-making," which has a broader meaning. Indeed, policy-making entails both decision-making and also activities relating to the long-run development of the enterprise.

Early observers of general management examined policy-making by studying and writing case studies of firms in the private sector.[8] In law, the academic study of cases was used even earlier. The case-study method has also been used with differing formats in political science and public administration. In these areas observers have examined policy-making as a pluralistic process, reflecting the democratic political system.[9] Still others have chosen to focus on public policy as an outcome of bureaucratic political maneuvering. Graham Allison's *Essence of Decision,* a study examining the Cuban missile crisis, is one example; another might be a work focusing on the making of foreign policy.*

Managing the Resource Allocation Process, a study by Joseph Bower that appeared in 1970, is concerned with the "general management processes by which major strategic plans are formulated and investments made in large companies."[10] This work analyzes these processes through four case studies of one large multidivision, multitechnology private firm, using a general management approach.

In the public sector, planning, resource allocation, and budgeting should all be considered in contemplating a research format. Some observers, however, feel that key public decisions in fact occur in "increments," and that these increments are more suggestive of "muddling through" than of the image usually suggested for the planning and resource allocation process.[11] If one accepts

---

*There are many examples of use of the case technique to study activities within the federal government. One is provided by Philip Selznick, *TVA and the Grass Roots: A Study in the Sociology of Formal Organization* (Los Angeles: University of California Press, 1949). Selznick chose a format of institutional analysis to examine the interaction between a federal agency and its environment.

Examples of observers' focusing on public policy as an outcome of bureaucratic political maneuvering are provided by Graham T. Allison, *Essence of Decision: Explaining the Cuban Missile Crisis* (Boston: Little, Brown, 1971), and by Morton H. Halperin et al., *Bureaucratic Politics and Foreign Policy* (Washington, D.C.: Brookings Institution, 1974).

"incrementalism" as a hypothesis, it follows that policy-making in the public sector moves in sequential steps from a first decision to a final outcome—a discontinuance or reversal of effort on a program is possible at any point. Stated this way, "muddling through" in the public sector may in reality be very responsive to the objectives of the democratic form of government.[12]

The role of public budgeting should also be considered in this context. Many observers see little coordination or comprehensive planning in the making of public budgets.[13] They find it hard to link policy analysis and budgeting under the "muddling through" hypothesis. In fact, one political scientist quipped that the "shotgun marriage between policy analysis and budgeting should be annulled." In discussing the implementation of planning-programming-budgeting systems (PPBS), this observer goes as far as to say "PPBS has failed everywhere and at all times."[14] Another unenthusiastic expert on public budgets believes that the use of analytical PPBS techniques in decision-making is really a "museum piece . . . exuberantly displayed for outsiders, but a 'hands off' practice bars their use in actual decisions."[15]

Public policy-making and the control of budgeting have been addressed from several vantage points with various results.[16] A study by Thomas Lynch examines attempts to institutionalize policy analysis in the federal government by focusing on the implementation of PPBS in three agencies. This study generally agrees with the "muddling through" hypothesis. Within the Department of Transportation, however, it found "praise for PPBS as used in the Coast Guard."[17] Lynch reports that the public management process of the Coast Guard involves both comprehensive planning and coordination. Hence the agency chosen for study is one that, in the opinion of some, has a policy-making system that involves more than chance.

IMPORTANT POINTS TO WATCH

In parts 2 and 3, the development of several key ideas and concepts should be noted and referenced against the six categorical charges and the three research questions posed earlier. These points should also be examined by asking this question: How does the Coast Guard, as a federal agency, learn over time? These concepts all represent patterns and trends; in part 4 I will argue for their continuity over time. Here is a list of these key ideas and concepts:

1. the dual-role strategy;
2. the multimission concept;
3. the opportunities and threats faced by the structure;
4. the patterns of centralization and decentralization;
5. the development of human resources;

6. the development of physical resources;
7. the development of political resources.

Both the dual-role strategy and the multimission concept play vital parts in the evolution of the Coast Guard as a federal agency and are important in understanding its strategy and policy processes. To review, the dual-role strategy commits the Coast Guard to serve with the navy in time of war and national emergency and to act as the principal federal agency of the United States for maritime law enforcement, marine safety, and the protection of marine transport in time of peace. The multimission concept involves sharing resources across multiple roles and missions and permits the Coast Guard to use many of the same human and physical resources in an array of federal programs.

The opportunities and threats this agency has faced in its nearly two hundred years of existence provide excellent material for analysis. Part 2 examines them as they affect the evolution of strategy and structure, and part 3 provides case studies of specific challenges and threats.

The pattern of centralization and decentralization is also important, both for the early years when the Revenue Marine was growing and diversifying its services to the public and in 1915, 1939, and 1942, when the Life Saving Service, the Lighthouse Service, and the Bureau of Marine Inspection and Navigation were acquired and assimilated into the modern Coast Guard. (See table 1 and Appendix 1.) The structure's evolution in the years following World War II into an organization capable of managing a portfolio of roles and missions is also very important.

The next focus of parts 2 and 3 is on the way the Coast Guard develops its human, physical, and political resources. The historical development in these three important areas sets the stage for the strategic profile of the Coast Guard that is planned for the 1980s.

Of greatest importance, probably, is the learning process the Coast Guard has gone through as it has grown into its complex task matrix of roles and missions. Who were the proponents of these roles and missions? What opportunities or threats stimulated action in these areas? Who were the adversaries? What events provided opportunities or threats? As the strategy and policy processes of the Coast Guard developed, who were the agency's key actors? How did they become institutionalized during the process?

The answers to these questions should satisfy the primary objective of the book—to better understand the process of managing a federal agency by examining a detailed case study of the Coast Guard. Before concentrating on the Coast Guard, however, I shall further examine the elements of general management theory as it applies to the public sector.

Chapter 2 hypothesizes a general management model that should prove useful both in conceptualizing the management process and in relating administrative theory to actual events in the development of the Coast Guard. Some readers may want to skip this chapter and go directly to the discussion of the development of the strategy and structure of the Coast Guard that begins with chapter 3. Others will find chapter 2 an important prologue and an aid to the theoretical deductions that will be drawn in chapters 11 and 12.

2 GENERAL MANAGEMENT IN THE PUBLIC SECTOR

GENERAL MANAGEMENT THEORY

This chapter discusses general management theory and develops a model for conceptualizing general management in a federal agency. To link this and the preceding chapter, one should visualize the simple stimulus-response model posed for the general management process of an entire enterprise. Recall that the research questions of chapter 1 broadly probed the differences in the nature of the stimuli and responses present in the public and the private sectors, in hopes of providing theoretical implications for the proposed case study of the Coast Guard.

After a discussion of the role of the market mechanism and competition as a stimulus in the private sector, the first research question asks if there is an analogous stimulus in the public sector. Assuming that such a stimulus can be identified, the second research question goes on to examine the set of responses available to the public-sector organization. Assuming that both identifiable stimuli and feasible responses do exist, the third research question asks the potential for transferring management technique from the private situation to the public.

One soon realizes that existing general management theory does not deal explicitly with the stimulus motivating an enterprise. Instead, it deals with the responses available to general managers in directing the fate of their enterprises. Since competition and the market mechanism are implicitly accepted as the stimulus for effective general management in the private sector, a review of theory for this sector is a good place to begin to examine the general management process. It will help us identify the responses available to general managers.

GENERAL MANAGEMENT THEORY
FOR THE PRIVATE SECTOR

General management theory for the private sector concedes that in successful situations the process of directing an organization is anticipatory. The process must be *proactive* and *innovative*. The organization must act on environmental forces, not merely react to them. The process is really the motive force—or response—to the stimulus of the market mechanism and competition. The motive force drives the organization to identify consumers, to segment its market, to develop identity and competence, and to strive for perpetuity. The overall responsibility for managing this process in the private sector rests squarely with the general managers of the organization.[1]

The Strategic Process. The concept of strategy, the cornerstone of general management theory, provides a model that is important in mapping the strategic process. An early study of the role of strategy in large organizations defines strategy as "the determination of the basic long-term goals and objectives of an enterprise, and the adoption of courses of action and allocation of resources necessary for carrying out these goals."[2] Another study is even more specific. It defines strategy as the "pattern of major objectives, purposes, or goals and essential policies and plans for achieving those goals, stated in such a way as to define what business the company is in or is to be in and the kind of company it is or is to be."[3] This key concept enables general managers to set the course and speed of their organizations.*

When the concept of strategy is applied to an organization, four components of strategy should be considered: (1) market opportunity available to the organization: (2) organizational competence and resources; (3) organizational values and aspirations; and (4) the organization's acknowledged public and social responsibility.[4] A strategic decision is therefore concerned with the long-term development of the organization. Strategic decisions must attempt to foresee external or exogenous events that will have future influence. But effective forecasting is not the only element of the strategic process. It must also include planning and resource allocation, and it should take place within the constraints

---

*The first definition of strategy is from Alfred D. Chandler, Jr., *Strategy and Structure* (Cambridge: MIT Press, 1962), p. 13. The second definition is from Kenneth R. Andrews, *The Concept of Corporate Strategy* (Homewood, Ill.: Dow Jones–Irwin, 1971), p. 28. Note that the first definition even refers to an "enterprise" rather than to a "firm" or "business," implying that the definition applies to either the private or the public sector.

Richard Vancil offers a definition of strategy that is even more specific than the first two. He states that "the strategy of an organization, *or of a subunit of a larger organization,* is a conceptualization, *expressed or implied by the organization's leader,* of (1) the long-term objectives or purposes of the organization, (2) the broad constraints and policies, *either self-imposed by the leader or accepted by him from his superiors* that *currently* restrict the scope of the organization's activities, and (3) the *current* set of plans and near-term goals that have been adopted in the expectation of contributing to the achievement of the organization's objectives." See Richard F. Vancil, "Strategy Formulation in Complex Organizations," *Sloan Management Review"* 17, no. 2 (1976): 1–2.

of the four components of strategy. An effective strategic process should develop the resources needed to bob and weave faster than changes occur in the external and internal environments.

The strategic process in the private sector poses several questions that are central to any analysis. The most obvious general question is this: *"Quo vadis* in three, ten, or twenty-five years?"* The only way to answer this is to pose more questions:

1. How will the economic, social, political and technological environments change?
2. How will goals and objectives change over the period under consideration?
3. What will the organization be able to do well, and by comparison better than anyone else?
4. What external and internal demands from the present to the future will be closest to what the organization does well?
5. Will the organization be able to clearly define these demands and segment them into markets?
6. Since competition and the market mechanism are the stimulus for the strategic process, it is important to identify the competition. Who will be the competitors?
7. What risks will the organization have to assume?

The quality and effectiveness of the answers to these questions are vital to the strategic success of the organization.

The first two questions probe the demands of both the external and the internal environments and what the future holds for the organization. The third examines what an organization does well—its skills or competence. Some have called this *corporate competence* or used a term that describes a public as well as a private organization—*distinctive competence.*[5]

Indeed, the concept of distinctive competence is very valuable to the strategist. It helps him identify the human, physical, and even political or marketplace resources that an organization acquires as it grows and develops its own identity and *character.** When strategists consider the future of the organization, they should use the distinctive competence—the resources available to the organization—to the greatest possible advantage to meet the changing demands of the external and internal environments.

*Philip Selznick discusses the *character* of an organization in *Leadership in Administration: A Sociological Interpretation* (Evanston, Ill.: Row, Peterson, 1957), pp. 38–56. On p. 42 Selznick states that in examining character "we are interested in the *distinctive competence or inadequacy* that an organization has acquired. In doing so, we look beyond the formal aspects to examine the commitments that have been accepted in the course of adaptation to internal and external pressures." Selznick goes on to describe how *distinctive competence* was developed and applied by several organizations in both the public and the private sectors. In fact, he uses many government and military examples.

Kenneth Andrews further develops this notion and terms it *corporate competence*. See Andrews, *Concept of Corporate Strategy,* pp. 38, 89–102.

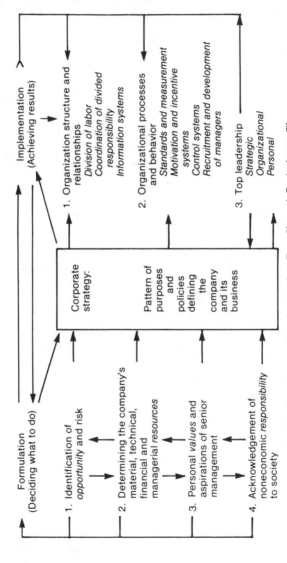

FIG. 3. A model of policy formulation and implementation. From Kenneth R. Andrews, *The Concept of Corporate Strategy* (Homewood, Ill.: Dow Jones-Irwin, 1971), p. 41.

20

The Formulation and Implementation Phases.   There are two important, and importantly distinct, phases of the strategic process—formulation and implementation. The organization responsible for directing strategy is the *structure*.[6] Its task is to "convert the intellectually formulated strategy through . . . organization into an operationally effective one."[7]

During the formulation phase, answers are sought to the last three of the strategic questions. In the process, strategic alternatives are "formulated" and serious consideration is given to the consequences that will develop if the alternatives are in fact "implemented." During the implementation phase, however, all activity shifts to administering the strategy that was formulated earlier. Implementation takes on an operational orientation and differs markedly in its demands from formulation, which had an intellectual orientation.

One study of strategy and the strategic process, by Kenneth Andrews, develops a model that will help us visualize the discussion so far. This model, figure 3, illustrates the key role corporate strategy performs in linking the formulation and implementation phases. It points out that in the formulation phase four steps are taken that are simply "what to do" decisions. In implementation, three more steps are taken that involve "commitments to achieve results."[8]

The strategic process usually is both complicated and difficult, since people, tasks, and even the organization change as conversion proceeds. As the strategist quickly sees, the intellectual formulation of strategy is not enough. To be successful, a strategist must develop an operationally effective course of action. The reality of examining alternatives and considering the prospective consequences of each for resources and tasks is the challenge and responsibility he faces.

Studies of the Strategic Process.   Several studies of general management go beyond conceptual models and spell out a series of steps to map the strategic process. These steps form an algorithm, a route to a solution of the strategic problem.[9] One such study, by Peter Lorange and Richard Vancil, views strategic planning as a process designed to coordinate the efforts of those assigned responsibility for the long-term development of an organization.[10] The authors feel that there are two important, and linked, dimensions to strategic planning in a large, diversified organization: "One is vertical and operates through three organizational levels: headquarters, the divisions, and their functional departments. The other is chronological; as the process moves from level to level it also moves through three cycles: setting corporate objectives at the top, setting consonant business objectives and goals in the divisions, and establishing the required action program at the functional level."[11]

This study of strategic planning describes existing systems in many organizations and makes comparisons. For example, goal setting is usually "top-down" in a small organization and "bottom-up" in a new planning system in a large organization. For a large organization, these observers describe a process where strategic options are refined as strategic planning moves from level to level through the three cycles. The process starts out in a very general form as a centralized staff sends material to the divisions and on to functional areas, then narrows as more detailed plans are sent back to the centralized staff for more specific determinations. As the planning matures, the goal-setting changes from a bottom-up mode to a process of negotiation.[12]

When we consider general management in the private sector, we must take into account organizational diversification and even acquisition of other organizations. In fact, a great deal of descriptive research examines "the important role played by diversification in the strategies of large industrial firms. . . . These studies provide ample evidence that the typical industrial firm, both in the U.S. and abroad, no longer operates in a single industry, but rather is active simultaneously in several, and in many cases numerous, different business areas."[13] Many of these studies document the importance of strategies that involve both growth by acquisition and growth by internal diversification, and they also report the structural changes that have accompanied these strategies.[14]

Still other studies describe the behavior of managers in the general management process.[15] For example, in Joseph Bower's detailed study of resource allocation within a large, decentralized private firm, Bower examined the behavior of managers through four case histories. He found that in the highly diversified organization he examined the top executives frequently are reacting to strategic options that have already been identified, culled, and developed by managers lower in the hierarchy.[16] Bower's study vividly portrays the complexities involved as an organization interacts with its external and internal environments. It traces proposals as they pass from formulation to implementation within the structure and examines the behaviors of managers in dealing with opportunities and threats over extended periods.

This same study of resource allocation focuses on the manager and the top manager as they interact within a large organization. It points out that the manager is in fact pursuing both "corporate and personal goals guided by a structure that helps him relate the two."[17] As such, the designs and dictates of the structure motivate him to meet dual goals, creating a climate in which he must function. Often a manager succeeds because he has developed exceptional personal influence. In the same vein, top managers often base decisions on their perception of a manager's personal "track" record and not entirely on the merit of his proposals. The study gives a name—*structural context*—to the ambience created by this motivating force.* Understanding this concept further helps one understand the stimulus for managers and general managers.

---

*Joseph Bower uses the term *purposive manager* to describe the individual manager who responds to structural context. Bower assumes the personal goals of the manager are economic wealth and power to influence affairs. He points out that the purposive manager "can further his own objectives by meeting the objectives of his corporation." See Joseph L. Bower, *Managing the Resource Allocation Process* (Boston: Division of Research, Harvard Business School, 1970), p. 73.

Bower's discussion of the purposive manager helps integrate the various discussions of "eco-

This resource allocation study develops three other key concepts that become important in considering the processes of planning, resource allocation, and budgeting—the concepts of *definition, impetus,* and *context.* Definition refers to the degree to which the proposal is defined in terms of strategy, structure, and relationship with external and internal environments.[18] Impetus refers to a manager's personal commitment and willingness to stake his reputation and future career on the success of the proposal.[19] A manager or a group of managers will often advocate and supply impetus to a proposal they have defined, then find that the proposal is affected by the forces of context.[20] Context is the conjunction of external and internal environmental forces affecting a particular proposal as it becomes a part of strategy. These forces often cannot be anticipated in the early stages of planning and policy-making, and this uncertainty adds to both the risk and the opportunity. Coping with and managing this uncertainty is a vital managerial function that is not always well performed:

There are many executives who enjoy the privileges of office but are unwilling to assume the responsibilities. They relish the symbols of power, forgetting why they've received them.

The privilege, the status, and the titles that accompany it are yours to enjoy for the duration of the office. Wear your epaulets lightly. The corporation gives them to you as a reward for accomplishment, and as tools to help you work more effectively in the future. They're not hereditary, nor do they indicate you're a better human being than anyone else.[21]

Favorable structural context, however, should help the general manager do his job well. Privileges and symbols of power provide strong motivators for diligence to those who aspire to them. If the general manager uses them wisely and rewards the accomplishments of subordinate managers, he will enhance the organizational climate.

As one can see, general management theory for the private sector does deal with the strategic response options available to general managers in directing their enterprises. Indeed, it deals extensively both with what managers should do and with how they should do it. Examinations of strategy and structure, management processes, and the response of general managers to the external environment have helped further the study of the general management process in the private sector. I hope that my research will help us in examining the same process in the public sector and in answering the categorical charges levied and the research questions posed in chapter 1. Before looking at the theory for the public sector, I shall discuss the systems approach to general management theory.

---

nomic man'' and ''administrative man'' and allows the reader to reconcile these differing views and understand the climate in which the general manager functions. It also integrates the various discussions of the maximizing model of economic behavior of Alfred Marshall with the satisficing model of James March and Herbert Simon, presenting a very pragmatic theory of the general manager and the organization he manages.

POLICY-MAKING MODELS AND THE
SYSTEMS APPROACH

"General systems theory" is a method of developing a theoretical framework for analyzing multiple interrelationships. The systems approach is particularly useful for visualizing how interrelationships both inside and outside the system affect the process of management.* Like most models in the social sciences, this analogue is not a one-for-one mapping of reality—it is a conceptualization, an abstraction, not an exact likeness of the situation being modeled.

A Systems Model. A simple "input-output" systems model will be used here to map the management process.† The term "system" has been defined as a "set of interrelated elements."[22] Semantically the term conveys order; each element of the system has a function. It operates in a larger environment, and inputs are required to sustain it. Inputs may be demands or supports.** Demands require the system to provide specified outputs. They are manifested as requirements, mandates, or laws and as opportunities and threats (negative opportunities). Support inputs, which help the system process demand inputs into the specified outputs, consist of human, physical, and political resources. The system is the transformation or conversion process.

The system through which this transformation occurs in the Coast Guard is conceptualized and idealized in its most basic form in figure 4. The structure of the Coast Guard—its missions, programs, self-interests or values, and its human, physical, and political resources—affects the actual operation of the transformation process. The environment includes the executive branch of the government—the president, the Office of Management and Budget, the secretary of transportation, and other agencies; the legislative branch—the Congress, and all the relevant committees; and the nation—the various constituencies and the general public that the Coast Guard serves.

A vast array of environmental dimensions surrounds the system. These are most often sorted into four categories: economic, social, political, and technolog-

---

*The utility of general systems theory for modeling the process of management is discussed in several management texts. See, for example, Richard A. Johnson, Fremont E. Kast, and James F. Rosenzweig, *The Theory and Management of Systems,* 3d ed. (New York: McGraw-Hill, 1973), and John P. van Gigch, *Applied General Systems Theory* (New York: Harper and Row, 1974). Two of the early sources on general systems theory are Ludwig von Bertalanffy, *General System Theory* (New York: George Braziller, 1968), and Kenneth Boulding, "General Systems Theory: The Skeleton of Science," *Management Science* 3 (April 1956): 197–208.
†Input-output systems, conceptually allowing data input to the structure, have become ubiquitous in the literature. Input-output systems are often adoptions of the work of David Easton. For example, see "An Approach to the Analysis of Political Systems," in *Introductory Readings in Political Behavior* S. S. Ulmer, ed. (Chicago: Rand McNally, 1961), pp. 136–47. See also David Easton, *A Framework for Political Analysis* (Englewood Cliffs, N.J.: Prentice-Hall, 1965), and his *The Political System* (New York: Alfred A. Knopf, 1953).
**Daniel Katz and Robert Kahn describe the two categories of inputs as production and maintenance. See *The Social Psychology of Organizations* (New York: John Wiley, 1966), pp. 32–33.

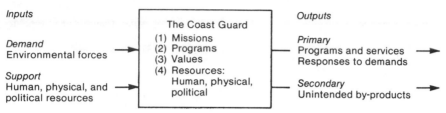

FIG. 4.   An abstract model of the Coast Guard system.

ical. The inputs supplied by the various internal and external environmental pressures interact with the structure of the system and are transformed to outputs that are returned to the environment. Primary outputs are the programs and services that result from the system's objectives; secondary outputs are unintended by-products such as pollution and demographic change that also affect the total environment surrounding the system. Secondary outputs must be closely monitored. Indeed, with policy-making systems they have the potential to be more significant than the primary outputs in affecting the environment. The effect of outputs on future inputs, and hence on system performance, is known as feedback.

A system is considered "closed" if no material enters or leaves it or if decisions made within the system are not affected by input and output. Conversely, a system is considered "open" to the degree that it receives inputs from outside the system and to the degree that its decisions are not predetermined.[23] When the system operates in a constantly changing external and internal environment, decisions cannot be automatic. Certainly in this way the Coast Guard is to some degree an open system. Ideally, decisions must anticipate and respond to changing environments and to changing external and internal forces.

A Policy-making Model.   The abstract model presented in figure 4 can now be developed into a more complete input-output model. One text focusing on the general management process conceptualizes a general model that serves as an example of the policy-making process.[24] The model is presented as figure 5. Both figure 4 and figure 5 are of the input-output format, but figure 5 is circular in nature. It is an input-output version of the formulation and implementation model presented in figure 3, but with output now fed back to the environment, where it can affect future input. The system can now monitor and modify its own output by evaluating actual performance against desired performance.

In open systems, people and processes become intertwined in what is often referred to as a "sociotechnical" system. People operate the system; but, as part of the management process, a good deal of their behavior is induced by the

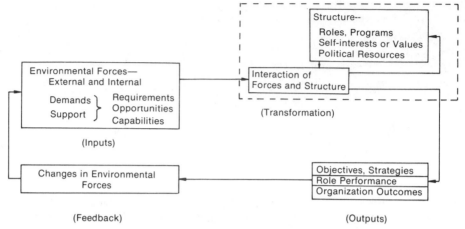

FIG. 5. A descriptive model of policy-making. From Frank T. Paine and William Naumes, *Strategy and Policy Formation* (Philadelphia: W. B. Saunders, 1974), p. 48.

system they run. This operator-system interaction is a two-way street. Open systems usually operate in an environment that is multifaceted and, at best, hard to define.*

In examining the process of managing the Coast Guard, I shall focus both on the historical evolution of the Coast Guard's organization, roles, and missions and on the recent formulation and implementation of two of its major programs. Naturally these programs fall within the usual constraints of being economically sound, socially acceptable, politically feasible, and technologically possible. They are really the response—in the sense of the stimulus-response model discussed in chapter 1—of the general management process within the Coast Guard and are outputs of an open system. To be cost-effective, they should be logical extensions of the Coast Guard's distinctive competence as an organization, and, ideally, they should add value to the environment.

Management Systems.   As in most open systems, one can categorize four subsystems at work within the Coast Guard. These subsystems transform inputs and are called management, organization, information, and resources. The first major subsystem is *management*. Of the four, it is the most important, for it directs the transformation of both demand and support inputs into the desired output. In fact, it should determine what the outputs will be. The functions of management involve forecasting, planning, organizing, selecting resources, establishing and maintaining controls, and evaluating results.†

*For an excellent review of the literature in this area see Raymond G. Hunt, "Technology and Organization," *Academy of Management Journal* 13, no. 3 (1970): 235–52. Hunt discusses the interrelationships between technology, structure, and behavior.
†The basic functions of management were described as such by Henri Fayol in a book first published

The second major subsystem is *organization*. It can be viewed as the process of structuring and allocating tasks. Many organizational forms are possible; each has the primary objective of accomplishing tasks assigned by management. Organizations may be centralized or decentralized, and large organizations may be both centralized and decentralized at the same time. In the general systems analogy, management is the brain or transformer; organization is the body or structure.

The third major subsystem is *information*. Where management is the transformer and organization is the structure, information subsystems allow the organization to move and execute the action directed by management. A few examples of information systems include: human—personal and developmental; physical—operating and supporting; and political—scanning and supporting. The management process has become dependent on these systems, and for management to be efficient and effective, information subsystems must be well developed.

The fourth major subsystem is *resources*. Human, physical, and political resources are the support inputs that help the system transform demand inputs to meet the objectives established by management. Political resources are supports necessary to help produce and deliver outputs. Resources are utilized by the organization and monitored by information systems. Resources serve as the energy—work over a time period—used to respond to information systems, to organization, and to management.

All four of these subsystems must be attuned to the external and internal environments of the system for which they function. As I mentioned, any relevant environment has economic, social, political and technological dimensions. Economic considerations alone may vary from macroeconomic concerns of the overall economy to the microeconomic concerns of a firm or an industry, to changes in an agency's budget brought about by a sudden shift in fiscal policy. Examples of environmental factors that can serve as demand inputs and have an effect on a system are social considerations such as changes in demography, education levels, and value systems. Political considerations that serve as demand inputs can run the gamut of public policy toward business, from the changing views of the opinion-setters in any relevant microcosm of life to the shifting priorities of the national agenda. Technological considerations obviously can change the methodology, transformation, production, and distribution process of any economic, social, or political endeavor. Changing technology therefore must be monitored—there should be no surprises.

---

in 1916 in Paris. It was published in English in 1949: Henry Fayol, *General and Industrial Management,* trans. Constance Storrs (London: Putnam, 1949).

The functions were popularized in the 1930s by Luther Gulick, who gave managers an early acronym, POSDCORB, referring to planning, organizing, etc. See Luther H. Gulick, "Notes on the Theory of Organization," in *Papers on the Science of Administration,* ed. L. H. Gulick and L. F. Urwick (New York: Institute of Public Administration, Columbia University, 1937), p. 13.

Application of the Policy-making Model. The policy-making model discussed so far has application in either the public or the private sector, since both must consider factors that have a long time frame and also wide impact for the future. Policy-making allocates human, physical, and political resources to follow strategy and achieve objectives. The internal environment of management, organization, information, and resources can now function as a transformer, or processor, of inputs to outputs. The required transformation is directed and monitored by the same planning, policy-making, and resource allocation processes that allow the corporation or agency to be proactive and innovative. Figure 5 treats demands on management and the attendant organization "both as *external* environmental pressures, opportunities or threats (e.g., public policy, public opinion, unions) and *internal* environmental pressures (e.g., subordinates, peers)."[25] Support may come from a wide array of external or internal constituencies and interests.

The complexity of the management processes is evident in figure 5. Changes in any of the economic, social, political, or technological dimensions of the environment are important demand inputs that might affect management and structure, and changes in the availability of human and physical resources cause variations in support units. These inputs thus must be monitored for their effect on roles and programs, self-interests or values, political resources, and components of structure.

There are unlimited possibilities for interaction between the various forces and the structure. Many elements of an organization's environments are interdependent, and any changes in one environment will affect others. Such changes will then feed back and cause further change; conflicts lead naturally to reexamination and negotiation. A public-sector example of feedback is the change that a new national economic policy might bring in regulatory programs, which in turn could affect economic policy. Another is an exogenous cut in a department budget that adversely affects a program the executive branch is advocating.

Objectives, strategies, role performance, and organizational outcomes are all outputs of the model. These outputs cause many changes in the environment, which are fed back as inputs of still more environmental pressures. Because the model tries to conceptualize the dynamic process by which management tries to deal with an environment, it is often described as the environmental model.

The environmental model allows one to visualize a manager or a group of managers as a team that makes policy by seeking opportunities, or by following a detailed step-by-step process, or by adapting incrementally to the existing base of operation.[26] Policy-making involves choices between many conflicting self-interests and values. Programs are often "devised to provide a course of action in response to some stimulus or pressure."[27] The conflicting self-interests and values of the managers involved are important to the interaction of pressures and structures. Role demands on managers and the interacting behavioral patterns that result are central to the transformation that takes place in the input-output model of figure 5.

The role demands and values of managers, and indeed the whole functioning of the model discussed so far, imply that there are important differences in application of the environmental model within each sector. In the environmental model, policy-makers are bound by unavoidable constraints. One text points out that policy-makers must "find solutions to policy issues that will (1) satisfy environmental demands or requirements, (2) win external support . . . and internal support . . . , and (3) partially satisfy self-interests."[28] Even though coordination and planning have been described as "muddling through," policy-makers should be sensitive to their environment when deciding effective strategy and policy. Any strategies developed must fall within a range of constraints, sometimes broad and sometimes specific.

Setting objectives and developing strategies to achieve them are important parts of policy-making as modeled by the systems approach. This process must take into account the external environment as it exists and as it is forecast for the future. It must also take into account the internal environment, including the complex array of distinctive competence, resources, values, and aspirations. External and internal support must be aligned. Objectives, the specific statements of the goals to be achieved, are often hard to formulate clearly and even harder to verbalize so that they are easily understood. Indeed, the strategic process is neither simple nor easy.

GENERAL MANAGEMENT THEORY
FOR A FEDERAL AGENCY

One way to examine the effectiveness of the systems approach in conceptualizing public management is to adapt the environmental model to a federal agency. This brings into focus several marked differences between general management theory for the two sectors. A thorough understanding of these differences is an important part of adapting the environmental model to the particular world of a federal agency, for these surroundings have their own unique constraints that evolve from law, tradition, and administrative practice. These constraints affect inputs, outputs, and the transformation process of the model as well.

First, there are differences in the demand and support inputs of the two sectors. In the private sector a demand exists for goods and services. In the public sector there is also a demand, but it is for government programs and services. In the public sector, both demand and support inputs are diffused through the complex set of institutions and institutional processes that makes up the government. These institutions include the Congress and the congressional committees, the president and the executive agencies, and the general public and special interest groups.

Second, there are differences in the nature of the stimulus for innovation in the private sector and in the public sector. The stimulus for innovation is really a demand input, but it is markedly different from the demand for goods and services or for programs and services. The stimulus for innovation is a demand for the efficient and effective production of output.

In each sector there is a stimulus for self-preservation and self-perpetuation, but their natures are different. In the private sector this stimulus is the market mechanism and competition. In the public sector its nature is not so clear; in fact, the first research question asks whether the stimulus is analogous to the market mechanism and competition. It may be more of an instinct for survival—a form of individual and organizational Darwinism.

Why is it that a threat to self-preservation and self-perpetuation takes different shapes in private and public organizations? In theory the private firm is threatened by the consumer sovereignty that supposedly characterizes the market mechanism. To survive and prosper, the firm must anticipate the demands of the marketplace. In the public sector the major threat is not so much consumer or voter or taxpayer or even citizen sovereignty as the sovereignty of the executive, legislative, or judicial branch. And the payoff matrix for performance is completely different. To succeed in the public sector, one must vigilantly tend to the multiple demands of the president and the executive branch, the Congress and the committee structure, and the public and the interest groups. And, in addition to tending to these demands, a federal agency also must keep an eye on opposing camps, because some other agency may steal a march. This form of threat creates a significant difference in the stimulus for innovation and in the way a federal agency behaves.

Third, there are differences in primary and secondary outputs in response to demands. Whereas the primary outputs of private firms are goods and services, the primary outputs of federal agencies are programs and services. Although secondary outputs of firms can be beneficial, they are usually oriented to by-products and tend to affect the physical environment—for example, pollution and demographic change. Secondary outputs of federal agencies are policy-oriented and tend to affect the external economic, social, or political environment. Private firms tend to measure outputs in terms of profits and the "bottom line." Public organizations tend to measure output in terms of values and the degree of consensus that was reached in achieving the output.

Fourth, in a large federal agency the transformation process involves more group and institutional actors than in a private firm, and the institutional and political processes differ. It is important to consider the role of bureaucrats and the dynamics of their interaction with representative government. Despite these differences, however, there are similarities in the ways a firm and a federal agency scan their environments to determine the needs of their market or their public.[29]

These differences help delineate and define general management theory for a federal agency. But any list of differences would be incomplete without a note on the essence of the United States government. Established as a reaction to the excesses of an eighteenth-century monarchy, the American democratic system emphasizes checks and balances. Indeed, the Constitution does more to limit arbitrary power than to promote organizational efficiency. The pluralistic nature of this government in itself provides a key difference between the general management processes of a federal agency and those of a private firm.

The second research question asked, What is the set of feasible responses available in the public situation? The responses of a federal agency to the stimuli it receives—whatever the stimuli are—are probably the same general management responses, or options, open to a private firm. Some of the general management theory for the private sector firm discussed earlier in this chapter probably applies to a federal agency. For example, the concept of strategy can be applied to some extent. The four components of strategy for a firm would be modified for a federal agency to fit the following dimensions: (1) the nation's aspirations, values, and ideals; (2) the opportunities and threats confronting the federal agency; (3) the federal agency's distinctive competence and resources; and (4) the federal agency's acknowledged public and social responsibility.[30] The key ideas of strategic analysis and the concepts of the formulation and implementation phases also apply.

We must further explore possible transfers of general management theory from the private to the public situation, but this is the task assigned to the third research question. Care must be taken not to oversimplify or overgeneralize the complexities of the policy-making process in the public sector. As one political scientist points out, " 'power' is always held by a number of persons rather than by one; *hence policy is made through the complex processes by which these persons exert power or influence over each other.*"[31]

General management theory for a federal agency must reflect not only administrative theory but the principles of government as well.[32] Indeed, a study of the dynamics of federal organization points out that an understanding of the workings of the federal government is an important part of any model of the general management process for the public sector:

Established organization doctrine, with its emphasis on structural mechanics, manifests incomplete understanding of our constitutional system, institutional behavior, and the tactical and strategic uses of organizational structure as an instrument of politics, position, and power. Orthodox theories are not so much wrong when applied to the central issues of executive branch organization as largely irrelevant.

Executive branch structure is in fact a microcosm of our society. Inevitably it reflects the values, conflicts, and competing forces to be found in a pluralistic society. The ideal of a neatly symmetrical, frictionless organization is a dangerous illusion.[33]

At this point in the discussion it is necessary to develop a conceptual model to represent the functions of the general management process for a federal agency. Although a simple model of so complex a process is doomed to be not only too abstract but also to some extent an illusion, it will help us in pursuing the research questions and probing the categorical charges posed in chapter 1.

A GENERAL MANAGEMENT MODEL
FOR A FEDERAL AGENCY

The conceptual models of figures 3, 4, and 5 have all been borrowed from literature on the private sector. To apply to a federal agency, the environmental model of figure 5 requires considerable adaptation. The following discussion will reconstruct figure 5 to reflect the management of a federal agency. The new model appears as figure 6.

The "environmental forces" box at the left side of figure 6 is a good place to begin examining this new model. Every federal agency receives inputs from its external and internal environments. Inputs may take the form of a demand or a support or may be solely informational. Or they may be a stimulus analogous to the one posed in the private sector by the market mechanism and competition. The environmental forces these inputs represent can be categorized as economic, social, political, or technological, but often they are a mixture of these categories.[34] These forces may take the form of opportunities, threats, or requirements or may even be a distinctive competence.

The agency structure appears in the middle of figure 6. The structure incorporates the technical means of the agency—the resources and the distinctive competence discussed earlier—along with its roles, programs, interests, and values. One study of federal organizations stresses the importance of the structure as a determinant of agency power. "Shared loyalties and outlook knit together the institutional fabric. They are the foundation of those intangibles which make for institutional morale and pride."[35] After all, is not the distinctive competence an agency develops its stock-in-trade?

Matching the national needs and technical means inputs is the first step in developing the objectives, strategies, role performance, and organizational outcomes that are the output of the process at the bottom of figure 6. The national needs inputs come from the constituents of the agency, shown at the top of figure 6, whose roles will be discussed shortly. The technical means of the agency appear at the right and are really its distinctive competence—the synergy of its human, physical, and political resources and the credibility it has acquired.[36] Another study of federal organizations stresses the importance of this means-needs match. One way to examine this match is to ask, Can this agency perform this role better than anyone else?[37]

The needs of an agency's constituents are really the sources of its power base as an institution. Basically, these constituents group into three categories: (1) the public or special interests, either generally or through specific executive branch agencies; (2) the Congress, either generally or through specific committees; (3) the president, either generally or through specific executive branch agencies.[38] To formulate public policy effectively and to preserve its power base, the means a federal agency can use to implement policies under consideration must be matched with the needs of these constituents.

The three categories of constituents are important to a federal agency not only for the power base they provide, but also for their heterogeneous support. The extent of this heterogeneity is an important determinant of any agency's freedom of action and independence. Broad freedom of action can result from a varied set of programs serving the diverse needs of many constituents. A government agency, by developing multiple sources of support, can build an "enclave of independence."[39] By building such an enclave and by listening to its varied constituents, it can adapt its planning, policy-making, and resource allocation processes to ensure that it is responsive to changing national needs and mandates.

Let us briefly examine the nature of each constituency and the power it represents. Consider first the general public or the special interests. The general public often has only a vague idea of national needs unless these needs become sharply focused by publicity or catastrophic events. The public as a group often knows little about a specific agency unless it has gained publicity and built a reputation for its abilities in a specific need area.

Special interests are subgroups of the general public that have become organized around a particular issue or issues or who are naturally organized because of their common interest in an industry, a profession, a cause, or a movement. Special interests have detailed knowledge of their needs as they perceive them, and they usually know what agencies can help them gain the action they seek.[40]

Next consider the Congress. The Congress can be thought of as a general group, and the same principles noted for the general public then exist to some degree. Congressmen try to keep abreast of national needs, personally and through their staffs. But Congress can also be thought of as a network of its committees, and in this context the principles noted for special interests apply. Indeed, congressmen on the various committees become very interested in the issues facing their committees, and they team with the special interests and the involved agencies to form almost a "subgovernment" for the particular issue or area in question.

Three specific types of committees wield great power—the legislative or authorization committees, the appropriations committee, and the budget committee. The important role each plays in relating national needs and technical means and in working with the agency structure will be described in detail in chapter 4.[41]

The last source to consider is the president, either generally or through specific executive branch agencies. The president can be, and often is, the most powerful of the three sources, for he is the chief executive of any agency. The president's relationship to an agency and his influence over its programs have been the subject of many studies. Although this relationship and influence vary, the president is always vitally important.[42]

The objectives, strategies, role performance, and organizational outcomes

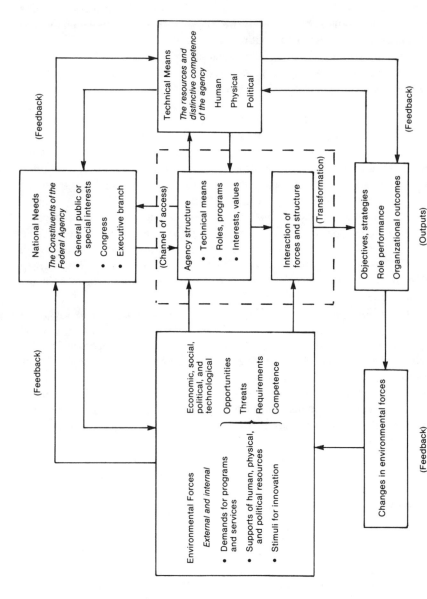

FIG. 6. A general management model for a federal agency matching national needs and technical means to deliver an optimal mix of services to the public.

34

that are the products of the agency should all be, as stated earlier, economically sound, socially acceptable, politically feasible, and technologically possible. Many institutional role players interact with the three main sources of constitutents on certain issues, with the institutions acting as stabilizers afterward. Often public policy and the resulting changes are created through the political process and "the dance of legislation" that bring new laws into being.*

The input-output model and the systems approach can now be adapted to a general conceptual model of a federal agency generating policy and change in the public environment.† The model is depicted in figure 6. Basically, the distinctive competence of an agency—its expertise as an institution—is matched with the needs of a constituency. The agency provides that constituency with a channel of access to government during the transformation process. Conflict, negotiation, and accommodation as well as alliance, bargain, and compromise all mark the internal political process in which needs and means are married and public policy emerges.

Using figure 6 as a model, one can take into account all the factors surrounding each issue and proposed policy and weigh their relative merits. Both the dynamics and the importance of each issue are considered. Some issues have short "staying power," whereas others remain alive for long periods and command great attention. Anthony Downs, an observer of large bureaucratic organizations, describes this process as the "issue-attention cycle."[43] He delineates five distinct phases within this dynamic process: (1) the preproblem stage; (2) alarmed discovery and euphoric enthusiasm; (3) realizing the cost of significant progress; (4) gradual decline of intense public interest; and (5) the postproblem stage.[44] A careful analysis of an issue that is itself an input to the model of figure 6 can identify the stage of the issue-attention cycle a particular policy has reached.

Figure 6 shows a federal agency providing a channel of access to constituents who want certain public policies adopted. The agency is involved in the conflict, negotiation, and accommodation phases of policy-making. Of course this model is simplified; many more elements of the governmental system are involved. It will be useful, however, in further describing the process of managing a federal agency.

---

*The "dance of legislation" is a descriptive phrase from the writings of Woodrow Wilson. Eric Redman uses this phrase as the title of a book describing his efforts in Washington as a staff assistant to Senator Warren Magnuson. Redman captures the essence of the complex processes that influence the creation of public policy by presenting the case of the "doctor-distribution" law. Redman worked on this law from its earliest legislative stages. See Eric Redman, *The Dance of Legislation* (New York: Touchstone Books, 1974).

†For a representative discussion of the theory behind the model presented in figure 6, see both public- and private-sector literature. The model is influenced by the work of Andrews (fig.4) and that of Paine and Naumes (fig. 5). It is also influenced by the work of Charles E. Lindblom, *The Policymaking Process* (Englewood Cliffs, N.J.: Prentice-Hall, 1968), and Francis E. Rourke, *Bureaucracy, Politics, and Public Policy,* 2d ed. (Boston: Little, Brown, 1976).

One can see that managing in the public sector is both complex and dynamic. Its effectiveness and responsiveness, the primary outputs of the model of figure 6, are constantly scanned by the external environment. This monitoring may cause future modifications of the process if it is either ineffective or unresponsive to still-changing needs and means. With any one policy, an agency may be constantly moved from one phase to another in the issue-attention cycle.[45]

To manage and create public policy, a federal agency can generally draw power from four sources—the expertise and mandates of the institution, the needs of its constituents, the vitality of the organization, and the quality of its leadership.[46] The definition of public management presented in chapter 1 recognized the importance of skillful leadership in orchestrating the "procedural tasks." Effective leadership is an important factor in assessing agency power; but it is only one factor. Francis Rourke states that leadership of an agency should be measured with respect to a particular issue: "In appraising the role of leadership in an administrative agency, it should be recognized that leadership in public administration, like leadership in any organizational context, is to a large extent situational, dependent that is on factors in the environment other than the leader himself."[47]

Indeed, the situational importance of external factors cannot be stressed enough. Emphasis should be placed on the distinctive competence, expertise, and existing mandates of an agency in a particular area, and the needs of its bureaucrats should be kept in mind as well. One should also keep in mind that the needs of an agency's constituents can be channeled through any combination of its sources of power. Finally, an agency can draw power from its own vitality as an organization. Organizational vitality is an elusive yet all-important factor in public management. It depends on the sense of mission and ésprit developed both by outside supporters and by those participants—the bureaucrats—inside the agency. Vitality, too, can be situational; it can vary between issues.

APPLYING THE MODEL TO THE RESEARCH

The model in figure 6 can be viewed from two distinct perspectives: first, from the overall vantage point of a federal agency delivering programs and services to the public; and, second, from the perspective of an individual participant within the agency. Both perspectives will appear in the following chapters.

Looking at the entire Coast Guard, one realizes that its planning, policy-making, and resource allocation processes must consider the knowledge, skills, reputation, and capital plant that exist to serve its constituency. The structure should seek to take on those programs and services that the Coast Guard can carry out more effectively than anyone else. The distinctive competence and credibility of the Coast Guard should be important factors in developing proactive and innovative public policy and programs.

The vitality of the Coast Guard in providing public service at present and in the future must also be considered along with the heterogeneity of its support. All these forces must be orchestrated into the strategic process for every issue that arises with the most skillful leadership possible. This is the challenge in managing a federal agency.

This challenge introduces the second perspective, that of the individual participant. The individual may be a top leader or a manager far removed from the top of the structure—the roles played by all participants within the Coast Guard as they try to be proactive and innovative bear careful scrutiny. Wherever the manager is situated, however, he carries a large share of the responsibility for the behavior of the structure if indeed it is to be proactive or even innovative.

Observe the ambience, or structural context, the Coast Guard creates for individual participants. To what degree are these individuals able to develop definition and impetus for their programs? How are they affected by the forces of context? Admiral Hyman Rickover's commitment to nuclear propulsion for submarines, for example, was an intense, and ultimately successful, application of impetus. Although the proposer of a new program and its ultimate "champion" need not be the same, one observer points out that "Rickover's skill in defining and promoting his ideas is legendary."[48] On the other hand, General Billy Mitchell's commitment to air power as an offensive military weapon is an example of the full measure of personal risk involved in applying impetus in an organizational setting. Although General Mitchell's vision of the strategic role of the airplane was ultimately vindicated, he had to face not only a court martial but the scorn of his peers for acting as the champion of air power. In Mitchell's case, definition and impetus were present, but context was not. Carefully observing the behavior of individuals involved in the process of managing the Coast Guard is an important part of the research design.

When I discussed the research design in chapter 1, I singled out several key points. Examining these points and observing the function of the model of figure 6 should help us understand the process of managing the Coast Guard. Each part of the book in turn should present different pieces of the evidence necessary to answer the categorical charges levied and the research questions posed in chapter 1. Probing these charges is the primary objective of the next eight chapters; if satisfactory answers to the research questions are also developed, all the better. The actual answers to the charges and the questions will not be explicitly taken up until chapters 11 and 12.

MANAGEMENT PROCESS

3 THE PLANNING PROCESS

THE ROLES OF STRATEGY
AND STRUCTURE

The object of this book is to present a detailed case study of the Coast Guard from which theoretical implications may be drawn. To present such a detailed case study, one should recognize at the outset the key roles that *strategy* and *structure* have played in the development of the Coast Guard as a federal agency. Alfred Chandler's study *Strategy and Structure* defines strategy as "the determination of the basic long-term goals and objectives of an enterprise, and the adoption of courses of action and allocation of resources necessary for carrying out these goals." This same study defines structure as "the organization devised to administer these enlarged activities."[1]

These definitions certainly have transferability from the private to the public sector, at least for the Coast Guard. Until the 1950s, the diversification of the Coast Guard was the result of the dual-role strategy and the multimission concept. In following this strategy in the early years, the cuttermen of the Revenue Marine diversified internally by adding new missions to Alexander Hamilton's concept of revenue collection. After the Cleveland Commission threatened to disband the Revenue Marine during 1912–15, the Congress in 1915 added the existing Life Saving Service to the Revenue Cutter Service, the name assumed by the Revenue Marine. The 1915 act named the expanded organization the Coast Guard and made the military officer who had headed the Revenue Cutter Service its head. (For an expanded account of these events, see Appendix 1.)

After 1915, diversification occurred both internally and through acquisition. In 1939 the Coast Guard acquired the Lighthouse Service, and in 1942 it took over the Bureau of Marine Inspection and Navigation (BMIN). The transfer of BMIN was made permanent in 1946. After World War II diversification again occurred internally through the dual-role strategy and the multimission concept. In this period the task of the Coast Guard expanded to managing a portfolio of programs. In 1967 an act of Congress moved the Coast Guard intact from the

Treasury Department to the Transportation Department as the water-mode administration.

Both the dual-role strategy and the multimission concept came into being and evolved along with the Coast Guard, and they were applied to many key decisions and turning points. To administer the strategy and concept, the Coast Guard devised a structure that is both centralized in Washington and decentralized through the field organization. This structure is by its very evolution sensitive to the force of events and issues, and it interacts with both the external and the internal environments.

As stated earlier, when we consider strategy in the normative sense we should ask two important questions. First, What must be done? What are the demands of the external and internal environments? The second really comprises three questions: How are resources allocated to implement strategy? How does the structure function to implement strategy? How are strategic responses shaped? These questions will be pursued in sequence.

The model of figure 6 is helpful in describing the management process. First, the Coast Guard identifies national needs in its area. These needs are the demands of the various publics to be served—its constituents. They are identified by the structure's management processes. Second, the Coast Guard identifies the means—its distinctive competence—that ideally equip it to fill these needs. These means are the type and number of its human and physical resources—the very "character" of the organization. The resources are identified by the structure's programming processes.

The very heart of managing the Coast Guard is identifying the national needs closest to the means of the agency, then matching the means and needs in response to the environment. This matching process is a part of the agency's planning, policy-making, and resource allocation processes; it is depicted by the model of figure 6. The structure, at the center of the model, assesses its technical means (its resources) and the national needs (its constituents) and looks for the best matches.

In the adversary system of American democracy, the Coast Guard structure is in large measure responsible for this matching process, since it controls the major issues of the agenda and presents its own justifications at each stage. Before I describe further the management process of the Coast Guard, with its planning, programming, and budgeting systems, let us consider the role of descriptive theory.

DESCRIPTIVE THEORY AND THE
COAST GUARD

Figure 6 is mainly a descriptive model as opposed to a normative model. It attempts to describe how a federal agency *actually* makes decisions as opposed to the way it *ought* to make decisions. Indeed, many of the management theories discussed in the last chapter are themselves descriptive theory, concerned with the way decisions really are made.

Descriptive theory is often classified into that involving individual choice, typified by most economic theory shaped for the individual decision-maker, and that more applicable to most organizational settings, based on collective choice.[2] The case researchers who describe the policy-making process; the institutionalists who, for example, examine distinctive competence; the incrementalists who examine muddling through; and even the advocates of the bureaucratic politics theory all develop forms of descriptive theory that are classified as collective choice.*

Incrementalism, for example, is a theory of collective choice. It deals with the way a group of individuals or even a federal agency makes a decision and then adapts or adjusts the decision in response to the forces it experiences after the first decision is made. The discussion of the "issue-attention" cycle in chapter 2 points out that many of the issues an agency deals with go through a cycle of relative importance, and decisions made by a group or an agency fluctuate with this cycle. The proponents of incrementalism point out that, although the process can be termed muddling through when looked at from a distance, it may actually be quite responsive to the democratic system of government.[3]

One way of discussing the categorical charges made in chapter 1 is to describe the behavior of the Coast Guard as a federal agency. For example, could this behavior be described as muddling through? One researcher of government bureaus, William Niskanen, describes the "supply" structure of the bureaus, the "demands" they face, and the environment in which they function.[4] The development of the strategy and structure of the Coast Guard reflects a continuing pattern of stimulus over the years that is very different from the private-sector stimulus of competition and the market mechanism. In weak form this public stimulus is the threat of a budget cut, in stronger form the threat of a loss of one or more programs, and in severe form the threat of outright liquidation or loss of identity as an agency. Though the stimulus is a basic and even a negative force, it has had significant impact on the agency's behavior. Table 2 lists the dates and nature of some of the more important applications of this stimulus. (Table 1

---

*For a discussion of various descriptive theories, see Frank T. Paine and William Naumes, *Organizational Strategy and Policy*. 2d ed. (Philadelphia: W. B. Saunders, 1978), pp. 16–19, 30–49. The work of the case researchers might be best illustrated by the followers of Edmund P. Learned, C. Roland Christensen, Kenneth R. Andrews, and William D. Guth, *Business Policy* (Homewood, Ill.: Richard D. Irwin, 1965); that of the institutionalists, by Philip Selznick, *Leadership in Administration* (Evanston, Ill.: Row, Peterson, 1957); that of the incrementalists, by Aaron Wildavsky, *The Politics of the Budgetary Process*, 2d ed. (Boston: Little, Brown, 1974), or Charles E. Lindblom, *The Policy-making Process* (Englewood Cliffs, N.J.: Prentice-Hall, 1968); and that of the bureaucratic politics theorists, by Graham T. Allison, *Essence of Decision: Explaining the Cuban Missile Crisis* (Boston: Little, Brown, 1971).

TABLE 2
Dates and Nature of Some Important Stimuli

Date	Stimulus
1797–99	Creation of the U.S. Navy threatens the separate identity of the Revenue Marine.
1801	President Jefferson threatens the Revenue Marine by calling for a smaller government.
1829	President Jackson indirectly threatens the existence of the Revenue Marine.
1840–43	Senate Commerce Committee threatens the existence of the Revenue Marine.
1878–94	Several events threaten the existence of the organization, then known as the Revenue Cutter Service.
1912–15	Cleveland Commission threatens to disband the Revenue Cutter Service.
1918–20	Events again threaten the independent existence of the organization, now known as the Coast Guard.
1932–36	Winding down of the Rum War threatens the existence of a larger Coast Guard.
1946–48	Return of the Coast Guard to the Treasury Department and the pressure for a smaller postwar military combine to threaten the nature of the postwar Coast Guard.
1956–58	Many forces combine to call for a smaller Coast Guard budget.
1966–67	President Johnson calls for the Coast Guard to move from the Treasury Department, its home in the executive branch since 1790, to the newly formed Department of Transportation.

provided a chronological listing of the most important organizational events in the evolution of the Coast Guard. For more detail, turn to Appendix 1 for an expanded list.)

The response pattern displayed by the Coast Guard in each instance is similar if not identical to the private sector responses well modeled by many of the collective-choice theories discussed in chapter 2. The Coast Guard, through the response patterns of many years, has built a store of human, physical, and political resources that have combined to give the agency its distinctive competence and character.

The dual-role strategy and the multimission concept have become cornerstones of the character of the Coast Guard. The role of leadership is very evident, particularly in the cases of Frederick Billard, Russell Waesche, and Alfred Richmond, who served as commandants during 1923–32, 1936–46, and 1954–62. Each in his turn played an important part in shaping the agency he headed.

SOME INSTANCES OF INEFFICIENT PERFORMANCE

One may feel that descriptions will be given only of Coast Guard behavior that at the time seemed laudable, or over an extended period was clearly shown to be in the national interest. Examples exist, however, of behavior that, while contributing to the expansion of the Coast Guard, was *not* in the national interest, or at least was suspect under the charges categorized in chapter 1.

These examples of inefficient performance can be selected from "operational" areas, where the Coast Guard was mandated to deliver services to the public, or from the "regulatory" areas, where the Coast Guard was required to protect the public by attempting to prevent disasters. They largely illustrate instances when the Coast Guard continued programs that had outlived part of their usefulness. The public would have been better served if the resources in these areas had been cut back or reallocated to more useful programs.

Instances from operational areas include the performance of Life Saving stations during the 1920s and 1930s, the Aids to Navigation program in the late 1940s and early 1950s, and the Ocean Station program in the 1960s. An instance from the regulatory area is the administration of the Merchant Vessel Safety program in the years immediately following World War II.

When the Life Saving Service was combined with the Revenue Cutter Service in 1915, the missions and physical environments of the two services seemed very similar. But the commandant of the Coast Guard found out in the 1920s that the two services were in fact still operating autonomously. There was almost no practical way to share or reallocate resources, or even to utilize separate resources to achieve the same effort jointly.

During the years between the world wars, the Life Saving operation experienced no real threat to its existence. The technology of saving lives in danger off the coast did not change, and the surfmen of the former Life Saving Service were quite content to practice the skills that had existed at their stations since the turn of the century. Politically and socially, no major accident created an issue that reflected directly on the surfmen or indirectly forced them to alter their long-practiced ways.

Administratively, the Life Saving stations answered to Oliver Maxham, who had succeeded Sumner Kimball. Kimball had headed the Life Saving Service for nearly forty years. Although Maxham, a civilian, reported to the Coast Guard officer who served as commandant, his tenure was longer, and he personally retained many of the political resources the Life Saving Service had gained before its merger into the Coast Guard. The merger was far from an acquisition.

A glimpse down the hall of the Coast Guard headquarters in Washington in 1925 would have given one a good idea of how autonomous the Life Saving Service had remained. The commandant occupied a corner office, and on one side of it was an office containing four Coast Guard officers with their desks pushed together to form one big desk. In the office on the other side was Oliver Maxham. Although the title on the door read "Chief, Division of Operations," in reality Maxham was in charge of the Life Saving districts. Any mail affecting cutter personnel or operations went to the officers at the four desks; any mail affecting the Life Saving districts went directly to Maxham.

Although some economists or political scientists years later might talk of bureaucratic supply structures and demand functions, and resultant trade-offs, little such action occurred in the Coast Guard between the wars.[5] In fact, the commandant and his cutter officers planned in the 1930s that any contribution they would make to a future national emergency would be in antisubmarine and convoy duty—the tasks they had performed well during World War I. After World War II broke out in Europe and Asia, the "destroyer" deal with Great Britain and United States Navy operations lowered the national need for Coast Guardsmen to man antisubmarine patrols. Many unanticipated tasks were assigned to the Coast Guard in 1940, however, and one of the first was manning small boats in the surf to carry out amphibious assaults.

Amphibious warfare was a made-to-order national need to fully employ the skills of the surfmen of the former Life Saving Service. Men from Life Saving stations from Maine to Florida were deployed on faraway shores in the European and Pacific theaters of operations. Once the surfmen had been deployed by the wartime need, the autonomy of their former operation was never restored. After World War II the advent of the helicopter and teamed operations of cutters and aircraft working in consort offshore spelled the end of the Life Saving operation as it had been. Many of the resources were reallocated for use in other mission areas of the larger Coast Guard, where they were used to save lives in far different ways.

There were similarities in the operation of the Aids to Navigation program and the Merchant Vessel Safety program in the years immediately after World War II. The first program came to the Coast Guard through the acquisition in 1939 of the Lighthouse Service; the second program came through the final acquisition in 1946 of the Bureau of Marine Inspection and Navigation. In both programs there was some difficulty in recruiting Coast Guardsmen from "regular" Coast Guard duties to work in the "new" areas called for under the multimission concept. This problem was mainly one of perception of relative prestige, or even a narrow view of the "calling of a true sailor." As had been the case with the Life Saving stations after World War I, neither program experienced any important technological change or attention-getting natural disaster in the first ten years after World War II. During this period both programs held a good share of resources, but to a large extent they languished. An exception to this, of course, was radio navigation, a specialized area of aids to navigation to be described at length in chapters 5, 6, and 7. As with radio navigation, both the Aids to Navigation program and the Merchant Vessel Safety program experienced many external forces and issues from the 1960s on, and the stimulus of these experiences changed the programs dramatically. Indeed, the Marine Environmental Protection program, the focus of chapters 8, 9, and 10, was a child of the old Merchant Vessel Safety program.

The final case of inefficient performance is the Ocean Station program in the 1960s. This program came into being with the need for radio transmission and weather reports and other military services in the days just before World War II and called for the biggest cutters of the Coast Guard. It was continued after the war and handled two dramatic rescues of transoceanic airliners, one in 1947 and another in 1956. Many important services, including weather reports and navigational aids to aircraft, were supplied in the early postwar years, but by the 1960s this program had outlived its usefulness. Yet it continued with only minor cut-backs during that period, on the rationale that it had some international financing as well as marginal utility in several areas. In truth, one major reason for its retention was that it was the primary justification for maintaining a fleet of large cutters whose command was deemed the capstone of a seagoing officer's career. Assignment to these cutters was also considered excellent training, and command of one was often a prerequisite for promotion to the rank of rear admiral. With great reluctance, the Coast Guard completely discontinued the program in the early 1970s.

THE STRATEGIC PROFILE

Before examining the details of the planning process, one should consider the strategic profile that the Coast Guard developed. "Every company, whether it has an explicit strategy or not, has a *strategic profile*."[6] With these words, observers of the general management process point out that "critical choices" made over many years shape the strategic profile. Such critical choices made by and for the Coast Guard since 1790 have formed a definition of the Coast Guard in its own eyes and with the government and publics it serves.

The dual-role strategy and the multimission concept are examples of critical choices. The dual-role strategy was first tested by the Senate Commerce Commit-tee in 1840. It was found to be in the public interest then and has been found so in many tests since. Resource-sharing over varied programs or missions is at the heart of the multimission concept. This decision was first made by early revenue cutter captains. Over the years, these choices were of course constrained by the external and internal environments and by available resources.

The strategic profile of the Coast Guard evolved into the following general objectives:

1. To minimize loss of life, personal injury, and property damage on, over, and under the high seas and waters subject to United States jurisdiction.
2. To facilitate waterborne activity in support of national economic, scientific, defense, and social needs.
3. To maintain an effective, ready, armed force prepared for and immediately responsive to specific tasks in time of war or emergency.
4. To assure the safety and security of ports and waterways and their related shoreside facilities.
5. To enforce federal laws and international agreements on and under waters subject to United States jurisdiction and on and under the high seas where authorized.
6. To maintain or improve the quality of the marine environment.
7. To cooperate with other government agencies and entities (federal, state, and local) to assure efficient utilization of public resources.[7]

These strategic objectives define what must be done by the Coast Guard. They can be related to the programs of the Coast Guard; for example, the program to protect the marine environment is encompassed in objectives 2, 4, 5, and 6. The objectives interact with demand inputs and the strategic forecast to shape the Coast Guard in the manner discussed in chapter 2 and illustrated by figure 6. The policy-making systems used by the Coast Guard structure further elaborate and quantify these objectives to make them useful in the decision-making process.

As the Coast Guard enters the 1980s it is engaged in the following missions: law enforcement, protecting lives and property, aiding marine commerce, promoting maritime safety, protecting the marine environment, conducting marine science activities, and maintaining readiness for military operations. In these years the Coast Guard workload closely parallels increases in population and real growth in the gross national product. This growth is manifested in increased maritime and commercial activity and in the growing use of bays and harbors as recreational areas. Economical and safe water transport, and enforcement and administration of boating safety and water-quality legislation are major long-range goals of Coast Guard nonmilitary programs.

A strategic profile also includes the base of resources available, both human and physical. Coast Guardsmen have always been an essential part of the base; certainly they are critical to the multimission concept. In 1980 the human resource base included approximately 6,400 officers, 31,800 enlisted men and women, and 6,900 civilian workers.[8] Numbers alone, however, do not convey the experience these people have in making the multimission concept effective. The versatility of Coast Guard resources has often led to new roles.

Estimates of the value of the physical assets were last calculated in 1975. These assets, totaling nearly five billion dollars, include cutters, aircraft, shore stations, and electronic equipment. Their 1975 value is shown in table 3. The versatility of these assets has also led to many new public services. For example, the capabilities of the cutter *Bear* led to missions in icebreaking and marine

TABLE 3
Value of Coast Guard Physical Resources, 1975
(in billions of dollars)

Asset Type	Percentage of Total	Value of Total Coast Guard Assets by Type
Shore plant	0.42	1.959
Cutters	0.43	1.957
Electronics	0.04	0.163
Aircraft	0.11	0.532
Total	1.00	4.611

Source: Programs Division, Office of the Chief of Staff, U.S. Coast Guard Headquarters. Estimates of value in 1975, exclusive of land.

science. The capabilities of cutters and later aircraft have developed and expanded search-and-rescue and law-enforcement roles. The versatility of Coast Guardsmen and their equipment is well illustrated in the development of Loran-C and of the Marine Environmental Protection program.

The resource base is funded by an annual appropriation that is divided into several categories. The two main categories are the operating expense budget (termed operating expense) and the capital budget (termed acquisition, construction, and improvement). The budget allocations for the major categories for 1973 to 1980 are displayed in figure 7. The actual and estimated Coast Guard budgets for these categories are presented in table 4. As one can see, the total Coast Guard appropriation topped one billion dollars for the first time in 1976.

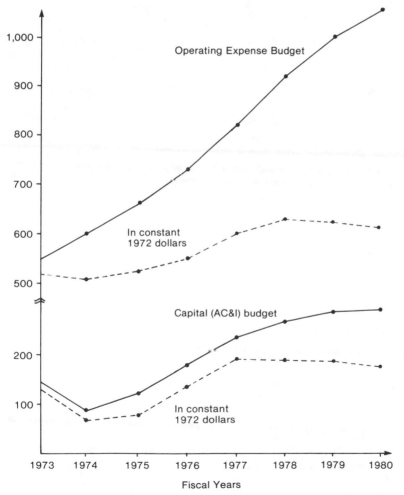

FIG. 7. Major Coast Guard budget categories, 1973–80. Data supplied by Budget Division, Office of the Chief of Staff, U.S. Coast Guard Headquarters, 15 February 1979.

TABLE 4
Actual and Estimated Budgets of the Coast Guard, 1973–80 (in thousands of dollars)

Fiscal Year	Operating Expenses	Acquisition, Construction, and Improvement	Other	Total
1973	548,441	131,550	140,059	820,050
1974	589,163	75,500	137,760	802,423
1975	660,085	108,376	164,984	933,445
1976	738,054	166,100	201,597	1,105,751
1977	838,383	236,000	233,435	1,307,818
1978	924,035	256,000	244,013	1,424,048
1979	989,561	286,617	266,610	1,542,788
1980[a]	1,037,175	284,361	314,510	1,636,046

[a] Estimated.

Source: Budget Appropriation History, Budget Division, Office of the Chief of Staff, U.S. Coast Guard Headquarters, 15 February 1979.

The strategic profile of the Coast Guard is constrained by both the environment surrounding the structure and by the resources available, as is shown in figure 6. The constraints of the external environment include executive orders and policies, and laws and legislative mandates. These "constraints" also can be, and often are, viewed as challenges and opportunities as well as threats. The mandates include Title 14, United States Code Annotated, containing the statutory authority for the Coast Guard. The code contains provisions outlining the general organization, functions, and responsibilities of the service as well as its relation to other federal agencies. The constraints of the external environment also include economic, social, political, and technological factors. The constraints of the internal environment include the Coast Guard's aspirations, values, ideals, and acknowledged social responsibility as well as its distinctive competence and resources.[9]

THE PROGRAM STRUCTURE

The Coast Guard's strategy, policy-making, and resource allocation processes use the program as the basic building block. As such, programs are the basic units, and the primary output, of the system. The Coast Guard *Planning and Programming Manual* defines a program as "a major Coast Guard endeavor defined in terms of specific actions and resource allocations required to reach an objective."[10] Each of the seven strategic objectives encompasses one or more programs, and a program may contribute to more than one objective.

The headquarters program structure is designed to administer both the programs and the resource base. The structure contains fourteen operating programs and thirteen internal supporting programs. Together the operating and support programs represent the total output of the Coast Guard. A full list is presented in table 5. The next few charts and tables should help one visualize and understand the program structure of the Coast Guard.

Responsibility for approved Coast Guard programs rests with the commandant, who directs the program structure. Reporting to the commandant through the chief of staff are program and support directors at headquarters in Washington and also two area and twelve district commanders in the field. This Coast Guard organization, in use in 1980, is presented in figure 8. Responsibility for the various programs and supports mentioned in table 5 lies with program and support directors, listed in table 6. Each director is chief of one of the offices shown in figure 8.

This structure has become more complex since World War II, and the complexity has accelerated since the early 1960s. The addition of the program and support areas has tended to expand the headquarters structure horizontally.

TABLE 5
Program and Support Areas

Program Area	Program	Acronym
Search and rescue	Search and Rescue	SAR
Aids to navigation	Short Range Aids to Navigation	AN
	Radio-navigation Aids	RA
Bridges	Bridge Administration	BA
Marine safety	Commercial Vessel Safety	CVS
	Recreational Boating Safety	RBS
Marine environmental protection	Port Safety and Security	PSS
	Marine Environmental Protection	MEP
Ocean operations	Ice Operations	IO
	Marine Science Activities	MSA
	Enforcement of Laws and Treaties	ELT
Military operations and preparedness	Military Operations and Preparedness	MO/MP
Reserve training	Coast Guard Reserve Forces	RT

Support Area	Support	Acronym
General support	General Administration	GA
	Personnel Support	GAP
	Engineering Support	GAE
	Financial Management, Personnel, Supply, and Automatic Information Systems Support	GAF
	Research, Development, Test, and Evaluation Support	GRD
	Medical Support	GAK
	Legal Support	GAL
	Safety Program Support	GAS
	Civil Rights Support	GAH
	Public and International Affairs Support	GAA
	Retired Pay	RP
	Intelligence and Security Support	GAI
	Communications Services Support	GAC

Source: U.S. Coast Guard, *Planning and Programming Manual* (CG-411), p. II-2.

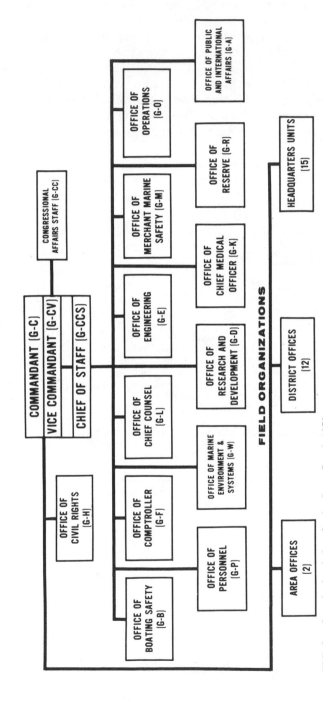

FIG. 8. Organizational chart for the Coast Guard, 1979.

52

The first real change came in 1946 when the Bureau of Marine Navigation and Inspection (BMIN) was permanently acquired. It became the Office of Merchant Marine Safety and was given the same status as the Office of Operations. When new programs developed, they were added horizontally at the program level at headquarters. One example, discussed further in chapter 9, is the creation of the Office of Marine Environment and Systems in 1971. Conversely, older and less effective programs, such as the Ocean Station program, discussed earlier in this chapter were phased out by transferring their resources to other programs.

As the concept of managing a portfolio of programs came into being, considerable internal competition for resources developed. This concept is critical to a full understanding of how the Coast Guard manages, and it should be kept in mind as we examine the management processes.

At headquarters the organization is centralized and has the characteristics of both a program and a matrix organization. In the districts, the organization generally parallels headquarters in functions, but it is somewhat more compact, as befits its emphasis on operational over administrative matters.

Operationally, in the field, the organization is rather decentralized. At headquarters, the commandant and the chief of staff are mainly concerned with meeting the objectives of the Coast Guard and with managing the total Coast Guard system. Although ultimate responsibility rests with the commandant, his chief of staff is charged with the day-to-day management of the resource allocation system.

Armed with strategy and policy guidance from the commandant, the chief of staff is responsible for the coordination, development, and evaluation of all Coast Guard programs. Although initial stimulus for new programs generally comes from outside—from the Congress or the president—new programs are actually formulated and implemented from within the Coast Guard structure. In his resource allocation role the chief of staff is assisted by three divisions who have key roles in planning, programming, and budgeting.[11]

The Plans Evaluation Division (G-CPE) may be simplistically described as being concerned with the agency's long-term development.* The concerns of CPE are strategic; it looks to the future, assesses national needs, and weighs them against the distinctive competence of the Coast Guard. It is specifically charged with looking at the time period from beyond the next two budget years to the far horizon of Coast Guard planning. As such, CPE examines both the threats and the opportunities in the external environment and relates them to the concerns of the internal environment and the structure. Its focus is generally on events three or more years in the future.

The word "evaluation" in CPE's name, however, relates to an important concept. This division evaluates plans that are prepared by all the program

*The letter G in the staff acronym G-CPE was applied by the Department of Transportation. G stands for Coast Guard, as CPE stands for Office of Chief of Staff, Plans Evaluation Division. The staff acronyms and the names of the offices appear in figure 8.

directors, comparing them with the basic objectives and examining them against the future environment forecast for the Coast Guard, to assist the chief of staff in his coordinating role. The decision to have plans developed by the program directors was deliberate and allows the chief of staff to concentrate on coordination, overall development, and evaluation.

While CPE's focus tends to be long term, the focus of the Programs Division (G-CPA) is current operations. CPA is concerned with the present budget year and with the budgets for the next two years. Under the aegis of CPA, program plans move from plans to funded programs. In CPA the action becomes intense, for, as Byron said, "Ready money is Aladdin's lamp." All the program directors who have a stake in developing new programs, or in altering current programs, also have a crucial interest in the resource allocation work of CPA.

The Budget Division (G-CBU) is primarily concerned with the Coast Guard budget for the current year. In budgeting terminology, CBU is concerned with the "execution" of the current budget. It works closely with CPA to coordinate the funds available in one year with the stream of funds for the next two years. One individual who in successive years was chief of first CBU and then CPA made an interesting analogy about the two divisions. He compared them to relay sprinters exchanging a baton in a passing lane. The baton is the budget, and the passing lane is the period of the OMB and congressional stage budgets. The length of the passing lane—the transition period from a programming to a budgeting orientation—is illustrated in figure 9.

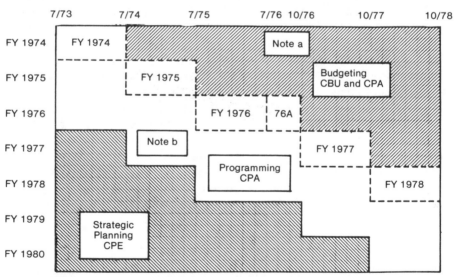

FIG. 9. The broad transition in time between program and budget orientation: (*a*) The fiscal year changed from a beginning date of 1 July to 1 October in 1976. This created a 1976 and a "1976A" budget, the latter lasting three months. (*b*) The transition from planning to programming is not nearly as clear as the transition from programming to budgeting.

While the divisions in the Office of the Chief of Staff focus on overall Coast Guard objectives, the office chiefs, who are the program and support directors, are concerned with the demands of their individual programs.[12] As was shown in figure 8, the office chiefs are one organizational level below the chief of staff in the program structure. Each operating or support program has a director, usually the rear admiral who is the chief of the related office at headquarters. It is not uncommon for a program director to oversee the activities of several generally related programs.

A list of program and support directors and managers is given in table 6. The directors are assisted by program or support managers, who are generally captains and division chiefs. Each manager is intimately involved with his operating or support program; he works with it every day. The program is often his sole responsibility. The manager is a key figure in the program structure; he is

TABLE 6
Program and Support Directors and Managers

Program	Director	Manager
Search and Rescue	Chief, G-O[a]	Chief, G-OSR
Short Range Aids to Navigation	Chief, G-W	Chief, G-WAN
Radio-navigation Aids	Chief, G-W	Chief, G-WBR
Bridge Administration	Chief, G-W	Chief, G-WBR
Commercial Vessel Safety	Chief, G-M	Deputy, G-M
Recreational Boating Safety	Chief, G-B	Deputy, G-B
Port Safety and Security	Chief, G-W	Chief, G-WLE
Marine Environment Protection	Chief, G-W	Chief, G-WEP
Ice Operations	Chief, G-O	Chief, G-OOC
Marine Science Activities	Chief, G-O	Chief, G-OOO
Enforcement of Laws and Treaties	Chief, G-O	Chief, G-OOO
Military Operations and Preparedness	Chief, G-O	Chief, G-OMR
Coast Guard Reserve Forces	Chief, G-R	Deputy, G-R
Support	Director	Manager
General Administration	G-CCS[a]	Chief, G-CPA
Personnel Support	Chief, G-P	Deputy, G-P
Engineering Support	Chief, G-E	——[b]
Financial Management, Personnel, Supply, and Automatic Information Systems Support	Chief, G-F	Deputy, G-F
Research, Development, Test, and Evaluation Support	Chief, G-D	Deputy, G-D
Medical Support	Chief, G-K	Chief, G-KMA
Legal Support	Chief, G-L	Deputy, G-L
Safety Program Support	G-CCS	Chief, G-CSP
Civil Rights Support	Chief, G-H	Deputy, G-H
Public and International Affairs Support	Chief, G-A	Deputy, G-A
Retired Pay	Chief, G-P	Deputy, G-P
Intelligence and Security Support	Chief, G-O	Chief, G-OIS
Communications Services Support	Chief, G-O	Chief, G-OTM

Source: U.S. Coast Guard, *Planning and Programming Manual* (CG-411), p. II-2.
[a] See figure 8 for the full names of the offices of each program director, etc.
[b] Each functional engineering division is a support manager for its appropriate areas.

expected to be a partisan advocate for the program. A list of all the actors will be convenient before their interaction is described in this and the next seven chapters.

As program or support directors, the office chiefs are really a centralized staff reporting to the commandant. While many of the offices at headquarters are defined according to the program structure, some also have limited responsibilities to the field.

In the field, the two area and twelve district commanders have basically decentralized responsibilities for their geographical regions. In administrative situations, district commanders report to the office chief who has responsibility for the particular situation. They report to the chief of staff if the situation spans the areas of two or more office chiefs or program directors. In operational situations the district commanders report to the area commander, who in turn is responsible to the commandant. This combination of program and support areas, on the one hand, and operational and administrative situations, on the other, creates a matrix of program and operational structures.

THE PLANNING PROCESS

The planning process the Coast Guard uses is a modification of a planning, programming, and budgeting system (PPBS). PPBS was first used by the Department of Defense in 1961.[13] Conceptually, PPBS embraces the entire spectrum of resource acquisition and allocation, from long-term planning to budgeting. An executive order made PPBS mandatory for all civilian agencies in 1965. The system did not last long, however, except in the Department of Defense and the Coast Guard.[14]

The planning process is often generalized into one of three categories: "top-down," "bottom-up," or "interactive." The Coast Guard planning process is diagramed in figure 10. It is an "interactive" process. As the figure shows, the commandant has a continuous and involved dialogue with both the program directors and the district commanders at each stage of the planning process.[15] The process involved at each of the points depicted in figure 10 will be

TABLE 7
The Four Organizational Levels of the Coast Guard Structure

Organizational Level	Responsible Officers
Coast Guard–wide	Commandant and chief of staff
Multiprogram	Chief of staff and Plans Evaluation and Programs Division
Program	Program and support directors and program and support managers
Field	Area or district commander and staffs

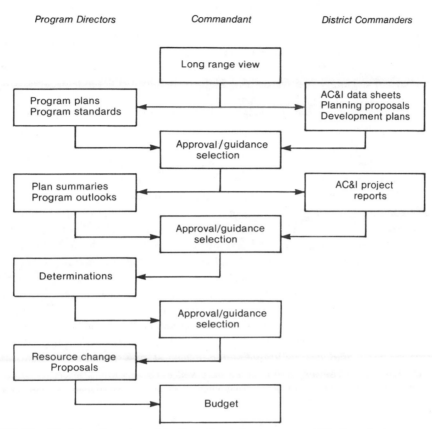

Program Directors *Commandant* *District Commanders*

FIG. 10.   The interactive nature of the Coast Guard planning process. This figure depicts many events in the planning process as it occurs in the Coast Guard. Many terms, such as the long-range view, program plans, or determinations have not yet been defined. They are presented here to depict the flow of events and to provide a convenient reference for later discussions. From U.S. Coast Guard, *Planning and Programming Manual* (CG-411), p. I-2.

discussed later in this chapter. As detailed as the figure seems, it does not fully model planning, programming, and budgeting, which together form the modified PPBS system used by the Coast Guard. Nor does it, for example, explicitly model the four organizational levels through which the various interactions take place.

These four distinct organization levels are listed in table 7. Consider the planning processes that go on at these levels. Coast Guard–wide planning is directed by the commandant, assisted by the chief of staff and his Plans Evaluation, Program, and Budget divisions. Multiprogram planning is centralized; it is directed by the chief of staff. Multiprogram planning must coordinate program planning and at the same time search for gaps and overlaps between existing programs.

On the other hand, program planning is decentralized. It is directed by program and support directors. Program planning corresponds in many ways to divisional planning in a large firm. Field planning is still more decentralized. Here the area and district commanders are responsible, and their efforts often must cut across several program areas. The whole purpose of the planning processes is to define and develop effective programs that are responsive to the national need.

So far only the internal actors in the planning process have been introduced. The interactions between them are of course complex. The external actors, however, are every bit as important, if not more important, and further increase the complexity of the process. Basically, the external actors can be grouped as members of the executive branch, the Congress, or the public. These constituencies were discussed in chapter 2 and appear there in the model of figure 6.

Within the executive branch, the Coast Guard is part of the Department of Transportation, and the secretary of transportation is the immediate supervisor of the commandant. The Office of Management and Budget is the president's principal means of supervising programs and budgets. In the Congress, authorization and appropriations committees are concerned with budgets. Also, the entire Congress can exercise any of its constitutional powers to require action in the executive branch. Finally, the public in general, or a special public interested in a particular program, can become involved in the planning process.[16] Examples include recreational boaters, waterway operators, the marine industry, and environmentalists.

THE PROGRAM PROCESS

The program process that follows and interacts with the planning process is also in some ways like an art. The range of environmental demands, the conflicts, the timing, and the large number of participants all add to its complexity. No one participant totally controls the program process. For example, unexpected external events, such as the *Titanic, Morro Castle, Torrey Canyon,* or *Argo Merchant* incidents, can reverse decisions and change emphasis.[17] But more predictable trends, such as the public demand for boating safety, can also alter priorities for resources. In many ways the program process is a microcosm of the democratic process.

The program process, however, is adversary in nature. A program or support manager proposes a course of action. The chief of staff, normally through CPA, renders a preliminary decision on the proposal. The program manager then may appeal before the decision is sent on to the chief of staff. When the proposal is presented to the chief of staff, roles are *reversed:* CPA becomes the proposer and the chief of staff is the reviewer; and so on.[18]

Throughout the process of developing programs and managing the Coast Guard, participants progressively change their roles. Such role reversal is a critical concept. One can best understand this by noting the number of times it occurs in the following description of the program process and the effect it has on the strategic choices the Coast Guard makes and on the final product of the budget.

The program process begins within the program structure. The initial proposer is the program manager; he is the advocate. The commandant is the final decision-maker. At the very beginning the Coast Guard sets the agenda of what will be proposed at each stage and the "broad boundary" of what the Coast Guard will do in the future. The responsibility of matching national needs and Coast Guard means thus rests squarely on the structure.

Each year the commandant proposes to the secretary of transportation those programs he feels are most necessary. The commandant and his staff and the secretary and his staff go over the budget. Now the commandant is the advocate and the secretary is the decision-maker. Role reversal has taken place. The request the commandant presents is called the preview stage budget.* During the review and subsequent modifications by the secretary of transportation, the budget is in the forecast stage.

During initial review by the Office of the Secretary of Transportation (OST), attention is on policy-making as much as on aggregate budget amounts. For example, in the 1977 preview the Coast Guard proposed constructing a new 270-foot cutter. That year the Department of Transportation review paid greater attention to the justification for the new cutter—the missions it would perform—than to the projected cost of twenty-four million dollars per cutter. The secretary, however, is not unmindful of overall dollar amounts being requested. There are general, though preliminary, budget targets for the department as a whole.

After the OST stage, the secretary becomes the advocate for the Coast Guard budget as it is sent forward to the Office of Management and Budget (OMB) as part of the overall Transportation Department budget. Role reversal has again taken place, and OMB is now the decision-maker. The budget at this point is called the OMB stage budget. Here aggregate numbers become vital. In preparing the president's budget, OMB weighs departmental as well as Coast Guard requests against national priorities as set by the White House. After submission of the executive budget, another role reversal takes place and the executive branch becomes the advocate. The Congress is now the decision-maker. This period in the program process is called the congressional stage. The timing of these stages is shown in table 8.

At each stage the Coast Guard interacts with the external environment—with the executive branch, the Congress, or the public. The budget, which is

---

*The preview stage budget takes the name of the year when it is submitted to the secretary of transportation, for example, the 1980 preview.

TABLE 8
Approximate Timing of the Major Stages in a Budget Cycle

Date	Responsible Agent	Event
Spring 1978	Commandant	Issue long range view
March 1979	Commandant	Approve and issue program plans
May 1979	Commandant	Issue plan summaries
October 1979	Commandant	Issue determinations
February 1980	Chief of staff	Complete scoring of resource change proposals
March 1980	Chief of staff	Serve on coordinating board for preview budget
May 1980	Commandant	Deliver preview budget to secretary
August 1980	Commandant	Deliver OMB stage budget to secretary
September 1980	OST	Prepare program memo to OMB
October 1980	OMB	Hold OMB hearings
November 1980	OMB/OST	Assign marks
December 1980	OST	Perform final OST review and pass on budget
January 1981	President	Send executive budget to Congress
Spring 1981	Congress	Hold congressional hearings
October 1981	Commandant	Issue budget to operating units

Source: Programs Division, Office of the Chief of Staff, U.S. Coast Guard Headquarters. Prepared in January 1979. See U.S. Coast Guard, *Planning and Programming Manual* (CG-411), p. A-1.

merely "a written plan for resource allocation," is the subject of the process.[19] The plan must change in response to all the inputs and pressures it receives from those who participate in the process. It is important to understand the complexity and nuances of these inputs and pressures and to see how they shape resource allocation in the Coast Guard.* Consider next how planning and resource allocation are affected by the demands of the environment.

PLANNING ACROSS FOUR LEVELS OF STRUCTURE

The Coast Guard identifies national needs that fall within its distinctive competence. These needs are the demands of the environment, identified by the planning processes used within the structure. Although final responsibility for

---

*It is important to consider the two important dimensions to this process discussed in chapter 2. The work of Richard Vancil and Peter Lorange clearly focuses these two dimensions. The first is "vertical and operates through ... organizational levels. ... The other is chronological; as the process moves from level to level it also moves through ... cycles." See Richard F. Vancil and Peter Lorange, "Strategic Planning in Diversified Companies," *Harvard Business Review* 53, no. 1 (1975): 81.

One individual in the Office of the Chief of Staff stressed to me that time is the critical dimension. He drew an analogy between a budget and a leaf floating down a gutter toward a sewer on a rainy day. Then he asked me to keep in mind that he has to watch three leaves (budgets for three separate years) at one time.

planning rests with the commandant, he assigns the daily management of these tasks to the chief of staff. In turn, the Plans Evaluation Division functions as an evaluator, monitor, and catalyst.

CPE finds that one of its most important tasks is coordinating planning activity at the four organizational levels. Another important task is providing Coast Guard planners, at all levels, with a synthesized projection of the future environment in which the Coast Guard will work. This synthesized projection, the "long-range view," will be discussed shortly.

In this way CPE helps Coast Guard planners identify national needs. The planners at each level then identify the means—the distinctive competence—that ideally equip the organization to fill these needs. CPE then has the task of assuring that program plans are in fact responsive to these national requirements.

In viewing the planning subsystem, the focus shifts from the larger, interactive planning system of figure 10 toward the subsystems of figures 11 and 12, which show planning activity at each of the four organizational levels of Coast

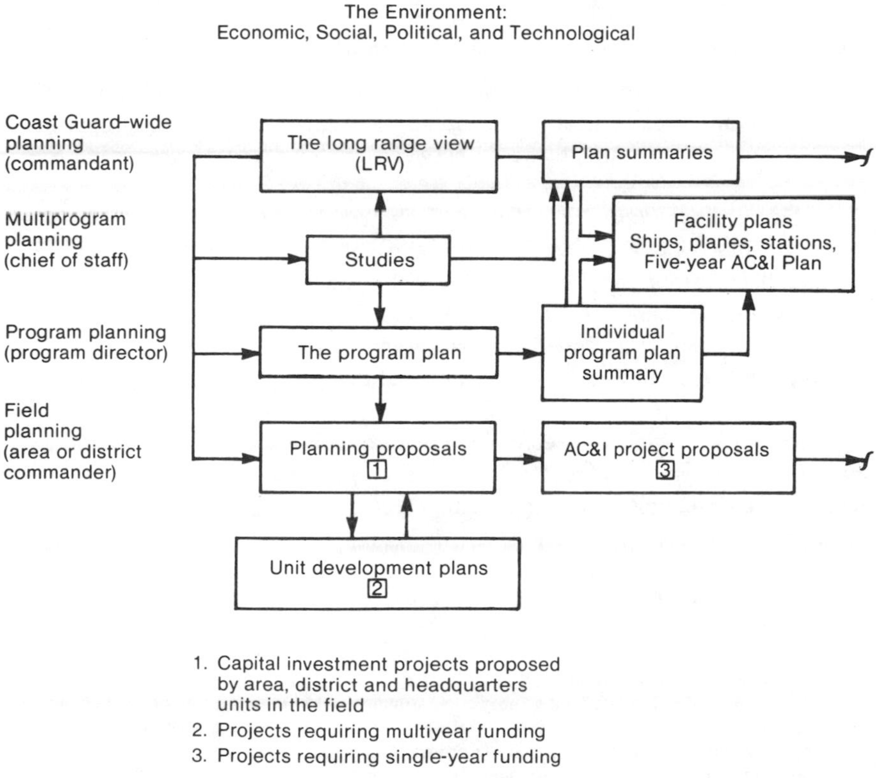

The Environment:
Economic, Social, Political, and Technological

Coast Guard–wide planning (commandant)

Multiprogram planning (chief of staff)

Program planning (program director)

Field planning (area or district commander)

The long range view (LRV)

Plan summaries

Studies

Facility plans Ships, planes, stations, Five-year AC&I Plan

The program plan

Individual program plan summary

Planning proposals 1

AC&I project proposals 3

Unit development plans 2

1. Capital investment projects proposed by area, district and headquarters units in the field
2. Projects requiring multiyear funding
3. Projects requiring single-year funding

FIG. 11.   The planning process, showing organizational levels in the initial phases.

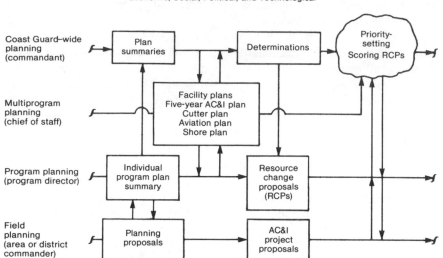

FIG. 12.   The planning process, showing organizational levels in later phases.

Guard structure listed in table 7. The "plan summaries," "planning proposals," and "determinations" are all shared between planning and programming.*

Coast Guard-wide Planning.   During early winter of each year, CPE develops its long range view (LRV).[20] Initially, the LRV is a group project in CPE. "Generalists" from the Plans Branch and "specialists" from the Systems Branch work together on it. The early drafts reflect many kinds of input, including comments on LRVs of previous years. Input is solicited from all program and support managers and directors. The area and district commanders are asked for their comments.

Economic, social, and technological forecasts are considered by the Systems Branch. Contractual assistance in developing forecasts and trends is obtained to ensure objectivity and completeness. For example, economic and demographic forecasting models are used. Many scenarios of possible future environments for the Coast Guard and the various program areas are proposed. Gradually, a new LRV takes shape. The chief of staff, the vice commandant, and

*The plan summaries, planning proposals, and determinations are all important documents in the step-by-step planning and programming subsystems. Inputs for the actual drafting of these documents come from each of the four organizational levels. Note that portions of the drafting of these documents occur within both the planning and the programming subsystems.

The content and role of the plan summaries, planning proposals, and determinations are discussed later in this chapter. The determinations, being the written guidelines of the commandant for the following budget year, lend their name to a phase in the planning and programming process.

the commandant all spend time considering critical choices and molding the final version of the LRV. Each spring the commandant signs the LRV, and copies are distributed throughout the Coast Guard. The LRV can be considered a periodic "global rethink" of the agency's future.*

The LRV discusses the future—the economy, the nature and scope of marine activities, and the most probable public expectations of the Coast Guard. It is the entry point in the models of figures 10, 11, and 12. It is also the first stage in a planning cycle, as presented in table 8, providing a common view for planners at each of the four organizational levels. It is helpful in coordinating planning and is the basis for individual program plans. It furnishes both an overview of the future environment and projections for each of the Coast Guard program areas. In 1979 the LRV included for the first time short, specific "policy-guidance" statements in each area of Coast Guard interest.

Often, the external or the internal environment signals that a particular issue or concept needs further attention, usually because it involves a threat to, or an opportunity for, effective public service. If the issue cuts across several program areas or has wide impact, an "issue study" is ordered by the commandant or the chief of staff. A "lead" program manager is usually assigned to direct the study. If the issue has particular bearing on a given program, an issue study can be initiated by a program or support director. CPE monitors all issue studies.

Many of the elements of the planning system cause only minor change or adjustment in a budget from year to year, but the particular conditions under which a study is initiated may require much larger adjustments. For this reason a study is a very important part of the Coast Guard wide planning system; it often leads to a major change in a program or even signals the beginning of a new program.†

Many of the current programs have excellent program plans based on studies of past years and sophisticated projections of future trends. Note in figure 11 that studies serve as input to plan summaries, the program plan, and planning proposals. Studies also affect the positions taken in the LRV. The only constraints to a study are the precept under which it is initiated and the broad guidelines of the LRV.

*"Global rethink" is a term popularized by some of the management studies begun during the Carter administration. See "Making Government Simpler Is Complex, Carter's Aides Find," *Wall Street Journal*, 6 June 1977, pp. 1, 29.

The timing of the LRV varies somewhat each year, depending on other priorities of the particular year. In 1979, for example, it was published at the end of August. It is actually planned and written in draft form earlier in the year.

†An "issue study" can represent a "top-down" recognition of an *opportunity* or a *threat* in the external or internal environment. Within the Coast Guard structure, an issue study normally has license to take a macro, or global, view of all the issues involved. The top-down nature of a study carries an implicit political clout that influences the structure and encourages development of proactive and innovative strategic responses.

By definition, issue studies "involve more than six man-months of in-house effort or more than $30,000 of consultant's time (if done by contract)." For a discussion of issue studies see U.S. Coast Guard, *Planning and Programming Manual* (CG-411), 21 July 1977, p. I-7.

Program Planning. The LRV provides a common projection, and Coast Guard–wide planning provides coordination for all programs. Important work also goes on at the program level, however, that can more correctly be called planning. Here the individual "program plan" is developed and the "bottom-up" phase of the planning process begins. Starting with the current state of their programs, program managers develop plans for actions they consider necessary to ensure that public needs are met.

Program plans are usually explicit and detailed over at least a ten-year horizon. These plans may call for new policy decisions, innovations in operations, reallocation of existing resources, or changes in the type and amount of resources. The program plans are developed around "program standards"—quantified expressions of specific tasks, together with a measure of performance for each task, that are necessary to attain the most effective level of a program's objective. Alternative levels of operations are considered, along with their implications for success in meeting this objective. Based on the program plans, support plans are then developed for the internal assistance needed to implement the program plans.[21] The multimission concept of shared resources has an obvious application here.

Program planners are not constrained in any way.* Some program plans are of far better quality and far more detailed than others. Funding and studies, priorities, and competitive reasons explain some of the variations. In some cases the ability of the participants is clearly different. Often the effort that goes into preparing program standards determines, to a large extent, the worth of the program plan. Also, the concepts of definition and impetus come into play at this stage and prove essential.

The next step in "bottom-up" planning begins with the development of the plan summaries. The program plan travels up two organizational levels. After a review by CPE, it must be approved by the commandant, usually by March or April. The plan summaries are then reviewed by CPE and in May are approved by the chief of staff. The plan summaries have three advantages:

1. They concentrate the thrust of the programs on specific goals.
2. They relate the goals of each program directly to the seven Coast Guard–wide objectives.
3. They establish the beginnings of quantification of program effectiveness and coordination. This in turn is a major element in evaluating program success.[22]

---

*Planning at this stage is not constrained, since the "bottom-up" phase of the process is just beginning. See "Resource Allocation in the Coast Guard," an address given by the chief of staff of the Coast Guard, Rear Admiral Robert H. Scarborough, to the corps of cadets at the United States Coast Guard Academy, 21 February 1976, p. 7. However, after the process continues and plans move up the four organizational levels, the "determinations" issued by the commandant constitute strategic guidance and the beginning of the "top-down" process. After "determinations," program planners are constrained for the budget year in question.

These advantages prove very useful to the commandant and the chief of staff when program planning is integrated. They also prove particularly valuable during later phases when difficult decisions must be made on the allocation of resources.

Field Planning. Planning as discussed so far goes on within the headquarters structure. Yet the vital link in any management system is feedback from the points where services are delivered. Field input may take several forms. An area or district commander, or the commanding officer of a large unit—such as the Coast Guard Yard at Curtis Bay, Maryland, or the Coast Guard Academy at New London, Connecticut—can develop a "planning proposal." The purpose of a planning proposal is to develop from the field commander plans for changes to an "existing situation or an existing plan at any unit under his command." Each planning proposal must do the following:

1. Identify the problem.
2. Explain why a change is necessary.
3. Present feasible alternative solutions to the problem and analyze each, supplying cost data.
4. Recommend a solution and explain why it is recommended.
5. State the effect if the proposal is not approved.
6. Discuss the environmental effects of the proposal.[23]

When a planning proposal is received at headquarters, it is studied by the concerned program director and by CPE and CPA. Before drafting a reply to the field commander, the program director is responsible for coordinating his answers with those of other concerned program directors and the chief of staff. To obtain approval, the proposal must be consistent with the appropriate program plan and the LRV.

When a planning proposal requiring new capital funds is approved, there are two paths for implementation, depending on the cost of the project. If it requires a capital investment of less than seventy-five thousand dollars, a field commander may implement it as soon as funds can be set aside from the local operating expense budget. The costs of the vast majority of projects, however, exceed seventy-five thousand dollars. This classifies them as capital projects or, in the government terminology mentioned earlier, as acquisition, construction, or improvement projects (AC&I).* AC&I projects must be submitted to the Con-

---

*The practice of having a dollar cutoff on approval authority is, of course, standard in industry and the government. Capital projects exceeding a certain amount have been sent by the Coast Guard to the Congress for explicit approval ever since the cutter-building program of 1843–46.

Subverting dollar cutoff levels on approval authority occurs in the public sector as well as the private sector. See U.S., Congress, House, Committee on Government Operations, Hearings before a subcommittee, 87th Cong., 2d sess., *Illegal Actions in the Construction of the Airfield at Fort Lee, Virginia*, 13–29 March 1962, pp. 9–318.

gress and approved by the authorization committee as well as the appropriations committee. When headquarters approves a planning proposal, therefore, the field generally goes ahead and prepares the more detailed "AC&I project proposal report." This report is carefully scrutinized by the appropriate program director, the engineering support director, and the programs division. The field receives a reply approving, disapproving, or requiring revision of the report.[24]

A planning proposal serves two important functions. First, it provides a "bubble-up" link between decentralized field planning and centralized Coast Guard-wide planning. Second, it avoids squandering valuable design and engineering work on projects that will not be approved.

For large field commands that have extensive capital facilities, such as the Coast Guard Yard or Academy, a "master plan" for the command is required. This is called a development plan.* It reflects the real practical consideration that large capital investments must be scheduled over a number of years because of the inherent limit of the overall executive budget. The plan includes a site development plan, general design data, a financial plan, and a construction schedule. It is reviewed by the program director, by the engineering support director, and by the Plans Evaluation Division and Programs Division. The plan must be approved by the chief of staff.

Invaluable field input, particularly for the program areas, is gathered through less formal channels as well. Many programs require statistical information on operating facilities or on the workload, and reporting systems for this purpose are becoming more prevalent. New attempts are constantly made to gather field inputs and help measure program performance.† This area is the key to further progress on program standards and on effectiveness measures in general.

Fitting field input both into the overall policy-making and planning systems and within the time frame of the budget cycle is difficult. The development plans and the planning proposals are inputs to the program plan and ultimately to the plan summaries. Sometimes the field structure feels there is a lag in integrating their inputs into Coast Guard-wide planning. Although some lag is probably inevitable, it is usually overcome by discussions between the commandant and his area and district commanders in the field. More often, the discussions occur between the chief of staff and the district commanders. Coordination at this level between the programs competing for resources is often necessary and increases the effectiveness of each organizational level.**

*Planning proposals, AC&I project proposal reports, and development plans do *not* include plans for new cutters or aircraft. The planning for cutters and aircraft is centralized at headquarters in the cutter and aircraft plans, which will be discussed later in this chapter as a part of multiprogram planning.
†One example of a performance model for an individual program is reported in U.S. Coast Guard, *Marine Environmental Protection Program: An Analysis of Mission Performance,* report no. CGWEP 1-76, August 1975. This report analyzes Coast Guard oil pollution statistics and establishes effectiveness measures and performance standards for the Coast Guard Marine Environmental Protection program. This report will be discussed further in chapter 10.
**Beside frequent formal and informal communications between the commandant and his area and

Multiprogram Planning.   The approval of the plan summaries in May indirectly begins another task. Once the individual program plans have been summarized, the needs for the various resources of the Coast Guard must be coordinated and summed. Here the dual-role strategy and the multimission concept of the Coast Guard place an extraordinary demand on planning and resource allocation.

Many of the human and physical resources of the Coast Guard are used during the same year for accomplishing the objectives of two or more programs. For example, aircraft flying fishery patrols are often diverted to search for lost ships or even to track oil spills. Shore stations are often involved in operational programs such as search and rescue and at the same time have a schedule of law enforcement or aids to navigation duties to perform. And, of course, military preparedness is always required and must not be forgotten when other duties are planned.

Having resources ready to deploy for multiple programs is cost-effective for the nation. Having the Coast Guard ready to serve with the Navy Department has also been a valuable asset. In the terms of an organizational advocate, the multimission concept and the dual-role strategy make "the Coast Guard uniquely cost-effective in comparison to other federal agencies."[25] To administer this concept effectively and to implement the strategy, however, multiprogram planning is necessary. The "facility plans" shown in figures 11 and 12 integrate the requirements of the various programs and make up a major part of the multiprogram planning flow.[26]

The facility plans integrate the Cutter, Aviation, Boat, and Shore Unit plans. These plans were first developed in response to a congressional request in the late 1950s. The problems the Coast Guard had in gaining approval for aircraft purchases during the 1958 budget appropriations hearings were partially met by an aviation plan prepared at that time (see Appendix 1).

By 1980, facility plans had grown to include the requirements for operational hours for ships, boats, and aircraft and for operational networks for ships, boats, and aircraft, and for shore facilities. These requirements are the demand. They are taken directly from the needs expressed in the program plans. In turn, these needs reflect actual levels of service provided to the public. The facility plans go on to list the hardware available—that is, the supply. The gaps between supply and demand are then categorized.

Most plans are based on detailed research. In some cases, simulations have been developed of the requirements placed on the hardware by the program plans. Two such simulation models cover the Search and Rescue program and the Enforcement of Laws and Treaties program. Both simulations were developed and updated by the Office of Operations at headquarters.

---

district commanders, a conference of all Coast Guard admirals is convened once a year to discuss problems. It usually lasts one week and is held in October, three months before the beginning of the critical desision period of another budget year.

Facility plans are necessary because no one program or even program area should dominate any given operational unit of the Coast Guard. The matrix of resource-sharing that results from the dual-role strategy and the multimission concept is complex, but it enables the various programs of the Coast Guard to function with the available resources.

Many trade-offs are involved. These compromises between conflicting interests are the essence of multiprogram planning. For example, the Search and Rescue program will have definite ideas about the most effective cutter to fulfill its own requirements. On the other hand, the Military Readiness, Enforcement of Laws and Treaties, and Marine Environmental Protection programs may all have marked variations in their requirements for cutters. The cliches about committees, horses, camels, and compromises often surface. Compromises are made, however, and a cutter plan, boat plan, aviation plan, and shore units plan are drawn up.

One output of these plans is the number of new cutters, boats, aircraft, and shore units required to operate the various programs. This output helps produce a capital-budget plan for the next five years. This plan is called the "AC&I five-year projection."[27] It is a "compilation of all AC&I projects which, in the opinion of the Coast Guard, will require funding within the immediate future."[28] Figures 11 and 12 map how capital projects may be submitted as single-year or multiyear requests.

The AC&I five-year projection meets one important goal of multiprogram planning—providing the Coast Guard with the resources necessary to carry out its various programs. The second important goal of multiprogram planning is to coordinate planning at all levels. Figure 12 shows that a comparison of the facility plans and the plan summaries are the final inputs to the "determinations," the next milestone in the policy-making and planning systems.[29] The determinations will be discussed as the first phase of the resource allocation process, the subject of the chapter that follows.

4 THE RESOURCE ALLOCATION PROCESS

INTERNAL RESOURCE ALLOCATION: GUIDANCE, APPROVAL, AND SELECTION

Chapter 3 introduced the actors. It also traced the planning process as it interacts with the changing external and internal environments and as it moves through time and through the four levels of the structure. The internal planning process attempts to identify "a picture of what the ideal Coast Guard would look like," if limitless resources were available to meet the needs of the nation.[1]

Because few if any resources in the real world are limitless, here I shall describe the dynamics of the resource allocation process, focusing on both the actors and the internal and external processes. To adapt and to compete in the public sector, the Coast Guard attempts to identify the *means*—the resources and the distinctive competence—that will optimally equip it to fill the *needs* of the nation as defined by the planning process. At this point the means are precisely identified in terms of both the human and the physical resources required to match these needs. Identifying and tagging resources makes up a large part of the resource allocation process as modeled in figure 6.

A bridge between planning and resource allocation is reached at the first "guidance, approval, and selection" decision point. This is illustrated in figure 13, a slightly modified version of figure 10. At this point in internal resource allocation—often called programming in the public sector—the primary function is narrowing the options developed during planning. One difficulty of programming is that the ideal does not involve competing for scarce resources.

As the programming cycle starts, this competition begins in earnest. Although planning starts as a "top-down" process with the long range view, it changes to "bottom-up" as it progresses through the four levels of the structure, identifying the responses open to the Coast Guard. As resource allocation starts, the process again becomes "top-down" when choices are made between possible strategic responses. The programming process is formally under way when the commandant gives "top-down" guidance on choices for the next budget year.

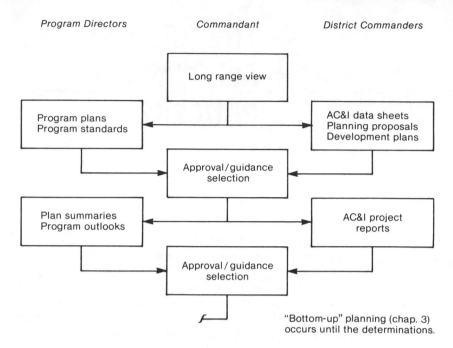

Program Directors   *Commandant*   *District Commanders*

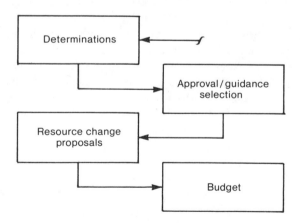

FIG. 13. The interactive nature of the Coast Guard resource allocation process. From U.S. Coast Guard, *Planning and Programming Manual* (CG-411), p. I-2. Some modification of figure 10 has been made to differentiate planning from resource allocation.

Until this point in the cycle, program plans, program standards, plans summaries, and program outlooks all are activities for which CPE is responsible at the multiprogram planning level. But a transition is occurring between planning and programming (shown in fig. 9) that shifts responsibility between the Plans Evaluation and Programs divisions. At this point the Plans Evaluation Division shifts to merely providing a long-range overview. The Programs Division is given responsibility for preparing a draft version of the important determinations. All activity at the Coast Guard–wide and multiprogram level shifts its focus from a few or many years in the future to just one twelve-month period—the next budget year.

A review of figure 13 will help us recall the timing of the budget cycle. Activity began when the commandant signed the long range view. The plan summaries, program plans, and standards were then approved by the commandant over the months that followed. The determinations now to be discussed were recycled and refined during the summer. The commandant issues the determinations in October; when he does so he shapes, for better or worse, the responses—the strategic choices of the Coast Guard. At this time the fiscal year being addressed is still twenty-four months away. This one fiscal year, however, becomes the focus of all programming activity.

THE DETERMINATIONS

The determinations are depicted in figure 14, which shows the involvement of the Coast Guard–wide, multiprogram, and program planning levels in the makeup of determinations. (Figure 14 is the same as figure 12.) The Coast Guard *Planning and Programming Manual* discusses the activity at this stage:

The preparation of draft Determinations by each Program/Support Manager is the initial programming action in the budget formulation process. . . . The basic purpose of the Determinations is, through dialogue with the Commandant and Vice Commandant via the Chief of Staff, to reach agreement on those goals and achievements which are to receive emphasis in the upcoming budget cycle. Determinations are a major function of the decision-making process in the Coast Guard, and one of the few that provide a direct access to and a direct response from the Commandant. Because the Determinations involve the Commandant personally, the form and format they take may change as required to enhance their comprehensiveness and usefulness.[2]

To generalize, determinations are a mechanism through which the commandant sets priorities and chooses the responses of the Coast Guard for the upcoming budget year.

More specifically, each program manager works initially with his program director to draft a "determination" for his program. These drafts set the agenda for an annual discussion between individual program managers and the comman-

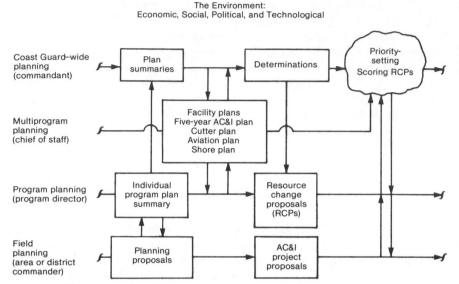

FIG. 14.   The resource allocation process, showing organizational levels.

dant. Rear Admiral Robert H. Scarborough, appointed vice-commandant in 1978 and chief of staff from 1975 to 1977, describes the process:

Program Managers propose the agenda which normally consists of the actions laid out in the first year of their 10-year, long-range plan. The discussions center on operational and management concept changes the program managers wish to implement in the upcoming budget.

The Program Manager thus sets the agenda for these discussions. Concepts rather than costs are discussed in these meetings. For example, a discussion might concern the Program Manager's Proposal for improved buoy position accuracy—not how much it will cost. The result of these meetings is written general guidance by the Commandant on those programs or activities he would like emphasized in the upcoming budget, together with an indication of both those items he is willing to consider further in the formulation of the next budget request (i.e. future fiscal years) and those he wishes deferred or cancelled. . . . The players in this direct interchange are the Program Managers and the Commandant. The latter's strong personal role at the outset of budget request formulation is an important feature of our system. A feature, I might add, that is relatively uncommon in federal government.

Because issues, not dollars, are the subject of these discussions, there still remains a very formidable task of paring down. . .to budget realities—the setting of internal priorities.[3]

Drafts of the determinations from each program area are then sent to the Programs Division. They are first studied by the reviewer assigned to the specific program area and then discussed over a "round-table" session of other reviewers and the chief of the Programs Division.* Several informal discussions take place between the reviewers and the program and support managers whose areas they cover. Members of the Plans Evaluation Division also participate in determinations meetings to ensure that "single-year" decisions are consistent with long-run plans.

After a final meeting of all of the reviewers, the chief of the Programs Division "provides the Chief of Staff with an analysis of [the determinations], highlighting major budget initiatives, strategy, policy decisions needed, conflicts, etc."[4] The chief of the Programs Division then recommends broad areas of thrust for the chief of staff to emphasize in his covering statement for the draft of the determinations. Final staff preparation of the determinations begins when the chief of staff holds hearings with the individual program manager and directors. The chief of staff then sends his recommendations for the determinations to the commandant.

The determinations are a goal-setting process; the early drafts were a "bottom-up" process. Later, the process includes negotiation, and still later the commandant gives strategic guidance and the process becomes "top-down." Both the commandant and the vice commandant spend considerable time going over the determinations. In recent years several days have been spent, and a great deal of written material has been produced. At this point the commandant is pragmatically shaping the short-run future of the Coast Guard, in the sense of the model of figure 6.†

The beginning pages of determinations spell out the broad areas of thrust to be taken. For example, for fiscal year 1976 the following points were singled out:

1. *People*   A basic concern for the well-being of and workload on our people is a factor in almost every program area. Of concern in *all* programs is the lack of sufficient personnel allowances to do the jobs that must be done. In today's economy there will *never* be enough for a 100% effort, but in many of our programs—especially the ones with newly legislated burdens—we are at 50% or less of what we need. Couple this with the shortage of bodies for the allowances we *do* have, and we are in real danger of not being able to perform effectively in many areas.
2. *Plant*   One thing that has become patently clear with the application of our 5-year AC&I Projection and updating our Cutter and Aviation Plans is that the present level of AC&I funding is an order of magnitude out of step with what is needed to meet our expanding missions and plant obsolescence. Maintenance and utilization are also serious problems, made more so by skyrocketing costs and energy shortages.

---

*While Captain James S. Gracey was chief of the Programs Division (1969–74), he usually convened a daily "round-table" session of his division. His reviewers sat at a round table and dissected critical issues. Each reviewer was expected to present strategic options for issues within his area, then serve as an advocate for one alternative. Another reviewer or the programs chief then assumed the role of the opposition. Under the leadership of the programs chief, the reviewers quickly focused on problems and solutions. This round-table model was continued by Captain John D. Costello when he was chief of the Programs Division from 1974 to 1977.
†The commandant often holds final discussions with program or support directors and other key general managers in the area to help prepare key parts of the determinations.

3. *New Missions* and responsibilities have been imposed or are expected from legislation, treaty, and executive mandate. But the resources to go with them have not been provided in full measure. The nature of our role is changing to include a greater and greater proportion of regulatory and enforcement functions, while operational demands have not really diminished.[5]

The pages that followed in determinations for 1976 contained concise guidance for each program area, drawing upon the planning done at each of the four organizational levels.

Determinations set the stage for programming. The basic task at this point is summed up in the final paragraphs of the determinations for that year.

Somehow, we must find a way to present our situation to those who review our budget requests that will convey the conviction that we must break away from the confines of traditional budget "levels" if we are to grow in capability commensurate with the growing role in government that is expected of us and which we are best suited to perform.[6]

So far we have been discussing plans and budgets; but plans and budgets in the public sector are not necessarily linked. In government, plans, as the focus of the planning subsystem, respond to requirements. These requirements come from the president—in the form of executive branch orders and policies—and from the Congress—in the form of legislative branch mandates. For the Coast Guard the mandates include Title 14, United States Code Annotated, and require the agency to deliver specified services.

But federal budgets, the focus of the programming subsystem, often respond to budget envelopes. (An envelope is a share, or a projected percentage share, of an arbitrary appropriations figure for an area of government.) In reality then, *budget envelopes are not linked to plans:* when new services are mandated, a resource gap may exist. This is one of the large problems of programming and resource allocation. Another is the age-old decision about *where* the available resources will be used.

THE RCP: GUIDANCE, APPROVAL, AND SELECTION

Once the determinations are complete, much of the remaining work in programming and budgeting involves requesting resources. The RCP, or "resource change proposal," is a format for requesting resources that grew out of budget studies done in 1963–64. Each RCP, as its name implies, is a proposal to reallocate resources by an increase, a decrease, or a shift.

Most commonly, the RCP initiates the process of acquiring new resources. RCPs are shown in figure 14. They result from work done at the program level of the structure. RCPs begin every concrete and substantive change in a program, although their role differs markedly from the role of the study discussed in chapter 3.* In one officer's words, the RCP is "where the money is and where the battles are."[7]

An RCP is a document used within the Coast Guard, prepared by the program or support manager for discussion with the program or support director. The document itself consists of at least five pages plus a number of coded data sheets necessary for computer input. The first page of the RCP is a summary of alternatives, with the net change in money and personnel each requires.† The costs (or gains) for the budget year must be provided and the RCP must project both the incremental and the aggregate costs for a five-year period. The second page is an analysis of the goal or problem that provoked the proposal. It must provide a narrative description, a definition of quantitative criteria, and background information. An in-depth analysis of the desired course, along with background information on other alternatives, completes the RCP. The program managers are critically aware that the RCP must be a thorough, well-researched document that will form the "cornerstone" of the resource allocation process.[8] The program directors review and approve the RCPs prepared by their managers, then forward them to the Programs Division.

The chief of staff sets a date for submission of RCPs. He usually allows one month after the approval of determinations. Each year, approximately six-hundred RCPs are submitted. Table 9 depicts the aggregate value of RCPs submitted for capital projects during 1972–80. About half of the total value of projects requested survived the RCP process and remained in the budget when it reached the OST stage.

An elaborate scoring system has been developed for rank-ordering RCPs. RCP-scoring usually takes place in December and January. Reviewing six hundred RCPs each year places time pressure on all who must analyze them. The Programs Division assigns a numerical grade to each RCP submitted by the various programs. The "scoring process" algorithm contains a number of factors, and weights are assigned to each. A typical list of factors and weights is presented in table 10.

The weights are designed to favor proposals that are consonant with the long range view, program plans, program standards, plan summaries, and determinations. RCPs that are based on unequivocal mandates—for example, specified in

---

*Whereas a study may initiate a major program change, an RCP often makes more detailed, and sometimes minor, adjustments to a program. The mechanisms of the RCP are discussed in more detail in U.S. Coast Guard, *Planning and Programming Manual* (CG-411), 21 July 1977, pp. III-5, IV-2, 4, and Appendixes G and I-2. See also Thomas D. Lynch, *Policy Analysis in Public Policymaking* (Lexington, Mass.: Lexington Books, 1975), pp. 59–64.

†For most of the resource allocation decisions within the Coast Guard, the most significant resources are money and personnel. The number of people is important because manpower levels of the Coast Guard are set by law. Congress is also very concerned about points such as the officer/enlisted ratio that are affected by shifts in the aggregate number of people in each category.

TABLE 9
*Aggregate Value of Capital Projects Requested and
Approved, 1972–80 (in thousands of dollars)*

Fiscal Year	Value of RCPs for Capital Projects Submitted by Program Managers	OST Stage Capital Budget Request
1973	661,913	300,000
1974	403,109	215,283
1975	419,400	182,351
1976	488,080	231,627
1977	510,492	300,000
1978	671,574	385,434
1979	583,463	405,714
1980	530,027	425,897

Source: Programs Division, Office of the Chief of Staff,
U.S. Coast Guard Headquarters.

law or specifically required by the president—those that affect large numbers of
the public, and those that have favorable cost/benefit ratios also enjoy scoring
advantages. The relative importance of the factors is "tuned" by adjusting the
weights by which each factor will be multiplied. The weighting of each factor in
the scoring process algorithm is reviewed annually to allow shifts of emphasis in

TABLE 10
Factors and Weights Used in Scoring RCPs, 1975

Factor	Raw Score	Weight	Total Score
Contribution to long range goals or objectives	____[a]	9	____
Relationship to existing programs and resources	____	10	____
Mandate for carrying out action (e.g., law, presidential order)	____	13	____
Substantiation of need	____	5	____
Size of public benefited	____	10	____
Relationship of benefits/outputs to costs	____	12	____
*Effect on personnel workload	____	6	____
*Effect on present living conditions	____	5	____
*Effect on present working conditions and safety	____	7	____
*Impact on physical plant	____	5	____
*Impact on training programs and facilities	____	5	____
*Support managers preparedness to implement	____	5	____
Impact on environment	____	4	____
Effect on energy consumption	____	4	____
		RCP score[b]	____

Source: Programs Division, Office of Chief of Staff, U.S. Coast Guard Headquarters.
[a] A raw score is filled in by a particular evaluator.
[b] RCP score = summation of total score.
*These "effects" or "impacts" are internal to the Coast Guard.

meeting strategic objectives.* This bottom-up process has the advantage of combining strategic direction with involvement and interaction from many levels, leading to rigorous competition between programs. It makes incremental choices that are at the very center of the model of figure 6.

The chief of the Programs Division is assisted in applying these decision aids by program reviewers who are responsible for working with various program and support managers. As priority-setting continues, individual RCPs must satisfy higher and higher standards to remain in competition. Each RCP is scored for the first time by the program manager as he submits it to CPA. Once in CPA, each 1976 RCP was scored by the reviewer responsible for that program area and again by a panel composed of the three senior members in the division. Because the scoring system must deal with subjective material and values, the large and varied list of criteria is an attempt to reach a balanced and objective compromise. A program manager is understandably anxious that an RCP he submits survive, and his evaluation of its worthiness may be higher than that of an impartial observer. One can easily perceive the competition and conflict that occur within the structure, but the necessary match between national needs and organizational means is being struck, as depicted in figure 6.

THE PREVIEW BUDGET

As the list of RCPs is being compiled by CPA, each program director is asked to rank according to his own priorities all the RCPs he has submitted, as a final input. Some people in the program areas believe that the value of the RCP as a decision tool is not really proved. They think the six hundred RCPs submitted each year could probably be sorted within two weeks into the four cells of a matrix like that in figure 15. On the other hand, many more people argue that the RCP is a good tool, since it produces a centralized ranking of projects by priority. Indeed, table 11 enumerates four groups into which all RCPs are categorized during the sorting process used since 1976. Note that the total dollar value of RCPs submitted ordinarily far exceeds any expected budget level. Since the actual budget will fall between the B and the C category, eliminating category D is reasonable.

Finally, the staff of the Programs Division sits down to another round table, where the rank-ordered lists are discussed in detail. Each reviewer serves as advocate for the projects he considers. The remaining reviewers have a chance to

---

*The RCP has the potential to examine the base budget and since 1979 is used for this. The qualitative aspect of the RCP also must be emphasized. Along with numerous instructions on RCPs, the following caveat appeared with guidelines issued by the Programs Division: "The scoring system is not a precise mathematical procedure. It is a tool . . . just one of many considerations that will ultimately decide the priority of any given item. . . . Please use it in the spirit in which its use is intended."

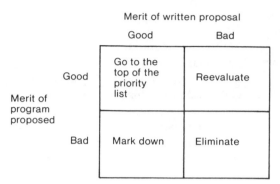

FIG. 15. A matrix for scoring RCPs.

speak for a higher or lower priority on any item. The chief of CPA often speaks as an advocate or adversary of various possible budgets. He tries to weigh the advice of his reviewers against the sum of all inputs he has received. The round table discussions are brutally frank, and an atmosphere of "what's best for the Coast Guard" builds up as critical choices are made. In this atmosphere the strategic responses of the Coast Guard are cast. Often examiners are asked to assume adversary roles in situations where CPA feels controversy may arise. In the terms of one examiner, a *bruta figuro* around the round table may prevent one at a later and more costly stage in the budget process.*

Between round-table sessions, reviewers in CPA seek input from each of the organizational levels that have developed RCPs. Area and District commanders are asked their priorities on AC&I projects. Field planners are queried. Program managers are asked their final preferences in regard to RCP ordering, and there is input from the multiprogram level as well. With these inputs, an RCP priority list is drawn up by the end of February, according to the schedule discussed in chapter 3 and presented in table 8.

At this point the chief of staff convenes the Coordinating Board, which is chaired by the deputy chief of staff. It generally consists of the deputy chiefs of the headquarters offices, all program and support managers, the chief of the office planning staffs, and the chiefs of the Programs, Budget, and Plans Evaluation divisions. The members are all the key captains within the program structure at headquarters.

The Coordinating Board has been termed a "court of appeals." Here the program managers can appeal projects they have advocated that failed to survive

---

*The language at a round-table session in the Programs Division is both frank and colorful—a hybrid of the jargons of budgeting, banking, ships, aircraft, and, in the case of *bruta figuro,* Italian. One program director liked to submit an RCP each year for a "yellow submarine." The program director claimed he did it so "those turkeys in CPA will have something to cut while my pregnant stuff gets stuck in the budget." A reviewer from CPA counters that this ploy is an example of the type of "fox [resource claimer] who needs to be kept out of the chicken coop [the resource pool being allocated]."

TABLE 11
Four Categories of RCPs Ranked by the Programs Division

Category	Characteristics by Rank
A	RCPs scored in the top 50 percent, and in the top 50 percent of the program directors' subjective priority list. (These RCPs will be top contenders for the preview stage budget. Emphasis will be placed on strengthening their justification.)
B	RCPs scored in the top 50 percent, but in the bottom 50 percent of the program director's priority. (These RCPs will be reviewed in depth as preview stage budget contenders. Clarification of the differences in scoring will be sought.)
C	Scored in bottom 50 percent, and in the top 50 percent of the program directors' priority. (These items will be reviewed further if better analysis is provided.)
D	Scored in the bottom 50 percent, and in the bottom 50 percent of the program directors' priority. (These items will not be reviewed further.)

Source: Programs Division, Office of the Chief of Staff, U.S. Coast Guard Headquarters. The exact technique for making these categories obviously varies from year to year.

a cut. This is the familiar reclama of the adversary process. At this point the effects of the cuts on the Coast Guard are argued. Since the priority list is essentially his product, the chief of CPA usually makes the principal response to the issues raised. In some instances adjustments are made in the priority listings, though they generally must be strongly supported by new "evidence" or reasoning, and there is some "trading off" of proposals above and below the expected budget request level. The Coordinating Board is reconvened at each stage in the budget process where resource shifts take place. Obviously the number of adjustments at successive board meetings is severely limited, commensurate with the progressive "firming" of the actual level for the budget being considered.

After review by the Coordinating Board, the priority list, with any modifications, is presented to the chief of staff by the chief of the Programs Division. All reclamas, both those accommodated and those not, are reviewed for the chief of staff, along with the rationale for each recommended action. At this juncture roles are reversed. CPA becomes the advocate of items on the proposed priority list—in reality a first draft of the upcoming Coast Guard budget request. Individual program and support directors also have the opportunity to submit written reclamas at this stage, and the chief of staff may make changes in the list proposed by CPA.

The same process is repeated with the commandant. Here the chief of staff, assisted by CPA, is the advocate in the adversary process. Each of these reviews is rather long—on some occasions taking a full day. This review permits the commandant and the chief of staff the full opportunity to direct the Coast Guard budget. It also allows both officers to become familiar with individual items and trade-offs in the upcoming budget. As soon as the commandant approves the priority list, a preview budget is drawn up. In May the preview budget is delivered to the Office of the Secretary of Transportation.

At this point the commandant is the advocate. His familiarity with the process by which the list was drawn up aids him in his advocacy at later stages. This advocate-adversary process has served Coast Guard top management well, as is attested by various departmental, OMB, and congressional reviewers who have been associated with the Coast Guard. The Coast Guard's advocacy of its budget has been characterized as informed, complete, and accurate by each of these outside sources.

This process places time pressure on both the Programs Division and the Budget Division. They must know each component of the preview budget in minute detail, for they will have to reassemble the various parts in thousands of different combinations as the budget passes into the next four stages. Not only must people and capital be envisioned, they must be carefully coordinated with time, which now becomes equally important, if not a controlling variable. As the budget passes through the next stages, culminating in its enactment into law and its execution, the chief of the Budget Division assumes responsibility for the budget from the programs chief in the "baton-passing" analogy mentioned earlier. Close cooperation between CPA and CBU becomes increasingly important.[9] At this point the Coast Guard is prepared to discuss in detail with outside reviewers the strategic responses chosen—at least for the next budget year.

EXTERNAL RESOURCE ALLOCATION:
THE OST STAGE

The Office of the Secretary of Transportation (OST) and the Office of Management and Budget (OMB) make the first two reviews in the external resource allocation process. Here the executive branch directly examines, discusses, and adjusts the Coast Guard budget. The policies of the president and the Department of Transportation serve as guidelines by which Coast Guard programs are examined and measured. These two review stages are the first opportunities for outside constituents to directly influence the new Coast Guard budget. During these two stages the budget is transformed from a general, policy-orientated one to a detailed, line-item one.[10]

In May the Coast Guard sends the preview budget to the assistant secretary of transportation for programs and budget. This preview budget includes:

1. A highlight statement of the thrust and direction of the administration's programs for the upcoming year. . . .
2. An identification and analysis of each major program change in existing programs or new program proposals that . . . are of such significance that they should be considered by the Secretary. . . .
3. Summary tables conforming to the appropriation structure . . . showing this administration's preliminary estimates of budget authority, obligations, and positions.[11]

The deputy secretary goes over the preview budget. He is assisted by his Offices of Budget and by Planning and Program Review. During June formal and informal meetings occur between Coast Guard and OST officials at several levels. There is extensive communication between members of the Coast Guard Programs and Budget Division and their counterparts in the Office of the Assistant Secretary for Programs and Budget. Simultaneously, discussions take place between the commandant and the deputy secretary.

As I mentioned earlier, the OST review is primarily concerned with policy-making and with issues that have significant influence on programs rather than with dollar levels and specific line items. The commandant defends the Coast Guard budget at the review. Active participants in the departmental review include each of the assistant secretaries. The secretary, by not actively participating, frees himself to act as an arbiter of any major differences between the Coast Guard and his staff in the review. In one sense the preview budget parallels the Coast Guard determinations process.

After the review of the preview budget, the secretary of transportation provides general policy guidance. Because there has been continuing dialogue between the department and the Coast Guard over the year, however, the policy guidance of the secretary rarely leads to significant changes to the ongoing preparation of the budget request for the next year.

In July the Coast Guard submits a departmental stage budget. It is derived directly from the priority lists approved by the commandant and is submitted to the secretary. Specific line items then become the focus of discussions between CPA and CBU, representing the Coast Guard, and the staff of the assistant secretary for programs and budget, representing the Department of Transportation. By mid-July specific dollar ceilings, or "marks," are given for the seven individual appropriations that together constitute the Coast Guard budget.* The categories are:

1. Operating Expense
2. Acquisition, Construction, and Improvements
3. Alterations of Bridges
4. Retired Pay
5. Reserve Training
6. Research, Development, Test, and Evaluation
7. State Boating Safety Assistance.

The dollar ceilings are based on general guidance about the total federal budget limit provided by OMB to the Office of the Secretary of Transportation. Since OST ceilings are imposed three to four months later than Coast Guard estimates, the Department of Transportation has the benefit of more recent OMB feedback on these ceilings. The pressures of the postwar budgetary process are even more evident during the OST and OMB reviews, particularly the latter.

In the late 1970s, the Coast Guard experienced on average a 10 to 15 percent

---

*"Mark" is the budgeting term for the aggregate amount allowed for a given appropriation.

cut in its aggregate budget total during the OST stage, although this percentage varied widely both from year to year and across individual appropriations categories. When OST policy guidance and marks are finally received, the Coast Guard has forty-eight hours to appeal to the secretary. Once the appeals, if any, are settled, the Coast Guard priority lists must be revised to conform with OST policy guidance. The budget then must be revised to conform with the budget ceiling. It is necessary to rearrange many items. Within the Coast Guard, the revised budget and priority lists constitute the agenda for another meeting of the Coordinating Board. The Programs Division is the focal point for this realignment.

By late August the commandant usually receives the decision of the Coordinating Board. He reviews and approves the revised priority lists and directs the Coast Guard Budget Division to assemble the OMB stage budget. The Programs Division prepares justification folders for each item in the AC&I (capital) budget and helps to assemble the detailed budget.

Rearrangement of items at a Coordinating Board meeting, or at any stage of the resource allocation process, is an important part of the Coast Guard system. In fact, the flexibility of this system was proved again when zero-base budgeting (ZBB) was instituted within the Department of Transportation during the 1979 budget cycle. At the time the Coast Guard was able to merge ZBB objectives with its existing system.*

A ZBB approach was used with the 1979 budget by requiring the submission of RCPs for the lowest 5 percent of base resources from each program area. These RCPs—called XRCPs—had to compete in the priority lists and in the scoring processes with RCPs for new requirements. This change, although incremental in form, allowed the competition of the resource allocation process to spread to the base budget. If the commandant wanted to take an even broader look at the base, this marginal-analysis approach could be extended to a greater percentage of the base budget. In fact, such an incursion into the base could help implement the strategic choices that supposedly are the heart of the process depicted in figure 6.

---

*Zero-base budgeting was discussed by presidential candidate Jimmy Carter during the 1976 presidential election campaign. President Carter has stated that his interest in ZBB was first provoked by an article by Peter A. Pyhrr in the *Harvard Business Review*. See a later book by Pyhrr, *Zero-Base Budgeting* (New York: John Wiley, 1973).

The ZBB approach appeared to offer an answer to the problems presented by base-budgeting systems in the public sector; by 1980 the approach was the subject of considerable disappointment. Supposedly, the base budget is inflexible; it does not experience the same competition for resources as do changes to the base. Or does it? The answer to this in fact partially answers the first research question of chapter 1; it will be discussed at length in chapters 11 and 12.

The ZBB approach also offered promise of dealing with "uncontrollable" expenditures. Uncontrollable expenditures refer to those budget items that are required by a law, over which a federal agency has no budget control. In this case, ZBB could merely identify the legal conflicts these items present to the appropriations process that is described in this chapter.

THE OMB STAGE

In September the commandant reviews the assembled budget and works with the deputy secretary in preparing a covering letter to the Office of Management and Budget. The material initially submitted to OST was general in nature. The material submitted to OMB, on the other hand, is specific and detailed. This submission requires extensive justification by CPA and CBU. At the OST level, the Coast Guard initially spoke primarily in terms of programs. During the OMB stage, however, these programs must be presented in the standard federal budget format. The transition from program proposals to a budget has been described as follows: "The principal hallmarks of a budget as opposed to program proposals are documentation and preciseness of format. In a budget, each schedule must interlock mathematically with every other schedule, and differences between fiscal-year columns on all schedules must match the program justification as to timing, benefiting activity, and exact object, as well as rate of obligation and expenditure."[12] Money does not come from Congress in one lump sum; it is grouped according to the seven separate appropriations mentioned. The Operating Expense appropriation is broken down into the program areas, such as Search and Rescue, Aids to Navigation, and Marine Safety. These program areas are roughly equivalent to Coast Guard missions. In the OMB stage budget, funds requested must be arrayed in matrixes by appropriation and by program. The key documents prepared during this stage are a "digest" for each appropriation that "gathers new programs in some logical sequence with a cross reference to budget activities."[13] A narrative describes and justifies the budget increases by line item.

Once the budget is submitted to OMB, it is reviewed and becomes the subject of a hearing held in September or October. One examiner is assigned to the Coast Guard's budget. In OMB's relatively flat organization, the examiner is a member of the Office of Economics and Government, only three levels from the OMB director. The examiner reviews the Coast Guard budget in preparation for the hearing. Detailed discussions are conducted before the hearing by the Coast Guard's Programs and Budget divisions and the OMB officials concerned. In fact there is a continuing dialogue during the year between CPA and CBU and the OMB examiner. This dialogue makes the examiner generally familiar with Coast Guard operations.

The hearing is held at OMB to examine the specifics of the Coast Guard request. The principal witnesses are the commandant and the deputy secretary. This hearing is relatively informal, generally lasting two to three hours. The budget hearing is followed by more intensive informal meetings between the examiner and CPA and CBU. At this point, *the Coast Guard budget request is clearly subject to national economic policy and political considerations*. The marks the Coast Guard receives reflect the president's overall strategy for the

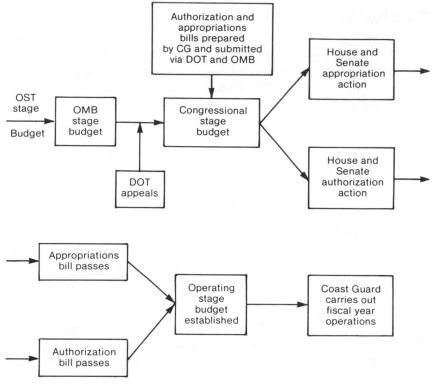

FIG. 16.   The budgeting system.

upcoming budget year. These marks are often an overriding factor, no matter how the policy-making process has worked up until this point.

Sometime in November the Coast Guard will get marks from OMB. These marks may come down, as from OST, in the form of guidance to cut a certain amount, or specific "redlining" of certain items, or inclusion of more resources in others.* The guidance can apply to policy-making, as pointed out by the Coast Guard chief of staff: "For example, in Fiscal Year 1975, when we proposed conversion of the nation's electronic navigation system to Loran-C, the OMB decision on that request spoke specifically to the policy ramifications. In that instance, OMB agreed with our proposal and overruled the suggestion by other agencies that another system be adopted."[14] The secretary may appeal these marks to the director of OMB. He may also appeal directly to the president, if he so chooses, although this is rare. Such an appeal did occur on the 1977 budget, when Secretary Coleman personally appealed several items directly to the president.[15]

---

*"Redlining" is the budgeting term for removing a specific budget line item.

Figure 16 partially maps the budget process through the external stages. The Coast Guard must revise the budget to reflect all decisions during the OMB stage, then prepare it for submission to Congress. CPA updates the justification sheets after seeking the review and approval of the Coordinating Board, the chief of staff, and the commandant. Next, the chief counsel of the Coast Guard is called to draft the budget legislation. At this point CBU puts the budget into the required format for submission to Congress. This preparation of the material marks the beginning of the most politically complex stage of the budgetary process, the congressional stage.

THE CONGRESSIONAL STAGE

In January the Coast Guard budget goes to Congress. At the congressional stage the budget is the written plan for resource allocation for activities for the fiscal year beginning in October, only nine months away. The budget at this stage is a product of the adversary process in the executive branch. It represents a judgment by OMB of the best match of national *needs* and Coast Guard *means,* tempered by economic, social, and political demands, as depicted by the model of figure 6. At earlier stages it may have been appealed by the commandant or by the secretary. At this juncture, however, the Coast Guard budget is one part of the president's budget for the upcoming year.

At this point we can formulate only partial answers to the first and second research questions; the potential stimulus of threats is only implicit in this description of the resource allocation process. In the response mechanism, however, this becomes much more explicit.

The Coast Guard budget is reviewed in part by different appropriations and authorization committees in both houses of Congress. The appropriations committees ordinarily are the scene of the more critical action. In addition, certain parts of the budget require passage of a separate act by the authorization committees before final appropriations action can be taken. Operating expenses, personnel strengths, procurement of cutters, aircraft, and shore stations, and projects costing more than seventy-five thousand dollars require such prior authorization. Reserve as well as active duty strength must also be authorized. In the House, authorization hearings for all but the strength of the selected reserve are held by the Subcommittee on Coast Guard and Navigation of the Merchant Marine and Fisheries Committee. In the Senate they are held by the Merchant Marine Subcommittee of the Committee on Commerce, Science, and Technology. Selected reserve hearings are held by the House and Senate Armed Services committees.

In the past the authorization process generally has not involved any substantive changes. For example, the Merchant Marine and Fisheries Committee is concerned that the Coast Guard get what it needs to carry out its programs as the committee sees them. In more recent years, however, particularly with the increased attention paid to marine environmental protection and fisheries resource conservation, the authorization committee has shown an increasing tendency to make substantive changes in the Coast Guard bill when the committee view differs from the president's view of matters within its cognizance. Members of the authorization committee see themselves as experts on their assigned agencies and feel they give valuable advice to the members of the appropriations committee. The appropriations committees, however, perceive the role of the authorization committees in a somewhat different light.[16]

After the authorization, the Coast Guard's budget must go through the appropriations committees of both the Senate and the House. Senators serve on more committees than members of the House, and they do not have as much time to become expert in particular areas of the budget. Also, senators recognize that the House usually gives the budget a thorough going over before sending it on. Often the Senate Appropriations Committee acts as the appeal body, much as the commandant, the secretary, and the president did in earlier stages. For this reason the Senate Appropriations Committee appears more generous.

The most rigorous scrutiny of the Coast Guard budget request takes place before the Transportation Subcommittee of the House Appropriations Committee. Hearings before the subcommittee are extensive and detailed, usually lasting three days. Questions run the gamut of Coast Guard activities. The appropriations committee has an excellent reputation for hard work, fairness, and effectiveness, and membership on the committee is sought after. Once appointed, members usually serve on one subcommittee for several terms and become experts on the agencies whose budgets they review.

The Budget and Impoundment Act of 1974 requires each subcommittee to remain within an established congressional ceiling. In effect, the subcommittee takes a role for the legislative branch much like the position OMB takes for the executive branch. Here, too, through the influence of the budget committee, the Coast Guard request must be weighed against national economic, social, and political demands.[17]

Each appropriations subcommittee has a staff, in addition to the staffs of the individual congressmen. It is this staff that has working contact with persons in the Coast Guard. The staff does the research for the committee members and often prepares questions to be used during the hearings. The staff members are a vital link between the Coast Guard and the congressmen, and so the agency makes a special effort to see that they are well informed.

With an understanding of the roles of the House Appropriations Subcommittee and its staff, one can better understand the significance of the various actors during the budget hearings. Once the budget is submitted to Congress, the Coast Guard is on its own to support itself at the committee level. This reflects the rapport and confidence between commandants and secretaries of transportation and attests to the quality of the Coast Guard's defense of its requests. A great deal of preparation naturally takes place before both the authorization and the appropriations hearings. The committee staff members will get together with the Programs and Budget divisions to prepare for the hearings. At this point the full range of interests of the constituents of the Coast Guard and the public can affect the process, in the manner described by figure 6. For example, extensive congressional hearings on loran and on Tanker Safety are discussed in chapters 7 and 10.

On the day of the hearings, the commandant goes to the "Hill" accompanied by other witnesses, primarily the office chiefs and the chiefs of the Programs and Budget divisions. The commandant is flanked at the witness table by the vice commandant, the chief of staff, and the chiefs of the Programs and Budget divisions.* National needs and the means of the Coast Guard to fill them are discussed. A recent chief of staff stated that "the House Hearings often represent the most detailed examination of our request in the whole process outside of the Coast Guard. . . . The familiarity of Members of our Subcommittee with the specific details of Coast Guard operations is surprisingly complete."[18]

The appropriations subcommittee often relies heavily on the expertise of a particular member in a particular field. It is not uncommon to hear "statements such as: 'I will leave the questioning to our great expert on. . . . ' "[19] This is possible because members of the subcommittee often concentrate their efforts on one segment of overall Coast Guard operations.

After the hearings, any "for the record" submissions must be prepared. The Budget Division coordinates the activities and ensures that all material is prepared on time. Generally speaking, the material submitted for the record for the House Appropriations Committee will be extensive. This committee feels that it must supply an extensive record to fellow congressmen. The members try to anticipate all the questions that might arise on the floor of the House and to answer them in the record, and their success is impressive. For example, for the 1974 budget, there were forty "for the record" submissions. These were not simple questions requiring "yes or no" answers, but involved questions requiring detailed answers.

Throughout its presentation, the Coast Guard is mindful that the final determiner of priorities within the executive branch is the president, irrespective of the views of the agency. This of itself is an obvious but important difference between the strategic processes of the two sections. Cuts are frequent. When they are made, the house usually does not provide specific policy guidance, which is distinctly different from the case with many OMB cuts. Instead, it ordinarily allows the commandant to select what will be dropped, and again Coast Guard structure has some flexibility.[20]

Although the appropriations committee generally cuts budget requests, there are instances when the House as a whole disagrees and actually raises the amount appropriated. For example, a public demand for an increase in the Marine En-

*Daniel Elliott in his portion of the research conducted at the Coast Guard Academy and in Washington in 1973–74 described in detail the various activities surrounding the Coast Guard budget hearings on the Hill. For a general description of budgetary strategies on the Hill, see Aaron Wildavsky, *The Politics of the Budgetary Process*, 2d ed. (Boston: Little, Brown, 1974), pp. 63–126.

vironmental Protection program was one reason behind an increase the House made in this area. This program is the case example in chapters 8, 9, and 10. The Coast Guard's formal task during the questioning in Congress is to remain consistent with the president's budget.

The usual task of the Senate Appropriations Committee is to concentrate on those items that are dropped from the budget after the House hearings and that the Coast Guard particularly wants restored. The Senate hearings often serve as a court of appeal from the House cuts. The Senate frequently restores some portion of what the House has cut, but "there is no consistent pattern regarding how these differences are ultimately resolved. On any specific issue, the position of either Committee may be finally approved by the Congress."[21]

When it has passed committee, the appropriations bill containing the Coast Guard budget request goes to the floor of the House, where it is defended by the chairman and ranking minority members of the appropriations subcommittee. A conference committee consisting of representatives of both House and Senate concentrates on items in dispute between the two bodies, if there are any. This process has been discussed at length by several observers.[22]

During the approximately six months of congressional review, both constituents and the public have access to the Coast Guard budget. The executive branch and the legislative branch also have their opportunity to examine and adjust the match of national needs and Coast Guard means that the budget represents—as illustrated by figure 6. At this point the general public and specific constituents have an excellent opportunity to be heard.

For example, the Loran-C issue [the subject of chap. 7] was fully examined by the various Committees. Many opinions from public groups both for and against our proposed funding of the system were heard. In that situation, the Committees ultimately agreed with our position and funds were subsequently appropriated. The important lesson, however, is not our success, but rather that individual constituencies or interest groups can and do participate in the process.[23]

After the Coast Guard budget request passes both houses and the differences are resolved by the conference committee, it goes to the president for his signature. When the president signs the appropriations bill it becomes law. The Coast Guard receives full obligational authority for the budget as a written plan for resource allocation for the coming fiscal year, subject (not by law but by presidential mandate) only to restrictions that may be imposed by OMB. These restrictions would be set through the establishment of personnel and outlay ceilings and the apportionment of funds. At this point the Budget and Impoundment Act of 1974 also could be exercised.

THE BUDGET EXECUTION STAGE

The final step in the process of resource allocation in the Coast Guard is the budget execution stage. The changes to the congressional stage budget made in

Congress, and any adjustments initiated by the Coast Guard, are now incorporated into the final budget document known as the operating stage, or "OPSTAGE," budget. It is this budget the Coast Guard will be working with during the fiscal year. The responses—the actions—of the Coast Guard for the next budget year are final.

Although the Coast Guard legally has the authority to obligate funds and make outlays as soon as the president signs the budget bill, OMB stipulates that before any funds are spent, each agency must submit a financial plan outlining its spending requirements for the fiscal year. The document actually submitted to OMB is known as an apportionment schedule, and OMB is said to "apportion" money to the Coast Guard.

Before submitting the Coast Guard's apportionments schedule to OMB, headquarters must receive apportionment requests from the field units. To give these units some idea of the total dollar figure upon which to base their estimates, headquarters issues "planning factors" to the field units[24] shortly before the beginning of a new fiscal year. They include:

1. A listing of the Operating Expense changes and capital projects included in the congressional stage budget.
2. A similar listing of the Operating Expense items expected to be included in the budget for the year following.
3. A list of major projects for the unit.[25]

After funds are apportioned to the Coast Guard by OMB, the agency distributes them to the program and support managers at headquarters, and to the area and district commanders in the field, in the form of allotments. After receiving the planning factors, their financial staffs work out the flow of funds for each quarter of the year.[26]

Invariably, adjustments or reordering of some priorities requires the reprogramming of funds that have been allotted. This is a natural result of the constantly changing external and internal demands placed upon the Coast Guard. The rate of change across the diverse mix of programs is increased by the continued application of the multimission concept and the dual-role strategy. When reprogramming of any substance does occur, the secretary informs the chairman of the appropriations committee, and the commandant advises the other committee chairman.

RESOURCE ALLOCATION, THE MODEL, AND THE RESEARCH QUESTIONS

Coast Guard structure, the center of the model of figure 6, is in fact the center of the resource allocation process that links the planning process to the actual events that occur during the coming budget year. The description in this chapter of the functioning of the resource allocation process—or programming and budgeting—demonstrates how the structure attempts to respond to inputs of national needs and technical means as well as to environmental forces and agency strategy and objectives. The model of figure 6 is representative of the planning and the resource allocation processes.

The structure responds to a full array of external and internal demands and implements the strategy developed by the Coast Guard. The structure has four distinct levels, as depicted in table 7, all involved in the policy-making and planning systems that direct resource allocation. These systems first monitor changing conditions and influences. They focus on national needs in areas close to the means of the agency—the resources and the distinctive competence of the Coast Guard. When these needs are identified—needs the Coast Guard feels it can meet better than anyone else—the systems program the Coast Guard means that are necessary to fill them.

The three research questions posed in chapter 1 can be answered at this point. But they can be answered more fully if we use specific cases to illustrate planning and resource allocation in terms of the challenges of the environment, as is done in part 3.

III THE CHALLENGE OF THE ENVIRONMENT

5 THE NAVIGATOR AND THE CHANGING TECHNOLOGICAL ENVIRONMENT

CHALLENGE AND THE EXTERNAL ENVIRONMENT

We have seen the concepts and mechanisms the Coast Guard developed in the 1970s in an attempt to anticipate and manage the opportunities and threats posed by the continued challenge of the external environment. Part 3 presents two case studies of how the Coast Guard structure has dealt with opportunities and threats in specific areas over extended periods. The first case deals with the Coast Guard Aids to Navigation program. "Loran," the radio-navigation system whose name is an acronym for long-range navigation, took shape amid the rapidly changing environment of World War II. The changes in technology that occurred at this time threatened to affect the Coast Guard profoundly.*

Loran might not have become a Coast Guard program had it not been for the Coast Guard's acquisition of the Lighthouse Service in 1939 (see table 1 or Appendix 1). The Coast Guard then made a case for merging the resources, responsibilities, and functions of the two services. The merit of this position, and the value of absorbing the Lighthouse Service's human and physical resources into the Coast Guard, were proved during the development of loran, discussed in this chapter and the two that follow.

The second case deals with the Marine Environmental Protection program (MEP), which grew in anticipation of the great upsurge in transport of petroleum

---

*The word *technology* when used in this chapter has the same meaning discussed in chapter 1. Technology is "not simply a 'machine,' but a systematic, disciplined approach to objectives, using a calculus of precision and measurement and a concept of system that are quite at variance with traditional and . . . intuitive modes." See Daniel Bell, "Trajectory of an Idea," in *Toward the Year 2000,* ed. Daniel Bell (Boston: Houghton Mifflin, 1968), p. 5.

Peter Drucker points out that, since the beginning of World War II, the development of new products, processes, or services from technology has proceeded at such speed and penetrated to such depth as to bring forth new industries, government programs, values, and concepts of knowledge. See Peter F. Drucker, *The Age of Discontinuity* (New York: Harper and Row, 1968). See also Donald A. Schon, *Technology and Change* (New York: Delacorte Press, 1967).

both across the ocean and through United States coastal waters. The cuttermen of the Revenue Marine had been concerned years before with protecting marine commerce from the hazards of the natural environment. The Coast Guard's acquisition of the Bureau of Marine Inspection and Navigation, made final by Harry Truman in 1946, greatly strengthened the Coast Guard role in this area and provided many of the resources necessary for the development of the Commercial Vessel Safety program.

MEP called for protecting the natural environment from the hazards of commerce. Although this was a new role, the Coast Guard was able to follow the multimission concept and utilize many of its existing resources in developing a new program that would anticipate the needs of the nation in this area. The development of the Marine Environmental Protection program is the focus of chapters 8, 9, and 10.

These two case studies describe both environmental forces and their effect on Coast Guard structure and also the agency's strategic responses.

A third case study, provided in Appendix 2, describes developments within the Coast Guard at one point in the process of preparing offshore-fishing policies during the mid-1970s. It attempts less explanation than the other cases, and it stops all the dynamics of the case at one decision point. The presentation in the third case gives no interpretations but allows the observer to assess the action.

NAVIGATION SYSTEMS
AND WORLD WAR II

Historically, marine navigators have been reluctant to accept new systems, since they desire to avoid the risks of unproved systems and prefer to depend on tradition. This reluctance is particularly true for celestial navigation, a central skill of the navigator since the early days of civilization.* World War II dramatically changed this dependence on the sun, stars, and moon, which are not available in poor weather and take time and skill to use.

By 1939 loran loomed as a promising radio-navigation system, offering an

---

*The voyages of Captain James Cook of the Royal Navy in the Pacific Ocean between 1768 and 1779 have been said to mark the dawn of modern navigation. Armed with a special clock and a nautical almanac, Cook could use celestial navigation to a degree undreamed of by Magellan. Many of these techniques were documented in the first edition of *The New American Practical Navigator*, published by Nathaniel Bowditch in 1802, when he was twenty-nine years old. The techniques of Bowditch won him many honors, including an honorary doctorate from Harvard College and election to the Harvard Corporation. These techniques remained largely the state of the art in navigation until World War II.

A parallel to navigators' reluctance to change is found in Elting Morrison's description of the changes in gunnery procedures under way in the United States Navy at the turn of the century. See Elting E. Morrison, *Men, Machines and Modern Times* (Cambridge: MIT Press, 1966), pp. 17–44. Morrison lists five conditions that often are prerequisites for change. He also discusses Alfred Thayer Mahan's comments on reform of a military service.

all-weather, automated technique for plotting positions accurately and quickly. The technology underlying it was not new; loran was one of many instances in which World War II provided the impetus to recognize and develop existing technology.

As early as World War I, sound waves from cannons had been monitored from three different spots so that the differences in arrival times could be used to fix the location of enemy artillery. This developmental time lag was common in technological innovations of the period. In fact, the average delay between a technological discovery and its commercial application was thirty years before World War I and sixteen years between the wars, but only nine years after World War II.[1]

The Battle of Britain sorely taxed the will of Great Britain and the strength of the Royal Air Force. The introduction of radar and ground control techniques for both aircraft and antiaircraft fire helped shift the advantage in the air war from Germany to Great Britain. The natural progression of techniques called for a better radio-navigation system for the Royal Air Force when the RAF took the offensive and bombed the Continent, particularly at night and in bad weather.[2] The British, under the leadership of Robert J. Dippy, hurriedly developed a radio-navigation system that they named Gee. They intended Gee as an aid to navigation for high-flying aircraft. Radar had a range of fifty to one hundred miles, but Gee promised to extend this to three hundred miles.[3]

UNITED STATES INVOLVEMENT

At the same time a group in the United States spanning government, industry, and academia was formed to examine radio-navigation applications for the military. This group became known as the Microwave Committee. The committee conceived a pulsed radio-navigation system that later became known as loran. The first formal definition of the system was made in October 1940.

American scientists from the Radiation Laboratory at Massachusetts Institute of Technology and the Bell Laboratories of American Telephone and Telegraph Company in New Jersey became very interested in new radio-navigation systems. They traveled to England and discussed possibilities with those working on Gee for the RAF. Because the United States was still a neutral country, they returned home and began developing their own concept for a radio-navigation system. The National Defense Research Committee (NDRC) of the Council of National Defense strongly backed this independent effort. Among the members of NDRC were Alfred L. Loomis, Karl T. Compton, and Lee DuBridge.

NDRC members were very influential. Alfred Loomis, for example, was not an engineer, but had been highly successful on Wall Street. He had frequent contact with the White House, and he used this access to gather support for radio-navigation technology. Karl Compton, as president of Massachusetts Institute of Technology, had many high-level contacts and considerable political influence. Karl Compton's brother, Arthur Compton, was active in the atomic bomb project, and later became a major force at Los Alamos. In the 1950s Lee DuBridge became science advisor to the president of the United States.

The War and Navy departments in Washington obviously were interested in the possibilities raised by radio-navigation systems. The military worked closely with NDRC on plans for research and, if a practical system could be developed, plans for the actual construction and operation of chains of loran stations. Wartime supplied the final impetus to begin developing a technological innovation whose scale and impact would be large.[4]

By spring 1941 Melville Eastham of the General Radio Company and Jack Pierce of Harvard were assigned to a group at the Radiation Laboratory of Massachusetts Institute of Technology. This group was commissioned to pursue the concept of radio navigation. The principle is fairly simple. Loran measures the difference in arrival time of two radio signals transmitted from geographically separated stations. The pulse from the first station, called the master, triggers the second station, the slave, into transmitting a similar pulse after a set delay. Ships or airplanes are fitted with portable loran receivers to pick up these signals. According to the fixed locations of the two sending stations, each measured difference in time defines a unique hyperbolic "line of position" on the surface of the earth.* This concept is depicted in figure 17. Knowing the elapsed time difference, a navigator refers to a loran chart and selects his line of position. His actual position will be somewhere along this curve. By taking a similar time-difference reading from a second pair of stations whose curve intersects that of the first pair, he obtains a definite geographic fix. Figure 18 shows this process using one master and two slave, or secondary, stations to form the station pairs.†

Although Coast Guard officers had been skilled navigators since the first patrols of the Revenue Marine cutters, their interests did not extend to the design and operation of marine navigation systems until the Lighthouse Service was acquired in 1939. In the mid-1920s the Lighthouse Service had acquired the Airways Division of the United States Post Office's air mail services. The Lighthouse Service proceeded to develop all the principal radio- and light-equipped airways, which were used for years to come. Later the Lighthouse Service set up, as a separate agency within the Commerce Department, what was the beginning of the Federal Aviation Administration.

The Airways Division was considered glamorous by young engineers in the 1930s, and it attracted many good people. When the Coast Guard acquired the Lighthouse Service many senior Coast Guardsmen wanted to disperse to field jobs the Lighthouse Service people who had been assembled in Washington. The

*Because these imaginary lines are widely spaced on the earth's surface, a user can select the appropriate one without difficulty.
†The term "slave station" gave way to "secondary station" much later, but to simplify the description of loran I will use the term secondary in the rest of this chapter and the next two chapters.

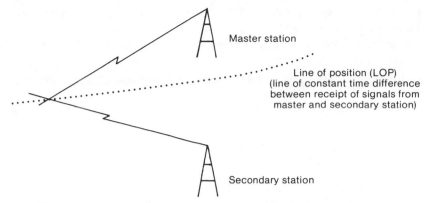

FIG. 17. Line of position from a master and a secondary station.

commandant and the chief of the Office of Engineering for the Coast Guard wisely kept the Lighthouse engineers in Washington, integrating them with the naval and marine engineers of the Coast Guard to form an expanded Office of Engineering at Coast Guard headquarters.

The Coast Guard's first contact with loran did not come through the Lighthouse Service, however; it came through an intergovernmental request for the use of two former life-saving stations for a special project. In March 1941, as Eastham's group at MIT raced to produce the American version of Gee, NRDC requested that the Coast Guard make stations at Montauk Point, Long Island, New York, and at Fenwick Island, Delaware, available as sites for pilot transmitters.[5] Both stations were in remote areas, on points of land overlooking the ocean, and at opposite ends of an important sea-lane—in this case the approaches to New York harbor.

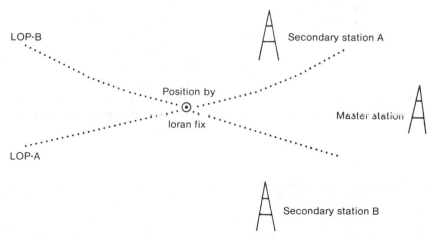

FIG. 18. Obtaining a loran fix from two lines of position.

Under the sponsorship of NRDC, transmitters were placed on Montauk Point and Fenwick Island, and a receiver was designed and tested at the Bell Transoceanic Monitor Station at Manahawkin, New Jersey. The trial and error process of developing the technology of loran had begun. As with any technological innovation involving a large and complex system, the development phase was tedious.

COAST GUARD INVOLVEMENT

In May 1942 a key decision was reached. Direction of the project by MIT's Radiation Laboratory in Cambridge and the chief of naval operations (CNO) in Washington was kept separate, but the close working relationship between MIT and CNO was retained. As a result of this decision, the vice chief of naval operations asked Russell Waesche, Coast Guard commandant from 1936 to 1946, to assign a "ranking Coast Guard officer possessing radio and electronics experience" to serve as project coordinator.[6] Because of the secrecy then surrounding the project, the Coast Guard knew little about it or about what progress had been achieved.

Why, at this critical juncture, did the navy suddenly ask for a Coast Guard officer? A vital part of the answer lies in the distinctive competence the Coast Guard had attempted to build. Russell Waesche had been able to add to this organizational competence by acquiring the Lighthouse Service, and in the process he acquired many electrical engineers with a great deal of technological experience in the emerging field of electronics. When the navy had serious doubts about the validity of the test results from the Fenwick and Montauk stations, these doubts raised questions about what priority should be assigned to the American version of Gee.

Given these problems, who should Vice Admiral Waesche nominate? Rear Admiral Park, a former chief engineer of the Lighthouse Service, was familiar with the systems engineering work Lieutenant Commander Lawrence M. Harding had done with the Airways Division. Park recommended Harding, and the former Lighthouse Service electrical engineer was assigned to the Navy Department.* When Harding arrived at the Office of the Chief of Naval Operations, he found that many of the navy officers concerned with the project had flown with him on tests of radio systems he had developed for the Airways Division.

Lieutenant Commander Lawrence Harding had become a Coast Guard offi-

---

*The background of Lawrence Harding itself tells a story of one way the Coast Guard was building its *distinctive competence* as a federal agency. The way the Coast Guard developed the Coast Guard Academy in the 1930s and 1940s relates another way.

The concept of distinctive competence and the role it plays in the development of an organization is developed by Philip Selznick, *Leadership in Administration: A Sociological Interpretation* (Evanston, Ill.: Row, Peterson, 1957), p. 42.

cer in 1939 along with many on the staff of the Lighthouse Service. When Harding first reported to CNO, it was evident to him that many in the navy thought the resources committed to Gee should be shifted to the radar project. Harding was asked to justify continued support for the Gee project.

Commander Harding quickly found that a frequency in part of the spectrum used by the Gee system was already taken by other transmissions and was thus unsuited for any long-range application. This explained the problems encountered in the Fenwick-Montauk tests. Armed with this information, Harding was assigned to the Radiation Laboratory as the naval representative. He was granted wide authority over activity both in Cambridge and at the necessary field locations.

When Commander Harding arrived at the Radiation Laboratory with navy orders, he was surprised to be greeted so warmly. The researchers were depressed over the Fenwick-Montauk test results, and they looked to Harding for solutions. An office had been prepared for Harding at the laboratory, and he was urged by both NDRC and the Radiation Laboratory to take over the daily management of the Gee project. Harding convinced the Radiation Laboratory that he could help the project more by serving as the CNO representative in Cambridge. The approval of this relationship by both CNO and MIT proved to be an important decision.

Commander Harding was ordered by CNO to "determine by any suitable means, whether the transmission of long range pulse waves could be developed into anything of immediate value to a nation whose merchant shipping was being sent to the bottom at an alarming rate, and whose Navy, after Pearl Harbor, was totally inadequate to cope with the demands of convoy coverage."[7] Lawrence Harding found himself in charge of the military application of a revolution in aids to navigation. The Coast Guard and the newly acquired Lighthouse Service were entering a period when the needs of war and the means of technology would produce rapid changes in radio navigation.

Many people became involved with the project. Admiral Furth of CNO, Rear Admiral Julius A. Furer, coordinator of research and development for the navy, other naval officers, officers from the Royal Canadian Navy, scientists and engineers from Bell Laboratories and the Radiation Laboratory all joined in the search for a system that would effectively extend the two-hundred-mile range of the radio beacon. Commander Harding arranged for tests of a receiver aboard both a blimp in the air and a ship at sea. These tests not only confirmed the promise of the system but also revealed its all-weather potential.

Of all the likely supporters of the American version of the Gee project, Admiral Ingersoll, at the time commander-in-chief of the Atlantic fleet, was in the fore. Admiral Ingersoll often visited the Radiation Laboratory for briefings and demonstrations. Karl Compton of NDRC and MIT also frequently attended Commander Harding's briefings. Compton knew Harding from the days when Compton had been president of MIT and Harding, as a student, had been presi-

dent of the MIT Radio Society, which operated an experimental radio station. Admiral Holland of the Royal Navy also became very interested in the project. All three of these men influenced the high priority ratings the project established in Washington.

Admiral Furth of CNO was the key man controlling the necessary resources. The worldwide demands for resources placed on Admiral Furth in 1942 were obviously enormous, but he gave Commander Harding every support, from assignment of dirigibles and special aircraft to special rail express trains with construction supplies. In the first months after Pearl Harbor, priorities for resources were hard to obtain, but Harding mustered the necessary backing at every step in the expanding project.

At this point Commander Harding formally suggested that the new system be called "loran," mainly to protect the project's secrecy, and the acronym was accepted by both the navy and the Radiation Laboratory.* Commander Harding, however, played a much larger role than merely naming the new navigational system. In any large formal organization, a new development of this magnitude may be doubted, if not openly resisted, even during wartime. When such an innovation succeeds despite such opposition, some program champion normally both makes the new idea work technically and also gains acceptance for it from potential users. Lawrence Harding was clearly the initial champion of loran. He also assumed the roles of project manager and "gatekeeper" to help expand the acceptance of the loran concept.[8]

The next phase in the development of loran involved more extensive field testing. Two more sites were selected, both in Nova Scotia. While these stations were being built, Commander Harding teamed with Donald MacMillan, an experienced Arctic explorer, to study likely locations in the Canadian Arctic and Greenland, so as to stretch the range of the system out across the western Atlantic.† As sites were located, the scope of the loran project expanded beyond the research and testing stage.

THE CONSTRUCTION OF THE LORAN SYSTEM

By mid 1942 the formulation phase of the loran project was well defined, and implementation was beginning. More human and physical resources were

---

*Security was a major concern in 1942. "Jamming" studies were not conclusive, and many thought the enemy might try to use the emerging radio-navigation system. The security problem was compounded by the large number of small contractors that had been utilized at the Radiation Laboratory. Commander Harding knew that Captain Sam Tucker of the navy had coined the word "radar" for security purposes. Harding coined the word "loran" primarily for the same reason.
†Donald B. MacMillan had worked for Rear Admiral Robert E. Peary. In fact, he was one of Peary's chief assistants for the Arctic expedition that reached the North Pole on 6 April 1909.

needed. The wartime environment finally provided full political support for the project. Further backing came from NDRC, the joint chiefs of staff, and from each of the services. Through Commander Harding and the early use of the Montauk and Fenwick stations, the Coast Guard became involved in a new system that changed the scope of services in the Aids to Navigation area. Vice Admiral Waesche was able to see another positive result of his acquisitive strategy.

Secrecy still shrouded the project, however, and few outsiders learned the total potential of the system being developed. For example, before equipment was installed at Montauk Point on Long Island, Commander Harding called Lieutenant Loren Brunner, the Coast Guard district electronics officer in New York, and Lieutenant Paul Trimble, the district supply officer, to Cambridge to be briefed on the loran project. Both Brunner and Trimble were graduates of the Coast Guard Academy and had benefited personally from Waesche's expansion of the postgraduate education program for officers. Indeed, Brunner had just received a master's degree in electrical engineering from Massachusetts Institute of Technology. Brunner and Trimble worked on the loran system at the Montauk station, but because of the secrecy of the project, they could not tell even their supervisors about their work.

One center of activity in developing human resources for the loran project was the loran school that was established at MIT. Another was at each of the first few working stations, where the individuals—such as Lieutenant Brunner and his technicians—operating the equipment were rapidly becoming experts in a brand-new field. Still other centers were wherever Commander Harding, his deputy Commander David Cowie, and other staff officers on the loran project happened to be as they traveled, championing the new system and briefing military staff on its possible applications. Experts and technicians were being developed as the system grew, and through this process the Coast Guard was acquiring the human resources so essential to the expansion and diffusion of a new technology.

Physical resources were also badly needed. Equipment and transportation were required to build the new stations. The frustrations of obtaining physical resources for a project of this scope were formidable, even by wartime standards. The Arctic climate, even during summer, was far from hospitable. As the fall of 1942 set in, weather became even more of an obstacle. Laying foundations and other construction required special design and preparation for the Arctic. Coast Guard and navy personnel were assigned to the loran project, and by December construction had started as far away as Greenland. The electronic equipment, station facilities, and newly trained men from loran school all had to be ready to meet the target dates for the stations to go "on the air." Under the leadership of Lawrence Harding the loran project was making progress, and in the process the Coast Guard was helping develop a new navigation technology.

In June 1943 a decision was made to forgo the use of loran for the invasion of Sicily and southern France because time was too short to prepare the equipment. At the same time a decision was made to have loran sites and mobile teams ready for future invasion and forward area operations. In meeting these deadlines, the Coast Guard would gain early experience in managing and deploying a complex technological system.

THE WORLD WAR II SCOPE OF THE
LORAN SYSTEM

The scope of the loran system was truly international, with civilian implications as well as immediate military uses. Since the war was global, many potential station sites involved negotiations with allied governments. Selecting and clearing the necessary frequency band was one task. The immediate military uses included navigation for both ships and aircraft, and bombing and bombardment. Consequently, loran stations were in demand for the Gulf of Alaska and the Pacific as well as for the Atlantic and Europe. Before the war was over in the Pacific, loran stations were in operation on some islands even before Japanese resistance there was formally terminated.

The north Atlantic chain that began with the experimental stations in New York and Delaware in March 1941 continued to grow until it spanned eleven stations by May 1944. Table 12 lists the stations, their locations, and the organizations operating them. Six stations were operated by the Coast Guard, three by the Royal Navy, and two by the Royal Canadian Navy.[9]

As soon as the north Atlantic chain became operational, Admiral Holland of

TABLE 12
Locations and Operators of Atlantic Loran Stations, 1944

Location	Operator
Fenwick Island, Delaware	U.S. Coast Guard
Montauk Point, New York	U.S. Coast Guard
Baccaro, Nova Scotia	Royal Canadian Navy
Deming, Nova Scotia	Royal Canadian Navy
Bonavista, Newfoundland	U.S. Coast Guard
Battle Harbor, Labrador	U.S. Coast Guard
Frederiksdal, Greenland	U.S. Coast Guard
Vík, Iceland	Royal Navy
Skuvanes Head, Faeroe Islands	Royal Navy
Mangersta, Hebrides	Royal Navy
Sankaty Head, Nantucket	U.S. Coast Guard

Source: Malcolm F. Willoughby, *U.S. Coast Guard in World War II* (Annapolis, Md.: United States Naval Institute, 1957), p. 156.
Note: These stations are part of what was later called the Loran-A system. The distinction between Loran-A and Loran-C is explained in chapter 6.

TABLE 13
Locations and Uses of Alaskan and Aleutian Loran Stations, 1944

Location	Use
Alaskan chain	
Saint Matthew Island	Single secondary[a]
Saint Paul Island	Double master
Umnak Island	Single secondary
Cape Sarichef[b]	Monitor
Saint George Island	Monitor
Aleutian (western Alaskan) chain	
Attu	Single master
Amchitka	Single secondary
Adak	Monitor

Source: Malcolm F. Willoughby, *U.S. Coast Guard in World War II* (Annapolis, Md.: United States Naval Institute, 1957), pp. 158, 160.
Note: These stations are also part of what was later called the Loran-A system. The distinction between Loran-A and Loran-C is explained in chapter 6.
[a] As noted earlier, secondary stations were originally referred to as slave stations.
[b] Replaced by Saint George Island.

the Royal Navy again visited the Radiation Laboratory at MIT. He greatly encouraged Lawrence Harding and his team by bringing reports of the effectiveness of loran in the north Atlantic. In fact, Holland called the American loran system ''a war winner'' because he felt it did for the Battle of the Atlantic what the Gee system had done for the Royal Air Force in the early days of the war—made maximum use of limited resources against an unsuspecting enemy. The U-boat commanders began to report to Germany that the allies could record their location in a fashion that let them peer through the ocean surface almost as if it were a window.

In the same period another chain of loran stations was constructed and placed in operation in Alaska and across the northern Pacific. This chain was built and operated solely by the Coast Guard. There were construction difficulties in Alaska as well as in Labrador and Greenland. In Alaska, however, the Coast Guard could rely on facilities such as the lighthouse at Cape Sarichef, on Umnak Island, and on the local knowledge that had been acquired by the Revenue Marine and Lighthouse Service from their Alaskan experiences dating back to the 1870s. Table 13 lists four of the Alaskan stations and their uses, as well as three stations that were built in the Aleutian Islands of western Alaska. These three stations were also built totally by the Coast Guard.[10] These additional stations began the process of extending loran coverage across the Pacific Ocean.

In November 1943, just as construction of the Alaskan and Aleutian stations was beginning, vital invasions were occurring at Tarawa and other Japanese-held outposts in the Gilbert Islands. By then a joint loran planning committee of the joint chiefs of staff was established. The committee called for an expansion in both the number of loran stations serving the Pacific and the geographic coverage. The coverage would have to move rapidly across the Pacific to Australian waters, then upward to support the attack against Japan.[11] The task was formidable indeed.

By late 1943 the national need for a system to accommodate the wartime demands for accurate all-weather navigation was falling more and more to the Coast Guard. The war in the Pacific made such a system far more necessary there than in the Atlantic. The Coast Guard was proactive and innovative in meeting this need. The personnel who had already served on stations in the Atlantic formed the nucleus of expanding human resources needed to establish the Pacific stations.

The MIT loran school was moved to the Coast Guard training station at Groton, Connecticut. By June 1944 the school was preparing classes of twenty technicians each in a ten-week course, with new classes graduating every five weeks.[12]

Despite the enormous scope of the loran project, it remained a military secret throughout the war. This was brought home to Captain Alfred C. Richmond shortly before the Normandy Invasion of 6 June 1944. Richmond, who served as commandant of the Coast Guard from 1954 to 1962, was taking a noontime walk from his London headquarters where he headed the Coast Guard hearing unit. That morning he had returned to General Eisenhower's headquarters a top-secret plan for D-Day that had been mistakenly sent to Richmond's Coast Guard office.

On his walk Richmond met a Coast Guard lieutenant he had never seen before and asked him his assignment. After great hesitation, Lieutenant T. D. Winters, a Coast Guard reserve officer on duty with the Royal Navy to help with the north Atlantic loran chain, said he would reveal his assignment only inside Richmond's office. Even then he did so only after searching the office for electronic listening devices. Lieutenant Winters finally revealed that he was in charge of selecting a site and building a loran station. He carried a briefcase full of money and top-secret plans. Although Richmond was fully aware of the Normandy plans and reported directly to Vice Admiral Waesche, the lieutenant's story came as a surprise—he had been unaware of the Coast Guard's role in loran.*

Considerable design work was being done to modify and improve the loran system; this will be discussed in chapter 6. To build the stations the Coast Guard

---

*As Captain Richmond's experience in London showed, the Royal Navy was very concerned about maintaining the secrecy of the loran system. The same attitude prevailed in the United States.

In one incident a Radiation Laboratory staff member mentioned a new system called loran in the club car of a Boston-to-Washington train. Another passenger phoned the Federal Bureau of Investigation, and an agent arrived at the laboratory the next day. Lawrence Harding discussed this incident with Lee DuBridge of NDRC, who handled the situation effectively. The staff member disappeared from the Radiation Laboratory. This became known and had a great effect on keeping the project secret.

had to assemble and coordinate a wide array of physical resources. Transmitters, shelters, antennas, furnishings, and power all had to be obtained and shipped while the secrecy of the project was maintained.

The structure that handled this began with ad hoc command units and construction detachments that traveled to the sites. They in turn were supported by the decentralized field organization that Admiral Waesche had assembled before the war. The supply depot at Alameda, California, the district supply staff at Seattle, and the Coast Guard base at Sand Island in Hawaii all became centers of activity. The Coast Guard acquired a cargo ship, *Menkar,* to carry supplies to the sites. Centralized direction of the loran project rested with the commandant in Washington, through the general supervision of the Civil Engineering Division of the Office of Engineering.

Coordination with other agencies was important. The Hydrographic Office had to survey each site thoroughly and pinpoint the location of the transmitting antenna so that loran charts could be prepared with overlaid lines of constant time differences.[13] Work had to be coordinated with the navy, army, and army air corps. Some coordination was required with foreign governments, including the Netherlands, Australia, Great Britain, Denmark, France, and China. International agreement had to be obtained for frequency bands. Electronic navigation had certainly expanded the technology of light and sound that had been the mainstay of the Lighthouse Service before the radio beacon emerged after World War I.

On 25 November 1944, 111 B-29s bombed Japan—becoming the first raid on the Japanese capital since the Doolittle raid of 1942. The Hawaiian, Phoenix, and then the Marianas loran chains provided navigational support for the air and sea offensive against Japan. Table 14 lists the stations involved in these chains.

TABLE 14
Locations and Uses of Some Pacific Loran Stations

Hawaiian chain		*Marianas chain*	
French frigate shoals	Single secondary	Guam	Double secondary
Niihau	Double master	Saipan	Single master
Hawaii	Single secondary	Ulithi	Single master
Kauai	Monitor	Ritidian Point	Monitor
Phoenix chain		*Japan chain*	
Baker	Single secondary	Iwo Jima	Double master
Gardner	Double master	Okinawa	Single secondary
Atafu	Single secondary	Tokyo	Single secondary
Canton	Monitor		
Kwajalein	Single secondary		
Majuro	Double master		
Makin	Single secondary		
Majuro	Monitor		

Source: Malcolm F. Willoughby, *U.S. Coast Guard in World War II* (Annapolis, Md.: United States Naval Institute, 1957), pp. 161, 163–65, 168.
Note: These stations are also part of what was later called the Loran-A system. The distinction between Loran-A and Loran-C is explained in chapter 6.

The Marianas chain was completed in February 1945, and provided primary navigational support for the aircraft of the Twenty-first Bomber Command. By early June 1945, before Japanese resistance on the islands had ceased, Coast Guard loran stations on Iwo Jima and Okinawa were on the air providing a single line of position from the closest possible location to the Japanese mainland.[14]

THE FUTURE OF THE LORAN SYSTEM

The accomplishment of Coast Guard operators and engineers in developing an idea for loran into a technology that spanned major portions of the world is an achievement of which they are proud. In a mere five years, they created a loran system that utilized and developed existing technology to fill a national need. Admittedly, wartime pressures greatly accelerated this development and made the accomplishment politically possible. But the events that occurred, including landing in hostile territory, fighting both frigid and tropical climates, and developing and operating state-of-the-art equipment, was no small task. Lawrence Harding, by the end of the war a captain in the Coast Guard, was indeed a successful program champion and project manager.

At war's end, the decision had been made to turn over the operation of loran to the Coast Guard. Also, a decision was made to remove the secrecy and make loran available to other nations and to public marine and air interests. This decision was followed by worldwide publicity and the system's eventual worldwide acceptance for navigation wherever signals could be received.

The Science Services Organization of Washington, a consulting firm serving the media, selected loran as one of the ten most important secret developments of World War II. This award bestowed well-deserved prestige upon the Coast Guard, Captain Harding, and his loran project team. The top three secret developments were the atomic bomb, radar, and loran. Malcolm Willoughby, devoting an entire chapter of his *U.S. Coast Guard in World War II* to loran, singles out the development of the system as one of the great contributions of the Coast Guard during World War II.[15]

After the war, an important question arose from both within and outside the Coast Guard about the role a loran system should play in a world at peace. After all, much of the use of loran had been for bombing and for military operations in bad weather when commercial activity might not have been undertaken. Certainly the extent of postwar commerce would be less than the enormous, unprecedented volume of wartime sea activity. Some argued that many skilled navigators, who could call on both radio-navigation systems and the more traditional celestial navigation techniques of Nathaniel Bowditch, would be available to navigate the more limited postwar commerce. Seldom has man given up a new technology, however, once he has become accustomed to using it.

The mere existence of seventy-five loran stations providing a radio-navigation system for ships and aircraft probably was the most important argument for its postwar existence. At the peak of the war coverage had extended to more than one-third of the earth's surface, providing the first all-weather system of navigation. Loran's accuracy had been proved to navigators around the world by its success in pinpointing convoy rendezvous and making landfalls, as well as by the devastating effects of more accurate bombing. To navigators, there could have been no retreat from the technological innovation that had become known as loran.

6 THE DEVELOPMENT OF THE POSTWAR LORAN SYSTEM

NAVIGATIONAL NEEDS
IN THE POSTWAR
ERA

When the question of loran's future was analyzed after the war, the scope of the loran system that was already a fait accompli was an important consideration. Some loran stations were easily closed. But many were kept on the air because of both continued military requirements and growing civilian demands for an accurate commercial navigation system with all-weather capability. The Coast Guard recognized that the opportunity cost of abandoning the loran system would be high.

There was a great deal of talk in 1946 that the Decca system, developed by an American, Harvey Schwartz, but used by the British during the war, might be an ideal postwar system. The characteristics of Decca will be explained later. Basically, it was good for short-range coastal navigation. To many people in 1946 its advantage was that the user of the system paid for it by renting a receiver from Decca. In concept the Decca Company was much like a cable television company. Another benefit some saw was the capital structure of the basic company; it was a profit-making venture. The concept of "user charges" for navigation, however, went against an American tradition. Since the early years of the Lighthouse Service, aid-to-navigation services in America had always been financed by the government and were ostensibly free to the user.

A question arose in the Treasury Department in 1946 and 1947 over the funding of the loran system. The conservative role of the Treasury Department, informally established by the pressure of the Employment Act of 1946, led the Treasury to look for budget reductions to set an example to expansionary departments in the postwar budgetary process. With the postwar Coast Guard budget a major portion of the Treasury Department budget, new Coast Guard programs such as loran presented an obvious opportunity for a reduction or outright deletion. In fact, during the 1947 House Appropriations Subcommittee hearings, Representative John Taber of New York, a ranking member of the Coast Guard subcommittee in 1946 and a member when the Coast Guard was still within the committee's jurisdiction in 1941, was not even fully aware of how loran worked:

Mr. Taber. These loran stations are stations that provide radio beams, are they not?
Captain Richmond. No, Sir: loran is a navigational aid to permit a plane or a ship that has proper equipment to fix its position. It is a long-range navigating aid. . . .
Mr. Taber. Is it not a radio-beam activity?
Captain Richmond. No Sir.[1]

Despite the lack of knowledge of loran in Congress and the substantial cut the Coast Guard took in its 1947 budget proposals at both the Treasury and the Bureau of the Budget, the Coast Guard decided loran was an important program with important constituents. Quite probably this decision reflected short-run concerns more than a strategic output from the model of figure 6. The Coast Guard, however, went to the appropriations subcommittee in the March 1946 hearings with 57 percent of its capital budget request of slightly more than four million dollars allocated to one item—relocation and modernization of loran stations.* Despite short-run concerns, the Coast Guard felt strongly that loran would be important in the future of navigation. The experience of the Coast Guard before the subcommittee that year was a harbinger of events to come.

Captain Alfred Richmond, who had first learned of loran by chance in London in 1944, by 1946 had become chief of the Budget and Requirements Division at headquarters. Commander Paul Trimble, who had worked at the first loran station at Montauk Point in 1942, assisted Richmond as chief of the Material Budget Section. It was Richmond's task to advocate the need for physical resources for the loran system to the subcommittee:

The eight stations requiring relocation and modernization will require permanent construction to house personnel and equipment for efficient operation of the units. The units to be relocated were established on a temporary basis, using Quonset Huts for barracks and operations buildings in order to get the units on the air in the shortest period of time. After a period of 2 years or less these buildings are deteriorating to the extent that replacement will be required, even though relocation is not accomplished. The average cost of each unit will be $215,000.[2]

---

*The Coast Guard presented to the House Appropriations Subcommittee in March 1946 a request for a fiscal year 1947 operating expense budget of $129,185,000, a great reduction from the fiscal year 1946 appropriation of $468,007,707, the Coast Guard's last budget as part of the navy. The $129 million already represented a cut of more than $51 million from the level the Coast Guard had originally requested from Treasury and the Bureau of the Budget for fiscal year 1947.

The March 1946 request to the appropriations subcommittee also included a separate request of $4,715,000 for "construction projects." This request reveals the priority the Coast Guard placed on operating the loran system. Of the amount, $2,690,000—57 percent of the capital budget request—had been allocated by the Coast Guard for "relocation and modernization of eight stations in the loran system." See U.S., Congress, House, *Hearings before the Subcommittee on Appropriations on the Coast Guard Appropriation Bill for 1947*, 79th Cong., 2d sess., 19–20 March 1946, pp. 6, 14–15, 111–12.

The appropriations subcommittee, and in particular ranking members such as representatives John Taber, Emmet O'Neal, and Frank Keefe, who had served on the subcommittee when the last prewar Coast Guard budget appeared, were, at the least, surprised by the changes in the postwar Coast Guard. In the last budget the prewar subcommittee had reviewed, the Coast Guard had yet to fully consolidate the Lighthouse Service. By 1946 it was operating a worldwide navigation system. The subcommittee questioned the priorities of the postwar Coast Guard.

PRIORITIES WITHIN THE COAST GUARD

Even to many Coast Guardsmen, the loran program and the Commercial Vessel Safety program of the newly acquired Bureau of Marine Inspection and Navigation seemed wide departures from the Coast Guard that had existed before the war. Departures they were! The national need for these programs and their proper scope and scale had to be determined through the postwar budgetary process, both inside and outside the Coast Guard. At first glance the problems of the day seem to fit well within the bounds of the parameters of the model of figure 6. At the time, however, they took on a far more immediate concern.

Within the Coast Guard, the rapid demobilization of 1946 created an enormous problem of human resources. Where would the Coast Guard get skilled technicians to man the loran stations? Good electronics technicians were in demand in industry, and the benefits of civilian life in 1946 far outweighed the prospect of being assigned to a remote loran station.

Commander Walter Capron and Lieutenant Commander Loren Brunner, at the time assigned to the Enlisted Personnel and to the Electronics Engineering divisions at headquarters, solved this problem by developing a two-year educational program for technicians who would reenlist. Technicians who chose this program were sent to the Radio Corporation of America (RCA) Institute to study electrical engineering. Sending enlisted men to such a school was an enormous innovation in 1947, but it was effective in retaining the needed quotas of electronics technicians. More important, the Coast Guardsmen assigned compiled fine academic records at RCA and went on to give the Coast Guard an electronics competence unrivaled in other military services.

The loran issue was resolved in the budgetary process. The critical point occurred during the 1948 budget hearings before the House Appropriations Subcommittee. The subcommittee demanded an independent study of the "organization and operations" of the Coast Guard and "its relationship with other government agencies."[3] This study, begun in March 1947 and completed in January

1948, became known as the Ebasco Report. The report was generally supportive of the loran system and recommended that the Coast Guard seek specific legislation mandating that it be part of Coast Guard services.*

Captain Richmond, by then chief of the Planning and Control staff at Coast Guard headquarters in Washington, served as chairman of the steering committee to review the recommendations of the Ebasco Report. Because of wartime demands, the loran program had been established without the authorization legislation so necessary in peacetime. The Coast Guard now had to seek congressional authorization and support for loran. The agency had come to consider assisting marine transportation on and above the water a clear Coast Guard mandate, assumed after it acquired the Life Saving Service, the Lighthouse Service, and finally the Bureau of Marine Inspection and Navigation.

In 1947, however, there was inherent danger in naming any one radio-navigation system in legislation. The technology of radio navigation was still changing rapidly, and many people both outside and inside the Coast Guard questioned whether loran would become the dominant system. The Coast Guard considered these dangers, yet decided that loran had the greatest potential for meeting the needs of marine transportation. The agency thus committed itself to electronic aids to navigation.

Captain Richmond saw to it that legislation mandating an Aids to Navigation program was submitted to the Congress. The Congress approved, and the Coast Guard mandate for this service to the public was spelled out in the new United States Code, enacted in 1949. With the support of Congress and the code, the budgetary support of Treasury Department was ensured. The Coast Guard had finally won for the loran system the political resources that go with the peacetime support of both the executive and legislative branches—backup the system lacked during the early postwar years. Loran had finally gained a secure place as a Coast Guard Aids to Navigation program. It had also gained international support.

The strategic match of national needs and organizational means had been consummated, in the manner described by figure 6. The interaction of environmental forces and actors provides a much greater depth to the events, however, than do the simple concepts of this model.

The loran program had been threatened with budget cuts and even with termination, and it had come through the threats improved physically and technologically as well as economically and politically. Some of the national and international support for the loran system should be discussed in detail.

---

*The Ebasco Report became a significant milestone in the development of the Coast Guard. Alfred Richmond and Irwin J. Stephens played important roles in developing the report, which both outlined a postwar direction for the Coast Guard and ordered the Treasury Department—the supervisor of the Coast Guard in the executive branch—and the Coast Guard to carry out this direction. See Ebasco Services, Incorporated, *Study of United States Coast Guard* (New York: Ebasco Services, 1948).

NATIONAL AND INTERNATIONAL
DEMAND FOR LORAN SERVICES

In 1944 an international conference held in Chicago resulted in the formation of the Provisional International Civil Aviation Organization (PICAO). By
September 1946 PICAO had developed an eleven-nation agreement to provide
both ships at sea and aids-to-navigation systems as services for aircraft flying
across oceans. The United States was a party to this agreement. In line with this,
President Truman mandated that the Coast Guard supply cutters to man several
ocean stations, and that it provide loran coverage where possible. In the process
loran was developing a user group that included not only the military but commercial aviation, merchant shipping, and fishermen as well. The Coast Guard
was the leader in a new technology and a new service, and the list of its constituents was growing.[4]

In the United States, the Defense Department, the marine industry, airlines,
fishermen, and smaller groups who had access to the large surplus of loran
receivers after the war all wanted the service continued. By the end of the war,
seventy-five thousand receivers had been built by various companies, and the
Hydrographic Office had produced more than two million loran charts. Potential
users of the loran system abounded. The public, too, supported loran.[5]

By 1947 the International Civil Aviation Organization (ICAO) was established, gathering together many international groups interested in transoceanic
air traffic. Soon thereafter, ICAO called attention to the international acceptance
loran enjoyed with aviators by specifying loran as a required aid to navigation for
transatlantic flights. The United States was a leading force in ICAO. For many
years, ICAO funded the operating costs of a number of the stations listed in table
12.

National navigation needs created a demand for Coast Guard resources.
Some of the resources to satisfy this demand came through internal reallocation
from older, less responsive programs toward newer, more effective programs
that better answered national needs and the specific demands of constituents.
This reallocation was an important part of the internal dynamics of the structure,
as depicted in figure 6. Loran is a good example of a more effective program
whose resources increased.

Remember that the internal reallocations of 1948 to 1950 came at a time
when Coast Guard resources were particularly scarce. Although reallocation was
painful, it definitely was a learning process for the Coast Guard structure, which
had to adopt the dual-role strategy and multimission concept. Certainly a small
part of loran funds in this period did come from incremental additions in the
operating budget, specified as increases for loran within the Aids to Navigation
program. These additions became possible because of the congressional mandate
the Coast Guard received through the Ebasco Report.[6] The Treasury Department
and the Bureau of the Budget had to approve and back these increases, however,

and to the extent that fiscal policy considerations became overriding in any one budget year, this check served as a damper on congressional support.

This internal reallocation of resources between Coast Guard programs is an example of the multimission concept at work. The Coast Guard organization in the postwar period was larger through its acquisition of three organizations between 1915 and 1946, and it was becoming more effective as a matrix for shifting human and physical resources between changing programs. It was the task of the structure, discussed in chapters 3 and 4, to assume a proactive and innovative stance, develop alternatives, make judgments on each, and act on these judgments by shifting resources to the most effective programs. Since loran had been a very effective program, its growth shows the structure working effectively. The model developed in figure 6 appears to be a good paradigm for managing a federal agency, at least in the case of the postwar loran system.

DEPLOYMENT OF LORAN FOR THE KOREAN WAR AND THE COLD WAR

The Cold War that began in earnest after the outbreak of the Korean War greatly strengthened the demand for radio-navigation systems, and loran was again called on to fill important military needs in the Pacific. The air war over Korea demanded more precise navigation, and a new chain of loran stations was built across the western Pacific to refine coverage for that area. At first these stations were temporary, with equipment in electronic "trailers." The response of the Coast Guard to the sudden new demand was both pragmatic and "incremental." The stations were made permanent when it became more obvious that a need for military aircraft in the area would exist for some time.[7]

The rapid deployment of loran systems during the Korean War was possible because of the multimission concept and because of the nature of the new technology the Coast Guard was developing. The skilled technicians of loran were able to respond, assisted by Coast Guard physical resources. For example, the Coast Guard Yard at Curtis Bay, Maryland, had the necessary plans and technology to build the "trailers," because they had performed the same service during World War II.

By the mid-1950s the postwar loran system was well established. Loran chains existed across a good deal of the Atlantic, and in the Pacific they stretched across the Hawaiian, Marshall, Mariana, Philippine, and Japanese islands. Some of the Pacific loran stations carried the names of familiar World War II battlegrounds—Guam, Saipan, Ulithi, and Iwo Jima. A station was even built in Pusan, Korea.

As I explained earlier, a minimum of three stations are needed to send the signals to determine a position in a given area. Because of the frequency and pulse width used, the stations must be situated away from industrial areas and along the coastline. To maximize the area receiving loran coverage, they must be separated as far as possible, within other considerations.* As a result of these restraints, the stations are often placed in somewhat isolated areas.[8]

An average station during the 1950s was manned by approximately twenty Coast Guard enlisted men, typically a mix of skilled electronics technicians and support personnel. The station was commanded by a junior officer, usually fresh from his first assignment aboard a Coast Guard cutter. Many were Coast Guard Academy graduates; some were former technicians who had graduated from officer candidate school. The Coast Guard expanded its policy of developing junior officers by assigning them to an independent command—a loran station. This policy worked well in the postwar years, and the Coast Guard experienced little trouble in operating the far-flung loran system. Indeed, the effectiveness of the wartime system and the loran net that evolved in the 1950s was attested to by Gifford Hefley in 1972: "The merit of the wartime system is evidenced by the fact that it is still in service in many areas. Of course numerous improvements have been made but the system we know today . . . is, in all major respects, identical to the one which was first flight-tested in 1942."[9]

But potential applications for radio-navigation technology were changing during the late 1950s. Other systems were available. In fact, toward the end of World War II, operational requirements in Europe and the Pacific demanded radio-navigation coverage at greater ranges, and over land as well as water. Some of the new systems were sponsored by other agencies and would compete with standard World War II loran; one new system was conceived then that would operate at a much lower frequency. The low-frequency system promised a greater range and the ability to propagate well over land. This idea, however, had remained experimental until the mid-1950s, when a system called "Cytac" was tested. Tests revealed that Cytac could yield both the longer range and the higher accuracy that had been sought.[10]

A NEW NEED FOR LORAN

After the Russians launched their Sputnik satellite in October 1957, the navy established an operational need for a long-range, high-accuracy radio-navigation system. The navy wanted coverage extended to the eastern Atlantic and to specified advanced areas of operation. At first the need was created by the Atlantic Missile Range—for tests of satellites and missiles. Because of the distinctive competence the Coast Guard had displayed in developing loran in the Atlantic and the Pacific and operating it in the postwar years, it was only natural

---

*This technical constraint to be near a shoreline does not apply to another version of loran technology, known as Loran-C, which operates on a much lower frequency. Loran-C was first used in the late 1950s and is discussed in the rest of this chapter and in the chapter that follows.

that the agency should operate the low-frequency radio-navigation system required to fill the new need.

Loran satisfied still another national need. From 1957 to 1960 the missile and satellite programs of the Atlantic Range demanded and received top priority. As had happened in 1942, three Coast Guard stations were selected for the trials of the low-frequency system. The master station was located at Carolina Beach, North Carolina, and secondary stations were established at Jupiter Inlet, Florida, and Martha's Vineyard, Massachusetts.

Because the various systems being discussed were all versions of loran, the names Loran-A, Loran-B, and Loran-C were developed by the Coast Guard.* Loran-A was the name given to the standard system that had been used in the Atlantic and the Pacific during World War II, and for commercial as well as military navigation after the war. Loran-B designated a short-lived version of Loran-A developed for laying minefields and for special navigational purposes. Loran-C was the name given to the lower-frequency, higher-range loran that emerged from the Cytac tests.[11]

There were problems, however, to be worked out in the Loran-C system, as with any technological system of its scope. For example, the original tests during World War II on what had become Loran-C were done at frequencies of 160 and 180 kiloHertz. Frequency management is a very complex area, with both national and international dimensions, involving domestic agreements and international treaties. The Coast Guard worked at length on this, and final agreement was reached for operation of Loran-C at 100 kiloHertz.

Many problems of physical resources had to be solved. For example, the transmitters necessary to send the Loran-C signal evolved through three major design generations. Indeed, all three designs were in use at one station or another as the system expanded and were still in use in the late 1970s. In 1959, however, obtaining a transmitter that was both accurate and reliable was a major concern. Tests had to be run on the new loran-C system to iron out any systems-development problems. During testing, the Martha's Vineyard Station was moved to Nantucket. The systems development problems were solved, with much of the work centering on the East Coast chain as a model.

Solving the problems of physical resources was not the only or the most important facet of the story of Loran-C. Human resources proved to be a very important part of the distinctive competence the Coast Guard brought to radio navigation. The role of program champion and manager that Captain Lawrence Harding undertook during World War II was filled in the late 1950s by Captain Loren Brunner and Commander Helmer Pearson, who served as chief and as assistant chief of the Electronics Engineering Division at Coast Guard headquarters in Washington. While Brunner and Pearson were in charge of Loran-C for

*By 1957 Loren Brunner had become a captain in the Coast Guard. Captain Brunner selected the names Loran-A, Loran-B, and Loran-C to differentiate the loran systems available at the time. The letters A, B, and C indicated the sequence in which the systems were developed.

the Coast Guard, they assembled an able team from within and outside the Coast Guard.

An important ingredient was the diversity of education and experience that team members brought to the Electronics Engineering Division. For example, Captain Brunner had been able to earn his master of science degree in electrical engineering from MIT in 1942 as a result of Admiral Waesche's expansion of postgraduate education for officers after 1936. In the late 1950s Captain Brunner and Commander Pearson in turn emphasized the postgraduate education program for young officers. Through their foresight, they recruited good officers for the loran program who would continue its success in years to come. They also reaped dividends from the skilled technicians who at one time or another had attended the RCA Institute program that Brunner had started after World War II.

The list of those involved in electronics and loran within the Coast Guard from the days of Loran-A is long, and if we mention names we risk leaving out many whose contributions were at least as important as those discussed. Rear Admiral Peter Colmar had been involved in loran for most of his Coast Guard career. David Haislip, Elmer Lipsey, Alfred Manning, Carl Mathews, Cort Pohle, Joseph Stewart, and James Van Etten all had considerable experience.

The technological and managerial leadership demonstrated by these advocates of advancing radio-navigation technology was only one aspect of the human resources the Coast Guard was building. During World War II the loran school, first at MIT and then at the new Coast Guard Training Center at Avery Point in Groton, had trained a generation of able radiomen and electronics technicians. By the mid-1950s, many of these were graduates of the RCA Institute. Many then attended officer candidate school, and went on to careers as Coast Guard officers. Between general duty tours, these officers were available to the Electronics Engineering Division as commanding officers of loran stations and for other key assignments within the loran project. Part of the success of Loran-C as a system is due to the education and personal development of these men. In turn, the Coast Guard's success with the multimission concept was very much related to its policy of developing human resources. The new resources related well with the new technology. A synergy was building.

The physical and human resources necessary to develop the radio-navigation program even further were clearly available by the mid-1950s. But political resources and the structural context were not yet ready.* Funds for Loran-A were available, but tight. Loran-A as a system, however, had acquired further international support. In the late 1940s the International Civil Aviation Organization had required Loran-A as an aid to navigation on transatlantic flights and had even funded the operation of some Loran-A stations. In the late 1950s

---

*For a discussion of the meaning of the term *structural context,* see Joseph L. Bower, *Managing the Resource Allocation Process* (Boston: Division of Research, Harvard Business School, 1970), pp. 72–73, 78–79. See also the discussion in chapter 2.

the North Atlantic Treaty Organization (NATO) nations added to this international demand by adopting Loran-A as an international aid to navigation. NATO funded the construction of stations in several locations, including Greenland, Iceland, Norway, and Portugal.

A CHANGE IN STRUCTURAL CONTEXT

In the three years from 1957 to 1960, a great change in structural context took place. Where funds for Loran-A had been tight, the budgetary mood toward radio navigation suddenly changed. Loran was no longer simply another Coast Guard program competing for resources in the postwar budgetary process. Suddenly, Loran-C became an important project demanded by the Department of Defense (DOD), and it was given top priority. DOD and the Congress agreed that a national need was at stake, and they recognized that the Coast Guard had the technical means to fill it. All the physical and human resources that could be used to achieve the objectives of an effective, longer-range Loran-C system were made available to the Coast Guard, which was designated operator for the Loran-C system. This time the dynamics of the model of figure 6 moved in a far quicker fashion. A strong national need was "pulling" a program through the system.

The human and physical resource problems to be surmounted in expanding the Loran-C system were huge. Examples are many. The demand to provide skilled technicians led Captain Brunner to establish a Loran-C school at the Coast Guard Training Center at Avery Point. Lieutenant Commander Cort Pohle was placed in charge of the school, which quickly increased the number of technicians available.

Time again became the navigator's bane. The latitude of any position on earth could be well defined, but the longitude was hard to pinpoint—readings were often from a quarter mile to two or three miles out of location. This meant that, as Loran-C spread across the Atlantic, the available maps were wrong—or at least inconsistent with the positions available from Loran-C signals. The Coast Guard's Electronics Engineering Division had to redraw charts that identified the locations of islands and even continents such as Africa. The tail was wagging the dog.

The task of first placing Loran-C "on the air" and then rapidly expanding the system to meet DOD needs fell to Captain Brunner and the team he assembled from his post as chief of the Electronics Engineering Division. After the transmitting station moved from Martha's Vineyard to Nantucket, a crash program of design work on the system components was undertaken.

Many interrelated projects with tight schedules made the Electronics Engineering Division look much like a war room before an invasion. Tasks ranged from negotiations with foreign governments to replacing large transmitting antennas that had fallen. Calibration and accuracy checks on the East Coast chain that served as a model for future Loran-C chains were successfully completed in June 1962. Little time was available then to celebrate this first Loran-C achievement, though, for other chains had to be established across the Atlantic. Considering the time pressure to develop the first chain, however, the East Coast chain has had an excellent operational record since 1962.

COMPETING NAVIGATIONAL SYSTEMS

Obviously the demands from the Defense Department for Loran-C coverage for extensive areas were made for important military reasons. After the successful trials of the East Coast chain, Loran-C chains were established in key locations around the world—an enormous undertaking. The wide scope of Loran-C coverage by 1972 is shown in figure 19. Table 15 lists the various Loran-C chains by name, with the location of the master station of each chain, as they existed in 1972.[12]

With the building of the Loran-C network, the Coast Guard became the active operator of two loran systems, Loran-A and Loran-C. Loran-C stations were manned either by Coast Guard personnel, as had largely been the case with Loran-A, or by citizens of the countries in which they were situated. Many of the experienced Coast Guardsmen assigned to Loran-C stations were the same indi-

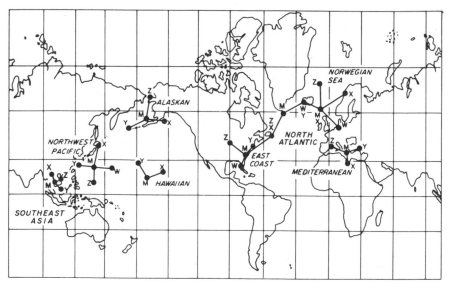

FIG. 19. Locations of Loran-C chains, 1972. From Gifford Hefley, *The Development of Loran-C Navigation and Timing* (Washington, D.C.: U.S. Government Printing Office, 1972), p. 83.

TABLE 15
Loran-C Chains and the Locations of Their Master Stations, 1972

Chain	Master Station
North Pacific	Saint Paul, Pribilof Islands, Alaska
East Coast	Carolina Beach, North Carolina
Central Pacific	Johnston Island
Mediterranean	Simeri Crichi, Italy
North Atlantic	Angissoq, Greenland
Norwegian Sea	Ejde, Faeroe Islands
Northwest Pacific	Iwo Jima, Bonin Islands
Southeast Asia	Sattahip, Thailand

Source: U.S. Coast Guard, *Loran-C User Handbook* (CG-462), August 1974.

viduals who had worked with Loran-A in the past. Through their work with Loran-C, they gained even more valuable experience with radio navigation. And United States Coast Guardsmen at overseas stations usually raised less military apprehension than navy or air force personnel might have caused.

Those who worked with loran generally felt that their system for radio navigation was the best technology available in the world. Although most of those in the Coast Guard who developed Loran-C had also worked on Loran-A, there were some internal, bureaucratic differences, and competition grew between the advocates of Loran-A and Loran-C within the agency. Both groups, however, felt that loran as a system would grow and find commercial application if it were ever given the chance to demonstrate its ability.

At first Loran-C was limited in actual use to military applications. Any commercial user of the system would have to invest in a receiver, then maintain it. The first receivers were expensive, complicated, and frequently unreliable. Transmitters at loran stations, in contrast, were reliable and created a high-quality signal. Since operational units of the Defense Department were the primary users, they could well afford to acquire and maintain the receivers.

But, since the receivers were used primarily in classified applications, Defense gave little feedback to the Coast Guard about problems with the receivers, and so Coast Guard engineers focused on the part of the system for which they were responsible—improving the technology of the transmitters. At first this silence about receiver problems retarded the development of a practical Loran-C receiver for private use.

Loran-C services—the signals—provided by most of the stations shown in figure 19 and table 15 slowly found users in the private sector and in industry. The familiar pattern of the military developing a technology for a specific use, followed by its diffusion and use by industry, had occurred with Loran-A, but with Loran-C both the cost and the technology of the receiver formed a barrier to entry into the system. This problem was solved in increments. Coast Guard engineers, skilled from their work on Loran-A and Loran-B, were at work on the Loran-C system, and they realized the receiver was the key to making the system available to more users.

The statutory responsibility of the Coast Guard for maritime navigational aids was first clarified after the Ebasco Report in 1948. Since the initial promulgation of Title 14 of the United States Code in 1949, areas of responsibility within the federal government for aids to navigation were formally spelled out. By the 1970s, Section 81 of Title 14 gave the Coast Guard responsibility to establish, maintain, and operate maritime navigational aids "to prevent disasters, collisions, and wrecks of vessels and aircraft." This mandate is broad; the critical guidelines are presented in table 16. The mandate covers use by the armed forces, as determined by the Defense Department; by maritime commerce; and by air commerce, as requested by the Federal Aviation Administration. Section 81 points out again the number of constituents the loran system had acquired. In radio navigation, the Coast Guard had achieved a needs-means match.

In 1970 the Department of Transportation published its *National Plan for Navigation*. For the first time one plan outlined a specific order for developing, implementing, and operating navigation systems to satisfy civil aviation and maritime requirements. The civil maritime requirements were developed for three broad areas—the high seas, the coastal confluence zone, and harbors and estuaries. Geographically, the mandate of Section 81 covers the domestic area of the United States, the United States coastal confluence zone, and certain designated areas such as territories and overseas military bases.[13]

TABLE 16
Responsibility of the Coast Guard for Aids to Navigation

In order to aid navigation and to prevent disasters, collisions, and wrecks of vessels and aircraft, the Coast Guard may establish, maintain, and operate:

(1) aids to maritime navigation required to serve the needs of the armed forces or of the commerce of the United States;

(2) aids to air navigation required to serve the needs of the armed forces of the United States peculiar to warfare and primarily of military concern as determined by the Secretary of Defense or the Secretary of any department within the Department of Defense and as requested by any of those officials; and

(3) electronic aids to navigation systems (*a*) required to serve the needs of the armed forces of the United States peculiar to warfare and primarily of military concern as determined by the Secretary of Defense or any department within the Department of Defense; or (*b*) required to serve the needs of the maritime commerce of the United States; or (*c*) required to serve the needs of the air commerce of the United States as requested by the Administrator of the Federal Aviation Agency.

These aids to navigation other than electronic aids to navigation systems shall be established and operated only within the United States, the waters above the Continental Shelf, the territories and possessions of the United States, the Trust Territory of the Pacific Islands, and beyond the territorial jurisdiction of the United States, at places where naval or military bases of the United States are or may be located.

Source: United States Code, Title 14, Section 81.

The national need for effective navigation involves a broad range of considerations. The changing technology available to fill the need has been discussed at length in this chapter. Many competing systems for radio navigation, each with differing characteristics, have also been developed. These systems are compared in table 17.

This table shows that the many competing radio navigation systems have different features. All use the hyperbolic principle described at the beginning of chapter 5. Loran-A has a ground wave range of 700 to 900 miles and fix accuracy of 0.5 to 2 nautical miles. Loran-C, on the other hand, operates at a much lower frequency, which extends both its range and its accuracy.

Omega operates at a still lower frequency (in the very low frequency band) and extends the range still farther, to 5,000 nautical miles. The accuracy of the Omega system is between 1 and 2 miles, less than the 0.1 to 0.5 mile accuracy of Loran-C. Differential Omega is a variation that involves correcting Omega signals by local monitor stations. For various technical reasons, the accuracy of Differential Omega varies with the distance of the receiver from a monitor station and with the time of day. Decca, on the other hand, a system of British design mentioned at the beginning of chapter 5, has a frequency band similar to that of Loran-C. Decca has the accuracy of Loran-C but is range-limited to approximately 100 to 150 nautical miles at night.[14]

The policy-making process of choosing navigational systems that will both proactively fill the national need and also be cost-effective became increasingly complex. Competing navigational systems were a stimulus for developing technology, but they were costly for the government to provide when needless

TABLE 17
Characteristics of Competing Radio-navigation Systems, 1974

System	Wave	Frequency	Range	Accuracy (at range) ($2\sigma \simeq$ limit of errors 95% of the time)
Loran-A	Pulsed hyperbolic	1850–1950 kHz	700–900 nautical miles (n.m.)	1 to 5 nautical miles (n.m.) at 400 n.m.
Loran-C	Pulsed hyperbolic	90–110 kHz	1,200–1,500 n.m.	0.1 to 0.5 n.m. at 800 n.m.
Omega	Continuous wave hyperbolic	10–14 kHz	5,000 n.m.	2 to 5 n.m. at 3000 n.m.
Differential Omega	Continuous wave hypberbolic corrected by monitor	10–14 kHz	Function of communication path	0.5 to 2 n.m. at 100 n.m.
Decca	Continuous wave hyperbolic	70–130 kHz	100–150 n.m. at night	0.05 to 0.25 n.m. at 100 n.m.

Source: H.R. Document no. 93–30, 93d Cong., 2d sess.; *Hearings before the Subcommittee on Coast Guard and Navigation of the Committee on Merchant Marine and Fisheries on H.R. 13595;* 26, 28 March, 25 April, 1974, p. 94. Accuracy column has been adjusted from that appearing in H.R. Doc. No. 93–30 by Captain William Roland.

overlaps in service resulted. From the point of view of potential users, the question whether to invest in a radio-navigation system by buying a receiver and learning how to use it was complex and confusing with so many systems available. The government was faced with choosing between competing navigational systems, and another bureaucratic battle loomed.

This choice between systems went back to 1941 when loran first emerged, and it recurred in the 1950s. In fact, Captain Loren Brunner recognized that the rapid development of Loran-C for the Atlantic Missile Range in the late 1950s would again bring up the familiar question: Which system is best? Captain Brunner saw to it that a definitive study was made. The independent consultant firm of Jansky and Bailey, widely respected in maritime electronics, was hired and produced a report titled *Engineering Evaluation of the Loran-C Navigation System*. Although the report was prepared in 1959 for the Coast Guard, the funds for the study came from the Navy Department. Jansky and Bailey found that:

The capability of the U.S. East Coast Loran-C system to satisfy certain special purpose requirements for highly accurate position fixing over very great areas has been demonstrated. It is *recommended* that Loran-C systems be created in other areas of the world to satisfy similar special purpose requirements. . . .

It is recommended that Loran-C systems be operated in a manner to encourage their use for general purpose long-distance radionavigation by all potential users.[15]

The many and varied users of the competing navigational systems, mentioned in the 1959 Jansky and Bailey study, indeed did become a key in the development of the systems in the 1970s. Basically, they were the same three constituencies interested in radio navigation—the military, industry, and the small users, including independent flyers, fishermen, and sailors. The military and industry had the resources of their large organizations to advocate the system they favored, as well as to acquire the receiving equipment for that system. Designers and manufacturers of equipment, of course, also became formidable advocates of the particular systems in which they had a stake. The small users, largely fishermen and private planes, usually had neither the time, the resources, nor the inclination to become involved in the competition between systems. They wanted to get from one place to another and to know where they were by the cheapest and easiest method.

When the cost-effectiveness of government support of several competing radio-navigation systems was raised by the Office of Management and Budget in the 1970s, each of the arms of the government developing a system should have been asked how its system filled the national need, and how its organization could fill this need with the means and distinctive competence available to them. For policy-making there were also other considerations, such as radio-frequency allocation and international diplomatic aspects.

The Interagency Radio Advisory Committee (IRAC), consisting of representatives of the various government departments, determined the assignment of frequencies to federal agencies. Of course the Federal Communications Commission was interested, since it regulated all the frequencies assigned to commercial use by IRAC. If radio-navigation stations had to be located in another country, or if another country became interested in some aspect of a radio-navigation system, the State Department also became actively involved. All these factors were considered.[16]

7 THE ADVOCACY OF THE LORAN-C SYSTEM

STRUGGLING WITH A DECISION

The General Accounting Office (GAO) and the Office of Management and Budget (OMB) together helped define the problems of organization and overlap posed by competing navigational systems. Since the early 1970s OMB and the Office of Telecommunications Policy in the executive office of the president had recognized that the combined cost of overlapping navigational systems was simply too high.

OMB made this known to the Coast Guard and asked for an examination of the issue and a recommendation. In February 1972 the director of the Office of Telecommunications Policy (OTP) wrote to the secretaries of defense and transportation recommending that the Omega system be approved as the general-purpose navigation system for the United States. OTP proposed standardizing "the minimum number of long distance radio navigation aids . . . in the interest of frequency conservation, overall economies, and avoidance of unnecessary duplication." At the time, both secretaries responded to OTP that selecting Omega "would have been premature since its implementation was incomplete, as was the verification of its capabilities."[1]

The OTP proposal represented a threat to the existence of the loran system. Individuals within the Coast Guard realized that a new direction in navigation planning was needed, however, and they started to examine how overlaps could be eliminated. After all, the Coast Guard itself had responsibility for operating two radio-navigation systems, Loran-A and Loran-C. Two internal groups intimately involved in this analysis were the Programs Division and the Systems Development Branch of the Electronics Engineering Division. Captain James S. Gracey of the Programs Division and Commander William F. Roland of the Systems Development Branch were important in the analysis, and the program manager for Aids to Navigation also played a central role as they struggled to decide which navigation system the Coast Guard would advocate.

In 1969 Polhemus Navigation Sciences, Incorporated, had completed studies on radio-navigation systems for the Coast Guard. Polhemus worked for the Coast Guard "to evaluate the candidacy of the three hyperbolic radio navigation aids . . . to satisfy the requirements for safe and economic operation in the CCR [coastal confluence region] waters of the Untied States including Alaska," and to examine the cost-benefit and user requirements for the northwest Atlantic area as well.[2]

The coastal confluence region proved to be one key to segmenting the varying demands of different users. The region was defined as the area including domestic waters contiguous to major land masses, where transoceanic traffic converges and heavy interport traffic exists.* It extended from the boundaries of inner-harbor entrances seaward fifty miles, or to the hundred-fathom line, whichever was farther from shore.[3]

As pressure mounted for a decision to use only one radio-navigation system, the complexity of a decision of this magnitude became more obvious to all involved. Was the same system most effective for the coastal confluence region and the high seas, for military and civilian use, and for aviation as well as maritime uses? The question was not only one of the Coast Guard's advocating Loran-C and the Defense Department's advocating Omega because these were the systems they sponsored. At some locations many systems and users were involved. For example, Decca was operated in the United States for the Federal Aviation Administration, and it could be argued that Decca was a "user pay" system. The question was what system was in the best interests of the nation. Yet the interests and reputations of the sponsoring agencies were at stake. Clearly, the issue posed a serious threat to an important Coast Guard program.

In later testimony before Congress, William Polhemus, himself an experienced navigator and president of Polhemus Navigation Sciences, Incorporated, described the mounting struggle:

A number of professional groups both within the U.S. Government and from among equipment manufacturers and the user community had become convinced that a single radio navigation aid could be provided which would fully satisfy the requirements of high-seas, coastal confluence region and the rivers, harbors and estuarial areas.

This opinion, held primarily by advocates of Omega, resulted in considerable pressure being placed on the Secretary of Transportation to obtain a declaration that Omega would be implemented as the national navigation aid.

At the same time, the advocates of Decca were standing on very firm ground resulting from some 25 years of successful operation of their equipment in European, Canadian, and Far Eastern waters.

This equipment is regarded very highly by knowledgeable marine navigators, and

---

*Later in this chapter this area is referred to as the coastal confluence zone. The terms coastal confluence region and coastal confluence zone have been used interchangeably in documents published by the government and industry.

rightfully so. Its ability to satisfy extremely demanding performance requirements is well known.

Department of Defense use of Loran-C in southeast Asia and recently completed, jointly sponsored NASA/DOT flight tests have confirmed its inherent capability to meet the requirements we are concerned with.

Activities of the British government's Royal Air Force, several departments of the Canadian government and the increasing use of Loran-C by civil marine and aircraft operators on and over the North Atlantic indicate something of the diversity of applications to which the radio aid may be put.[4]

Because of the impending decision to choose one system as the national navigation aid, Robert Cannon, assistant secretary of systems development and technology for the Department of Transportation, indicated to the Coast Guard in fall 1971 that "its known advocacy of Loran-C required that an impartial evaluation of these radio aids should be completed by a non-DOT agency."[5]

Commander William Roland of the Systems Development Branch prepared the way for such an evaluation. Working with the program manager for Aids to Navigation and the Office of the Chief of Staff, Roland conceived the Loran-70s program as a new initiative for the Coast Guard in aids to navigation. In Commander Roland's eyes Loran-70s consisted of three requisite tasks. First, existing Loran-C chains needed improvement by upgrading obsolescent equipment in service at several transmitting stations. Second, a plan was needed for implementing Loran-C coverage for the entire United States coastal confluence zone. Third, a plan was needed to phase out Loran-A after Loran-C coverage was available. Roland recognized that a period of overlap when both Loran-A and Loran-C signals would be available was a necessary part of any phase-out plan.

Commander Roland realized the significance of Cannon's request for an impartial evaluation. A requirement was made that the organization doing the study "must be known to have absolutely no explicit or implicit association with the promotion of any one of the candidates, yet it must be knowledgeable of the practices of navigation and competent in the field of operational requirements. Further, it was to have demonstrated access to the user community so that its needs might be fully recognized." Whoever would do the study should play the same impartial role that Jansky and Bailey had played for Captain Brunner in 1959. Polhemus Navigation Sciences, Incorporated, was selected. Their report, "Radio Aids to Navigation—Coastal Confluence Region," was completed in July 1972. It proved to be an important decision tool.[6]

DISTINCTIVE COMPETENCE PAYS A DIVIDEND

The Coast Guard knew Loran-C was extremely accurate and had good range for military applications; they realized the problem was lack of an inexpensive and reliable receiver, which effectively barred its use by private sailors and fishermen. These potential users regularly traveled in the coastal confluence region and needed Loran-C services. The maritime users, however, in most instances already had Loran-A equipment and wanted that system continued, particularly if they could avoid the expense of any new radio-navigation receiver. The lack of a suitable Loran-C receiver was critical. The problem was the Coast Guard had to serve multiple constituencies with different needs. The different needs were clear; did the agency have the technological means to fill them? The Coast Guard structure again faced the matching process described in chapter 2 and depicted in the model of figure 6.

Commander Roland was as keenly aware of this problem as was the head of the Office of Engineering, two levels above him in the structure at headquarters. Rear Admiral Pearson, chief of the Office of Engineering, had been Captain Brunner's principal assistant in the hectic days of the late 1950s when Loran-C was developed. Helmer Pearson had been a strong advocate of Loran-C and had helped develop the system and the human resource team discussed in the last chapter. Pearson had four alternatives to turn to for research and design work.

The first two alternatives were the Coast Guard Electronics Engineering Center (EECEN) at Wildwood, New Jersey, and, to a lesser extent, the Washington Radio Station in Virginia. Both did developmental work for the chief of the Office of Engineering and the Electronics Engineering Division. EECEN had gained expertise on receivers from repairing and testing them over the years. EECEN's excellent reputation, however, was built in other areas, and manufacturing techniques were not its specialty. Pearson could also turn to the recently created Coast Guard Office of Research and Development at headquarters. His fourth alternative was to foster development of the necessary technology by contracts with private industry. Several seed-money contracts were written. What the Loran-C system lacked was a reliable receiver that could be sold commercially at a reasonable price. For navigation equipment, reliability was as important as price. Lacking such a receiver, the argument for the system benefits and cost-effectiveness of Loran-C could not be made.

The seed-money contracts were a departure from Coast Guard practice in this area. Time, however, was of the essence. These important contracts were handled by Commander Roland of the Systems Development Branch and his assistant, Lieutenant Commander David Freese. They sought industrywide proposals for a receiver that could be mass-produced and marketed to dealers for approximately $2,000. Roland's challenge resulted in new receiver-manufacturing techniques at lower costs. Contracts were awarded to two companies to produce "low-cost" Loran-C receivers. For a small government investment, these lower-cost receivers allowed large segments of the public—such as fishermen, boaters, and small mariners and aviators—entry to the more accurate Loran-C system. They were also the first step to gaining the political support of these groups for Loran-C and to arguing the commercial as well as military benefits of the system.

The strongest competitor of Loran-C in the coastal confluence region was Differential Omega. Decca was second. Differential Omega was advocated by the navy-sponsored Omega Office in the Department of Defense. In an attempt to be totally objective in recognizing the capabilities of this system for the region, the Coast Guard contracted with Beukers Laboratories for a study of Differential Omega. This study was completed in May 1972.[7]

By 1973 the Coast Guard had become convinced that the two critical variables for selecting a radio-navigation system were where the signal was to be received—that is, location—and how accurate a fix was required from the signal—system accuracy. The location variable could most easily be resolved by segmenting two areas, the coastal confluence region and the high seas. Looking at these variables, was one system the best? This was the heart of the question. It would be a struggle to decide, because a decision would require the concurrence of the Department of Transportation, the Department of Defense, the Office of Management and Budget, and the Congress. Many would be unhappy whether Loran-C or Omega was selected.

The Coast Guard decided that the accuracy requirement varied for the high seas and the coastal confluence region. In fact, many users in the coastal confluence region had far more stringent requirements than others. A sample of these requirements is provided in table 18; many had originally been established by national and international meetings held in 1945 and 1946. As the table reveals, some industrial users require an accuracy of fifty feet. Probably most significant were the potential accuracy requirements for a Vessel Traffic Control System, discussed in chapter 9. After the *Torrey Canyon* wreck and the Santa Barbara well blowout, sensitivity to the necessity of better offshore safety had been greatly increased. Many were clamoring for Vessel Traffic Systems—later to be called Vessel Traffic Services—which were possible under the Ports and Waterways Safety Act passed in 1972.[8] This is an important example of a linkage between the Coast Guard Aids to Navigation and Marine Environmental Protection programs.

TABLE 18
Most Stringent Accuracy Requirements: Coastal Confluence Region

---

1. *Interface with Possible use in Vessel Traffic Systems*
   a. Harbor entance and approach sea-lanes
   b. Restricted coastal sea-lanes
   Requirement: less than one mile down to fifty feet
2. Oil exploration, pipe-laying, and oceanography
   Requirement: fifty feet, repeatable
3. Fishing
   Requirement: fifty feet, repeatable

Source: H.R. Document no. 93-30, 93d Cong., 2d sess.; *Hearings before the Subcommittee on Coast Guard and Navigation of the Committee on Merchant Marine and Fisheries on H.R. 13595;* 26, 28 March, 25 April, 1974, p. 94. Accuracy column has been adjusted from that appearing in H.R. Doc. No. 93-30 by Captain William Roland.

The accuracy requirements of any radio-navigation system input to a Vessel Traffic Services System promised to be highly important in the future. They were studied for many of the critical sea-lanes, such as New York Harbor, Chesapeake Bay, the Gulfs of Mexico and California, and the Valdez, Alaska, to Puget Sound, Washington route. The Aids to Navigation program manager and Marine Environmental Protection program manager were both part of the Office of Marine Environment and Systems, and much study and discussion took place. As the frequency and volume of cargoes passing through the sea lanes of the coastal confluence region increased, some of the vessel traffic lanes would become more and more crowded. For example, a two-mile-wide sea lane carrying two-way traffic could be constructed and its traffic pattern simulated. This was done, and the expected number of accidents were calculated using Delaware Bay traffic density. The analysis showed that navigation system accuracy of a quarter of a mile could greatly decrease the probability of an accident. The effect of navigation system accuracy is illustrated in figure 20.

Finally, the Aids to Navigation program manager and the Electronics Engineering support manager, along with Commander Roland's Systems Development Branch, determined that the Coast Guard should require continuous coverage, extending over the entire coastal confluence region, to an accuracy of one-quarter of a nautical mile. With this requirement set, the Coast Guard could take a definitive position on advocating a particular radio-navigation system.

EFFECT OF NAV SYSTEM ACCURACY

EXAMPLE: DELAWARE BAY

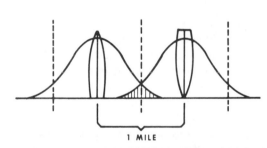

1 MILE

NAV ACCURACY	CHANCE OF BEING OUTSIDE 1 MILE LANE	CHANCE OF 2 VESSELS PASSING WITHIN 200 FT OF EACH OTHER	# OF EXPECTED "INCIDENTS" FOR 2 YEAR PERIOD
¼ NM (95%)	1/100	1/1,000,000	0
½ NM (95%)	1/20	1/1600	5

FIG. 20.   Effect of navigation-system accuracy in traffic-controlled sea-lanes. From H.R. Document no. 93-30, 93d Cong., 2d sess., *Hearings before the Subcommittee on Coast Guard and Navigation of the Committee on Merchant Marine and Fisheries on H.R. 13595,* 26, 28 March, 25 April 1974, p. 103.

In the summer of 1973 Commander William Mohin returned from a three-year assignment at the Coast Guard Activities for Europe Office in London. Mohin had been technically responsible for Loran-C in Europe; indeed, he had worked with radio-navigation systems continuously since his assignment as an executive officer of a Coast Guard cutter in the mid-1960s. Commander Mohin relieved Commander Roland as chief of the Systems Development Branch. At the same time, Rear Admiral James Moreau was assigned as chief of the Office of Engineering, relieving Rear Admiral Helmer Pearson. Moreau did not have Pearson's electronics engineering background, but he was known for providing strong impetus for positions he advocated.

By the time Commander Mohin became involved, the various groups within the Coast Guard had decided Omega was the most cost-effective and preferred system for the high seas. This decision revealed great objectivity, considering the threat to their own program. They then needed to choose either Loran-C or Omega for use in the coastal confluence region. If the Coast Guard were to advocate Omega for the coastal confluence region also, one system would dominate marine use. Loran-A could then be phased out and Loran-C continued only where required by military needs. Mohin reviewed the work that had been done internally and the Polhemus Report, completed the preceding summer. He felt that accuracy requirements were the crux of the case, and he agreed with the requirements that Commander Roland and his group had advocated.

Mohin was aware that the time for a decision was at hand. Within the Coast Guard, Captain James Gracey of the Programs Division and Captain John Costello of the Budget Division were preparing the 1975 budget. One of the initiatives scheduled for this budget was construction of new radio-navigation systems for the safe transit of vessels to and from the southern terminal of the Trans-Alaska Pipeline (TAPS) at Valdez. TAPS, which is discussed in chapter 10, had high national priority.[9] Because of the potential for catastrophic accidents and the unacceptable risk to the marine environment in the Northwest, the Coast Guard was giving high priority to demands for improved radio-navigation in the area. Commander Stephen Duca of the Programs Division was the examiner for this program, and he worked with Captain Gracey and Commander Mohin in determining the final budget detail.

During this period the Office of Telecommunications Policy (OTP) designated the Department of Transportation "lead agency of the interagency committee on navigation with DOD, Commerce, and NASA as participants." The first meeting of the committee was held in August 1973. Some differences existed between DOD and DOT. DOD was "attempting to coordinate its interservice navigation plans through the Defense Navigation Planning Group, sponsored by the Director of Defense Research and Engineering."[10] On the other hand, the Department of Transportation was focusing on its *National Plan for Navigation*,[11] which was "not concerned with defense navigation matters other than identifying those systems having civilian uses."[12] A resolution of the differences was necessary; the public policy process would determine the outcome. The distinctive competence it had developed in aids to navigation helped the Coast Guard decide which technology to advocate. The dynamics involved in managing a federal agency had reached a high stage of activity on the issue of radio navigation.

MAKING A DECISION IN THE
EXECUTIVE BRANCH

The Coast Guard determined that only Loran-C could meet the accuracy requirements for the coastal confluence zone. Omega was fine for the high seas, but it did not have the accuracy necessary in the heavily traveled coastal waters. Several meetings were held within the Coast Guard to make this policy decision final. Since the 1975 budget would call for construction of more Loran-C stations, this resolution had to be immediately cleared with the Department of Transportation. In the adversary process discussed in chapters 3 and 4, the time had come for the Coast Guard to advocate this decision to the department. If the ruling was favorable, the department would in turn advocate the decision before the Office of Management and Budget. One can trace Loran-C through this management process.

Now the commandant, Admiral Chester R. Bender, and the vice commandant, Vice Admiral Thomas R. Sargent, were the advocates for the Coast Guard position to the department. Incrementally, the Coast Guard was asking for authorization and funding to construct a Loran-C chain for the region along the United States Pacific Coast. This chain, which would cost nearly seventeen million dollars, would provide accurate navigation along a critical sea leg of TAPS. The larger issue was not the amount of funding but whether or not the new radio-navigation system should be a form of Loran-C. The department knew well that the Office of Telecommunications Policy, the Defense Department, and others favored Differential Omega.* The Department of Transportation would have to decide which position to advocate to the Office of Management and Budget.

Both formal and informal meetings on the issue involved officials at several levels in both the Coast Guard and the Department of Transportation. The Coast Guard vice commandant, Vice Admiral Thomas Sargent, was active at this stage. Briefings were also held for the joint chiefs of staff to indicate the Coast Guard position and obtain high-level support from the Defense Department. The Coast Guard held similar briefings for the American Institute of Merchant Shipping and for airlines, soliciting their comments and support.

---

*The advocates from the Office of Telecommunications Policy must have at least considered the views of Max Polk of OTP, a retired U.S. Navy captain who had headed the navy's Omega program before joining OTP in the area of navigation.

With an extensive background in civil engineering and command, Vice Admiral Sargent had most recently had experience with Loran-C when he was in charge of constructing a new chain in Southeast Asia. Captain Gracey and Commander Duca of the Programs Division, Captain Costello of the Budget Division, and Commander Mohin of the Systems Development Branch were among those from the Coast Guard who participated in meetings discussing the costs of the different proposals. Representing the Department of Transportation were the assistant secretary for systems development and technology, Robert Cannon, and Richard Beam of the same office, as well as Theodore C. Lutz, deputy undersecretary of transportation for budget and program review, and William F. Cass, analyst for Coast Guard programs.* The Department of Transportation approved the Coast Guard decision on Loran-C and in turn advocated this position to the Office of Management and Budget.

The informal hearings at OMB began in late fall 1973. Most of the Coast Guard and Department of Transportation officials who had discussed the issues surrounding this decision earlier were again called to various briefings and meetings at OMB. Roger Atkins, the OMB examiner for the Coast Guard, participated in most of these sessions, along with OMB colleagues with an interest in the navigation system issue. OMB clearly recognized that the Coast Guard was operating Loran-C overseas for a changing mix of Defense Department programs; this pattern would probably continue for some time, as it had with Loran-A. OMB knew the OTP position and the progress of the GAO study. It recognized the issue as presented by the Coast Guard and DOT—that is, that Loran-C should be the government-provided radio-navigation system in the coastal confluence zone. As an important decision factor, OMB focused on the necessity of accuracy within a quarter of a mile.

In December 1973 Admiral Bender, Vice Admiral Sargent, Captain Gracey, and Commander Mohin attended a discussion meeting at OMB, in the new executive office building across the street from the White House. During the meeting, officials from OMB produced a letter from the Naval Electronics Laboratories in California stating that by February the laboratories could give Omega accuracy identical to that of Loran-C.

Admiral Bender discussed this overture with his officers, then turned to the OMB officials with the reply, "Fine, we accept the test. We will have a cutter ready with Loran-C equipment installed, and will be ready to have equipment the navy proposes also installed. Then let's run a test and see." Proposing a physical

---

*Theodore C. Lutz came to the Department of Transportation from the Office of Management and Budget. The deputy undersecretary knew most of those at OMB who were involved in assembling the presidential budget; Lutz was very influential in the budgetary process.

William Cass had been a member of the Office of the Secretary since the first year of the Department of Transportation. Cass knew the Coast Guard well; he had retired from the Coast Guard with the rank of captain in January 1968.

challenge ended the verbal challenge. In large measure it also marked the turning point in the threat to Loran-C. The meeting adjourned with the presumption that the test would be run in February 1974.

Nothing more was heard about the proposed accuracy test. Two other important questions were asked of the Coast Guard while waiting for an OMB decision. The more important came from OMB, which wanted to know why the Coast Guard had not recommended Loran-A for the coastal confluence zone. Was not Loran-A a suitable alternative to Loran-C or Omega? This question touched off a good deal more review. Loran-A, the original loran system, had important advocates within the Coast Guard, particularly within the Electronics Engineering Division.

The review of Loran-A averred that "little engineering development has been done . . . in twenty years. As a result, there is considerable technical risk associated with achieving one-quarter mile accuracy with Loran-A."[13] Loran-A had poor propagation over land, and therefore it would require at least eight new stations to cover the coastal confluence zone. Even if the extra engineering work on the system were not included in the cost, it would not be cost-effective to build the eight stations, compared with the Loran-C alternatives. Even then its accuracy might not reach the standard proposed for Loran-C. The Coast Guard informed OMB in detail why it favored Loran-C over Loran-A.

The second question, from the General Accounting Office, involved a Coast Guard research and development project to investigate a navigational aid for rivers and harbors. GAO wanted to know why, when OTP advocated reducing the number of navigational aids, the Coast Guard was trying to develop still another one. GAO wanted to know how this project affected Coast Guard advocacy of Loran-C for the coastal confluence zone. The GAO question was quickly answered. The Programs Division, the Office of Engineering, and the Office of Research and Development rapidly exchanged data on the project. The rivers and harbors project was reported to be a minor effort within the Office of Research and Development that did conflict with the Loran-C project. It was determined that Loran-C had the potential to meet this need, and so the rivers and harbors navigational aid project was terminated and GAO was informed. When a policy issue is being debated at OMB and funding is on the line, a federal agency can move with surprising speed.

During the OMB phase, Deputy Undersecretary of Transportation Lutz was very helpful in advocating the Coast Guard position on the importance of Loran-C for the coastal confluence zone. He pointed out the civil nature of the system and the responsibilities of the Coast Guard under the Federal Water Pollution Control Act, as amended, and the Ports and Waterways Safety Act. He also recapitulated the other points made by the Coast Guard during the Department of Transportation review of the Loran-C issue. Finally, in early winter, OMB cleared the Coast Guard position. Before Loran-C could go forward to

Congress as a part of its budget, however, the Coast Guard had to obtain a statement of agreement on radio-navigation systems between the Department of Transportation and the Department of Defense.

The interdepartmental agreement between Transportation and Defense was completed at the level of the assistant secretary and deputy undersecretary. Another series of meetings was held between the two departments to work out details of the final agreement. Deputy Undersecretary Lutz again was very active, this time in seeing that the agreement was as realistic as possible.

Part of the agreement involved "turning on" Loran-C coverage for the coastal confluence zone along the West Coast. Station sites had to be selected, built, and equipped to go "on the air." An integral part of the package, however, was "turning off" Loran-A in other areas, as well as on the West Coast, which would reduce the number and cost of radio-navigation systems in use. This reduction was, after all, the original object of the choice between Loran-C and Omega for the coastal confluence zone. There was added political complexity because some important military and commercial users still felt they needed the Loran-A system.

A "Loran-C public awareness program" that began in early 1974 helped relieve some of the political pressure the Coast Guard still felt from commercial users of the Loran-A system. Lieutenant Commander Leo Schowengerdt of the Plans Evaluation Division of the Office of the Chief of Staff was assigned to head a special project staff in Washington. Schowengerdt in turn designated people in each Coast Guard field district to visit users in their areas and serve as "apostles" for Loran-C. The apostles gave demonstrations, talked to user groups, and visited as many individual members of the loran constituency as possible before the summer of 1974. Loran-C workshops held at Gettysburg, Pennsylvania, and Portland, Oregon, were outgrowths of their efforts. Work was done at Oregon State University on public education efforts necessary to smooth the transition from Loran-A to Loran-C. The public awareness program, however, did not consider the political pressure from military users. This was resolved by the interdepartmental agreement between the departments of Transportation and Defense.

Rear Admiral Warren M. Cone of the United States Navy, alternate co-chairman of the DOT/DOD Task Force on Navigation, summed up this interdepartmental agreement in his testimony before Congress in spring 1974. He testified that, because of the high expense of existing Omega receivers for aircraft, DOD had "extended the military user requirement for Loran-A services until December 31, 1977, or two years after the Joint Chiefs of Staff declare . . . some other worldwide navigation system . . . fully operational." One Loran-A chain, in Baffin Bay, Canada, was declared unnecessary after 30 June 1975. With this exception, Defense declared that "the Department of Transportation proposal for a minimum 5-year period before shutting down any Loran-A facilities fully accommodates the Department of Defense Loran-A phaseout plan."[14] This statement in effect provided for the "turn off" decision OMB, OTP, and GAO wanted for partially redundant systems. At the same time it allowed for a reasonable phase-in period for many commercial users to adjust from Loran-A to Loran-C. It was a policy statement that reasonably satisfied all the varied interest groups involved in the decision-making.

In his testimony to Congress, Rear Admiral Cone then went on to the portions of the interdepartmental agreement that dealt directly with the Coast Guard's decision to formulate expanded Loran-C coverage.

The Department of Defense fully supports the Loran-C replacement program in the Mediterranean as necessary to the continued fulfillment of a high priority military requirement.

Although there is no known military requirement for the construction of the new Loran-C facilities on the Pacific Coast, the Department of Defense recognizes the need for such an improvement for safety in the private sector and the obvious importance to the U.S. Coast Guard in exercising its responsibilities.[15]

With the interdepartmental agreement made, the Coast Guard finally had a definite timetable for "turning on" Loran-C and "turning off" Loran-A. The last step in the executive branch of government was complete.

CONGRESS EXAMINES THE DECISION

The final step in developing the loran system involved the Congress. Hearings would be held by both the authorization committee and the appropriations Committee. There were two key hearings in the House of Representatives. One was an appropriations hearing before the Subcommittee on the Department of Transportation and Related Agencies Appropriations, chaired by Congressman John J. McFall of California. The other, for authorization, was before the Subcommittee on Coast Guard and Navigation of the Committee on Merchant Marine and Fisheries, chaired by Congressman John M. Murphy of New York.

The hearings, triggered by the seventeen-million-dollar line item for construction of the West Coast Loran-C chain, proved to be the forum for resolving the executive branch decision to "turn on" Loran-C and "turn off" Loran-A. All groups had the chance to have their arguments considered. The hearings before the Murphy subcommittee were held on 26 and 28 March and 25 April 1974.

Chairman Murphy brought the issue into focus in his opening statement:

This morning we begin hearings on the fiscal 1975 money authorization for acquisition, construction, and improvement of the U.S. Coast Guard. The $114.1 million is $38 million more than the 1974 figure.

The members of this committee have continually worked for across-the-board increases in funding to give the Coast Guard a greater capability to save lives, prevent oil pollution, protect the interests of U.S. fishermen, and to provide the best in domestic and international navigational aids among their other worthwhile missions. . . .

Some of the items in the 1975 budget are of great significance in protecting our territorial waters against raids from foreign fishing fleets, protecting the West Coast from oil pollution when the gush of crude oil begins to flow down from Alaska, and replacing important navigational equipment needed to keep our Polaris and Poseidon missile submarines on target. These items include. . . .

Construction of a vessel traffic system at Valdez, Alaska. . . .

Two controversial long-range navigation programs, one of which has been the subject of Executive Branch vacillation for the past 6 years.[16]

The commandant of the Coast Guard was the first witness. Admiral Bender pointed to all major areas of Coast Guard capital budget thrusts. When he came to radio navigation, he reviewed all facets surrounding the important transit of vessels to and from the southern terminal of the Trans-Alaska Pipeline. He pointed out the gaps and deficiencies in radio-navigation coverage in the area and briefly discussed the arrangements to "turn on" Loran-C and "turn off" Loran-A.

How to solve these deficiencies involves a number of very complex considerations, such as differing user requirements, the economic impact on users of the services currently provided, the cost of establishing a new system and the potential of alternative systems to meet fix-accuracy, reliability and repeatability requirements.

There are several radio navigation systems which have been very carefully considered for selection. Loran-C is particularly suited and, pending final decision on this matter, must be considered the most likely candidate for selection.[17]

Commander Mohin then presented a detailed analysis of the Coast Guard choice of Loran-C.[18] Captain Costello, chief of the Budget Division, followed with a detailed ten-year estimate of the costs of four alternatives:

1. "Do nothing"—operate Loran-A "as is"
2. Extend Loran-A coverage throughout CCR*
3. Extend Loran-A coverage and increase accuracy to one-quarter of a mile
4. Provide Loran-C coverage in CCR, phase out Loran-A.[19]

The costs of these alternatives appear in table 19. Captain Costello pointed out that the first alternative was the least expensive in the short run; he then explained why the Coast Guard had selected the fourth, describing how Loran-C would be phased in and how this was reflected in the cost data:

In the phase-in period for Loran-C in the coastal confluence region, we plan to allow an extended period of overlapping operations. The analysis assumed that we would announce our intention to terminate Loran-A 5 years before we actually turn it off. During the final 2

*Captain Costello used the term "CCR" in his testimony because it had in error been printed on the slide that was being shown in the hearing room while he testified. The Coast Guard was using the terminology coastal confluence zone, or CCZ, not coastal confluence region, or CCR.

TABLE 19
Projected Costs for Fiscal Years 1975–84 for Four Alternatives
(in millions of dollars)

Alternative	Capital Costs	Operating Costs	Total Costs
1	33.7	39.9	73.6
2	46.7	48.3	95.0
3	51.7	48.3	100.0
4	49.1	45.6	94.7

Source: H.R. doc. no. 93-30; 93d Cong., 2d sess.; *Hearings before the Subcommittee on Coast Guard and Navigation of the Committee on Merchant Marine and Fisheries on H.R. 13595*; 26, 28 March, 25 April, 1974, p. 118.

years of that 5-year period, we would provide both Loran-A and Loran-C in the area of the coastal confluence region.

The reason for this is to allow the current user of Loran-A a reasonable period of time to amortize his investment in Loran-A equipment and a reasonable time to convert his navigational data to the Loran-C system.

We concluded from this analysis that not only was Loran-C engineering and operationally the preferred system but also from a cost analysis point of view it is the preferred solution.

Therefore the Coast Guard and the Department of Transportation have adopted the position that Loran-C should be adopted.[20]

Among the opponents of the proposed phase out of Loran-A were fishermen—important constituents in whom the Coast Guard had long been interested. Only recently the Coast Guard had been reminded of the conservative nature of fishermen and their power to get what they wanted. In about 1970 the Coast Guard had reversed the master and secondary roles of the Nantucket, Massachusetts, and Sandy Hook, New Jersey, Loran-A stations. This station reversal, of course, changed the numbers on the loran chart lines of constant time differences. When the Coast Guard sent out notices to change charts, they felt their responsibility to the public users of loran had been discharged. To their horror, they then found out that many fishermen did not use charts at all; they used little black books that contained only the time difference numbers of choice fishing spots! Even explaining how to add a constant to their readings to come up with corrected "black book" numbers did not mollify the fishermen. In exasperation, the Coast Guard met the need of the fishing public and returned Nantucket and Sandy Hook to their original master-secondary station roles.

Chairman Murphy asked if the Coast Guard had talked with the fishermen about the decision to declare Loran-C the system for the coastal confluence zone. Admiral Bender responded that the Coast Guard had "demonstrated Loran-C to the fishermen, but had not been able to do this on the west coast because it does not exist there." He pointed out the two-year overlap in coverage planned and the work under way to develop a better Loran-C receiver. He said that, although receivers then cost three to four thousand dollars, a "considerable increase in production" should bring the per-unit cost substantially lower. Congressman Gerry Studds of Massachusetts read a letter from the Seafood Producers' Association of New Bedford, citing the high cost of a Loran-C receiver and the desire of many fishermen in his district to retain Loran-A coverage.[21] A discussion ensued of the trade-offs between national pressures to reduce overlapping radio-navigation systems and the need for the accuracy of Loran-C. Both changing technology and the interests of the nation and the citizens the Coast Guard serves were consistent themes. Coast Guard structure was clearly trying to balance these conflicting needs as in the model of figure 6.

The first witness from outside the Coast Guard was William Polhemus, whose studies were mentioned earlier. The background and findings of the study by Polhemus Navigation Sciences, Incorporated were discussed. Chairman Murphy pointed out that the Office of Telecommunications Policy opposed Loran-C. Basically, OTP wanted the Department of Transportation to withhold any decision, whereas the Coast Guard felt a decision should be made.* Chairman Murphy read a letter from Clay Whitehead of OTP to OMB director Roy Ash, stating the OTP position. The letter was dated 3 December 1973;[22] the Office of Management and Budget had subsequently ruled in favor of turning on Loran-C in the coastal confluence zone.

The Department of Defense position on Loran-C was another significant area for the subcommittee to probe. Defense was represented by Rear Admiral Cone, who submitted a statement reflecting the interagency agreement worked out earlier between Transportation and Defense. Congressman Murphy questioned Admiral Cone at length about the advantages of various radio-navigation systems. Cone described extensive army and navy use of Loran-C; he even described a portable "manpack" Loran-C receiver the army was developing, at a cost of five thousand dollars per set. Cone stated that the cost per receiver should fall as receiver use rose, since Loran-C would have many private uses. Admiral Cone believed the Coast Guard should immediately begin construction of the West Coast Loran-C chain, to be ready for the large tankers traveling to and from Valdez, Alaska, in 1977.[23]

The subcommittee next heard F. J. Schafer, director of the Logistics and Communications Division of the General Accounting Office. Schafer summarized an extensive ongoing GAO study of radio-navigation systems available for maritime needs. The GAO had studied correspondence and reports and interviewed officials at the DOT, Coast Guard, DOD, Army, Navy, Air Force, Maritime Administration, Federal Aviation Agency, Office of Telecommunica-

---

*This last-minute request from OTP to delay a decision takes on added interest when one considers that OTP began the decision-making process by stating there were too many competing radio-navigation systems and that one should be singled out for increased government support while the others should be cut back.

tions Policy, and Office of Management and Budget. GAO generally supported the Coast Guard position:

Our study centered upon an apparent Coast Guard course leading to distinct marine radionavigation systems for (1) the high seas, (2) the coastal confluence, and (3) harbors and estuaries. However, recently, the Coast Guard decided in favor of two systems. No one existing system would satisfy all three areas. The Coast Guard believes that:

Omega is the most cost-effective solution . . . on the high seas. Loran-C can best satisfy the precision navigation requirements resulting from heavy traffic in the coastal confluence and harbors and estuaries, thereby eliminating the requirement for Loran-A.

We found no basis to question the two systems selected by the Coast Guard. We are providing information on these systems and observations on actions the Department of Transportation and the Coast Guard could take to (1) provide much needed authoritative information to manufacturers and users as the future operation of navigation systems and (2) improve coordination of the overlapping requirements and systems of the several Government agencies involved in the navigation field.[24]

Congressman Murphy thoroughly questioned Schafer on the GAO findings. Schafer stressed the importance of phasing out Loran-A and phasing in Loran-C and the need for coordination in planning navigation systems. He emphasized that technology was changing in this area, and that new applications serving the national need might soon be possible. For this reason Schafer urged that "the Department of Transportation assume the leadership because of the emerging and constantly growing commercial interest in radionavigation systems . . . for navigation or not as well as the Department of Defense's needs in the area."[25]

Many others testified for or against the Coast Guard decision to implement Loran-C for the coastal confluence zone. For example, James J. Reynolds, president of the American Institute of Merchant Shipping (AIMS), presented the views of an association representing the owners and operators of two-thirds of the oceangoing vessels serving America's foreign and domestic trade. AIMS not only supported the Coast Guard decision but expressed "strong support for the leadership exercised by the Coast Guard in developing vessel traffic systems in those areas of the United States which experience congested traffic conditions in their ports and harbors." Reynolds continued:

AIMS was a strong supporter of the Ports and Waterways Safety Act of 1972, which had its impetus in this subcommittee and gives the Coast Guard statutory authority to establish mandatory vessel traffic systems in U.S. waters where it determines such action to be proper.

In view of your oversight function associated with that legislation, AIMS would now like to discuss briefly the implementation of the act.

Vessel traffic systems should be federally directed and manned by trained Federal personnel with the expertise to assure that the controls themselves do not create maritime hazards. . . . Work on such systems is currently underway in New York, San Francisco, and Puget Sound, and we feel confident that the Coast Guard with all prudent haste will add other important areas to this list.[26]

When questioned by Congressman Murphy, Reynolds admitted that the operations committee of AIMS had argued the benefits and costs of various radio-navigation systems for years without strong agreement on any one system. But he stated that he felt the Coast Guard should decide, and that the users would then have to abide by the decision. He pointed out that the five-year period of changeover was ample to ease the financial burden of switching systems.

There were many other friendly witnesses. Carl Savit testified on behalf of the oil and geophysical contractors. Lloyd Higginbotham, James Van Etten, and Robert Bartlett of the Wild Goose Association also testified. The Wild Goose Association is an independent organization of individuals interested in national navigation capabilities. Higginbotham, president of the association, was the first of this group to testify:

The Wild Goose Association is comprised of approximately 350 members gathered from nearly all segments of government and industry which have interest in our national navigation capabilities. Our association is specifically interested in loran and we are of the opinion that loran and specifically Loran-C does now and can even more contribute to the national well being. . . .
Our concern, Mr. Chairman, is in the coastal confluence zone and in intercontinental and inland domestic navigation. It is the position of the Wild Goose Association that the specified accuracy requirements for the CCZ as presented in the National Plan for Navigation published by the Department of Transportation in April 1972 can be met with application of Loran-C.[27]

The rest of the testimony from members of this group thoroughly described their views; they clearly supported the Coast Guard position.

Some testified against the Coast Guard decision on Loran-C. For example, Edward Fraser, of Tracor, Incorporated, testified that "Loran-C is not the appropriate common radio navigation aid for the coastal confluence region and for the rivers and harbors, and . . . a decision at this time to begin the implementation of such a system would be ill advised."[28] Fraser specifically advocated a RIHANS system that was being developed by Tracor. RIHANS is an acronym for the rivers and harbors aid to navigation system project discussed earlier. The Coast Guard terminated its interest in RIHANS after the GAO inquiry, when it decided Loran-C could meet the rivers and harbors needs. Several other equipment manufacturers and users also testified.

Recall that the Office of Telecommunications Policy entered the decision-making process at several key points. Originally, OTP wanted one of the competing radio-navigation systems to be selected as the national system; after Loran-C was tentatively chosen for the coastal confluence zone, OTP took the position that selection should be delayed. Testifying before the Murphy subcommittee, Clay Whitehead, director of OTP, stated:

Although the system selections—Omega for high-seas navigation and Loran-C for the coastal and rivers and harbors areas—are still being questioned by proponents of other systems, the time necessary to develop and evaluate alternative proposals would delay any system implementation for at least two years. Therefore, OTP supports the DOT proposal for Loran-C expansion as primarily a civil maritime system for both coastal and rivers and harbors navigation.[29]

Clay Whitehead and Max Polk of OTP both gave detailed answers to a series of questions by Chairman Murphy both on Loran-C and on navigation in general.[30]

Besides those who had a specific interest in one of the candidate navigation systems, an important user still was concerned with the Coast Guard decision. Fishermen from New England—in particular Rhode Island and Massachusetts—made known their support of Loran-A and their opposition to Loran-C. It became clear that the phase-in period was the only concession they would receive. Although the examination of the Coast Guard decision for Loran-C was triggered by the need for authorization for the West Coast Loran-C chain, it appeared that Congress agreed with the more far-reaching advocacy of Loran-C.

The Subcommittee on Coast Guard and Navigation of the Committee on Merchant Marine and Fisheries finally approved the authorization bill, including nearly seventeen million dollars for the West Coast Loran-C chain. By so doing, the subcommittee effectively gave congressional approval to the Coast Guard decision to turn on Loran-C and turn off Loran-A after a phase-in period. Congressional approval was the final step in developing a policy and making a decision, a process that had begun within the Coast Guard structure more than two years before the subcommittee hearings. The decision had now been successfully tested against the demands of the external environment. During those two years the process of managing a federal agency had resolved many areas of conflict both outside and within the agency and provided an arena for negotiation and decision. Now the decision had to be implemented.

IMPLEMENTING THE DECISION

The first step in implementation was formal announcement of the decision as evolved by the policy-making framework of Washington. On 16 May 1974, Admiral Chester Bender, Coast Guard commandant, announced the details of the decision in New York City, aboard the cutter *Morgenthau*. Basically, the decision designated Loran-C as the government-provided radio-navigation system for the United States coastal confluence zone and brought about its implementation.

A key part of the Coast Guard announcement explained the phase-in period. Those who wanted Loran-A retained had insisted that Loran-C be turned on well before Loran-A was turned off. The Coast Guard stated that about five years' notice would be given before the United States decommissioned any Loran-A chain servicing primarily the coastal confluence region. Admiral Bender also promised that, once a Loran-C chain was operating satisfactorily, there would be a period of "simultaneous operation of the Loran-A and Loran-C systems for at least twenty-four months."[31]

The challenge during implementation was ensuring that the Loran-C system would be ready on time. The West Coast Loran-C chain was needed in 1977 for the scheduled opening of the Trans-Alaska Pipeline at Valdez. This deadline was real. Any departure from it would bring back the threat that had just been dealt with. With the phase-in policy announced, any scheduled turn off of Loran-A called for the Loran-C replacement to have already been in operation for two years.

The Systems Development Branch at Coast Guard headquarters had been actively involved in the decision-making process on Loran-C for four years. Initially, the National Plan for Navigation called for a decision on Loran-C in 1972.[32] The announcement in New York in May 1974 ended the struggle. The economic, social, and political environment had posed many threats; these threats were largely answered when Congress examined and approved the choice of Loran-C for the coastal confluence zone.

Though Commander Mohin had relieved Commander Roland only in the summer of 1973, Mohin and his branch had little time to savor the victory. They faced another challenge; the technological environment still posed major threats as well as opportunities. The Systems Development Branch quickly shifted their emphasis back to finding engineering solutions to the problems in Loran-C technology. It was their responsibility to have the West Coast Loran-C chain "on the air" before the Trans-Alaska Pipeline opened in the summer of 1977. Bill Mohin carried many of the same pressures that Lawrence Harding and Loren Brunner had experienced before him in similar periods of expansion of loran technology.*

At the time, two key contracts were outstanding. One was for a new monitor receiver, the other called for a prototype of a solid-state transmitter. Problems developed on both contracts. In addition, the Coast Guard Electronics Engineering Center at Wildwood, New Jersey, had been given the go-ahead to develop a new generation of Loran-C timing equipment.

The Systems Development Branch had two major tasks. First, they had to select all the basic equipment for use in the new Loran-C chain for the West Coast. In doing so they were keenly aware that equipment developed now would most probably be used in future chains. Second, they had to be sure the equipment would be available—serviceable and reliable—on time.

EECEN at Wildwood was given the task of designing and staging prototype timing equipment. Commander Donald Feldman convinced Mohin that it should be semiautomated. At Wildwood the equipment was referred to as "semi-automated or capable of operating in an unwatched mode"—that is, men were

---

*An overwhelming concern for protecting the marine environment, particularly on the sea leg of TAPS from Valdez to Puget Sound and the remainder of the West Coast, made the deadline for having the West Coast chain "on the air" a very real time pressure. This situation is discussed further in chapter 10.

not required to stand continuous "live" watches. Some of this equipment had been designed earlier, and some was designed in 1973. The semiautomated equipment, if successful, would free large numbers of technicians from loran stations and would be a major system innovation. To change the equipment required at this point in the project was a risk; but the expected benefits seemed worth it.

Once laboratory models of the semiautomated timers were tested, specifications for the equipment were drawn and sent to "time and materials contractors" for more detailed models and production copies. The contractors were also to produce manufacturers' drawings. The detailed models were again tested and refined. This iterative process allowed the Systems Development Branch to produce fairly sophisticated equipment on a tight time schedule. It also allowed for trial-and-error modifications without major contractual changes.

A goal had been set to unwatch—operate without a technician "watching" the loran transmitter—one station, Nantucket, by January 1974 to demonstrate the viability of the concept. With this accomplished and a favorable decision reached by Congress, all the secondary stations in the East Coast chain except Cape Race were semiautomated by August 1974. The Electronics Engineering Center again proved invaluable, as did the engineering professionalism of everyone involved.

Commander Mohin wrestled with two problems at this stage. The first centered on the operational strategy for Loran-C chains. By introducing the semiautomated timing and monitoring system, the number of men assigned to a station could be greatly reduced. This new strategy of operations not only was a major innovation, it held the promise of freeing large numbers of personnel. Based on the successful installation of equipment and operation of the East Coast chain in the "unwatched mode," Mohin decided to install semiautomated timing equipment in stations on the new West Coast chain and also around the world. He realized that with a relatively small capital investment he could free up as much as half the crews of the stations. The more capital-intensive operating mode promised to give Mohin the leverage he needed within the Coast Guard structure to meet his remaining goals.

The second problem involved whether to use a third-generation vacuum-tube transmitter or a solid-state transmitter for the West Coast chain. Captain Alfred Manning and Commander Roland had both invested considerable effort in supporting the development of a solid-state transmitter, and a contract had been let. But Mohin was afraid that the solid-state transmitter could not be produced and working on time. Mohin felt that, to meet the on-air deadline for the West Coast chain and at the same time introduce the new strategy of operations, a tube type of transmitter was needed. He did not have time to acquire one competitively. The Coast Guard therefore gave ITT a sole-source contract to build an updated version of an older, well-known tube transmitter, specifically modified to improve its performance when integrated into the system along with the semiautomated timing equipment.

A key to the success of the combination of semiautomated timing equipment and third-generation transmitters was that automation was first achieved on a small scale. Before 1974, EECEN had asked how the watch-stander could be eliminated at one station. One of the reasons the solid-state transmitter had been unsuccessful in 1974, when there was great time pressure, was that it was part of a large scheme—to automate and *unman* the entire transmitting station. Although the idea was outstanding, it was far too complex to manage with the technology then existing. In tests in 1973–74, the solid-state transmitter at best demonstrated poor reliability. Mohin selected the modified tube transmitter for the West Coast chain because he felt confident that with it he could meet the "on-air" deadline; by this time Mohin had the complete concurrence of his supervisor, Captain Manning, who had actively supported the solid-state transmitter project.

Later in 1974, Megapulse, Incorporated, demonstrated a far more advanced solid-state transmitter to the Coast Guard. Recognizing the complexities of the technology, the contracting process for state-of-the-art equipment, and the future needs of the loran system, Manning, Mohin, and Feldman conferred and decided to have Megapulse continue work on the solid-state transmitter. All hoped that it could soon be integrated into the operational network. Megapulse later delivered an impressive solid-state transmitter.

The new strategy of operation Mohin chose to introduce increased the technical problems of meeting the deadline for the West Coast chain. The initial tests of the new timing and control equipment indicated that the crew of a loran station could be reduced from nearly twenty-five to approximately nine. The significance of a manning reduction of this size was substantial; adopting the new strategy greatly eased the added pressures of redesigning equipment, changing operational concepts, *and* meeting the construction deadline at the same time. Implementing the decision to use Loran-C in the coastal confluence zone was even more involved than had been anticipated, if it was to be both technically innovative and on schedule.

Note that the funds for updating the timing equipment and in fact manufacturing the first models did not come through the resource change proposal or the acquisition, construction, and improvement processes discussed in chapter 4. The construction schedule and deadlines left no time for these processes. Once the potential savings from manning reductions became known, the new strategy of operation for the Loran-C system was immediately accepted. Funds were reprogrammed, mainly by the Coast Guard program manager for Aids to Navigation. Reprogrammed funds were diverted to acquire the new equipment. Loran was increasingly becoming a program with a high initial cost but a low operating cost. It was also becoming far less labor-intensive than it had been.

The new operational concept meant that, for the West Coast chain, the secondary station at Middletown, California, had all the monitoring and control equipment necessary to direct the chain. This innovation spread rapidly to the north Atlantic, Norwegian Sea, Hawaiian, Pacific, Mediterranean, and East Coast chains. Within eighteen months the Systems Development Branch, assisted by the Electronics Engineering Center, designed, contracted for, and installed new Loran-C timing equipment at operating stations around the entire globe.

The construction of a Loran-C chain on the West Coast was completed only four months after the original deadline. But implementing the decision to build the chain had further changed the loran system and opened up still more possibilities in the changing balance of national needs and technical means—two principal inputs to the model of figure 6. As Loran-C became more economical, and as its uses became more widely recognized, demands for the system increased. The proposed scope of the Loran-C network for North America alone is presented in figure 21.

FIG. 21.   Proposed scope of Loran-C coverage for North America, 1977. From U.S. Coast Guard.

In 1976 Commander Mohin was reassigned by the Coast Guard from the Systems Development Branch to head a newly created Radio-navigation Projects Office in the Office of the Secretary of Transportation. Commander Paul Pakos was assigned to head the Systems Development Branch, which still faced mammoth problems in implementing the changing loran system. Both Mohin and Pakos give great credit to the staff members of the Systems Development Branch and the Electronics Engineering Center who worked so hard to make the transition to Loran-C in the coastal confluence zone. The Loran-70s project, conceived by Commander Roland, had indeed come a long way.* Again, human resources of the Coast Guard made important contributions. These people and their successors continue to contribute to the distinctive competence of the Coast Guard in aids to navigation.

THE AFTERMATH

The reasons for deciding on Loran-C as the government-provided radio-navigation system for the coastal confluence zone were, in retrospect, straightforward. They are as follows:

1. Loran-C meets the accuracy requirements established.
2. It is the most cost-effective system.
3. It has been operationally proved.
4. Low-cost commercial receivers are available, and the cost is steadily decreasing.
5. It has high potential for future applications, since it is usable on land, is highly accurate, and has a long range.

By covering the coastal confluence zone, Loran-C provides an important externality to the nation. At the same time, it furnishes navigational service to more than two-thirds of the continental United States and more than 90 percent of its population.

Technological change usually brings forth new applications that transcend the need for which an innovation was first developed,[33] but such new applications often raise managerial objections because they go beyond the area the organization serves.[34] This certainly happened with Loran-C; a user constituency

---

*At least fifteen Coast Guard officers could be identified by name for their contributions as electrical engineers and project managers. The group spirit they displayed is noteworthy; Loran-C was a team project.

Indirectly, this group demonstrates the human resources of the Coast Guard. Many were graduates of the Coast Guard Academy, where their early preference for engineering was encouraged. Almost all had graduate degrees in electrical engineering and many years of experience with navigation technology. Many capable people followed in the footsteps of Captain Harding and Captain Brunner.

developed that was much larger than the original group of mariners and aviators. Transportation and inventory control of goods as they are shipped by one transportation mode then shifted to other modes until they reach the final distribution centers are huge potential applications. There are many others, made technically possible by miniaturized receivers that can be interrogated to "send back" their position at any time.

In 1978 the Department of Transportation introduced a midcontinent chain, bringing Loran-C service to most of the nation. The possible uses of Loran-C have been enhanced not only by the increasing geographic coverage, but by the growing realization of the potential of *retransmitted* Loran-C position information. This added feature means that not only will a receiver know its own location, but a remote unit can pinpoint where the receiver is. For example, the whereabouts of a police car equipped with Loran-C will be known to its central headquarters. This information can be used not only to keep track of the police car, but also to determine the location of an accident or other incident. A study completed by the New York State Department of Motor Vehicles in June 1976 found that "Loran C can technically, operationally, and economically satisfy the precise position identification requirements for selected operations in New York State."[35]

Other applications span the public and private sectors. Some reports have categorized these applications as automated vehicle tracking and monitoring, site registration and monitoring, and precise aircraft and ship monitoring. Government agencies that might integrate this technology into some of their public services run the gamut from the Post Office and Census Bureau to the departments of Justice and Agriculture. Private applications at present appear most promising in the transportation sector, where movement of goods and dispatch of services are involved.

Though repeatable position accuracy may pinpoint a position within 50 to 150 feet, a major barrier to the diffusion of Loran-C technology will be the payoff the application offers. This payoff will be determined by the cost of the loran receiver and the value of the information it provides. Figure 22 shows the declining cost of a Loran-C receiver over the 1970s. As with any electronic technology, mass production should make prices fall. As the price falls, usage should increase, further lowering the cost of the equipment. The economies of scale in effect here could change the entire complexion of the navigational services the Coast Guard supplies to the nation.

Many individuals within the Coast Guard involved with Loran-C were largely proactive *and* innovative in anticipating the needs of the public. The individuals produced the necessary services. The definition of the need for the program, the impetus to develop and advocate it against opposition, and the context that developed while the decision was formulated and implemented all are good examples of successful management responses of the Coast Guard.

These responses came in answer to a threat to cut back program funding

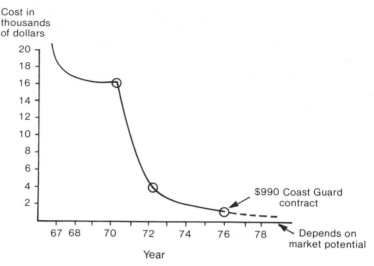

FIG. 22. The declining cost of Loran-C receivers, 1970–80 (data from U.S. Coast Guard). Land applications could potentially expand that market to several million users. With increased usage the price might be reduced to $200-$500, thus putting Loran-C in a class with citizen's band radio "position and communication."

or even dismantle all or part of the loran system. They could not have been developed without the human and physical resources and the distinctive competence of the Coast Guard in radio navigation. This competence, a heritage from the Lighthouse Service, the Revenue Marine, and the early days of World War II, had become formidable. The dual-role strategy had allowed the Coast Guard to nurture and further develop that competence in peace and in war. The multimission concept allowed the Coast Guard to reallocate these resources among programs, allowing a further expansion in specific competence.

In the future, some new technology such as satellite navigation is likely to be the stimulus for another threat that will bring further change, as will the changing needs of the public. Indeed, only two years after the hearings before the Subcommittee on Coast Guard and Navigation of 1974, such a prediction was made before the Senate Committee on Armed Services. Lieutenant General Alton D. Slay, air force deputy chief of staff for research and development, discussed a satellite network known as NAVSTAR Global Positioning System. Slay stated that it provided "10 meter positioning anywhere in the world." The chairman, Senator Howard W. Cannon, asked General Slay if the new system was "for use where you don't have Loran?" General Slay replied, "No; it is to replace Loran plus some other systems."[36] The timetable they discussed called for deployment of the satellite system by the mid-1980s. Adapting to the stimulus of varied threats and to the changing technical means and national needs will challenge the Coast Guard structure for years to come.

The loran system has been a source of materials to help us answer the research questions and the categorical charges. The problems of protecting the quality of the marine environment are also an excellent source of this kind of material and will be the focus of the next three chapters.

8 OIL AND THE CHANGING MARINE ENVIRONMENT

EARLY CONCERNS

From its early years as the Revenue Marine, the Coast Guard has been concerned with protecting marine transport from the hazards of the environment. Protection was the main objective of "winter cruising," the offshore patrols authorized by the Congress in 1837 (see Appendix 1). These patrols had been instigated even earlier by the local cutter captains as life- and property-saving efforts from cutters at sea.

The Life Saving Service also dealt with protection. It had been created by the Congress in 1878 as an answer to offshore disasters brought about by storms. The early concerns of the cuttermen and surfmen of these two agencies were mainly protective, aimed at saving life and property at sea during bad weather and periods of poor visibility. Mariners and the growing marine industry of the new nation benefited from these efforts and appreciated them.

Protection soon expanded to include prevention. In 1807 the voyage of the *Clermont,* powered by Robert Fulton's new steam boiler, signaled a period of change in marine technology. The sailing ship was eventually replaced. Ship hulls slowly changed from wood to steel, and propellers converted mechanical power to hydrodynamic power, driving the ship through the water. As various mechanical designs and hull arrangements were tried out, accidents became common.* Safety at sea became a concern of industry and the public, and

---

*As steam propulsion was introduced to ships, many interesting problems arose in shipbuilding, marine engineering, and the management of "steamship" companies. See, for example S. C. Gilfillan, *Inventing the Ship* (Chicago: Follett, 1935). By 1860, 15 percent of American tonnage was steam propelled, and the trend to steam and steel became irreversible. See chapters 4 and 5 of James P. Baughman, *The Mallorys of Mystic* (Middletown, Conn.: Wesleyan University Press, 1972). For an account of an entrepreneur who dealt in ships during this period, see James P. Baughman, *Charles Morgan and the Development of Southern Transportation* (Nashville: Vanderbilt University Press, 1968).

Congress searched for a solution, establishing a pattern of government concern for marine commerce.

Congress set a goal of preventing accidents in the first place and rescuing the victims if they did occur. And occur they did. Both the *Titanic* accident of 1912 and the *Morro Castle* accident of 1934 were external forces that had an important effect on the policy-making process. Prevention was less popular with mariners and the marine industry than protection, but it was a logical and necessary extension of government marine policy.

From 1790 to 1946 the Coast Guard became increasingly active in maritime law enforcement, safety, and facilitation of marine transport. Its acquisition of the Life Saving Service in 1915, the Lighthouse Service in 1939, and the Bureau of Marine Inspection and Navigation temporarily in 1942 and permanently in 1946 finally brought all the protective, preventive, and law enforcement functions of these agencies into the Coast Guard.

During these years the Coast Guard developed a strategy and structure that created its distinctive competence in these areas. The structure that emerged after World War II and the Ebasco Report of 1948 was shaped by the dual-role strategy and the multimission concept. This demanded that the organization be both a military branch of the armed forces, and at the same time handle the civil responsibilities of maritime law enforcement, marine safety, and marine transport.

External forces that led the Coast Guard to develop a marine environmental protection program include (1) tremendous growth in energy consumption after World War II, (2) growth in the size of tankers transporting both crude oil and refined products at sea; and (3) growing concern for the quality of the marine environment. Each of these will be discussed in turn.

One focal point within the Coast Guard as these forces grew in the years after World War II was the Office of Merchant Marine Safety, created at Coast Guard headquarters after the acquisition of the Bureau of Marine Inspection and Navigation. Although at first there were problems integrating this new function within Coast Guard structure, its addition added a preventive function to the protection and law enforcement functions the agency already performed under the direction of the Office of Operations. The combination of these three new functions meant that the Coast Guard examined the design, construction, operation, manning, and even the overall concept of marine transport. To do this it had to deal with industry (both management and labor), other government agencies, and international groups—all concerned with the safety of marine transport.* Despite the initial problems of integration, the new office was a busy center with

---

*Admiral Waesche not only argued for moving the Bureau of Marine Inspection and Navigation to the Coast Guard as early as 1936 but also participated from his deathbed in the behind-the-scenes discussions that preceded the final vote in the United States Senate in 1946 making the transfer permanent.

all its activities after World War II; external trends in worldwide energy consumption and transportation would make it even busier in the years to come.[1]

ENERGY AND THE ENVIRONMENT

In 1933 Standard Oil of California was granted a sixty-year exclusive concession for oil exploration on 320,000 square miles of territory within Saudi Arabia. This area was so rich in petroleum that even this large a company had to bring in partners to help finance exploration and production. Standard of California formed the Arabian American Oil Company to develop the Saudi oil fields. Aramco, as the new company became known, was legally a Saudi company, but decisions were typically made in its New York headquarters by an American executive committee.

Texaco was brought in as a partner before World War II. During the war the Saudi fields were unused. As the demand for petroleum jumped after the war, Aramco brought in Mobil and Standard of New Jersey as additional partners. Standard of California and Standard of New Jersey owned 30 percent each, Texaco also owned 30 percent, and Mobil owned the remaining 10 percent. The large multinational, multicompany oil supply business of the postwar era was under way.[2]

Petroleum is basically a four-stage industry. Exploration and production form the first stage, in which oil is located, then pumped to the surface from reservoirs beneath the earth. The second stage is transportation from the production field to the refinery. Refining constitutes the third stage. The fourth stage is transportation and marketing; the oil must be moved from the refinery and delivered to the final user. This four-stage process is depicted in figure 23.

Transportation of petroleum is a key part of the industry. Either tankers or a pipeline or a combination of the two are the usual movers of crude from the wellhead to the refinery where it is processed into various refined products. The product of this process is usually transported to its final user by tanker, pipeline, truck, or train, or by various combinations of these transportation modes.

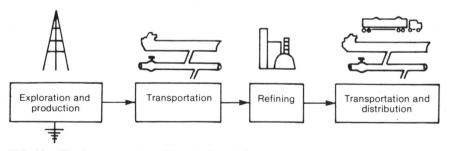

FIG. 23.   The four-stage nature of the petroleum industry.

Minimizing transportation costs is obviously one objective of any profit-seeking oil company. One obvious way to do this is to build refineries either at the site of the oil field or close to the final user. This strategy reduces or removes the cost of one stage of transportation. With the opening of the Middle East, and later the Iranian, oil fields, this collocation strategy became more complex.[3]

By 1955 the demands of both Japan and Europe for imported petroleum had grown rapidly. In Europe alone, consumption ten years after the war had quadrupled from 1938, the last year of peace before World War II. There was a demand for imported oil in the United States, too. A pattern was emerging of nations who were oil exporters and those who were forced to be importers. The imbalance caused an increasing demand for oil tankships—tankers—to haul crude and refined product across the oceans from the suppliers to the consumers.[4] But before examining tankers per se, we should discuss the seeds of the conflict between energy and the environment.

The growing national imbalances between energy production and consumption were at first a function of economic expansion in the industrialized nations after the war. These imbalances were aggravated as postwar explorations discovered new petroleum supplies farther and farther from the areas of high petroleum consumption. New discoveries in the Middle East, Iran, Venezuela, Indonesia, and even the North Slope of Alaska are all examples.

AN ENERGY OVERVIEW

Energy is usually measured in British thermal units (BTU) or in kilowatt-hours. The unit commonly used in aggregate energy statistics is the quad, representing one quadrillion BTUs. To give a more understandable perspective of relative energy usage rates, consider this comparison: it takes about 150 million BTUs to heat a house for a year and 100 million BTUs to run the average car for a year.[5]

Table 20 compares many of the common energy units and conversions; table 21 lists the annual energy consumption of the United States in 1970 from each of

TABLE 20
Energy Units and Common Conversions

Energy Unit	Conversion	Energy Unit	Conversion
1 joule	= 1 newton meter	1 barrel	= 42 gallons
1 foot-pound	= 1.356 joules	1 ton	= 7.35 barrels
1 BTU	= 1,055 joules	1 barrel/day	= 50 tons/year
1 watt-hour	= 3,600 joules	1 barrel	= 5.8 $(10)^6$ BTU
1 kilowatt-hour	= 3,413 BTU	1 cubic foot gas	= 1,031 BTU
1 $(10)^9$ BTU	= 1 billion BTU	1 ton lignite coal	= 20 to 40 $(10)^6$ BTU
1 $(10)^{15}$ BTU	= 1 quad	1 ton uranium 233	= 5.8 $(10)^{13}$ BTU

TABLE 21
Energy Consumption in the United States in 1970: Sample Calculations

Energy Source	Amount	BTUs	Quads
Petroleum	14.7 $(10)^6$ barrels/day	= 30 $(10)^{15}$ BTU/year	= 30 quads
Natural gas	59.5 $(10)^9$ cubic feet/day	= 21 $(10)^{15}$ BTU/year	= 21 quads
Coal	525 $(10)^6$ tons/year	= 16 $(10)^{15}$ BTU/year	= 16 quads
Hydroelectric power, etc.			= 1 quad
Yearly consumption			68 quads

the major energy sources, measured in units usually associated with the particular source and also in quads.

Energy consumption in the United States in the late 1960s and early 1970s rose more than 4 percent a year, an increase over the average annual 3.4 percent increase in demand reported for 1950–72. Even with increases of this magnitude, however, energy consumption in the United States as a fraction of aggregate world consumption has decreased from 44 percent in 1950 to 33 percent in 1968. Energy demand is indeed rising more rapidly around the world than in the United States.[6] The rate of increase in energy demand in the United States and in the world at large is obviously one key to any model forecasting the future for energy. Another key is the availability of energy.

The Demand Forecast. To predict energy consumption in the United States, we would have to prepare a demand forecast. Obviously, forecasting is not an exact science; in fact, one summary of recent forecasts cites eleven studies giving eleven different growth rates. A popular technique to resolve this difficulty is to prepare three or four alternative estimates based on different hypotheses, or scenarios, of the future. A report by the National Petroleum Council and the Energy Policy Project of the Ford Foundation both used the scenario method, as did the 1979 report of the Energy Project at the Harvard Business School.[7] The forecasts for domestic energy consumption from 1975 to 2000, as developed by the Energy Policy Project, are presented in figure 24 as examples of the possible range of consumption. This forecast is the demand picture I will use here.

The Supply Forecast. A supply forecast must examine available energy. Many geologic concepts and terms can be used to assess supply, taking into account both the probability and the cost of removing energy from the earth, as well as the price that energy will bring in the marketplace. Obviously, both military and national strategic interests, as well as corporate secrecy, cloud many of the available figures, which differ greatly depending on the source. The term ''reserves'' as used here will refer to estimates based on ''detailed geologic evidence, usually obtained through drilling,'' while ''recoverable resources'' and ''remaining resource base'' reflect estimates with ''less detailed knowledge and more geologic inference.''[8]

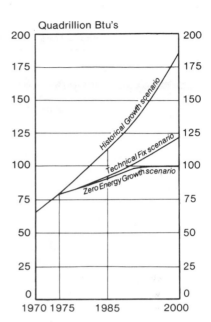

FIG. 24. Energy Policy Project scenarios for every use in the United States 1975 to 2000. From final report by the Energy Policy Project of the Ford Foundation, *A Time to Choose: America's Energy Future* (Cambridge, Mass.: Ballinger, 1974), p. 13.

The Energy Policy Project estimated worldwide reserves of petroleum at 3,680 quads, compared with a recoverable resource estimate of 14,400 quads and a remaining resource base estimate of 60,000 quads. Recall that in the United States in 1970, 70 quads were consumed for the entire year. By comparison, the remaining resource base estimate for coal is approximately 350,000 quads. The remaining resource base estimate for nuclear energy is at least an order of magnitude greater than for coal. The real dilemma in considering the supply numbers is not, however, in the aggregate amount; it comes in examining their geographical distribution. And it comes in remembering the comparative cost of recovering the other energy sources and the comparative importance that has been placed on petroleum as an energy source.[9]

Table 22 depicts the geographical distribution of the known oil reserves of the world in 1973. More than half the petroleum reserves exist in the Middle East, and only 5 percent are in the United States. The supply forecast then depends on the domestic supply available, in location and aggregate amount, and on the foreign supply—also in location and aggregate amount.

With the United States demanding more than a quarter of the petroleum consumed in the world each year, the heart of an energy forecast for the United States deals with the level of imports necessary to fill the demand after domestic production has been allocated. The supply forecast, therefore, involves looking at two aspects of supply: (1) the substitution of alternative energy sources for petroleum (coal, nuclear, solar, etc.), and the price level prevailing for each alternative source; (2) the imported petroleum required by the United States and

TABLE 22
Known World Oil Reserves, 1973

Area	Percentage
Middle East	*56%*
Saudi Arabia	21
Kuwait	10
Iran	10
Iraq	5
Other	10
Communist countries	*16*
Western hemisphere	*12*[a]
United States	5.5
Canada	1.5
Other	5.0
Europe	*2.5*
Africa	*11*
Indonesia	*1.5*
Other	*1*
Total	*100%*

Source: *Exploring Energy Choices,* a preliminary report of the Ford Foundation's Energy Policy Project, 1974, p. 176. Adapted with permission of the Energy Policy Project of the Ford Foundation.
[a] The actual extent of reserves in the United States, Mexico, and Canada, as in the world at large, is a subject of considerable controversy.

the world at large. The United States controls a substantial share of the world's coal reserves and (even after the events at Three Mile Island) holds the lead in nuclear power technology. If in the long run the nation switched to a new combination of energy sources, the strategic problem of petroleum dependence would diminish. I will not, however, further consider the first aspect of the supply picture.* Instead, to better understand the task of the Coast Guard's Marine Environmental Protection program, I will focus alone on forecasts for petroleum imports.

Petroleum Imports Required by the United States. By subtracting available domestic supply from demand, we can arrive at a forecast of petroleum imports.

*The possible range of energy supply estimates and demand forecasts has been the subject of a great deal of debate. See, for example, Morris A. Adelman, "Is the Oil Shortage Real?" *Foreign Policy,* no. 9 (winter 1972–73), pp. 69–107. See James E. Aikins, "The Oil Crisis: This Time the Wolf Is Here," *Foreign Affairs* 51, no. 3 (1973):462–90. See also Michael S. Macrakis, ed., *Energy: Demand, Conservation, and Institutional Problems* (Cambridge: MIT Press, 1974), pp. 273–400; and Robert Stobaugh and Daniel Yergin, *Energy Future* (New York: Random House, 1979), pp. 216–65. For a differing view, see Charles J. Elia, "Energy Expert Believes World Oil Surpluses to Persist through at Least 1982, Possibly 1985," *Wall Street Journal,* 23 December 1977, p. 19. Publishing their book six years after Aikins's article, Stobaugh and Yergin also argued for conservation, and even for use of solar energy.

Many of the variables in such an analysis have already been discussed. In September 1974 the National Petroleum Council (NPC) prepared a forecast of total crude and product imports to the United States for 1980 to 1990. Their forecast is also based on three alternative scenarios, which they term high, low, and medium import cases. The NPC forecast of 1974 is presented in table 23. Forecasts of necessary imports range from a low of 4 million barrels per day (MBD) in 1990 to a possible high of 12.5 MBD. One MBD of petroleum has an energy equivalent of approximately two quads a year. For comparison, the petroleum flow from the North Slope of Alaska could reach approximately 2 to 3 MBD, or four to six quads a year. The midpoint of the NPC forecast for imports to the United States over 1980 to 1990 is only slightly higher than import forecasts prepared by other groups. Certainly these imports depend on availability, cost, and the effects, if any, of conservation initiatives to say nothing of inflation and the ability of the United States to pay for the oil.

Petroleum Imports Required around the World.   The dependency on petroleum of the United States is, of course, not nearly as severe as that of Japan and Western Europe, although these relationships are changing. Figure 25 depicts the relative magnitude of petroleum imports, measured in MBDs, of the United States, Japan, and Western Europe from 1940 to 1973, the year of the Yom Kippur War in the Middle East. The American and Japanese import levels in absolute terms remained small, reaching the 6 MBD level only during the 1970s. Europe, however, reached the 6 MBD level in the early 1960s, and by 1973 its imports had surpassed the 15 MBD level, or 30 quads a year.[10]

An Environment Overview.   For many years the Coast Guard had been concerned with ships—protection and law enforcement at first, then prevention of accidents when the Bureau of Marine Inspection and Navigation became a part of

TABLE 23
Forecast of Total Crude and Product Imports to the United States, 1980–90

NPC Case	1980	1985	1990
High import	10.2	12.5	12.0
Low import	5.3	5.4	4.0
Medium import	7.8	8.4	8.1

Source: National Petroleum Council, *Emergency Preparedness for Interruption of Petroleum Imports into the United States... September 1974* (Washington, D.C.: National Petroleum Council, 1974), p. 11.
Note: All figures are millions of barrels/day (MBD); 1 MBD yearly is the approximate equivalent of 2 quads/year.

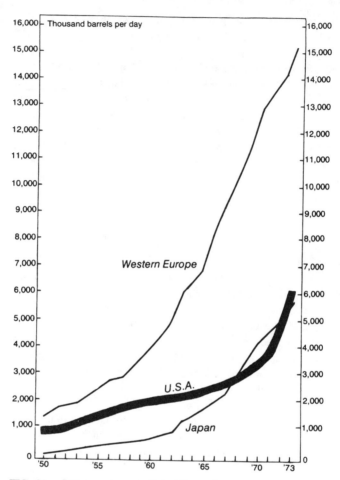

FIG. 25. Petroleum imports, United States, Japan, and Western Europe, 1950–73. From final report by the Energy Policy Project of the Ford Foundation, *A Time to Choose: America's Energy Future* (Cambridge, Mass.: Ballinger, 1974), p. 157.

the Coast Guard. The quality of the marine environment, however, had also been a concern from the early years.

When the cutter *Corwin* sailed to Alaskan waters in 1880–81, John Muir was one of the naturalists on the trip. At the time, Muir was working on an article, "On the Glaciation of the Arctic and Sub Arctic Regions."[11] Over the next decade Muir became a leading environmentalist, and by 1892 he helped form the Sierra Club. He became the first president of the club, and until his death in 1914 he published and lectured extensively to secure federal and state protection for the natural environment he loved.

Both the Refuse Act of 1899 and the early oil pollution laws gave the Coast

Guard law-enforcement roles in protecting water quality.[12] These laws, mundane at the time, had in practice become the responsibility of the staff of the captain of the port, which increased during World War II and again during the Cold War. As tanker traffic increased after the war, Coast Guardsmen assigned to the captains of the ports made regular harbor entrance and in-port surveillance patrols; they were among the first to notice the magnitude of oil pollution in the coastal waters.

The first in a postwar series of international Conventions for the Prevention of Pollution of the Sea by Oil was held in 1954 to examine this growing problem. The conference was held in London, and Coast Guardsmen, including the commandant, participated as members of the United States delegation. Amendments to this convention were made by successive conferences in 1962, 1967, and 1969.[13]

In the 1960s increasing concern was felt both across America and around the world that economic development and environmental protection go hand in hand. Economist Kenneth Boulding summed up the feelings of many when he pointed out that man's relationship to his environment was changing. No longer could the waste products simply be thrown away, as they had been in the "cowboy" or open-system economy that had once existed. Instead, producers would have to stop throwaways or pay a penalty if they occurred. Boulding termed the newer system a "spaceship economy."[14] More and more individuals and governments recognized that the free market pricing system "failed to provide incentives to protect society's common property in fresh air, clean water, and undergraded land resources."[15] In the United States, one of the leading groups advocating this position was the same Sierra Club that John Muir had founded more than seventy years earlier.

In 1967, as had happened so many times in the past, a catastrophic accident focused worldwide attention on a growing hazard that needed action. This time the hazard was the growing ocean trade in petroleum, and the potential victims were both water quality and the overall marine environment. On Saturday morning, 18 March 1967, the 118,000-ton tanker *Torrey Canyon* ran aground on Seven Stones, a reef sixteen miles from the southwest corner of England.[16]

At first the casualty brought attention not only to the threat that an entire cargo might spill, but also to the more everyday but insidious danger of using coastal waters to wash out "empty" cargo tanks and pump out bilges. In the United States, both Congress and the executive branch of government initiated their own investigations. Several other events added to the growing concern. The following March the *Ocean Eagle* grounded at the entrance to San Juan harbor in Puerto Rico. The ship broke in two, causing a spectacular spill much closer to home. Shortly thereafter, a tanker flying the Greek flag ran aground in the Bahamas. If national attention to the dangers of oil pollution needed further underscoring in the United States, the oil well blowout in the Santa Barbara Channel off California in January 1969 served this purpose well. This spill occurred on one of the most beautiful stretches of any American coastline, and damages have been estimated at more than five million dollars.[17]

The second stage in the issue-attention cycle discussed in chapter 2 had been reached. After these disasters, interest in the water-pollution issue and in overall environmental quality became great enough in the United States to lead to the passage of the 1969 National Environmental Policy Act (NEPA). This act established the Council on Environmental Quality (CEQ), an organization within the executive office of the president, to coordinate and develop national environmental policies and programs.[18] CEQ was also charged with publication of a National Contingency Plan for Oil and Hazardous Materials Pollution Control. NEPA also required all organizations of the federal government to prepare impact statements on proposed plans and programs that significantly affect the environment.

An executive branch reorganization of December 1970 created the Environmental Protection Agency (EPA) as an independent agency for research, monitoring, standard-setting, and law enforcement in the environmental area. Protecting the environment assumed high priority. Congress followed NEPA with two more laws, each of which had a strong influence on water pollution and, specifically, on the quality of the marine environment. The first was the Federal Water Pollution Control Act Amendment of 1972 (FWPCA). The second was the Ports and Waterways Safety Act of 1972. The combination of these two acts placed direct and indirect responsibility on the Coast Guard for assessing both the tankers that carried oil across water, and the systems for guiding them.[19]

These acts greatly expanded the scope of the Coast Guard's historic roles in maritime law enforcement, safety, and aid to marine transport. As had happened after much earlier catastrophes, both the protective and the preventive aspects of these roles were expanded. Implementing the acts led the Coast Guard to make a major change in its organizational structure by creating a new Office of Marine Environment and Systems in 1971. The activities of the new office, and those of Coast Guard personnel in developing both organizational and operational responses to the new legislation, are discussed at length in the next chapter. Now we need to explore the complexities of tankers and the international tanker markets to determine the nature of the external forces at work in this area.

TANKERS AND THE INTERNATIONAL
MARKET MECHANISM

Growing postwar demands for crude and for refined product occurred at increasing distances from the new sources of supply. This trend led to a growth in the number of tankers sailing the oceans and to an increase in their size. In the first years after the war petroleum imports to the United States were small and often came across the Caribbean from Venezuela. By the 1960s the number of tankers coming to ports in the United States had greatly increased, causing congestion in the coastal waters. Tankers bringing the oil were also far larger than their predecessors and, generally coming from the Middle East, sailed greater distances.

The postwar trend toward larger and larger tankers is described in Noel Mostert's book *Supership*.[20] The trend was first brought to public attention by the media after the *Torrey Canyon* grounding in 1967. This trend is the natural result of both the entrepreneur's desire to gain economies of scale on longer trips and the prevailing international market structure for tankers. Evidence clearly indicates that average cost for delivery of oil declines as tanker size increases.

Petroleum from the Middle East and other foreign markets come to the United States in tankers that are part of the international market structure. The international tanker market is differentiated from the United States coastal market by the Jones Act, which requires that cargoes shipped between ports in the United States be carried in ships flying the United States flag.* Since the quantities of oil indicated in even the "medium import" Case of table 23 have been imported for several years, and since the oil has arrived in ships available in the international market, the scale economies of the international market mechanism for tankers should be explored.

Zenon Zannetos, an economist, examined the nature of international tanker markets. He concluded that, although "on the basis of common sense and a priori characteristics [the markets] should be imperfect," in fact they operate like "perfectly competitive markets."[21] This is derived by a consideration of the basic elements of a competitive industry and by empirical data concerning price behavior and capacity changes over time.

There are four classic elements of proof of a competitive market. First is the existence of many competitors, none large enough to influence market price. Zannetos counted more than six hundred owners, none controlling more than 7 percent of capacity. A book by Morris Adelman entitled *The World Petroleum Market* points out that by 1972 the eight largest oil companies owned only one-fifth of tanker capacity. This study also reports that about one-third of aggregate tanker capacity becomes available for charter each year.[22]

The second element of proof is homogeneity of product. Although some design variations exist, tankers are in an economic sense containers, undif-

---

*The Jones Act, another name for the Merchant Marine Act of 1920, 41 Stat. 988, declares it be "the policy of the United States to do whatever may be necessary to develop and encourage the maintenance of . . . a merchant marine." This act carries the name of Senator Wesley Jones of Washington, a chairman of the Senate Commerce Committee. The Jones Act creates two separate markets for marine transportation—a coastal market for ships registered in the United States, and an international market for foreign ships.

An examination of this and other policies toward the merchant marine appears in Samuel A. Lawrence, *United States Merchant Shipping Policies and Politics* (Washington, D.C.: Brookings Institution, 1966); James R. Barker and Robert Brandwein, *The United States Merchant Marine in National Perspective* (Lexington, Mass.: Heath-Lexington Books, 1970); and Gerald R. Jantscher, *Bread upon the Waters* (Washington, D.C.: Brookings Institution, 1975).

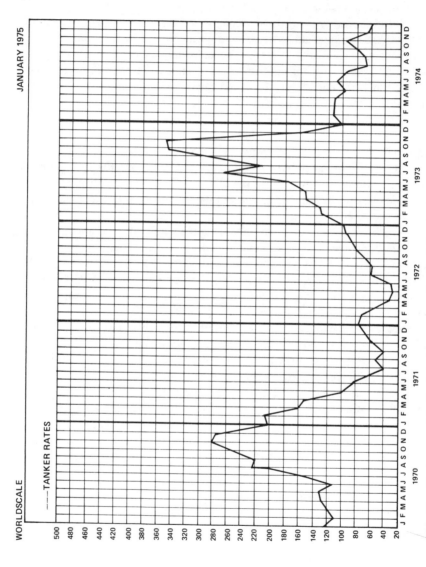

FIG. 26. Single-voyage Worldscale tanker rates (base Persian Gulf to Western Europe) for tankers between 40,000 and 99,999 DWCT (deadweight tons). From H. P. Drewry, Ltd. (shipping consultants), *Shipping Statistics of Economics* (London, January 1975).

162

ferentiated unless safety rules or other regulations in effect form a barrier to entry to the open market. The third element is ease of market entry. Adelman points out that relatively low capital barriers to the purchase of tankers and lack of advantage in owning a fleet rather than just one tanker remove two common economic barriers.

The fourth element is complete knowledge of market transactions by all economic agents. This is essentially true in the international tanker market, since chartering is brokered in centrally located markets in New York, London, and Oslo using standard rate scales. Worldscale, the current scale, allows price comparisons between charters on tankers of differing sizes for voyages on differing routes.* Edward Cowan's *Oil and Water: The Torrey Canyon Disaster* skillfully describes both the routine that tanker brokers follow and the flexibility they have in their daily chartering of tankers.[23]

Price data strongly support the notion that the industry is basically competitive. In the short run the single voyage, or "spot," rate is determined by aggregate supply and demand. The spot rate fluctuates as supply and demand shift. Owners are price-takers but can adjust to market conditions to the extent that system buffers—such as maintenance availabilities, voyage speed adjustments, and turnaround times—will permit.

In the competitive model, price expectations are important in the decision to build new ships. If a potential owner expects rising prices for ship charters, he will buy or build new ships. If a sudden decrease in ship demand comes—as from the initial OPEC oil embargo or the significant product price increases of the following years—tanker charter prices will fall. Orders for new building will disappear, and only those ships with operating costs low enough to adjust to the lower market price will remain in operation. Typical price data from the tanker marketplace are presented in figure 26.

Tanker owners who do not follow a strategy of committing their ships to "time" charters—the length of time can run to twenty years—will sooner or later be in the spot market. Then they will have all the problems of a price-taker in a competitive market. They must be concerned with marginal cost structures, technological and regulatory innovation in construction and in operating rules, and any other cost-saving that promises a downward shift in costs. Recognizing this is essential to understanding recent trends in tanker size and construction patterns.[74]

The increase in the size of tankers has come from a multitude of forces: by elastic price expectations in the years before the oil embargo; by shipbuilding innovations in Japan and elsewhere; by design innovation; and, most important, by the scale economies in crew and technical systems made possible by making

---

*Worldscale is a schedule of tanker rates based on a hypothetical ship. Issued by the International Tanker Nominal Freight Scale Association, Ltd., London, Worldscale has been in effect since September 1969.

the cargo sections larger and larger. A typical declining cost curve for oil transport on a long international voyage is depicted in figure 27.[25]

The declining average cost, represented in the figure as a function of "required freight rate," is of course a result of economies of scale.[26] In terms of manning, salaries, and most administrative costs, a 200,000-ton tanker is no different from a 50,000-tonner. The important economic distinction is that the larger tanker brings home substantially more revenue as a fraction of cost. Put simply, a larger tanker has a better return on investment, other things being equal.

Tanker owners, being businessmen in an international market, have sought to make a profit. Therefore in the tanker market described they had two options. Either they speculated on the spot market or they built larger and larger ships, often financed with the collateral of long-term charters obtained in advance. Sometimes they even "jumboized" existing ships, usually by cutting them in half and inserting another tank section in the "midbody," or middle of the tanker. This was done to the *Torrey Canyon.*

At the time of her grounding, *Torrey Canyon* was registered in Liberia and owned by Barracuda Tanker Corporation, a firm with an office in Hamilton,

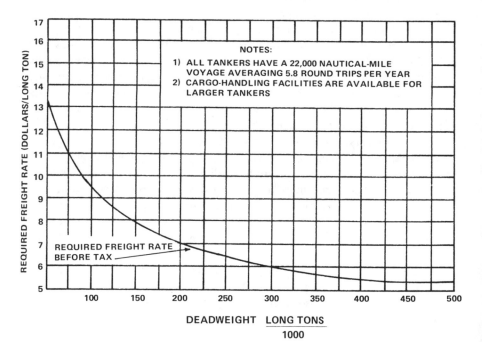

FIG. 27.   Required freight rate versus deadweight. From Joseph D. Porricelli and Virgil F. Keith, "Tankers and the U.S. Energy Situation: An Economic and Environmental Analysis," *Marine Technology,* vol. 11, no. 4 (1974). Copyrighted by the Society of Naval Architects and included herein by permission of the aforementioned society.

Bermuda, which had been organized by a group associated with the New York investment banking firm of Dillon Read. Barracuda in turn placed *Torrey Canyon* on a time charter to the Union Oil Corporation.[27]

Torrey Canyon was built by Barracuda in 1959 at Newport News Shipbuilding and Drydock Company in Virginia at a cost of nearly 17.5 million dollars. *Torrey Canyon* was jumboized in Japan in 1965, bringing her total cost to nearly 23 million dollars. When the "jumbo" plan was announced, *Torrey Canyon* and her sister ship, *Lake Palourde,* were made "the longest merchant ships in the world, with nearly double... carrying capacity."[28]

The original construction financing for *Torrey Canyon* came from the Manufacturers Hanover Trust Company, and Metropolitan Life Insurance Company assumed the permanent mortgage on the ship. Under a 1965 amendment to the time charter, Union paid $345,000 to Barracuda every three months, plus another $105,400 a month for expenses. The expenses "included $45,000 in wages, $10,000 for food, $7,000 in tonnage taxes levied by Liberia, and $20,000 for maintenance and repairs."[29]

These arrangements between the investors' group, Barracuda, and Union Oil may seem complex. In the international ship market, in fact, they are not. Many authors have written about the typical financial arrangements surrounding a ship that will sail from country to country. Edward Cowan's *Oil and Water* describes many of the participants and the arrangements that are made.

Tanker owners in the international market have of competitive necessity focused on the economic variables of cost and capacity. During the postwar boom in transoceanic oil traffic, competition in the charter market was a primary force in the increase in size of newly constructed tankers. Indeed, this growth in size became so rapid before the 1973 oil embargo that within sixteen years nine different tankers could successively be called "the world's largest tanker."

During this period the largest tanker grew from 56,000 tons to a mammoth 477,000 tons. If the largest tanker were simply to double from this size, the world would have a "megatanker."[30] Figure 28 compares the dimensions of a T-2 of the World War II era, the *Idemitsu Maru,* the *Nisseki Maru,* the *Globtik Tokyo,* and, finally, the gigantic *Esso Atlantic.*

The volume of orders for new tankers declined greatly following the softness in the charter market after the 1973 oil embargo. The percentage of larger tankers in the market has, however, increased greatly over the postwar years. In fact, the size of the average tanker in the world fleet increased from 40,000 tons in 1970 to the middle of the 50,000-ton range by 1974.[31] Table 24 indicates the large percentage of available tanker capacity made up by big tankers in 1974.

Different countries apply different standards and regulations to tankers registered under their flags. Obviously this leads to different operating costs. These standards and regulations not only span design and operating rules, but also specify the type of crew that will man the ship. Such broad and differing control over the human and physical resources employed in transporting petroleum

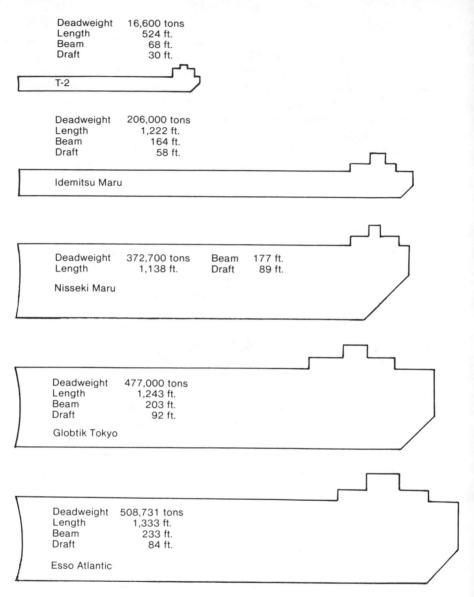

Deadweight   16,600 tons
Length   524 ft.
Beam   68 ft.
Draft   30 ft.

T-2

Deadweight   206,000 tons
Length   1,222 ft.
Beam   164 ft.
Draft   58 ft.

Idemitsu Maru

Deadweight   372,700 tons   Beam   177 ft.
Length   1,138 ft.   Draft   89 ft.

Nisseki Maru

Deadweight   477,000 tons
Length   1,243 ft.
Beam   203 ft.
Draft   92 ft.

Globtik Tokyo

Deadweight   508,731 tons
Length   1,333 ft.
Beam   233 ft.
Draft   84 ft.

Esso Atlantic

FIG. 28. The dimensions of some supertankers. From Louis K. Bragaw, Henry S. Marcus, Gary C. Raffaele, and James R. Townley, *The Challenge of Deepwater Terminals* (Lexington, Mass.: Lexington Books, 1975), p. 22, and the Exxon Corporation.

TABLE 24
Tonnage Range of Tankers in Operation, 1974

Tonnage Weight (Deadweight tons)	Percentage of All Tankers
10,000–60,000	30.9
60,000–100,000	16.4
100,000–150,000	8.6
150,000–200,000	3.2
200,000–250,000	26.4
250,000–300,000	12.3
300,000 and over	2.2

Source: C. Hayman, "What to Do with All Those Tankers," *New York Sunday Times,* 14 April, 1974, p. F-1; also, Fearnley and Egers Chartering Company, Ltd.

across the ocean leaves great room for variation. Not unexpectedly, tanker owners seek the countries providing the most favorable terms. By 1974, for example, Liberia, Britain, Japan, Norway, and Greece were the leading countries in tanker registration. The percentage of the tanker fleet registered in each country in that year is shown in table 25.

Any standard or regulation applying to tankers on international voyages should be part of an international agreement, binding on all nations registering ships. The essence of the tanker trade involves ocean voyages that cross the waters and harbors of different nations. Because tanker owners in the spot market are price-takers, it is important that each competitor bear the same added cost burden for complying with new standards or regulations. Without an international agreement on such rules, tankers registered with nations that do not enforce the standards or regulations will enjoy comparative advantage over tankers registered in nations that do enforce them. Such advantage allows the interna-

TABLE 25
Countries of Registry of Tanker Capacity, 1974

Registry by Country (flag)	Percentage of Total Deadweight Tonnage Available
Liberia	28.1
Britain	12.4
Japan	12.4
Norway	9.8
Greece	5.7
Other	31.6

Source: C. Hayman, "What to Do with All Those Tankers," *New York Sunday Times,* 14 April, 1974, p. F-1; also, Fearnley and Egers Chartering Company, Ltd.

tional market mechanism to work against tanker owners and industry in countries with strict rules and enforcement. This simple fact militates against tough international rules and leads to registering marginally passable tankers in the countries where they can most easily meet the standards and regulations that are applied.[32]

IMCO AS AN INTERNATIONAL ORGANIZATION

Since its founding after World War II, the United Nations has sponsored many organizations and programs. More than a dozen have a direct effect on shipping and maritime affairs. Many of these specialized agencies deal with special constituents and work with the Secretariat and the Economic and Social Council of the General Assembly. Figure 29 lists many of the agencies involved in this area and shows their interrelationships.

The Inter-Governmental Maritime Consultative Organization (IMCO) is one of these agencies. It has "the widest role in maritime affairs."[33] IMCO was officially formed in March 1958, ten years after a United Nations conference in Geneva proposed such a body. Although IMCO is one of the smallest of the United Nations agencies, it took a decade to receive ratification from the required twenty-one nations. At least seven of these nations could count at the time merchant fleets of over one million tons registered under their national flags.

IMCO has been largely a forum for maritime nations to present their positions and views. The rules it develops are those that are acceptable to all or nearly all its members. IMCO does not itself produce or enforce standards or regulations; it only recommends them. It is largely an advisory body or, as is explained by its name, a "consultative" organization.

IMCO has sponsored several important international conferences that have led to adoption or amendment of international conventions. These conventions include the Convention for Safety of Life at Sea (1960 and 1974), Convention for the Prevention of Pollution of the Sea by Oil (1954, amended in 1962, 1967, and 1969), Convention for Facilitation of International Maritime Traffic (1965), Convention on Load Lines (1966), Convention on International Regulations for Preventing Collisions at Sea (1972), Convention for the Prevention of Pollution from Ships (1973), and Convention on Watchstanding and Training (1978). IMCO has also sponsored a number of international committees and subcommittees that deal with technical, legal, and facilitation problems.[34]

By 1979, 106 countries were members of IMCO. Its staff and budget, however, remained modest. A professional staff of approximately fifty works at IMCO headquarters on Piccadilly in London. A great deal of the work of IMCO involves the findings of the committees and the agreements of the conventions. These committees and conventions have dealt largely with technical and legal

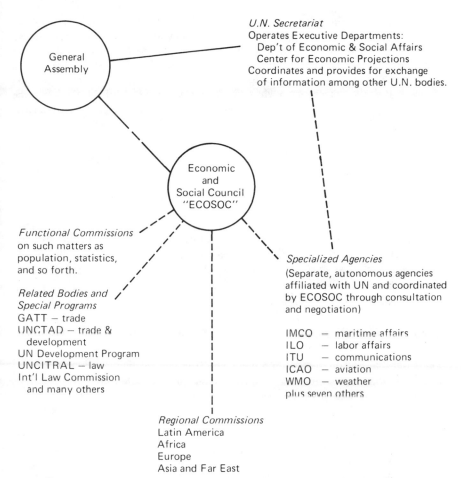

U.N. Secretariat
Operates Executive Departments:
  Dep't of Economic & Social Affairs
  Center for Economic Projections
Coordinates and provides for exchange
  of information among other U.N. bodies.

General
Assembly

Economic
and
Social Council
"ECOSOC"

Functional Commissions
on such matters as
population, statistics,
and so forth.

Related Bodies and
Special Programs
GATT — trade
UNCTAD — trade &
  development
UN Development Program
UNCITRAL — law
Int'l Law Commission
  and many others

Specialized Agencies
(Separate, autonomous agencies
affiliated with UN and coordinated
by ECOSOC through consultation
and negotiation)

IMCO — maritime affairs
ILO — labor affairs
ITU — communications
ICAO — aviation
WMO — weather
plus seven others

Regional Commissions
Latin America
Africa
Europe
Asia and Far East

FIG. 29. United Nations agencies dealing with transport matters. From Samuel A. Lawrence, *International Sea Transport: The Years Ahead* (Lexington, Mass.: Lexington Books, 1972), p. 34.

matters and have been very cautious in the economic and commercial areas. The Shipping Committee of the United Nations Conference for Trade and Development (UNCTAD), on the other hand, has done economic studies and looked at questions of trade policy.

The technical and legal focus of IMCO is understandable when one considers the varied economic and political interests of the many sovereign nations represented. This focus in fact dates to the final drafting of the IMCO convention, when ten countries filed declarations "stating in substance that their participation in IMCO was conditional upon that organization's refraining from intervening in the commercial and economic aspects of shipping." One observer sums up the relative power and outlook of IMCO:

Armed only with the power to suggest or nudge, IMCO has moved cautiously and has confined itself to technical and safety matters. Broad questions of international law and such sensitive economic issues as rates, routes and shipping conferences (associations of shipping companies, grouped by routes) have been beyond its ken. To be sure, that is hardly the fault, if it is a fault, of IMCO's secretariat or of the few hundred maritime specialists from the member states who comprise the working body of IMCO. One of the truisms of international politics is that governments are loath to surrender sovereignty; consciously or unconsciously, they have invested in IMCO no more power, and probably less, than they have imparted to the United Nations in general.[35]

A PATTERN OF OIL IMPORTS AND
SPILLS IN THE UNITED STATES

The *Torrey Canyon* and *Ocean Eagle* groundings in 1967 and 1968, and the oil well blowout in the Santa Barbara Channel in 1969 have all been discussed. These accidents, all catastrophic, focused public attention in the United States on the dangers of a large incident and, probably for the first time, on the collective damage possible from a multitude of smaller spills.

Soon after the *Torrey Canyon* grounding in March 1967, Great Britain called an emergency meeting of the IMCO Council. The council is a body that Edward Cowan calls "roughly equivalent to an executive committee." Cowan points out that Britain had two motives. The first was leadership and the appearance of action. The second, however, was far more substantive.

Having moved tardily to neutralize the source of the oil that had already contaminated the Cornish coast, the government needed to show all the dash it could.

Second, it was recognized by a few interested people in London and in other capitals, notably Washington, that the world-wide publicity generated by the most spectacular oil-pollution incident ever to occur could be used to forge a stronger U.N. maritime agency. By prompt action it would also be possible to use the *Torrey Canyon* publicity to propel through IMCO proposed safety regulations that had bogged down.[36]

The international shipping industry, the majority of tanker owners, and the governments of the maritime nations all realized that oil pollution of the seas and the attendant conflict between energy, economy, and the environment were issues that required immediate action.

In May 1967, less than two months after the grounding, the IMCO council met in London. More than one hundred delegates or observers attended the meeting. A legal committee was formed and charged with studying liability problems. A large research program was initiated "with a view to avoiding the hazards presented by the carriage of oil and other noxious cargoes."[37] Although some of the council's recommendations included items that were already under study, their impetus gave new vitality to the study efforts. For example, in January 1967 the Maritime Safety Committee, the key technical body of IMCO, had established a subcommittee for Ship Design and Equipment. This subcommittee became one focal point for studies of antipollution measures. An observer points out that IMCO "assumed an active role in the control of marine pollution and is the chief focus of international efforts toward this objective."[38]

Captain Robert I. Price, a Coast Guard officer and naval architect, was the United States representative to the Ship Design and Equipment Subcommittee. In a 1971 article in *Marine Technology* he describes many problems the subcommittee faced in devising antipollution methods that would be effective in the marine environment. Some prevention systems external to the oil tankship required consideration—for example, special training for tanker and port crews, port facilities for tank cleaning, and various navigational schemes. Included were ship separation lanes and vessel traffic systems for ports and waterways with high hazard potential. Still other studies concentrated exclusively on ship design and operation. Here attention focused on the tanker, that is, the "integrity and reliability of the cargo containment systems."[39] The Ship Design and Equipment Subcommittee and others working to develop solutions to the problem of oil pollution all realized that data on spills were badly needed.

Oil Spills. The oil pollution problem took on many dimensions. Some of the economic, social, political, and technological aspects have already been discussed. Large catastrophic spills like that of *Torrey Canyon* were one side of the problem, but small spills and discharges from oil transfer operations or other mishaps repeated many times were also important. Statistics on oil spills can be misleading because they are often dominated by a few large spills, obscuring both the incidence and the location of the smaller spills and operational discharges.

Spill statistics available to the IMCO committees and others studying the pollution problem in 1967 were not as accurate as those available later. In July 1967 the Coast Guard contracted with Battelle Northwestern to make a literature search on oil spills. The *Oil Spillage Study,* completed in four months, was well received and served as a basis for later work. A good many studies followed. Three Coast Guard officers published a paper in 1971, "Tankers and the Ecology," containing data on spills up to that time. Although the oil industry and environmentalists each had their own concerns, the general public seemed ambivalent. Some scientists debated the seriousness of the pollution issue and asked if it was a real threat. A more rigorous system for collecting spill statistics and carrying out research was necessary.[40]

One outcome of the passage of the 1972 amendments to the Federal Water Pollution Control Act was a far more rigorous requirement for reporting oil spills, combined with penalties for those who did not use the reporting system. The Coast Guard mounted a public awareness program to inform the public that spill reports had to be submitted. As a result, the quality and reliability of available oil spill statistics improved. The oil spill statistics collected by the

TABLE 26
Pollution of United States Waters, 1971-74

Characteristics of Spills	1971	1972	1973	1974
Total number of discharges of oil and other hazardous substances	8,736	9,931	13,327	13,966
Total gallons discharged	8,839,523	18,805,732	18,314,918	18,132,638
Number of oil discharges	7,522	8,380	11,003	11,440
Gallons of oil discharged	8,635,395	16,764,721	15,142,721	15,801,794
Average size of oil discharge (gallons)[a]	1,148	2,000	1,349	1,381

Source: Marine Environmental Protection Program: An Analysis of Mission Performance, U.S. Coast Guard, Marine Environmental Protection Division, NTIS, Springfield, Va., report no. CG-WEP-1-76, August 1975.
[a] The "averagfe size of oil discharge" figure is very misleading by itself. While the mean spill is about 1,500 gallons, the median is closer to an order of magnitude away—15 gallons.

Coast Guard for United States waters for 1971 through 1974 are presented in table 26.

The great increase in the number of spills reported for 1973 and 1974 compared with 1971 is in part a result of the new requirement in those years that spills be reported, in contrast to the less stringent requirements existing in 1971. The public awareness program also helped.* The spill amounts reported for 1974 probably give a good approximation of the real magnitude of the problem that existed in United States waters before 1972. Note in table 26 that oil constitutes approximately 90 percent of all the hazardous substances spilled.

The two key statistics are the number of incidents and the volume of pollutants discharged. The aggregate numbers, however, are misleading (see note a to table 26). Emerging from the statistics are three patterns—a few very large spills, a vast majority of small spills, and a subgroup of this latter category of small spills that recur frequently in the same geographical areas. The large spills require careful case-by-case examination. Most often this means looking at the design, operation, and route of a tanker. The frequent smaller spills must be examined by looking at tankers and transfer operations, a frequent source of recurrent spills. Smaller spills also took on increased importance in the 1960s because of the greater number of tankers bringing both crude and product imports to United States ports. The assumption that smaller spills are from "tanker and transfer operations," however, can also be misleading. Barges, storage facilities, and pipelines contribute more to spillage than do tankers.[41]

The Pattern of Oil Imports. One key to the pattern of oil spills in the United States is revealed by examining where, and in what numbers, tankers ply their

*The Coast Guard estimated that reports of spills received after the 1972 changes increased from 50 percent of the total occurring to more than 80 percent. The Coast Guard attributed this increase to improved public awareness of the new requirements.

trade. Another key is the size of the tanker and the country in which it is registered. Also important is knowledge of a tanker's spill record.

Estimates of the level of oil imports required by the United States in 1980–90 were presented earlier in the chapter and are detailed in table 23. These estimates are not markedly higher than the level of actual imports received during the 1970s. Most of these imports are needed to compensate for shortages on the East Coast of the United States, but many shipments for the East in fact arrive on the Gulf Coast because of the large refinery and transshipment capacity in that area.

Many models have been developed that simulate both the demand and the supply structure for oil in the United States. The demand forecast by sections of the country can be overlaid on the supply structure, with the difference between supply and demand estimates equaling the projection for oil imports for the area. Modeling of this type has been done for each statistical metropolitan area and, in less detail, for each Petroleum Administration for Defense (PAD) district.[42]

There are five PAD districts in the United States; their locations are shown in figure 30, a graphic model of the process of allocating supply to accommodate demand projections for 1985. This model predicts that 9.152 million barrels a day will be needed in 1985 in PAD I, along the East Coast. The model also predicts that 1.48 million barrels a day will be needed in PAD III, along the Gulf Coast. The model of figure 30 is not elegant, but it gives a way to examine the pattern of imports. It is borrowed from *The Challenge of Deepwater Terminals,* which appeared in 1975. This prediction is very close to the "balanced program" import level predicted for the late 1980s by the 1979 Report of the Energy Project at the Harvard Business School.[43]

The locations of PADS I and III have already been discussed; PAD II covers the Midwest, PAD IV the Rocky Mountains, and PAD V the West Coast. The locations of the major ports and waterways in these regions are also important. Although most of the nearly 10-plus million barrels per day necessary in the model are for the East Coast, the port areas there are limited by water depth in their capacity to handle large tankers with deep drafts.

The harbor of Portland, Maine, is deep enough to accommodate a tanker with a draft of more than fifty feet. Portland and Riverhead, Long Island, however, have the deepest harbors of any frequently used ports on the East and Gulf coasts of the United States. Most other harbors in the East and the Gulf of Mexico are limited to tankers drawing no more than approximately forty feet. This translates in carrying capacity to tankers well under 100,000 tons. New supertankers are thus excluded from the East Coast; the tankers calling in the East will largely be older tankers, small enough to navigate the shallower channels available. By 1980, large tankers were sailing into Long Island Sound and offloading their cargoes of oil to older, smaller tankers near the port of Riverhead.

Older tankers were built when safety and antipollution standards were not

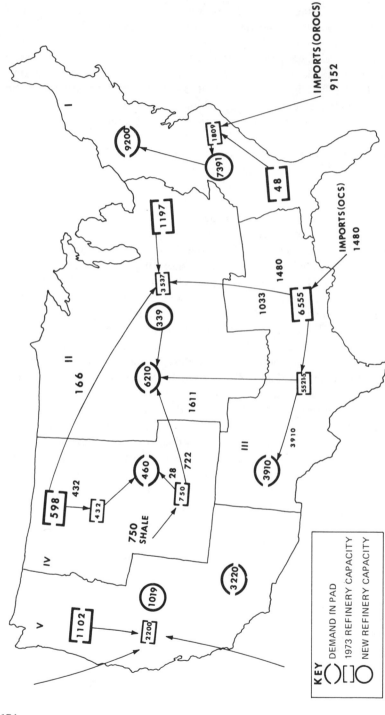

FIG. 30. Allocating petroleum supply to accommodate demand projections for 1985, by aggregate analysis over PAD districts. From Louis K. Bragaw, Henry S. Marcus, Gary C. Raffaele, and James R. Townley, *The Challenge of Deepwater Terminals* (Lexington, Mass.: Lexington Books, 1975), p. 34. Units in this analysis are millions of barrels a day (MBDs).

TABLE 27
Total Number of 50,000-Ton, 100,000-Ton, or 250,000-Ton Tankers Required to Carry Three Different Import Forecasts

	Number of Tankers Required for Imports[a]		
Size of Tanker	8 MBD[b]	10 MBD	12 MBD
50,000	1,510	1,888	2,266
100,000	755	944	1,133
250,000	302	377	452

Note: The estimate assumes a voyage from the Persian Gulf to the Gulf of Mexico, where approximately five round trips a year are possible.
[a] Numbers of tankers rounded to nearest integer.
[b] Million barrels of oil a day.

yet the public issue they have become since the *Torrey Canyon* grounding. A larger number of the older tankers were needed to carry a given quantity of imports than would have been the case with newer, larger tankers. This removed the threat of a massive spill possible from a supertanker, but it did increase congestion on the approaching waterways and within the ports.

Table 27 illustrates the aggregate number of tankers of three different sizes necessary if each size were to exclusively deliver three different import rates to the East and Gulf coasts. The table shows the massive number of tankers—more than fifteen hundred—required if an import rate of even eight million barrels a day were to be delivered to the United States in smaller tankers. For example, depending on the tanker size in use, this could represent the arrival of an average of nearly twenty-five tankers a day off the East and Gulf coasts. Obviously, the smaller the tanker used, the higher the arrival rate. In fact, a preponderance of the ships calling at United States ports in 1980 are transporting petroleum; the actual percentage in 1967 is listed in table 28, and this increased in the decade that followed.

TABLE 28
Percentage of Marine Traffic Carrying Petroleum at Major United States Ports in 1967

Port	Percentage	Port	Percentage
Seattle	44	Mobile	25
Portland	37	Savannah-Brunswick	42
San Francisco	75	Baltimore	25
Los Angeles	76	Philadelphia	53
San Diego	40	New York	69
Galveston-Houston	65	Providence	91
New Orleans–Baton Rouge	42	Boston	84

Source: James E. Moss, "Petroleum: The Problem," in *Impingement of Man on the Oceans*, ed. Donald W. Hood (New York: John Wiley, 1971), p. 383.

The rise in the number of tankers traveling off United States coastlines and entering domestic ports and waterways in the 1950s and 1960s led to an increased number of spills and a lowering of the quality of the marine environment during those years. As petroleum imports increased, the number of tankers increased further. Most of these ships were registered overseas. They tended to be smaller tankers with drafts shallow enough to clear United States harbors.

The nation needed a program to protect the marine environment. The response of the Coast Guard to this issue and the external forces surrounding it is described in the next two chapters, which show how Coast Guard structure translated national needs and its own technical means into a new program.

9 PROTECTION FOR THE MARINE ENVIRONMENT

EARLY ENFORCEMENT
OF LAWS TO PROTECT THE
MARINE ENVIRONMENT

By 1969 the Coast Guard was approaching a convergence between the national need to prevent marine pollution and its own means to provide such a program. After 180 years of attempts to protect marine transport from environmental hazards, the agency was ready to take on the complementary task of protecting the environment from marine transport. Environmental concerns, however, were not new to Coast Guardsmen. Indeed, the agency had been involved in this area since the 1870s, when John Muir and other environmentalists participated in Alaskan patrols. At that time, law enforcement and protection of the environment meant enforcing the fishing and seal-trade laws.*

The combination of protective and preventive roles in maritime safety assumed since 1946 allowed the Coast Guard to argue that protecting the marine environment was a natural extension of its multimission concept. By 1969 it was already performing law enforcement duties in the pollution area, armed with three different statutes: (1) the Refuse Act of 1899;[1] (2) the Oil Pollution Act of 1924;[2] and (3) the Oil Pollution Act of 1961.[3]

These laws, however, were difficult to enforce in actual situations. For example, the Refuse Act outlawed the discharge of pollutants other than municipal sewage into navigable water without a permit from the Army Corps of Engineers. The Coast Guard had used the Refuse Act in the late 1930s to

---

*The new Coast Guard role of protecting the marine environment from the hazards of transport was first discussed in chapter 1. The Marine Environmental Protection program is an excellent example of the process of matching national needs and the means of the Coast Guard.

The role that Captain Sidney A. Wallace played as chief of the Marine Environmental Protection Division at Coast Guard headquarters from the formation of the division in July 1971 until his promotion to rear admiral in 1975 will be discussed in this chapter. In a 1974 article that first discussed the notion of reversal of the historical and new Coast Guard roles, Wallace stated: "The marine environmental protection programs should be viewed in the context of long standing Coast Guard missions." Wallace had good reason for this argument. See S. A. Wallace, "To Fight to Save: The Environment," *Bulletin* 36, no. 1 (1974):41.

prosecute offenders in several pollution incidents in southern California. At the time, some tankers had either accidentally spilled oil or flushed their tanks near shore, so that oil washed up on the popular beaches of southern California. Coast Guardsmen who investigated the incidents found that oil spills were also in violation of a state fish and wildlife ordinance. This California law provided a legal tool to prosecute the violators. The Coast Guard combined the evidence of tide and current information with rudimentary chemical analysis of the oil from both beach and tanker to identify the offenders. This proved to be a harbinger of future enforcement battles.[4]

The Refuse Act fell into disuse after the 1930s. By 1969, however, the lack of other effective statutory tools to protect the environment led to an increased use of the old law. In fact, the Council on Environmental Quality reported eighty-one criminal actions under the Refuse Act in the last six months of 1971 alone.[5]

The problem with the Oil Pollution Act of 1961 was that it simply implemented the provisions of the 1954 International Convention for the Prevention of Pollution of the Sea by Oil. By later standards this convention had a great many loopholes. For example, it allowed tankers to discharge oil in the open oceans.

The Oil Pollution Act of 1924 was also difficult to enforce. This law required proof of willful or gross negligence, which was difficult to obtain in most cases, and impossible if the oil was spilled in the open ocean. As a result, the 1924 act was repealed in 1970.[6] The lack of effective legal tools was frustrating, and it became increasingly obvious that changes were necessary.

The Coast Guard faced the task of defining the expanding needs of the nation for marine pollution control. One can envision this task by recalling the model presented in figure 6. The structure had to ask how the means of the organization—its distinctive competence and its human, physical, and political resources—could be used to meet these needs. As a new program was shaped, it had to be measured against the dual-role strategy, the multimission concept, and character of the organization. Rear Admiral W. M. Benkert, whose role in the development of the Coast Guard Marine Environmental Protection program is discussed later in this chapter, summed up the challenge facing the structure in 1969 in remarks he made to the 1973 Conference on Prevention and Control of Oil Spills: "At our first conference in 1969 we were looking at a world-wide vessel traffic in oil of some 1.2 billion tons. . . . One can only ask, 'Are we winning or losing in our efforts to protect the environment? Where are we. . . . Where must we go?' "[7]

CHANGES IN COAST GUARD
STRUCTURE

By 1969 the Coast Guard took a proactive role in shaping policy for the marine environment. That year Admiral Willard Smith, Coast Guard commandant from 1966 to 1970, created a Marine Pollution Control Branch as a part of the Law Enforcement Division of the Office of Operations. At the time the change seemed small; events proved it was not. In fact, the Law Enforcement Division itself had only recently achieved autonomy as a division. It was a spinoff from the larger Port Security and Law Enforcement Division, a part of the Office of Operations throughout the Cold War era. Structural changes for a new program had begun.

The Marine Pollution Control Branch was charged with the following objectives, all directed toward the growing marine environmental protection needs of the nation:

1. General responsibilities in implementing a program to respond to the president's call for environmental protective measures.
2. The enforcement of antipollution laws; that is, the detecting, investigating, and reporting of marine pollution violations under their basic statutory authority.
3. Responsibility for responding to polluting spills in both a preventive and a curative way.
4. The abatement of pollution by Coast Guard vessels and shore stations.
5. Regulatory functions essentially directing the Coast Guard to issue and enforce subsequent regulations pertaining to pollution from vessels and harbor facilities.[8]

The Marine Pollution Control Branch of the Office of Operations, however, was not the only center within the Coast Guard structure that was looking at marine pollution. Both the Merchant Marine Technical Division and the Merchant Vessel Inspection Division of the Office of Merchant Marine Safety were well aware of the growing threat pollution posed to the marine environment. The district offices and the captain of the ports (COTP), as well as the Marine Inspection Offices (MIO) in the field also had to deal with the problem day by day.

The division of responsibility between the Pollution Control Branch and the Merchant Marine Technical Division in 1969 was more than a minor structural dichotomy. It was the start of a deep philosophical division between operational, port-oriented people and technical, ship-oriented people. Their conception of national needs and of the Coast Guard's means to deal with these needs often differed.

Rear Admirals Benkert and Robert I. Price, who were Coast Guard captains at the time, are examples of two Coast Guardsmen at work in this area in 1969. Captain Benkert was then officer in charge of marine inspection in New York, a post that made him head of the largest MIO within the Coast Guard. At the time he had more than twenty-six years of experience as a Coast Guard officer, including tours in merchant marine safety and command of four large Coast Guard cutters. Benkert had recently spent months on merchant ships observing actual practices. He was active in the operations of the port area and could sense the interests involved and the growing dimensions of the marine pollution problem. He knew the field problems at first hand.

In 1969 Captain Robert Price was a member of the Merchant Marine Technical Division at headquarters. His role as the United States representative to the Ship Design and Equipment Subcommittee of the Maritime Safety Committee of IMCO was discussed in chapter 8. He knew at first hand both the technical and the international problems.* The extensive operational and technical backgrounds of Benkert and Price are examples of the competence the Coast Guard could bring to bear on the growing marine pollution issue.

The human and physical resources available at the COTP and MIO offices were also an important part of the emerging program. Harbor patrols to enforce existing pollution laws as well as port security laws were already in operation. The myriad patrol boats and port security officers, along with the marine inspection personnel, served as a resource base to effect, at least initially, pollution patrols and inspections within the port areas.

The multimission concept adopted by the Coast Guard was again paying dividends. In fact, it was the only reason the Coast Guard was able to put an operational program in the field so quickly. Resources performing one task were simply told to perform the new pollution work as an "add-on." In the field, however, an argument erupted over whether "multimission" capability—the notion of *distinctive* competence discussed in chapter 2—and *technical* competence were at odds with one another. While this argument was taking place within the Coast Guard, however, still other events were occurring in Congress and the executive branch that would profoundly affect the quality of the marine environment.

ACTION IN CONGRESS AND THE
EXECUTIVE BRANCH

The growing national interest in the environment led to the passage of the National Environmental Policy Act (NEPA) of 1969[9] and to the creation of the Council on Environmental Quality (CEQ). NEPA required organizations of the federal government to prepare impact statements for plans and programs that would significantly affect the environment. CEQ is a part of the Executive Office of the President; it is charged with coordinating and developing national environmental policies and programs.

A law was passed in 1970 that placed direct responsibilities on the Coast Guard. Under the Federal Water Pollution Control Act (FWCPA), as amended

*Among the many accomplishments of Captain Robert Price was "A Study of Cost, Benefits, and Effectiveness of the Merchant Marine Safety Program," conducted by the Office of Merchant Marine Safety for the Bureau of the Budget as a fiscal year 1970 "Coast Guard special analytic study." The study was completed in May 1968 and approved by the commandant, the secretary of transportation, and the director of the Bureau of the Budget; it proved to be a definitive work.

by the Water Quality Improvement Act of 1970, the Congress stated that "it is the policy of the United States that there should be no discharge of oil into or upon the navigable waters of the United States."[10] Under this law CEQ was required to prepare a national oil pollution contingency plan.

In June 1970, CEQ published the National Contingency Plan for Oil and Hazardous Materials Pollution Control. Under the plan, the Coast Guard became part of a planning committee, the National Inter-Agency Committee, and part of the National and Regional Response Teams. The committee and the teams were "charged with the responsibility for the coordination and administration of cleaning up oil spills on the high seas, coastal and contiguous waters, and coastal and Great Lakes port and harbor areas."[11] The Coast Guard was to assume both on-scene commander and strike force responsibilities in case of an incident. An executive order that followed designated the Coast Guard as the appropriate agency to notify in case of a marine pollution incident.

The executive branch created the Environmental Protection Agency (EPA) in December 1970. EPA is an independent line agency created to maintain and coordinate research, monitoring, standard setting, and enforcement activities. It is responsible for the full sphere of clean air and water acts, including oil pollution control. EPA has mainly a single function—working for improved environmental quality. It cooperates with both federal and state agencies to achieve this objective. For example, it works with the Coast Guard on some research ventures and on some overlapping marine pollution responsibilities. Where overlaps occur, they "are handled through interagency agreements."[12]

THE CREATION OF A NEW OFFICE AT COAST GUARD HEADQUARTERS

NEPA and the congressional and executive branch action that followed in 1970 caused the Coast Guard to carefully examine its policies toward the natural environment. To deal effectively with the changing needs of the nation for port safety and environmental protection, Admiral Chester Bender, who became commandant in 1970 and served until 1974, initiated a major organizational change in July 1971. He created a program office of Marine Environment and Systems—with the staff symbol W—designed to coordinate both existing and new programs dealing with the marine environment.*

---

*Since the staff symbol M was already used by the Office of Merchant Marine Safety created in 1946, another letter was needed. An early planning memo had called the new group the "Office of Waterways and Port Facilities," and so the letter W was chosen as a staff symbol for the Office of Marine Environment and Systems when it was established.

Although Rear Admiral Benkert was the first chief of the new office, he liked to joke about the similarities and differences between M and W. When he later left the Office of W to become chief of the office of M, he referred to "W-types" as a bunch of "upside-down M-types."

The Office of Marine Environment and Systems was created by moving the existing Law Enforcement, Port Safety, and Aids to Navigation divisions from the Office of Operations to the new office. A new Division of Environmental Protection was added. The new office acquired the bridge administration function previously obtained from the Army Corps of Engineers as a part of the Department of Transportation Act. It also acquired the Ports and Waterways planning staff, a "new staff function with specific responsibilities in studying and developing the Coast Guard role in port and waterway management."[13]

Captain Benkert was promoted to rear admiral in 1971 and was appointed first chief of the new office. In this role he also became director of the Marine Environmental Protection program—with the program symbol MEP. Chapter 3 discussed the structure at headquarters and the role of the program directors.

The organizational change signaled by the creation of Marine Environment and Systems as a separate program office is significant. It is as important an organizational change as the 1946 creation of Merchant Marine Safety as a new office, separate from but at the same level as the Office of Operations. Until 1946, Operations had housed all Coast Guard programs serving the public.

The new Environmental Protection Division—with the staff symbol WEP—was important in developing the MEP program. The new WEP division chief became MEP program manager (see table 6). Sidney A. Wallace, who had just received an early promotion to captain, was selected to be chief of the new division. He had operational experience as an aviator and air station commander; he was an honors graduate of law school and held a graduate degree in political science as well. Captain Wallace commented on the role of his division:

The creation of the new Office, encompassing the responsibilities of several preexisting [Headquarters] divisions as well as the new baby, WEP, was an organizational innovation designed to gear the Coast Guard better to cope with public and Congressional demands for enhanced safety on our waterways and drastically improved protection of our navigable waters. By creating WEP, the Coast Guard took account of a relatively new consideration. Emphasis traditionally had been given to protection of vessels, cargoes, and people from the environment. Now emphasis was to be placed on protecting the environment in which marine commerce operates; i.e. the navigable waters of the United States.

The marine environmental protection program should be viewed in the context of long standing Coast Guard missions. Traditional programs, directed toward safety, have indirectly protected the environment by reducing risk of accidents which often can result in pollution. With the enactment of the National Environmental Policy Act in 1969, we were required to review all authority under which we operate—statutory and regulatory—with a view toward increasing environmental protection under these long standing mandates.[14]

The Marine Pollution Control Branch that was formed in Operations in 1969 was moved to the new division. Branches of Prevention and Enforcement, Pollution and Response, Environmental Coordination, and Program Review and Budget were formed within the new division. Captain Wallace became an active advocate of marine environmental protection.

At the time the Marine Environmental Protection Division was formed, several oil spills occurred. For example, a large spill occurred in Puget Sound during an oil transfer operation, and people in the state of Washington were understandably concerned. A larger spill, to be discussed later, had resulted from a collision in San Francisco Bay in January 1971.

Senator Magnuson of Washington, many environmental groups, port authorities, boat and property owners, and the general public who knew the water became greatly concerned with how such spills could be prevented.* The specter of oil pollution in United States waters was growing.

THE DEVELOPMENT OF THE MARINE ENVIRONMENTAL PROTECTION PROGRAM

The task of developing the new program took shape. At first the Coast Guard investigated how to prevent spills at their sources—during transfer operations and tank cleaning—and in cases of ship failures, collisions, and groundings in the waterways. A pilot study was soon begun, however, to develop both preventive and postspill strategies. Under Captain Wallace's leadership, the Marine Environmental Protection Division worked to develop mission standards, such as "conduct daily patrols of the essential harbor areas, by water, and during daylight hours and once during night hours." Such standards became part of the developing MEP program, concentrating on preventing frequent smaller spills. Vessel traffic schemes became another part, concentrating on preventing the collisions and groundings that lead to large, catastrophic spills.[15]

The Coast Guard began work on preliminary schemes for formulating and implementing vessel traffic services and systems. Although Long Beach, California, had begun a voice communication system in 1949, the ports of Hamburg and Rotterdam both had developed a full system of radar and communications by 1964. After the system was introduced in Rotterdam, the number of collisions occurring there declined fourfold, even though traffic in the waterway had increased.

Rear Admiral Benkert and Commander Ralph C. Hill, who was assigned specifically to look at vessel traffic systems, summed up some of the background:

For many years the Coast Guard has been pushing for permanent statutory basis for our port safety and security program—without notable success. Then on 20 January 1970 the USS *Yancey,* anchored off the Chesapeake Bay Bridge, tore loose from her anchorage in

*Senator Warren Magnuson, like Senator Wesley Jones before him, was both a powerful senator from the state of Washington and chairman of the Senate Commerce Committee. Although Senator Magnuson played a key role in earlier port security legislation, his interest in legislation affecting the quality of the marine environment takes on more importance in this and the following chapter.

high winds and knocked out three portions of the Chesapeake Bay Bridge–Tunnel Complex. . . . Congressman Downing of Virginia introduced the first Bill which included specific provisions for vessel traffic control.

In May 1970, the President, in his oil pollution message to Congress, urged enactment, among other things, of legislation directed at vessel traffic control. Shortly thereafter, the Department of Transportation submitted their own Ports and Waterways Safety proposal . . . H.R. 17830.

Testimony on H.R. 17830 favored the marine safety and environmental purposes of the Bill, but was almost unanimous in opposition to many provisions of the Bill. The general tenor was that it was too loosely drawn and too broad in scope.[16]

Even though legislation then appeared to be at a standstill, the Coast Guard continued research and development work on radar and traffic systems for ports and waterways. An experimental harbor radar project, begun with voluntary participation in San Francisco Bay in January 1970, was also continued. The Coast Guard announced plans to expand this system in stages until 1973 but pointed out that the "degree of *control* exercised will be limited until the Ports and Waterways Bill becomes law."[17]

One aspect of the emerging Marine Environmental Protection program that bothered both the marine industry and those within the Coast Guard was the need to assess penalties. Captain Wallace described some of the penalties: "Failure on the part of a polluter to report a discharge can result in a criminal penalty of up to $10,000 and/or one year in jail. The Coast Guard has authority to assess a civil penalty of up to $5,000 for each discharge. . . . Where a discharge occurs and the polluter is identified, a civil penalty must be assessed."[18]

Coast Guardsmen, however, identified themselves with protecting life and property and preventing disasters. Some therefore questioned the new "judge and jailer" role, feeling it was inconsistent with other Coast Guard missions. A favorite question was "Should the Coast Guard wear a white or a black hat?" The development of a Marine Environmental Protection program was bringing still another dimension to the multimission concept. Captain Wallace described the new approaches: "These new approaches are not always greeted with enthusiasm by those we regulate; nevertheless, we are enjoined to press these new iniatives in implementing the will of the Congress and stated policies of the Administration, hopefully without unduly burdening or harassing vital maritime commerce and public enjoyment of our water resources."[19]

The human resources of the Coast Guard—people—proved central to the success of the developing MEP program. People from all areas of the Coast Guard were called on to make the new program work. This strength in human resources was also evident during the development of the loran program; as then, mentioning certain individuals risks leaving out others whose contributions may have been at least as large. Even so, I will discuss a few individuals to illustrate the background and experience they brought to the program.

The background of Captain Sidney Wallace, who headed the Marine Environmental Protection program, has already been related. His branch chiefs were Commander Albert Stirling for Prevention and Enforcement, Commander Daniel Charter for Environmental Coordination, Lieutenant Commander George Brown for Pollution and Response, and Lieutenant Commander Allen Taylor for Program Review and Budget. All four had a good deal of experience as Coast Guard officers, and they also contributed diverse specialties and skills.

At the time, Stirling had eighteen years of service, including a senior tour in the Merchant Marine Technical Division. He held graduate degrees in naval architecture and marine engineering. Charter had sixteen years of service. He had been executive officer of a large cutter and had served as a commander in the Port Security program. Charter had been assigned to the Marine Pollution Control Branch formed in 1969, and he joined the new division when his branch was moved.* Taylor had eleven years of service, his most recent assignment having been in civil engineering work at Governor's Island in New York. Taylor had done graduate work both in civil engineering, specializing in the environmental and sanitary aspects, and in business administration.

Brown was the junior of the four branch chiefs in years with the Coast Guard, but he had essential firsthand experience with the problems the Environmental Protection Division faced. Only two years before, Brown had been commander of the Coast Guard Group at Santa Barbara. When gas and oil began escaping from the ocean floor near a Union Oil well off Santa Barbara on 28 January 1969, George Brown was ordered in as on-scene commander to direct the antipollution efforts. For his work at Santa Barbara, President Nixon awarded him the Legion of Merit. Brown was both a capable and a credible man to head the new Pollution and Response Branch.

MORE SPILLS BRING PUBLIC SUPPORT

A catastrophic incident again polarized public action. This time two tankers, the *Oregon Standard* and the *Arizona Standard,* collided in San Francisco Bay in January 1971. Tragically, though both ships could be seen on the experimental harbor radar installed by the Coast Guard in San Francisco the year before, the system was not advanced enough to prevent the collision.[20] As 1971 passed, the Environmental Protection Division received a greatly increased number of pollu

---

*The manner in which the Coast Guard develops specialists in new areas was discussed in chapters 5, 6, and 7. Lawrence Harding, Loren Brunner, and William Roland and William Mohin are themselves examples of the process over three "generations" of the development of radio-navigation technology.

The Marine Environmental Protection program is much newer to the Coast Guard than the Radio-navigation Aids program. The career of Daniel Charter is an example, albeit at an early stage, of the process of developing specialists. Charter received an early promotion to captain and was assigned as the operational commander of Coast Guard Group Long Island Sound. In the summer of 1978 he was assigned to Coast Guard headquarters as chief of the Law Enforcement Division.

tion reports, largely as a result of the new reporting requirement. By year's end, 8,736 reports of discharges had been received (see table 26), compared with only 3,711 the year before. Something had to be done.

After this most recent accident, the Coast Guard took a proactive and, it proved, an innovative, stance. In December 1971 the agency posted regulations to tighten standards for the design, construction, and operation of vessels and for bulk oil-transfer facilities. The regulations covered the vessel, its operation, and the transfer of cargo.[21] They were intended to reduce accidental or intentional release of oil into domestic waters during normal vessel operation and transfer operations, and at the same time to establish construction standards that would prevent oil outflows from minor accidents. Through 1971 the Coast Guard anticipated and prepared for major legislation to protect ports and waterways.

By February 1972 the Coast Guard began on a crash basis a formal two-stage Vessel Traffic System (VTS) study, aimed at greatly reducing the number of collisions and groundings. The objectives of this study were stated as follows:

1. Identify specific VTS program goals, anticipated benefits, and alternatives.
2. Analyze the potential VTS roles of federal, state, and local authorities, and private enterprise and recommend the most beneficial role for the Coast Guard.
3. Analyze the quantitative and qualitative factors to be considered in determining the needs for various levels of VTS in United States ports.
4. Prepare short- and long-range staffing and funding plans.
5. Prepare a management plan to use as a guide in planning, developing, and implementing new systems.[22]

Rear Admiral Benkert and Commander Hill delivered an important paper on VTS in April 1972.* They began by describing the San Francisco Bay tanker collision of the year before, which had happened under the eyes of an embryonic VTS:

We hope that by developing Vessel Traffic Systems in our major ports, we can prevent any similar occurrence in the future. This will be done as part of the continuing development of a National Plan for Navigation, the prime objectives being to "promote *safe* and *economic* movement of maritime traffic...."

We have just completed preparation of our budget estimate for fiscal year 1974 which include monies for several planned additional Vessel Traffic Systems. Again, final system designs in any particular port or waterway will be dependent upon:

1. The results of an outside contract study to be completed in December 1972;
2. The result of an in-house issue study on VTS for the Department of Transportation to be completed in December 1972;
3. The results of our continuing research and development in San Francisco;
4. The experience gained in operating the systems in San Francisco and Puget Sound;

---

*The acronym VTS stood for Vessel Traffic Systems in 1972. Later the Coast Guard changed this name to Vessel Traffic Services, although the acronym remained identical.

5. And, of course, the demonstrated, specific needs of the particular area, as determined by consultation with the maritime community.[23]

As a beginning the Coast Guard developed two pilot VTS programs in San Francisco Bay and Puget Sound in 1972. Tentative schedules were drawn up for systems for several other port areas. Near-term plans were drawn for the ports of Houston-Galveston (1974), New Orleans (1975), and New York (1976). These sites were selected based on their suitability and the need for experimental VTS systems in those areas. The Coast Guard also began work on a quantitative modeling structure to determine future sites.[24] It became increasingly apparent to the Coast Guard that enough public support existed on the marine pollution issue to bring about the legislation necessary for further protection of the marine environment. Both the national need and the technical means existed, and in the sense of the model of figure 6 the Coast Guard structure was ready to act.

MAJOR LEGISLATION IS ENACTED

The Congress also saw a need for action, and in July it enacted the Ports and Waterways Safety Act of 1972, giving the Coast Guard broad responsibility, including authority to regulate vessel traffic, port facilities, and vessel design and operation to prevent environmental damage. The act contained two titles. Under one, the secretary of the department under which the Coast Guard operates was authorized to "establish, operate and maintain vessel traffic services and systems for ports, harbors, and other waters subject to congested vessel traffic." A legal basis for VTS had been established.[25]

To further deal with marine pollution a second major piece of legislation was passed. The Federal Water Pollution Control Act (FWPCA) was amended in October 1972. It in essence *required* civil penalties for *any* discharge and gave the Coast Guard ample authority to regulate oil transfer at dockside as well as aboard tankers.[26]

Statistics showed marine pollution was mounting not only from a few spectacular spills but from the aggregate results of many small spills and operational discharges.* The Coast Guard studied alternative solutions. After long, detailed meetings with many constituents—including the marine industry, environmentalists, and other interested groups—it drafted regulations and solicited written comments, then submitted them to public hearings.[27] Rear Admiral Benkert, head of the Office of Marine Environment and Systems at the time, commented on Coast Guard action to implement FWPCA:

---

*On the one hand, between one and three spectacular spills account for approximately half of the total oil spilled in any one year. On the other hand, 90 percent of all spills are less than fifty gallons apiece. The preponderance of oil spilled in any one year clearly come from a small number of large spills.

Under the authority of the Federal Water Pollution Act, we issued on 21 December 1972, regulations (33 CFR 154–156) governing some aspects of the design, construction and operation of vessels operating in U.S. navigable waters and the contiguous zone, and governing certain portions of the design, construction and operations of onshore and offshore facilities engaged in the transfer of oil to and from vessels. Compliance with these regulations will reduce the probability of accidental discharges of oil and oily water during normal vessel operations, including the bulk transfer of oil and oily wastes to or from vessels.[28]

As Rear Admiral Benkert continued, he highlighted the increasingly dual nature of the Marine Environmental Protection program. At one level, spectacular spills resulted from collisions or groundings; at another level, many smaller spills occurred during tanker transfer operations or tank cleanings. Benkert commented on the relative danger of problems at each level:

Although collisions or groundings are spectacular and may create locally severe environmental damage, more significant and continuous degradation results from the regular and frequent discharges of oil into the water of the United States.[29]

The Ports and Waterways Safety Act of July and the amendment of FWPCA in October made 1972 a good year for legislative support. The Coast Guard was given both preventive and protective roles in regard to the transporting vessels and also the external systems that aid their navigation. In 1973 Rear Admiral Benkert explained to the Conference on Prevention and Control of Oil Spills what action the Coast Guard was taking:

Under Title I of the Ports and Waterways Safety Act, to expedite and, to the greatest extent possible, insure the movement of vessels in congested port areas, we are providing vessel traffic systems as fast as an orderly and rational program can proceed. The systems will monitor shipping in selected ports and advise or direct traffic as necessary to avoid collisions and groundings. . . . In studying the possible need for vessel traffic systems in a particular port, we are trying to develop criteria which will allow us to install the simplest and most economical system *if* a system is needed. . . .

Title II of the Ports and Waterways Safety Act requires that there be developed a comprehensive minimum standard of design, construction alteration, repair, maintenance and operation of liquid bulk carriers to prevent or reduce hazards to life, property and the marine environment.

The availability of data concerning the conditions existing on vessels and causal factors leading to vessel casualties is paramount in implementation of this title. The Commandant has, therefore, placed first emphasis on the gathering of more detailed data in the course of vessel casualty investigations and inspections and accelerating our plan for automating the files containing this data. The analysis of the data and . . . systems analyses then will provide the basis for regulatory development concerning vessel construction and operation with a view toward safety *and* economy. . . .

It is essential to recognize that our actions are not limited to U.S. vessels but to all vessels of any nation which desire to trade in U.S. Ports. . . . We are therefore deeply involved in drafting working documents for the forthcoming 1973 International Conference on Marine Pollution in order to obtain, to the greatest extent possible, multi-lateral agreement on methods to eliminate discharges of oil and hazardous substances.[30]

Some of the antipollution measures the Coast Guard formulated were preventive. Many were implemented ashore and would not go to sea with the tankers. The measures largely represented benefits and costs to the sponsor nation and thereby could be looked at purely from the vantage point of bureaucratic supply-and-demand analysis. A Vessel Traffic System is one example. Even then, foreign-flag tankers visiting United States ports would have to have the appropriate navigation and communications equipment to take part in the system. Many of the oil "containment systems" being studied would be installed on the tanker and thus would cross international lines with the vessel. Because of variations in the costs of the proposals and the *international* structure of the tanker industry, the issue was larger than any one government or federal agency could handle. IMCO thus had to play an important role.

AN INTERNATIONAL AGREEMENT IS REACHED

Providing antipollution measures in the international tanker market was one of the large issues dealt with at the IMCO-sponsored International Conference on Marine Pollution, held in London in October and November 1973. Delegates from seventy nations faced the problem that, if tankers of all registry were subject to the same additional antipollution measures, their costs in theory would rise proportionally. But, if some tankers were subject to environmental restraint and others were not, would not the workings of a competitive market tend to squeeze out the operator, industry, and nation complying with the restraint while increasing the volume of the operator without the restraint?

Economics and international politics were important considerations. What effect would tanker-installed antipollution measures have if applied to some tankers, but not all, in a perfectly competitive market? Tanker chartering is very sensitive to costs in a declining market; when costs rise, layups occur, particularly in the crunch since the deterioration of the tanker market in fall 1973.

If countries have different requirements and standards and hence impose a different cost structure on their tankers, the number of tankers registered in the country with the lowest standard may rise and the number registered in the country with the highest standards may decline until the effective world standard is the lowest set by any individual country of registry. This basic economic and political reality must have been tacitly recognized during the Marine Pollution Conference.[31]

An international agreement was important for other reasons. Even before this theoretical lower limit were to be reached, the countries of registry of tankers bearing costs not required of competitors would also suffer in trade balances, in fleet availability in time of emergency, and in employment in the domestic industry. At the same time, trade would go to the country less concerned. These problems are excellent examples of why international cooperation and agreement are necessary to overcome any ''compartmentation'' that may have been built into Kenneth Boulding's spaceship economy ideal, mentioned in the last chapter.

The 1973 International Conference on Marine Pollution concluded on 2 November. Russell E. Train, administrator of the Environmental Protection Agency and chairman of the United States delegation, termed the conference a ''historic milestone in the control of marine pollution.'' Admiral Chester Bender, Coast Guard commandant and vice chairman of the United States delegation, stated that the ''new convention can become a basis for Coast Guard enforcement and regulatory activity to control pollution from all vessels entering U.S. ports.''[32] Rear Admiral Benkert, Captain Price, and Captain Wallace all made important contributions. But the convention had to be ratified by the governments involved before it would become effective.

Russell Train stated that ''we can be proud of the fact that the two years of international activity culminating in this convention followed an United States initiative, made in 1970, calling on the nations of the world to take action to end ship-generated marine pollution in this decade.'' Some of the elements of the international agreement reached at the Conference are as follows:

A requirement that newly constructed oil tankers over 70,000 tons deadweight have separate tanks for cargo and ballast. . . .

Limitations on oil discharge from ships, including a complete prohibition on oil discharges within fifty miles of land.

Flexible amendment procedures to allow technical provisions to be kept up to date without traditional cumbersome treaty revision processes.[33]

Train went on to enumerate some ''important new legal duties'' that would be enacted to see that the regulations made under the convention were respected. Some of these duties require:

The Nation whose flag a ship flies must punish all violations by that ship.

In addition, Nations must either punish violations by a foreign flag vessel which occur in their waters or refer them to the state of the flag for prosecution.

Nations must deny permission to leave their ports to ships which do not substantially comply with the convention's construction requirements, such as segregated ballast tanks, until these ships can sail without presenting an unreasonable threat to the marine environment.

Nations which ratify the convention must apply its requirements to the ships of nations which do not ratify, as necessary to ensure that those ships do not receive favorable treatment, thus preventing a nation from obtaining competitive advantages by not joining the convention.

A system for settling disputes which arise under the convention through compulsory arbitration.[34]

The nature of the international tanker market and the way international shipping has developed as a business make international agreements a very important part of efforts to protect the marine environment from pollution. This is particularly true in the United States, where increasing quantities of petroleum are being imported. Of the crude oil and refined product imported, in the 1970s, *nearly 95 percent has come to the United States in ships registered in some other country.*

Rear Admiral Benkert was relieved in the spring of 1974 as chief of the Office of Marine Environment and Systems by his deputy, Captain Robert Price, who was promoted to Rear Admiral. Admiral Bender appointed Benkert to head the Office of Merchant Marine Safety. In a talk to the Marine Transportation Board of the National Research Council in 1977, Rear Admiral Benkert made clear the combined role of domestic legislation and international agreement: "We have been charged in the Ports and Waterways Safety Act with looking at the economic impact of our regulations in this field—the economic and technological feasibility of proposed regulatory action in connection with the whole picture. . . . In looking at any appraisal of vessels in the tanker industry, you must look at international considerations, in addition to domestic ones."[35] Recognizing from their backgrounds and work over the past ten years the international and domestic dimensions of the battle to protect the marine environment, Rear Admirals Benkert and Price set out to enforce the recent legislation and agreements. This required using the multimission resources of the Coast Guard.

COAST GUARD OPERATIONAL ACTIVITY

Chapter 3 described the program areas of the Coast Guard and listed the program directors responsible for each area at headquarters. The commandant and the program director, the chief of the Office of Marine Environment and Systems at headquarters, administer the MEP program in the field through two area and twelve district commanders. It is important to keep in mind that resources in the field are often shared by various programs, in keeping with the multimission concept. For example, a patrol boat scheduled to make a harbor surveillance patrol to check on pollution might also be asked to carry marine inspectors across a harbor, then suddenly be called back to search for some overdue recreational boaters.

In 1971 there were two distinct Coast Guard offices to accomplish regional and local responsibilities for each major port area. One office was headed by the captain of the port (COTP), the other by the officer in charge of marine inspection (OCMI). The COTP was the commander of the Coast Guard Group for the area in some cases, while the OCMI headed the Marine Inspection Office (MIO). Together the two represented the Coast Guard in the port area, and some overlaps, varying from region to region, did exist, caused by changing programs and responsibilities.

The OCMI is responsible to the District Marine Safety Division for the proper execution of all Commercial Vessel Safety programs within the territory assigned to the MIO. Across the country in 1971 there were forty-nine MIOs, generally performing the following tasks: vessel inspection, casualty and personnel investigation, licensing and certification of merchant seamen, shipment and discharge of seamen, and vessel documentation.[36] Counting all officers, enlisted men, and civilians, approximately fifteen hundred Coast Guardsmen are assigned to MIO duty at any one time. Assignments at MIOs usually run three to four years for Coast Guard military personnel, who generally alternate tours between Commercial Vessel Safety assignments and other programs of the Coast Guard.

In 1971 the COTP and group commanders were responsible for day-to-day duties to the District Operations Division. At the time there were fifty-four COTPs, with approximately fourteen hundred Coast Guardsmen assigned. The lengths of assignments to an MIO and a COTP are similar. The wide range of COTP functions include: (1) the protection and security of vessels, harbors, and waterfront facilities; (2) the enforcement of laws and regulations, including dangerous cargo, oil pollution, and tank vessel regulations; and (3) the rendering of aid to distressed persons, vessels, and aircraft.[37]

The Coast Guard field organization is basically decentralized. In the 1970s the agency developed the idea of establishing a Marine Safety Office in each geographical area, to improve services to local users of both the Marine Environmental Protection and Commercial Vessel Safety programs. The idea came from the multimission concept. In theory, the Marine Safety Office, MSO for short, combined COTP and MIO resources in a given area. In reality, the office created another organization level to provide the public with local services.

The MSO idea had advantages and disadvantages. Internally, the Coast Guard could combine both human and physical resources committed to several district programs, thus saving on people and equipment. Externally, the MSO did provide one Coast Guard office to a local community—marine industry, port authorities, boaters, fishermen, and the public at large.

The MSO combination, however, brought to the surface other issues inside the Coast Guard. COTP operations had grown from port security, and in the beginning from the post–World War II reorganization of many Life Saving Stations. The MIO operation, by contrast, was an outgrowth of the Marine Inspection Zones of the former Bureau of Marine Inspection and Navigation.

These different program backgrounds created some intraorganizational problems and professional jealousies, reminiscent of earlier consolidations of cuttermen and surfmen and even the integration of Bureau of Marine Inspection and Navigation or, for that matter, of Lighthouse Service personnel into the Coast Guard. Although by 1973 the advantages and disadvantages of the consolidation were clear to those at Coast Guard headquarters, the details of how the consolidation would be effected were not spelled out. A series of joint memoranda were signed at headquarters by the two supervising offices, Merchant Marine Safety—M—and Marine Environment and Systems—W. Each of these memos, however, reads more like a treaty than a simple organizational development initiative. As had happened earlier in the evolution of the Coast Guard, the development of a new program brought with it secondary policy issues.

The basic issues were: How broad in missions and geography should the MSO be? Should there be a zone command consolidating the MIO, the COTP, and the operational group commander? Secondarily, if the group and MSO were separate commands, should the MSO be an operational command on the water with its own boats, or should it rely on the groups and stations for support?

The significance of this dispute went beyond boats. If one had boats, they were liable to multimission use, and the door was open for a nonspecialist as commanding officer. Should M or W control the assignment of officers? Although this is a generality, M pushed for a narrow definition of the MSO, while W—the new kid on the organizational block—pushed for a broad definition that would open the door for new officers entering the program. The "battle" was reminiscent of earlier disputes for power, position, and status between "old" and "new" Coast Guardsmen. This negotiation between M and W was settled in 1974 by the vice commandant's decision to approve the specific details for a particular MSO advanced by the district commander of the area in question. At this point the "battleground" of the MSO shifted at headquarters from the planning staffs discussed in chapter 3 to the Office of Personnel, where the assignment and training of officers in the "Marine Safety" area was monitored (see fig. 8).

On paper, the MSO combination was designed to confront new challenges. But distances between separate offices, differences between industrial and recreational areas, and varied demands concentrated in either the Commercial Vessel Safety program or the Marine Environmental Protection program tended to partially or totally offset any advantage of centralization in some areas.[38] After the decentralization agreement reached by the vice commandant, local judgments were made for each area, and in some areas the COTP and MSO were left as autonomous offices. On balance, the organizational development initiative the MSO represented was successful, producing the predicted synergy.*

Under the guidance of the Marine Environmental Protection Division at headquarters, the Coast Guard developed a National Strike Force designed to deal with a polluting incident anywhere in the United States. The Strike Force, called for in FWPCA, included three strike teams. Each of the seventeen men

---

*In 1979 there were thirty-eight Marine Safety offices and ten Marine Inspection offices. The locations of these offices reveal the scope of their task. Across the Pacific Ocean in Guam and across the Atlantic in Rotterdam the offices answer differing problems as they respond to the needs of vessels that enter and leave the many ports and waterways of the United States.

placed on the teams by 1974 received extensive training in dealing with oil pollution. They were "specially trained and equipped for 'response,' . . . cleanup operations, and coordination of separate forces, both organized and volunteer."[39] District Offices and COTPs were made responsible for these duties for their regions.

The Atlantic team was positioned at Elizabeth City, North Carolina, the site of a large Coast Guard air station; the Gulf team at NASA's Mississippi test facility, Bay Saint Louis, south of New Orleans, and the Pacific team at Nevado, California, near San Francisco Bay. In his 1974 article, Captain Wallace, then MEP program manager, pointed out the roles assigned to the Coast Guard under FWPCA and companion executive order:

Surveillance and monitoring by ships, aircraft, and shore parties constitute a major part of Coast Guard efforts to detect discharges. When a discharge occurs, the primary responsibility for clean-up rests with the polluter. But, in the coastal region, the Coast Guard must monitor his efforts and, if they are judged inadequate, must take charge and effect the clean-up. This function is performed by EPA for navigable waters in the inland region. The Coast Guard administers a revolving Pollution Fund of up to $35 million which is used to defray clean-up costs, either where the polluter cannot or will not effect clean-up or where the polluter cannot be identified. The polluter, when known, must with certain exceptions and within specified limits of liability, reimburse this fund for the actual costs incurred by the U.S. government.[40]

With increased importance placed by law and executive order on cleanup of oil spills, a new industry specializing in cleanup seemed probable.* Owing to a lack of sustained demand, however, this industry never fully materialized. Instead, oil cleanup functions were taken over by closely related industries, for example, ship-service and tank-cleaning contractors. This meant that the only primary capacity for cleanup of catastrophic spills came from either large government activities or oil-spill cooperatives. Most cooperatives consisted of from four to ten oil companies pooling cleanup resources in a geographic area.

Often the commercial cleanup contractor industry, however, could respond effectively to inshore spills. Offshore spills were more difficult because transportation and equipment required a large investment, and the occasions when they could be used were far less frequent than for inshore spills. Therefore the Coast Guard was often placed in the position of taking charge of offshore cleanup.

This meant the Coast Guard had to further develop the Strike Force concept. By 1980 the three strike teams had grown to total seventy-two Coast Guardsmen. Each team was headed by a lieutenant commander. The teams were located at or

---

*An oil-spill cleanup industry first became possible in the early 1970s. The private firms in the area have been largely supplemented with cooperatives of oil companies. Nonprofit cooperatives have also grown. Each is a viable part of the total effort.

In many situations, however, the Coast Guard has had to step into a case. For a discussion of activity in this area, see Christopher M. Stone, "The Economics of the West Coast Oil Spill Clean-up Industry," M.S. thesis, U.S. Naval Postgraduate School, Monterey, California, 1974.

near air bases and were "air mobile." The "Force" acquired considerable experience in responding to hundreds of potential or actual spills during 1973–80. They carried specially designed equipment whose development will be discussed shortly. The Strike Force was asked for help and advice from countries as far away as Argentina, Norway, and Japan.

The key to the degree of success Coast Guard operations achieved in marine environmental protection was the development of the human, physical, and political resources necessary for the vitality of the MEP program. This development has many parallels with the early years of loran. The names and backgrounds of some of the early participants in the development of the program have already been given; the role of training and education for more personnel also should be mentioned.

In addition, the availability of physical resources deserves comment. In the early days of the program very little specialized equipment or operational doctrine had been developed to combat spills. As environmental protection increasingly came to mean protecting against both relatively smaller inshore spills and larger offshore spills, having equipment specially designed for each task became more and more important.

Finally, political resources were important. The external constituents of environmental protection included the organized environmental groups such as the Sierra Club and the Friends of the Earth; and fishermen, shoreline property owners, the boating public, and those with interests in shoreline and resort businesses—also strong advocates. The general public, even without a specific interest, was generally appalled at the specter of oil pollution and became generally interested in the issue. Taken together, there was strong public demand for protection of the marine environment.

The marine industry, on the other hand, offered some resistance; industry was more concerned about costs, and about its ability to pass the cost of pollution control on to the consumer. There was even some resistance to the Marine Environmental Protection program within the Coast Guard itself, particularly from those who thought it was either a fad or a "black hat" business that did not mix with the distinctive competence of the Coast Guard. Some correctly viewed the new program as a competitor for resources and status within the organization.

PROGRAM MANAGEMENT AND
RESOURCE DEVELOPMENT

Under the leadership of Captain Wallace, MEP program manager, the new program had excellent definition and impetus. Several catastrophic accidents focused public attention on marine pollution, rallying political resources and supplying context for the developing program. The congressional and executive branch mandates for control of marine pollution have been discussed; they pro-

vided a favorable budgetary climate. In 1974 Captain Wallace summed up the
early development of the MEP program:

The problems encountered in MEP in the past exist today, though in diminished dimension through the hard work and persuasive talents of a great many dedicated people, not
least those who were associated with the program at its conception well before WEP was
established. Coast Guard organization and modus operandi should be evolutionary in
nature, but resistance to change is understandably deeply imbedded. Innovating to effect
changes to meet the new challenges of MEP has been a painfully slow process. And
adapting program initiatives to the strictures of traditional organizational and command
relationships while still achieving program goals has been only partially successful. But,
on balance, much progress has been realized and more is clearly to come. Perhaps the
ability of the Coast Guard to meet the challenges of its environmental protection charter is
a measure of its ability to adapt to the changing needs of society and thus endure as a
viable, flourishing and versatile agency of the Executive Branch of our government.[41]

Program Management.   During 1971–73, Lieutenant Commander Taylor was
in charge of Program Review and Budget for WEP. Working with his division
chief, Captain Wallace, and the chief of the Programs Division, Captain James
Gracey, Taylor used with great success the resource change proposal and the
acquisition, construction, and improvement systems described in chapters 3 and
4. Although the environmental protection issue was clearly still in the stage of
"alarmed discovery and euphoric enthusiasm" nationally, Taylor's success at
winning resources may have caused him some long-run problems with people
within the organization who would have preferred to gain the new increments of
"bureau supply" for their own programs.

After 1973 the MEP program entered a more mature stage. This transition
was accentuated by the Yom Kippur War and the oil embargo of the winter of
1973–74. Also, the national mood for environmental protection was questioned,
particularly as rising energy prices and gasoline shortages changed some perspectives on the interrelated questions of energy, economy, and the environment. The
environmental protection issue had moved to the stage of "realizing the cost of
significant progress," and further increases in "bureau supply" would be harder
to achieve.[42]

In the fall of 1973 Lieutenant Commander John Harrald replaced Taylor in
the Program Review and Budget Branch. Taylor had displayed vision, optimism,
and the ability to take risks with a rapidly growing program; Harrald brought to
his new job the skills of a technocrat. Although he had not been to sea since his
initial tours following graduation from the Coast Guard Academy, he was fresh
from a second tour of postgraduate education, this time in environmental management. He understood the Coast Guard and MEP organizations and also the
threats and opportunities existing in the external and internal environments.

Harrald went to work on refining and developing systems for program
management. The Polluting Incident Reporting System (PIRS) had been de-

veloped in 1970 to collect and analyze data on spills. In 1973 Harrald contracted on a "sole-source" basis with Rensselaer Polytechnic Institute to expand PIRS to incorporate data on all Coast Guard enforcement, response, and pollution fund actions taken on each discharge. Mission Performance Standards were developed under this contract. A Port Safety and Marine Environmental Protection (PSS/ MEP) Activities Report was also devised, requiring, "operating units with Port Safety and Environmental Protection responsibilities [to report] their activities as they pertained to the prescribed standards."[43] The MEP program developed and implemented an effective information system on marine pollution. The system had the potential to analyze the international as well as the national implications of marine environmental protection.

The PSS/MEP and PIRS reports together served as inputs for the MEP Program Management System, depicted in figure 31. The system on paper is a dynamic one, allowing the program manager to make "budget-resource alloca- tion, program planning, and policy decisions requiring accurate and timely in- formation."[44] It also attempts to validate the mission performance standards mentioned in chapter 4 and required by the Department of Transportation as a budgetary tool. The system measures program cost-effectiveness—comparing program resources (bureau supply) with program demand and the competition of other programs—and as such is a viable tool for program management. This system is intended to validate, to the extent that this is possible, the efficiency and effectiveness of Coast Guard operational activity in MEP. It was also in- tended to win resources for the MEP program in the planning and resource allocation processes. Whether this most benefited those in the individual pro- grams, the overall Coast Guard, or the national interest only a longer-term assessment will tell. Will this system, for example, decrease resources when the issue reaches the "postproblem" stage? Or will it also allow the program man- ager to justify and retain program resources—bureau supply—after the demand for them diminishes?

Resource Development.   The MEP program director called on the Coast Guard Office of Research and Development to conceptualize and later develop specialized equipment. The objective was to limit quantities of oil discharged, to contain oil once it was in the water, and to recover it from the water. One of the first projects in 1971 was development of barrier systems to contain oil spills within a given area. A second project developed a device to recover oil from the sea, mainly by skimming and scrubbing.

Commander William Lehr of R&D (Research and Development) worked with Lieutenant Commander Brown of MEP, who represented the program man- ager. Contracts were let to private firms for both design and production work on the systems. Private consultants were hired for various phases of the project.[45] When work on a system reached the production phase, Brown worked with the Ocean Engineering Division, the support manager for the project.[46]

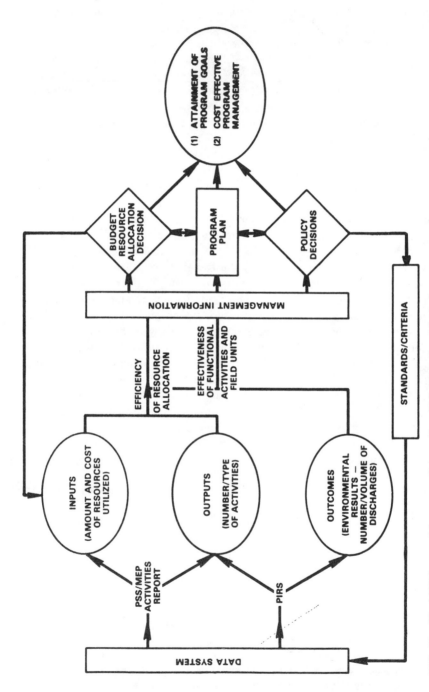

FIG. 31. The MEP Program Management System. From U.S. Coast Guard Study Report, *Marine Environmental Protection Program: An Analysis of Mission Performance* (Springfield, Va.: National Technical Information Service Report no. CG-WEP-1-76, August 1975), p. 5.

Being able to prove that an oil spill came from a given tanker or land source was essential to enforcing the Federal Water Pollution Control Act as amended in 1972. This had been a problem for the Coast Guard in prosecuting those who caused the oil spills in southern California in the late 1930s. A research project was initiated in 1972 at the Coast Guard Research and Development Center to develop a process to match samples from oil spills to samples from suspected sources.

Oils represent a complex mixture of many different organic compounds, and because each oil is different from others in composition, identification is possible by a unique chemical "fingerprint."* Employing several different methods of analysis, such as gas chromatography, infrared and fluorescence spectroscopy, and thin-layer chromatography, the R&D Center developed successful techniques to compare these fingerprints, which are accepted as evidence in court. The multimethod analysis approach has proved to be much more reliable than any single method.[47]

A network of laboratories was developed to apply the oil identification system in the field, allowing COTP and MSO personnel to perform comparison tests on oil samples near the scene of the oil spill. Electronic packages were developed for aircraft, allowing more efficient detection of oil spills from the air. In fact, this contributed to the demand for a new generation of "search" aircraft, and program supply did increase, although the planes were categorized as multimission resources and were shared with other Coast Guard programs. Operational doctrines were developed to allow the planes and the cutters of the Coast Guard to work together both in searching for oil-spill violators and in responding to spills when they occurred. Again, physical resources of other Coast Guard programs were shared to meet the demands of the new program—the essence of the multimission concept.

The Coast Guard's work in developing Vessel Traffic Services has already been discussed. VTS is a major technological and organizational innovation. Although the radar and communication systems were not new technology, deploying them in the field to guide the flow of marine traffic was a new application. In fact, the highly accurate radar being installed in several United States ports providing Vessel Traffic Services was specially modified for this.

Developing human resources was also fundamental to the success of the MEP program. Coast Guardsmen were aware of the importance of attracting junior officers into Commercial Vessel Safety after the final acquisition of the

---

*The "fingerprint" is a central piece of evidence in enforcing the various antipollution laws. Coast Guard personnel routinely take oil samples from all tankers entering United States ports so that they are readily available for analysis in the event of a spill. Analysis techniques have been sharpened until oil samples from different tanks on the same vessel can be separately identified, since there is always a small residue of previously carried oil, cleaning compounds, and such in the tanks, giving the oil in each tank a unique composition.

By 1972 the Coast Guard R&D Center was at Avery Point, in Groton, Connecticut, the same location used as the site of training loran technicians.

Bureau of Marine Inspection and Navigation, and of attracting electronics-oriented officers after the development of loran. The program champions of MEP faced many of the same challenges to "recruit" good people that the champions of earlier programs had faced. In the case of MEP, however, the program champions had as a guide the experiences of the earlier development of the other programs. Indeed, many of them—for example, Rear Admiral Benkert—were developed personally by alternating job assignments in operational areas and in the Commercial Vessel Safety program.

It is not hard to understand the mix of training and education that was developed; it had become a familiar pattern in the Coast Guard. Short courses were offered for both enlisted men and officers at a new Marine Environmental Protection School established at the Coast Guard Reserve Training Center, and moved by the 1960s to Yorktown, Virginia. In the late 1970s an advanced course was offered for supervisory and command personnel to help them handle new responsibilities in port safety, commercial vessel safety, and environmental protection. This course was jointly developed by the program managers in the three areas and proved to be a significant experiment in organizational change. A postgraduate degree program in environmental management was also set up to prepare junior officers for MEP assignments.

A potential career pattern for junior officers was begun.[48] Many junior officers were recommended for the program, and others sought out assignments in the area. Petty officers who had specialized in oceanography and marine sciences were also identified as well-qualified technicians for the Marine Environmental Protection program and were given the opportunity to transfer to the new area.

The success of the early advocates of the MEP program became well known by 1975, both inside and outside the Coast Guard. Through their sagacity the MEP program had come into being and had developed the resources to handle future challenges. The external pressures for the program had been strong, yet much opposition also had to be overcome. But these advocates had little time to reflect on their accomplishments, for even more change was to occur in the marine environment.

10 ANSWERS TO MORE CHALLENGES OFFSHORE

ANSWERING
THE DEEPWATER PORT
CHALLENGE

External threats and opportunities in the area of marine environmental protection challenged the Coast Guard several times during 1975–80. The growing demand for energy in the United States, coupled with increased consciousness of environmental quality, was at the root of each challenge. A pressing national need had arisen for offshore oil terminals, in water deep enough to service the large new tankers built in the 1960s and early 1970s.[1]

The dilemma over deepwater ports grew because the most economical supertankers had drafts of forty feet or more, and most United States ports could not handle even thirty-five feet. This in effect limited these ports to tankers of fifty thousand tons or less. Smaller tankers were predominantly older, with greater risk of spill. Obviously a great many smaller tankers in crowded ports and waterways also increased spill risks by raising the volume of traffic.

The United States had three alternatives: dredge deeper ports and waterways, build terminals offshore in deeper water, or accept the increased spill risks. Environmental considerations existing in the country in 1974 limited the first two alternatives. The third was also unacceptable. Yet offshore terminals had been built as alternatives to dredging in many harbors around the world. The United States needed to come to grips with this apparent conflict between environmental protection and the need for offshore ports.

The general scheme of a "deepwater port" is sketched in figure 32. Most such ports worldwide consist of platforms containing pumping stations, control rooms, crew accommodations, and connections to buried pipelines going to onshore tank farms. The platforms are usually flanked by a single-point mooring buoy, or a cluster of them, with underwater pipelines connecting the buoys to the pumping platform. The cargo hoses from tankers swivel, allowing the tankers to weathervane 360 degrees to face into the wind, waves, and current while continuing to offload.

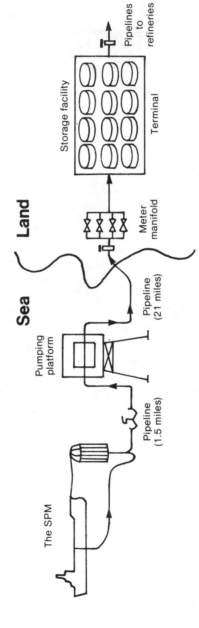

FIG. 32. The general arrangement of a deepwater terminal. The diagram shows a proposed method of bringing a large tanker to a single-point mooring buoy (the SPM) in water approximately one hundred feet deep. Oil would then be pumped through the platform to a land-based storage facility. From Kenneth G. Wiman, ''Deepwater Ports,'' *Bulletin* 37, no. 1 (1975): 44.

Some economists initially estimated that large tankers coming to deepwater terminals could save as much as 40 percent on transportation costs over smaller tankers, reducing the annual shipping bill by 1.5 billion dollars. They also estimated that in the first year the offshore ports would bring some thirty-five thousand new jobs and more than a billion dollars in capital investment to the regions hosting the ports. Some speculated that offshore oil ports could produce a tenfold reduction in the quantity of oil spilled.

Coast Guard structure anticipated the national need for offshore oil ports. In June 1974 Admiral Owen Siler became commandant. Realizing that a regulatory role for the Coast Guard was likely, he immediately established a Deepwater Port project under the Office of Marine Environment and Systems. Captain Kenneth Wiman, who was heading the Bridge Administration Division of the same office, was appointed project manager. A project staff was drawn from all the major program and support directors at Coast Guard headquarters, bringing many skills and points of view. The new project was charged with "development of regulations to cover license applications, port operations, safety equipment, construction, navigational requirements and other areas of vital concern."[2] Activity of the project staff anticipated deepwater port legislation.

On 17 December 1974 Congress approved the Deepwater Port Act. The congressional passage had been tedious, lasting several years. President Ford signed the legislation into law on 4 January 1975.[3] At the time twenty-three Coast Guardsmen were assigned to the Deepwater Port project. A way was at last open for the construction of offshore port facilities.

The responsibility for licensing deepwater port construction and operation was given to the Department of Transportation. The final congressional decision to place this authority with DOT and not with Commerce or Interior "resulted in part from extensive compromises worked out between affected committees of Congress and the results of the final House-Senate conference agreements."[4] The Coast Guard, however, had the distinctive competence and was prepared. Since the service was the major maritime agency within DOT, the secretary delegated the task of regulating the operations of deepwater ports to the Coast Guard.

The staff of the Deepwater Port project recognized that the licensing of ports not only would involve the new act, but would cut across other laws as well, including the Ports and Waterways Safety Act, NEPA, FWPCA as amended in 1972, and the Coastal Zone Management Act. The issues involved even spanned the jurisdictions of many cabinet departments in the executive branch and standing committees in the legislative branch, and they often crossed both national and local priorities.* The Deepwater Port project team had to deal with policy issues

---

*When the Maritime Administration was excluded from the Department of Transportation by the Congress during the 1966 passage of the DOT bill, the new department was constrained from conducting economic evaluations of proposals for the investment of federal funds in transport facilities or equipment in water resource projects by the language of Section 7(a) of the DOT act. The

daily. They soon recognized that at most two or three deepwater ports might be developed.[5]

Two industry groups showed active interest in developing terminals. Both had intentions for the Gulf area. The Louisiana Offshore Oil Port (LOOP) proposed a port eighteen miles off the coast of Louisiana in approximately one hundred feet of water. LOOP is jointly owned by Marathon, Texaco, Shell, Ashland, and the Murphy Oil Corporation. Seadock proposed a port twenty-six miles off Freeport, Texas, also in one hundred feet of water. Seadock is a corporation jointly owned by Cities Service, Continental, Crown-Central, Dow, Exxon, Gulf, Mobil, and Shell Oil. LOOP and Seadock both filed applications in December 1975.*

Their proposals both involved an array of single-point mooring buoys spaced about a mile and half from a pumping-platform complex, designed to pump the oil by a submarine cable and buried pipeline to a terminal several miles inland. LOOP proposed a facility that could handle a 700,000-ton tanker. The first stage of construction would give the complex a pumping capacity of 1.4 million barrels a day. This would cost $350 million, plus $80 million for a pipeline. A later stage could boost capacity to 3.4 million barrels a day. The oil storage facility would be twenty-five miles inland, near Galiano, Louisiana. Seadock proposed a facility capable of handling 2.5 million barrels a day, at an estimated cost of $700 million. This figure could jump to $1 billion if Seadock capacity was expanded to 3.5 million barrels a day.[6] For reference one may compare these capacities with the forecast of expected oil imports given in table 23.

The proposals of LOOP and Seadock offered a way to cut down the number of smaller tankers in United States coastal waters. They certainly "would curtail the practice of shifting U.S. bound cargoes from large to small tankers in the Caribbean, and the added expense it involved."[7] That tankers of more than fifty thousand tons were too large to navigate United States ports and waterways meant, among other things, that approximately three hundred tankers existing worldwide in the 200,000- to 300,000-ton range were effectively denied access

---

Deepwater Port Act, however, specifically called for DOT to compare the "economic, social, and environmental" issues at stake. For a discussion of the implications of this apparent conflict, see Henry S. Marcus, James E. Short, John C. Kuypers, and Paul O. Roberts, *Federal Port Policy in the United States* (Cambridge: MIT Press, 1976), pp. 170–71, 185–201.

For a discussion of the trade-offs between national and local, and economic and environmental issues, see Louis K. Bragaw, Henry S. Marcus, Gary C. Raffaele, and James R. Townley, *The Challenge of Deepwater Terminals* (Lexington, Mass.: Lexington Books, 1975), pp. 73–91, 101–5.

*When LOOP was formed in 1972, seven companies joined in the venture. At a high point there were sixteen partners. "One by one the others dropped out, frustrated by the obstacles encountered along the way. . . . Other oil companies know that, if someone else is forced to build the superport, they can always make use of it." See Anthony J. Parisi, "A Supertanker Bonanza: Texas, Move Over," *New York Sunday Times,* 20 November 1977, p. F-11.

There was also a change in the partner composition in the Seadock venture, as discussed later in this chapter.

to United States markets. These tankers, called VLCCs (very large crude carriers), were then relatively new, and the vast majority flew foreign flags. (See
tables 24 and 25 and fig. 28 for statistics.)

The Deepwater Port staff project processed the applications. An important
element in the decision was the potential for reducing the number of small
tankers calling at United States ports if offshore ports were established. For
example, if a deepwater port could service a VLCC of 250,000 tons, while a
regular United States port could handle only a 50,000-ton tanker, offshore tanker
traffic could be reduced by 80 percent, assuming a constant level of imports.
More figures are available for comparison in table 27.

Economic, environmental, and safety issues were also considered. The
economic issues are straightforward: there are large savings to be made on
VLCCs, but to take advantage of them, one must also make arrangements for
protecting the environment. This, of course, was considered both technically and
in terms of liability. A "liability of $50 million for each no-fault spill and
unlimited liability beyond that for a spill due to gross negligence or willful
misconduct" was established.[8] One business source reported that the Department
of Transportation estimated that profits on the port venture could return "70
percent on equity, while the industry says that 12–14 percent on total investment
are more realistic figures."[9] This same source said the key question is whether
expected returns of 30 percent on oil transportation investments are worth the
extreme financial risk represented by the threat of a large spill. The Interstate
Commerce Commission regulations, on the other hand, would limit total return
on investment to 7 percent.

On 17 January 1977 Secretary of Transportation William T. Coleman, Jr.,
offered licenses to both LOOP and Seadock to own, build, and operate the
nation's first deepwater ports. The application review process developed by the
Deepwater Port project of the Coast Guard included liaison with twenty-two
federal agencies, state and local officials, and public interest groups as well as
extensive environmental analysis and preparation of an environmental impact
statement."[10]

LOOP formally accepted its license on 1 August 1977 and was enthusiastic
about building the deepwater port. Construction was scheduled to begin in late
1978, after still more environmental data had been gathered. LOOP officials
predicted a throughput from the port of 1.4 million barrels a day (MBD) in the
early 1980s, building to a level of 3.4 MBD by 1989. A throughput of this
magnitude would provide the United States with half again the capacity of the
Trans-Alaska Pipeline.[11]

The Seadock proposal, however, did not enjoy the same good fortune.
Although Secretary Coleman offered a license to Seadock in January 1977, by
July Exxon had dropped out of the venture. Many felt this left the proposal "all
but dormant."[12] Hugh Scott, president of Seadock, stated in November 1977:
"We're trying to hang in, hoping to get some non-oil company participants.

Seadock is absolutely essential to the economy of Texas. Logic says it will have to be built. The only questions are by whom and when."[13]

Of course many important economic, social, and political issues surround the deepwater port question. For example, how long will imports continue, and at what level? Will changes in United States energy or economic policy or oil price levels and availability change these levels? These questions must be weighed against the more parochial issue of tanker size and traffic patterns in existing coastal ports and waterways. Any offshore port obviously must weigh its profitability prospects. The state of Louisiana and the LOOP project have examined these questions. They look to thirty thousand jobs by 1990, plus "an anticipated $6 billion worth of new refineries and other petroleum-related investments."[14]

The Louisiana Offshore Terminal Authority will regulate the complex ashore and the pipeline out to the three-mile limit. Beyond that, the Interstate Comerce Commission will regulate the port, which by law will be a "common carrier open to all."[15] Having accepted the license from the Secretary of Transportation, LOOP next must submit the final design and operating procedures for the port to the Coast Guard. The Coast Guard has played a very proactive and innovative role in the challenge of deepwater ports.

ANTICIPATING THE OUTER CONTINENTAL SHELF CHALLENGE

In the 1970s events changed rapidly on the outer continental shelf (OCS). These changes are a second example of challenges facing the Coast Guard during the 1980s. In the spring of 1976 the Office of the Chief of Staff was advised by the congressional liaison staff and the Office of Merchant Marine Safety that new legislation might well be passed affecting OCS operations. The Coast Guard already provided the nation many services in this area. To be proactive and innovative again, the structure had to anticipate the scope and nature of services needed on the OCS.

The first offshore well was drilled in 1947, some ten miles from land. From this start, the offshore industry developed rapidly worldwide. In the United States, offshore drilling expanded from the Gulf of Mexico to California, then to Alaska. The drilling in Prudhoe Bay, Alaska, led to the development of the North Slope and subsequently to the construction of the Trans-Alaska Pipeline (TAPS). The Alaskan fields could deliver an oil flow of approximately one-third the quantity of petroleum the United States imported, depending on the level imports reached.[16]

One economist estimated that expanded OCS operations off the East and West coasts could yield up to four million barrels a day, a flow rate greater than TAPS. The East and West coast OCS operation could yield the government a total of 200 billion dollars above environmental and extraction costs. One may recall the long battle over the TAPS environmental impact statement, subsequent court challenges and defeat of TAPS, and finally congressional action sanctioning TAPS. Environmental groups are not proponents of OCS development, either. They remember, as does the general public, the Santa Barbara well blowout of 1969. These groups exerted enough pressure through the 1970s to slow offshore development.

The Outer Continental Shelf Lands Act of 1953 gave the Coast Guard authority to regulate fixed structures on the shelf. Under this authority, the Coast Guard has issued regulations covering certain inspections, construction, and arrangement, lifesaving and fire-fighting equipment, operations, and safety zones. The Deepwater Port Act of 1974 and the Federal Water Pollution Control Act amendments of 1972 have also had an effect on offshore structures.[17]

The commandant discussed the possibility of OCS Lands Act amendments with the chief of staff. The chief of the Office of Merchant Marine Safety was asked to develop the immediate tactics necessary if the Coast Guard were assigned more duties. The Merchant Marine Safety planning staff developed a thorough analysis, including alternate scenarios, with implications in each case. A study done earlier by the Plans Evaluation Division of the Office of the Chief of Staff provided a good background. The new analysis defined the problem, reviewed the present regulatory regime and actions under existing authority, evaluated new legislative possibilities, then hypothesized probable tasks required under new legislation. The analysis finally examined the impact of the new tasks on the human and physical resources of the Coast Guard, both at headquarters and in the district and field organization.[18]

No new OCS legislation was passed by the Ninety-fourth Congress. The study group from Merchant Marine Safety, however, became so convinced of the magnitude of change coming on the OCS that they strongly advocated formal Coast Guard planning in this area, much as had been done for deepwater ports. They pointed out the key position of the OCS in President Carter's energy policy and the work already done by the Congress over three years of hearings. Oil and gas development and coastal zone management had been central items in the National Ocean Policy Study, and congressional action in this area could come any year.[19]

Merchant Marine Safety wanted the Coast Guard, externally, to anticipate and help shape policy in this area and, internally, to identify and make ready the human and physical resources necessary to carry out the needs of the nation as they developed. As had often happened in the past, the Commercial Vessel Safety program was moving into an expanded and, in some aspects, new jurisdictional area brought about by a changing economic, social, political, and technological environment. Now more than before the structure was trying to anticipate the national need, align the technical means, and effectively manage the change it brought.

TABLE 29
Tanker Accidents in or near United States Waters, December 1976 to February 1977

Date	Tanker	Registry	Cause of accident	Result of accident
11/15/76	*Argo Merchant*	Liberia	Grounding off Nantucket	7.6 million gallons of oil spilled
12/17/76	*Sunsinea*	Liberia	Explosion in Los Angeles harbor	9 deaths, 50 injuries
12/24/76	*Oswego Peace*	Liberia	Grounding in Thames River, Conn.	2,000 gallons of oil spilled
12/27/76	*Olympic Games*	Liberia	Grounding in Delaware River	134,000 gallons of oil spilled
12/29/76	*Daphne*	Liberia	Grounding in Guayanilla Bay, Puerto Rico	No oil spilled
12/30/76	*Grand Zenith*	Panama	Disappearance in winter storm off Cape Cod, Mass.	Believed sunk with crew of 38 and 8.2 million gallons of oil
1/4/77	*Universe Leader*	Liberia	Grounding in Delaware River	No oil spilled
1/5/77	*Austin*	U.S.	Unloading in San Francisco Bay	2,000 gallons of oil spilled
1/7/77	*Barcola*	Liberia	Grounding off Texas coast	No oil spilled
1/8/77	*Mary Ann*	Liberia	Explosion off Virginia coast during tank cleaning	Vessel disabled
1/10/77	*Chester A. Poling*	U.S.	Breakup during stormy weather near Boston	One crewman lost; no cargo on board
1/18/77	*Irene's Challenger*	Liberia	Breakup near Midway Island	3 million gallons of oil spilled
1/27/77	*Exxon San Francisco*	U.S.	Explosion while loading in Texas	Nearby tugboat sunk, 10 persons injured
2/24/77	*Hawaiian Patriot*	Liberia	Explosion 360 miles west of Hawaii	Sank after leaking 5 million gallons of oil; one crewman killed
2/24/77	*Marine Floridian*	U.S.	Smashing into bridge near Hopewell, Va., after steering mechanism failed	Tanker and bridge damage

Source: Associated Press, Editorial Research Reports, 11 March 1977.

MORE ACTION TO COMBAT OIL POLLUTION

Once more a major incident focused attention on oil pollution of the sea and surrounding shorelines. The distinctive competence and the human, physical, and political resources the Coast Guard had built in the area of marine enviornmental protection would all be called upon. On 15 December 1976 the Liberian tanker *Argo Merchant* ran aground on Fishing Rip, a shoal twenty-seven miles southeast of Nantucket, Massachusetts. Within a week the vessel broke apart, and by Christmas she had spilled her 7.6 million gallons of cargo into the Atlantic. The spectacle of the spill, and the *Argo Merchant's* record of eighteen previous accidents (some of them minor but nevertheless enough to be recorded in Lloyd's List) added to public pressure to combat oil pollution.[20]

Both the executive branch and the Congress sprang into action. In the three months that followed, both branches considered myriad proposals. As they developed proposals and considered the costs and benefits of marine environmental protection, the tanker controversy was reinforced by fourteen more tanker accidents in or near United States waters. Most involved Liberian-flag tankers. Table 29 lists the accidents during the period by country of registry, cause, and result of the accident.

Secretary of Transportation Coleman appointed a special Marine Oil Transportation Task Force soon after the *Argo Merchant* grounding. The task force issued a report on 11 January 1977, ten days before the change in administration, pointing out the dimensions of the problems confronting tankers. Many of the problems already discussed here formed parts of the report. One focus was the difference in appraisal and policy-making toward United States–registered tankers in the domestic market and flag-of-convenience tankers in the international market. For example, the report pointed out the divergent ages and conditions of tankers in the two groups. United States–flag tankers had an average age of more than twenty years, while Liberian-flag tankers averaged slightly over ten years old.[21]

The national need clearly demanded more action to combat oil pollution. Both the Congress and the executive branch searched for a more effective solution to an admittedly complex problem. After his election as president, Jimmy Carter identified the oil pollution problem as a first priority for his transition team preparing to assume leadership of the executive branch. In a press conference early in his administration, President Carter advocated "a stricter standard of ship quality maintained by all nations on an equal basis."[22] The president further emphasized his interest in the issue during his 2 February 1977 address to the nation. He called for "legislation which will reduce the risk of future oil tanker spills and help deal with those that do occur."[23] The Marine Environmental Protection program and the Commercial Vessel Safety program as well were again in the national spotlight, and the issue of marine pollution had returned to the stage of alarmed discovery and euphoric enthusiasm discussed in chapter 2.

A TASK FORCE IN THE EXECUTIVE
BRANCH

President Carter appointed United States Representative Brock Adams, a native of the state of Washington and at the time chairman of the House Budget Committee, secretary of transportation. Soon afterward, both the Department of Transportation and the Coast Guard would play active roles in decision-making in the executive branch.

An Interagency Task Force on Oil Pollution was established under the leadership of OMB, representing eleven departments and agencies. Included were State, Treasury, Defense, Justice, Interior, Commerce, and Transportation, along with the Federal Maritime Commission, the Environmental Protection Agency, the Federal Energy Administration, and the Council on Environmental Quality. A searching appraisal of the tanker business ensued.* The task force was to make short- and long-term efforts to develop a comprehensive package to combat accidental oil spills and reduce operational discharges.[24]

Initially the Interagency Task Force developed some sixty proposals, which were circulated through the responsible agencies and executive office staff for their input. The working papers were divided into six subjects: ships and ship systems; crew standards and training; oil pollution liability and compensation; international conventions; oil spill response; and a two-hundred-mile pollution zone.[25] The Coast Guard and the parent Department of Transportation had experience in all these areas. They stressed to the task force both the complexity and the international nature of the problems.

The Coast Guard and DOT were aware of strong feelings that international efforts had not been effective. They also realized that many felt unilateral action was the only viable alternative remaining to answer the national need for marine environmental protection. The Coast Guard was particularly concerned, however, with the possible effect of unilateral action on the agreements of past conventions—such as the 1960 and 1974 Safety of Life at Sea conventions and the 1973 International Convention for the Prevention of Pollution from Ships. The Coast Guard also was concerned that unilateral action might preclude possible advances during the IMCO Conference on Watchstanding and Training scheduled for 1978. The Coast Guard knew human error was a vital issue in tanker accidents at sea.[26]

The issues surrounding the tanker business are international and involve economic and political considerations as well as social and technological ones. The postwar trading partners of the United States, most of whom are NATO allies, plus Japan, are signatories to existing maritime treaties. If the United

---

*The Interagency Task Force was able to give the complexities of the tanker-safety issues higher-level attention across the executive branch than the Coast Guard ever could as a single agency. A highly visible ''accident'' had again highlighted the issue and brought action in the executive branch and soon would bring dramatic hearings in the Congress.

States imports nine MBD, this figure is more than one-third of the twenty-two MBD imported by the nineteen oil-importing nations who are members of the International Energy Agency. Any unilateral action by the United States not only would go against past IMCO agreements and preclude future agreement, but could also have repercussions in trade and other areas. For example, would trade retaliation occur? Would the international solutions the United States was proposing before the Law of the Sea Conference be affected? How could international solutions be proposed in one area while unilateral action was being taken in a related area?

HEARINGS IN THE CONGRESS

Senators Warren Magnuson, chairman of the Commerce Committee, and Ernest Hollings, head of the Ocean Policy Study, called for hearings before the Commerce Committee. Two days of hearings on Recent Tanker Accidents began on 11 January 1977. Opening statements were made by the chairman, Senator Magnuson, and by Senators Russell Long of Louisiana, Ted Stevens of Alaska, Ernest Hollings of South Carolina, and Harrison Schmitt of New Mexico.[27] On the first day, testimony was taken from Robert Blackwell of the Maritime Administration; Senator Edward Brooke of Massachusetts; Ambassador T. Vincent Learson, head of the Law of the Sea delegation; Russell E. Train, administrator of the Environmental Protection Agency; and Secretary of Transportation William T. Coleman, Jr.[28]

By the end of the second and final day—12 January—almost all of the major actors discussed in this and the preceding two chapters had been called on to testify, and many of the arguments already discussed had been heard. Among those called were Paul Hall, president of the Maritime Trades Department of the AFL–CIO and of the Seafarers International Union of North America, and Jesse Calhoun, president of the National Marine Engineers' Beneficial Association. Both union presidents were very influential in Washington. In a letter, Hall told the committee:

Obviously, Mr. Chairman, the mere use of United States–flag ships will not eliminate the risk of future pollution accidents. But an oil transportation system involving U.S.-flag ships will mean that, for the first time, the United States will have a larger measure of control and influence over the carriage of oil, thereby minimizing environmental risks.[29]

In his testimony Paul Hall pointed out:

Most of the foreign-flag vessels involved in our oil import trade are American-owned, flag-of-convenience ships. Their owners, principally the major American oil companies, register these vessels under the Liberian, Panamanian, or other such flags in order to escape American taxes, American labor, and American safety standards and requirements.[30]

He went on to press for legislation to require that more of the oil coming to the United States be carried in United States–flag tankers:

Congress has, in fact, recognized and attempted to provide a measure of protection against this situation through its passage, as you have indicated . . . of the Energy Transportation Security Act of 1974. This legislation ultimately would have reserved the carriage of up to 30 percent of America's oil imports for U.S.–flag vessels.[31]

The Energy Transportation Security Act of 1974 had been vetoed by President Ford, who spoke of its cost to the nation. The issues of economy and the environment, with all their political and social overtones, were again at center stage at the hearings.

Paul Hall went on to call for more vigorous enforcement by the Coast Guard of the Ports and Waterways Safety Act of 1972. Hall was much kinder to the Coast Guard, however, than Jesse Calhoun, president of the National Marine Engineers' Beneficial Association.* Calhoun lambasted the experience of the Coast Guard in marine transport, specifically stating that this experience had been in decline ever since the agency took over the Bureau of Marine Inspection and Navigation in 1946.

By this point in history, most of the old merchant marine people in the Bureau of Marine Inspection and Navigation and those hired by the Coast Guard in late 1940's or early 1950's are retired or right on the edge of retirement, and even those people were dealing in 14,000 or 16,000 ton tankers. They have, to my knowledge, nobody with experience on the large modern tankers.[32]

This comment, like others in similar hearings such as the 1947 Hearing that brought about the Ebasco Report, must have hurt Coast Guard pride and identity. It cut to the heart of the multimission concept and the strategy the Coast Guard had followed since Rear Admiral Waesche's first plan for acquisition of the Bureau of Marine Inspection and Navigation in 1936.

The distinctive competence the Coast Guard felt it had built in marine safety, and the human, physical, and political resources the agency had acquired over the years, did receive the advocacy before the Commerce Committee that the Coast Guard felt they deserved. It was not by coincidence that the man the

---

*In his testimony, Calhoun went into some detail on the owners of various Liberian-flag tankers. Although he admitted that ownership was hard to trace, Calhoun stated that some years before the explosion in Los Angeles harbor, the *Sunsinea* was at least partially owned by Peter Flanigan, who in the early 1970s was on the White House staff. See U.S., Congress, Senate, Committee on Commerce, *Hearings on Recent Tanker Accidents*, Part 1, serial no. 95-4, 95th Cong., 1st sess., 11, 12 January 1977, pp. 1–9.

The ownership of the *Torrey Canyon* and the *Lake Palourde*, both sister ships of the *Sunsinea*, was discussed in chapter 8. Barracuda Tanker Corporation, the firm owning *Torrey Canyon*, had been organized by a group associated with the New York banking firm of Dillon Reed. Peter Flanigan was an officer of Dillon Reed, and Douglas Dillon, Secretary of Treasury during the Kennedy administration, was a senior partner. For more detail see Morton Mintz and Jerry S. Cohen, *America, Inc.* (New York: Dell, 1971), pp. 234–35, 246–49.

Coast Guard called on to answer these charges was the chief of the Office of Marine Safety, Rear Admiral W. M. Benkert. It was also not a coincidence that his entire career, from the Coast Guard Academy to his current assignment, was a product of the Coast Guard's program of human-resource development.

Senator Hollings. I will get to the segregated ballast question in detail. But Admiral Benkert, can you give us some of your comments with respect to the competence of the USCG to actually promulgate safety regulations for tankers?

Rear Admiral Benkert. Yes, sir. I would be delighted, Senator. I have been associated for a number of years with our marine safety function in the USCG. When I haven't been at sea in the USCG, aboard ships, I have been involved directly with our marine safety programs.

I have working with me, sir, in our field offices and here in Washington, a large number of dedicated USCG and civilian personnel who are highly qualified, highly competent and, I might add, highly acquainted with the merchant marine, with the ships that operate in the merchant marine and with the personnel that operate our merchant vessels.

Senator Hollings. And that includes oil tankers.

Rear Admiral Benkert. Yes sir, including oil tankers. We have a number of officers in the USCG who are licensed officers of the merchant marine, and as Mr. Calhoun rightly said, we don't have 50 percent but we were not required by law to have 50 percent.

An agreement was made when the BMIN came into the USCG, in 1946, that the USCG would attempt to develop this type of percentage of our personnel with distinct merchant marine experience.

A law was passed, giving us the authority, setting up the ground rules for taking in this type of personnel into our business. We have recruited people under this, to the best of our ability.

We have a large number of officers. I don't have the number at my fingertips, but I have about a dozen of them working for me here right in Washington who are licensed merchant marine officers, a number of whom have sailed on tankers and who, in fact, are very well acquainted with this business.

Although I personally have not sailed in the merchant marine and I am not a licensed officer of the merchant marine, I have had a very wide association with the ships and the people. I have inspected ships, I have ridden ships, I have boarded ships both here and in foreign countries. I have working for me naval architects who are the equal of any naval architects in the country or any other country, and anybody that tells me that we do not have qualified people to handle this kind of problem, sir, I discount what they say entirely [33]

Rear Admiral Benkert's training and experience, discussed in chapter 9, lent weight to his answers.*

The Coast Guard, however, did not emerge from the 1977 hearings on

---

*Rear Admiral W. M. Benkert was even more direct in explaining the Coast Guard's role in marine safety to a nationally televised press conference shortly after the *Argo Merchant* broke apart off Nantucket. One reporter asked the admiral, who had been at sea for many years, what the Coast Guard was doing about marine pollution. In the pithy style of a mariner, Benkert said in exasperation, "We haven't been sitting on our asses!"

tanker accidents before the Senate Commerce Committee completely unscathed. One writer, in summing up the hearings, pointed out that some senators charged the Coast Guard with laxness "in enforcing regulations to ensure that incoming tankers are in good condition and manned by competent crews."[34] Some even claimed the Coast Guard "caved in to pressure from U.S.-owned multinational oil companies."[35] The Coast Guard denied these charges, but their very nature pointed out again the complexity of the underlying issues.

Oil spills were one of the issues discussed during hearings before the House Appropriations Subcommittee considering the Coast Guard appropriation for 1978. On 2 February 1977, Representative John McFall of California, chairman of the subcommittee, questioned Admiral Owen Siler, commandant of the Coast Guard, on regulations the Coast Guard had just released placing additional navigational requirements on tankers. Admiral Siler described the new regulations:

[They] have to do with the equipment that must be on the bridge of a vessel operating in the waters of the United States. They are things such as up-to-date charts, operating fathometers, operating radars, and to us they are commonsense type navigation regulations.

I think there are other things that can be done along this line. . . . I have a list here of the steps we are taking.

We are issuing some additional pilotage regulations.

We are revising the regulations that have to do with tanker men on inland vessels in particular.

We are revising the licenses that are necessary for a vessel to operate [as] a tank vessel.

The other regulations we have issued is the first step in requiring Loran-C on all vessels operating in the United States.

We have an item in this year's budget to put one more station into commission in the Great Lakes. In the past year we were funded for a Loran-C chain in the Gulf of Mexico area and it is only logical, it seems to me, that we would require that these vessels have this precise method of navigation when they come into our waters. If the *Argo Merchant,* for example, had used Loran-C, he certainly would not have been where he was.

Another regulation we plan to issue in the very near future is one to require collision avoidance radar as it is generally known. This is a device attached to a radar and gives an indication by some automatic plotting of whether a vessel in open water is going to pose a threat to your own vessel. This is not too helpful in port areas, but it should prevent collisions if properly used in the open oceans. It is simply a matter of avoiding the plotting on the bridge. If a proper number of people are on the bridge in the more restricted areas collision avoidance radar is not that much helpful.[36]

Other questions probed the value of Loran-C as a navigational device for tankers. The appropriations subcommittee agreed that it would be a very helpful all-weather navigational aid. Admiral Siler pointed out that the cost of $2,500 to $4,000 per ship "is a very low cost for the precision they will be getting."[37] The issue of crew qualifications was raised. Rear Admiral Benkert discussed this issue:

I do feel . . . 85 percent of our casualties that occur . . . are the result of some kind of human error, or a human misjudgment or lack of judgment, if you will, and this is the area . . . in our budget here that we are pursuing rather thoroughly, both on an international and on a national basis looking toward a greater training of personnel, a greater qualification and updating of personnel across the board.[38]

The attention tanker safety received in the Congress had international as well as domestic effect. The Liberian Shipping Council, an organization of sixty-two United States and foreign companies that own Liberian-registered ships, for example, created a task force of their own to "crack down" on safety requirements for tankers registered in Liberia.[39]

A PRESIDENTIAL MESSAGE TO THE CONGRESS

As testimony continued in the Congress, the Interagency Task Force on Oil Pollution completed its work and reported to the president. On 17 March 1977 President Carter sent a message to the Congress containing the recommendations of the executive branch to deal with the problem of marine oil pollution caused by oil tankers. The proposals covered six specific areas:

1. The President called for Senate ratification of the 1973 International Convention for the Prevention of Pollution from Ships.
2. The President directed the Secretary of Transportation to issue within 60 days proposed rules for ship construction and equipment standards.
3. The President ordered several actions to improve the qualifications of crews that man oil tankers entering U.S. ports. The President ordered the Departments of Transportation and Commerce to review the agenda for the 1978 Conference on Standards of Watchkeeping and Training.
4. The President directed that, starting immediately, each foreign flag tanker which enters U.S. ports will be boarded by the Coast Guard and examined to insure that the ship meets all safety and environmental protection regulations. Tankers will be boarded at least once a year and more often if necessary.

   The President directed that information gathered from the boarding program be fed into a U.S. Marine Safety Information System, which will be established to keep track of the accident and pollution records of all ships, U.S. and foreign, entering U.S. ports. Coast Guard information systems already contain some of this information for U.S. vessels. Since 94 percent of our imported oil enters the country in foreign tankers, it is important that information on these vessels also be available to Captains of the Port at all major U.S. ports. The President also directed that the proper Federal agencies initiate action to require that the names of tanker owners, major stock holders, and changes in vessel names be disclosed and be made available for inclusion in the Marine Safety Information System. This system will enable the Coast Guard to promptly identify tankers which have long histories of poor maintenance, pollution violations and accidents. Once identified, such tankers can be excluded from U.S. ports, if necessary.

5. The President called on the Secretary of Transportation to submit to Congress on the President's behalf the Comprehensive Oil Pollution Liability and Compensation Act of 1977, which replaces the current fragmented and overlapping systems of Federal and State oil spill liability laws and compensation funds with a single national framework.

6. The President directed the Coast Guard, the Environmental Protection Agency, and other responsible Federal agencies to begin plans for upgrading their capability to respond to, contain and mitigate the damaging effects of oil spills in cooperation with state and local governments.[40]

The president also directed the secretary of transportation, in cooperation with the Environmental Protection Agency and other appropriate agencies, to undertake several studies of other promising programs and techniques for reducing marine oil pollution. These studies included:

1. An evaluation of the costs and benefits of crude washing, a system that utilizes crude oil to clean cargo tanks.

2. An evaluation of design, construction and equipment standards for tank barges that carry oil.

3. A study of long-range vessel surveillance and control systems.

4. An evaluation of devices to improve maneuvering and stopping ability of large tankers, with research to include the use of a ship simulator.

5. A study of the fee-collection mechanism for the comprehensive oil pollution fund.[41]

The Tanker and Vessel Safety Act of 1977 was one of the bills considered by the Senate and the House.[42] It would establish airportlike approach patterns to ports and waterways, set crew training and licensing procedures, require the latest navigational equipment, allow for surprise tanker inspections, demand full disclosure of tanker ownership, and authorize the Coast Guard to turn away from United States waters any vessel not in compliance with high safety standards. It would also establish a two-hundred-mile pollution control zone. The reasoning behind this and similar legislative proposals was that, if airplanes could be tracked at thirty-five thousand feet, tankers could also be guided from remote distances and kept on safe courses. The basic rule of thumb of the legislation was that a ship would be barred from United States ports unless it met prearranged standards.*

---

*One excellent summary of the diplomatic arguments for and against barring a tanker from a United States port is presented in Thomas Oliphant, "We've Seen It All Before," *Boston Sunday Globe,* 16 January 1977, p. 47. This article touches on the issue of tankers entering Puget Sound laden with oil from the Alaskan pipeline, and the stands taken by Senator Magnuson of Washington and Governor Hammond of Alaska. The article states that "there are many steps that can be taken to regulate and police tanker traffic of whatever flag." It goes on to point out that it is important "that a ship doesn't get into an American port unless it meets certain standards."

COAST GUARD ACTION TO COMBAT
OIL POLLUTION

The commandant, Admiral Owen Siler, worked with his chief of staff, Rear Admiral Robert Scarborough, and his chiefs of the offices of Marine Safety and Marine Environment and Systems, Rear Admirals W. M. Benkert and Anthony Fugaro. They prepared position papers for the Interagency Task Force on Oil Pollution and made recommendations for the presidential message to Congress on marine pollution. Many other Coast Guardsmen at each of the four levels discussed in chapter 3 were involved. Among them were the DOT representatives to the OMB Task Force Working Groups: Conventions, Captain Hallberg; Ships and Ship Systems, Mr. Lakey; Compensation and Liability, Captain Bridgeman; National Response, Captain Schubert; and Crew Standards, Captain Emory.

The planning staffs of the office of Marine Safety and the office of Marine Environment and Systems had to develop the resource requirements necessary for the Coast Guard to implement the presidential initiatives contained in the message to Congress. They worked with the Programs Division in much the manner described in chapters 3 and 4.[43] They had to determine resource needs of both headquarters and the field organizations. The recently created Marine Safety Offices, along with the older OCMI, COTP, and Group organizations discussed in Chapter 9, provided a necessary framework to implement the presidential initiatives. The multimission structure provided a mechanism to add resources incrementally.

A challenge again came in identifying the increments that could be reallocated internally and those that would be sought through the budgetary process. The task of contributing to the presidential initiatives and determining how they would be implemented fell to the planning and resource allocation processes of the Coast Guard. As the Coast Guard waited for new legislation and resources, it again sought to answer the national need it saw emerging by reallocating resources internally, in a fashion like that described by the model of figure 6.

In fact, developing a marine environmental protection program had been an incremental process for the Coast Guard. Change came slowly.[44] The complexities of the tanker business and the international ramifications slowed any innovation in environmental protection. Rear Admiral Benkert described clearly the dilemma presented by the dichotomy in regulating United States- and foreign-flag ships: "We can regulate [United States-flag ships] and control them in most any manner we want to, sensibly of course, but it can be done essentially without international complications. But when you start talking about tankships you must talk of foreign-flag vessels because those are the vessels that are importing our oil."[45]

All of the economic, social, political, and technological considerations discussed in chapter 2 were involved in developing the program. Social and political pressures in the United States demanded an end to marine oil pollution. The public policy process had developed several laws, beginning with the National Environmental Policy Act of 1969, mandating that the executive branch become more concerned with the quality of the environment. In May 1977 Rear Admiral Benkert described Coast Guard action to combat oil pollution:

About 6 or 7 years ago the growing emphasis on environmental concerns within our country resulted in a number of important pieces of legislation, the major ones being the Federal Water Pollution Control Acts of 1970 and 1972 and the Ports and Waterways Safety Act of 1972. These placed a great deal of responsibility on the Coast Guard for an environmental appraisal of the carriage of inflammable, combustible, and hazardous liquids. What has evolved since then is an overlapping approach to all aspects of this type of marine transportation. We look at it both from a safety and an environmental appraisal point of view. We really have had to come to grips with this interface between environmental concerns and safety.[46]

That economic and environmental pressures often counterbalanced one another was another reason change was not rapid in the area of marine environmental protection. Technology also had to be considered. Rear Admiral Benkert again pointed out the tradeoffs:

There is another part of the problem which often gets lost in the shuffle. . . . We have been charged in the Ports and Waterways Safety Act with looking at the economic impact of our regulations in this field—regulatory action in connection with the whole picture. I need to stress that point. You can build a very safe tanker, and from an environmental impact point of view, a very good one, carrying right in its middle, very well protected, just *one* barrel of oil. But as you know other considerations enter the picture, namely economic and technological feasibility.[47]

The Marine Environmental Protection program, developed after the formal establishment in 1971 of the Office of Marine Environment and Systems and the new Marine Environmental Protection Division, came a long way when looked at with the perspective of the seven years that passed before the tanker spills of the winter of 1976–77. The program had many successes and some failures. The successes were largely in spills prevented and in effective spill responses. Where spills were prevented, no publicity was gained. Failures, however, were immediately known to the public when a Coast Guard lieutenant or petty officer in the decentralized field organization announced a spill and the problems in responding to it. The problems generally came from the large, spectacular spills, but the program to prevent smaller spills was, on balance, very successful.[48]

One way to illustrate a success of prevention is by an event such as the trouble-free arrival of the *Arco Juneau* in the summer of 1977 at a refinery near Cherry Point, Washington. This large tanker unloaded the first cargo of oil brought from the Alaskan pipeline outlet at Valdez, Alaska.[49] When the *Arco Juneau* made this maiden voyage, Coast Guard Marine Safety offices and Vessel Traffic Systems at both ends of the voyage were in place and operational.

The Loran-C stations necessary to provide accurate navigational coverage for the Gulf of Alaska, the inland passage, and the entire West Coast were "on the air," providing precise navigational signals to the navigators of *Arco Juneau*. Significant lead times were necessary to provide all these services, and the Coast Guard was ready when the pipeline opened. This example, however, depicts a domestic route, with United States-flag tankers and primarily United States shoreline services. (One Loran-C transmitting station is on Canadian soil.) If the oil instead had come across the ocean in a foreign-flag tanker, the prevention problem would have taken on a new dimension.

An illustration of success in the complex international tanker market is the conclusion of an international agreement in February 1978. Alan Butchman, deputy secretary of transportation and head of the United States negotiating team, announced the agreements that had been reached at the long-awaited 1978 IMCO conference. Basically, the conference placed the weight of the 106-nation IMCO body behind many of the tanker-safety rules advocated the year before by the Coast Guard. Indeed, many of these items had passed the Senate in 1977 in the federal Tanker and Vessel Safety Act. The controversial "double-bottom" requirement was missing from the tanker-safety package negotiated at the IMCO conference. A Senate maritime expert stated that "Congress isn't likely to push this provision, however, as the new treaties represent considerable tanker-safety progress."[50]

The provisions of the 1978 conference went a long way toward solving many of the complexities inherent in regulating an international market. They certainly were another large increment in the lengthy process of improving tanker safety and minimizing pollution. Yet the agreements reached at the conference are in effect a treaty and as such require ratification by the Senate. In the meantime, the Coast Guard proposed new regulations for tankers entering United States waters that will require enforcement of the provisions of the 1978 IMCO conference. Still further efforts should expand the safety and law enforcement responsibilities of the Coast Guard in the 1980s.

Many individuals within the Coast Guard involved with developing the Marine Environmental Protection program thus were both proactive and innovative in anticipating the needs of the public, even though complications arose. The program was well defined by its champions in the early years. Impetus was provided by many individuals, and the roles of some of them have been discussed. Most of those providing impetus—as in the case of loran—came from the second and third levels of Coast Guard structure.

As the years passed, definition became better, as the Coast Guard gained experience with the new program. The program champions of the early years of MEP gradually gave way to a larger-scale, more institutionalized program development effort. The program champions would not have been able to achieve the success they did, however, without the distinctive competence and resources available within the Coast Guard structure. One of the main battles of the champions was to win the use of these resources for the new program.

IV A THEORY OF DIFFERENCE

11 PUBLIC MANAGEMENT AND THE COAST GUARD

THE FINDINGS

This book provides a detailed case study of the process of managing one federal agency, the United States Coast Guard. In chapter 1 six commonly heard categorical charges were presented that challenge the efficiency and effectiveness of the general management processes used by public agencies. Three research questions were suggested to probe any theoretical implications of this detailed case study. By now one probably has formed some opinions about the validity of the categorical charges and arrived at some answers for the research questions.

ANSWERS TO THE SIX CATEGORICAL CHARGES

The first charge held that government organizations are good at adding new programs but poor at cutting them back or dropping them—that they are good initiators but poor liquidators. The strategy and structure of the Coast Guard and the diversification and acquisition patterns that developed—as pointed out in table 1 and Appendix 1 and discussed in chapter 3—cast doubt on the validity of this charge. The Coast Guard has not historically been reluctant to adapt its structure or shift its resources as national needs dictate.

Revenue collection, the agency's original program, gave way to protection, rescue, and other duties as time passed and national needs arose. Both the dual-role strategy and the multimission concept made this flexibility possible. The growth, decline, and elimination of the Ocean Station program provides a specific modern-day example of both the initiation and the liquidation of a program.

The development of the loran system and the Marine Environmental Protection program provide "longitudinal" case studies. The study of loran describes the shift in technology and approach in the aids-to-navigation area, from radiodirection finders to Loran-A, then to Loran-C. The study of marine environmental protection describes the changing interests of the Coast Guard in the areas of prevention of, and protection from, disasters in the marine environment. Both cases include many instances of the Coast Guard reallocating resources—or reassigning bureau supply—within the agency.

Many instances of initiation and subsequent liquidation of programs were the result of some important stimulus from the external environment, and the growth and decline of particular programs tended to follow the issue-attention cycle. A declining program, however, often required extra motivation to induce it to give up the resources it claimed, depending on just how flexible the Coast Guard structure was at that point and on the urgency of the stimulus.*

The second charge held that as government organizations grow in size and maturity they replace the client-centered human services characteristic of their early years with impersonal technology, systems, and procedures. Supposedly, as they become more aggregative and less personal, public agencies tend to lose track of the human reality of the people they were formed to serve.

A look at the labor intensity of the Coast Guard—a preponderance of the Coast Guard budget goes for human resources—and the roles played over many years by skilled people certainly casts doubt on the validity of this charge. The closeness of the Coast Guard to the sea and those who use it allows the agency to keep in touch with the people it serves, as is shown by the case studies of both loran and marine environmental protection.

As the Coast Guard changed its roles and missions and even acquired other federal agencies, individuals at many levels of the structure carried out the planning, the allocating, and often the delivery of services. The frequent transfer of Coast Guardsmen between various tasks and locations encouraged this. In fact, in the cases of inefficient performance cited in chapter 3, a failure to rotate staff or attract new people to the programs during the periods considered contributed to the poor showing. Despite new managerial and technological systems, the vital roles of individuals in developing and performing services speak for themselves. The behavior and career development of the Coast Guard leaders discussed emphasize that the agency values human services over managerial and technological systems.

The third charge was that government organizations with regulatory functions are co-opted over time by the very publics they were created to regulate. With only a single demand for their services and the same single source of support, the regulatory agency supposedly shifts to a captive rather than a super-

---

*The concepts of the *issue-attention cycle* and *bureau supply* come from Anthony Downs, "Up and down with Ecology: The 'Issue-Attention Cycle,'" *Public Interest,* no. 28 (summer 1972), pp. 38–50, and from William A. Niskanen, Jr., *Bureaucracy and Representative Government* (Chicago: Aldine, Atherton, 1971).

visory role. But when one examines the Coast Guard's long-term development one does not see much evidence to support this charge.

The varied roles and missions the Coast Guard has acquired provide a great breadth of constituents with diverse and sometimes opposing interests. The development of the Marine Environmental Protection program is an excellent example of this. Environmentalists and shoreline property owners who are eager advocates of this program hold objectives entirely different from those of the marine industry, which is primarily interested in another program of the Coast Guard—Commercial Vessel Safety. It would be very difficult for the Coast Guard as a federal agency to be the captive of such competing public constituencies, at least at the same time.

In practice these opposing pressures provide a dynamic model of the importance of heterogeneity of public support as a prerequisite to freedom of action for any federal agency, as demonstrated in figure 6. This heterogeneity is present in the Coast Guard generally not just in the areas highlighted in the example. The multimission concept tends to bring the Coast Guard political support from many diverse groups, as well as to provide a variety of assignments and applications for its "distinctive competence"—its human, physical, and political resources.*

The fourth charge held that, as they grow, government organizations become increasingly centralized in Washington, resulting in a lack of flexibility and responsiveness in the field where they deliver their services. The evidence presented in chapters 3 through 10 shows that this simply is not so for the Coast Guard. Although the agency formulates programs and makes strategic decisions in Washington, in most cases the structure implements these programs and makes operational decisions at the district, group, and unit levels. The many missions of the Coast Guard have in themselves precluded any such overcentralization. The Marine Environmental Protection program provides a good example, particularly the battle that developed over the "Marine Safety Office." The effectiveness of every operational unit has been increased by placing operational decision-making at the unit level.†

The fifth charge was that government organizations and their general managers contrive dubious threats to the nation that they claim their weaker programs can relieve or even answer if such weaker programs are strengthened rather than cut back or eliminated. By this very contrivance to justify retaining or expanding programs, federal managers are said to lose credibility with the public. Even the suggestion of this charge inflames opponents of public bureaucracy.

---

*The term *distinctive competence* comes from Philip Selznick, *Leadership in Administration: A Sociological Interpretation* (Evanston, Ill.: Row, Peterson, 1957), pp. 42–64.

†Throughout the development of the Coast Guard the structure has experienced periods of centralization and decentralization. The leadership style of a commandant and those with whom he interacts influences the degree of centralization, and the structure also develops its own patterns of centralized and decentralized operation to fit the climate and environment.

One can find numerous examples of this, with a long list of causal factors. The effect of the leader on the organization will be discussed in greater detail at the end of this chapter.

Elements of proof of this charge can be found in each of the instances of inefficient Coast Guard behavior described in chapter 3. Again, the case of the Ocean Station program applies. The two air-sea rescues that took place in 1947 and 1956 were real, even though the need for the cutters on ocean station duty clearly was decreasing over this period. The spectacle of an ocean crash by a commercial airliner, however, was sufficient threat—even though dubious—to keep the cutters on patrol longer than they all were needed. In the process, more large cutters were retained. The case of the Life Saving stations in the 1920s and 1930s also applies, for similar reasons. On the opposite side of the ledger, the threats in the loran and marine environmental protection areas were also real. Judgment on this charge should be reserved until the sixth charge is examined, because there is a definite relationship between these two charges.

The final charge, and probably the most serious, stated that government organizations lack the stimulus to effectiveness, efficiency, and innovation that is provided in the private sector by the market mechanism and by competition. This charge is predicated on the popular assumption that there is no public-sector analogue to the market mechanism and competition. If this charge is true, general managers in federal agencies have no motivation to search for efficiency and effectiveness or to innovate, and their agencies thus are doomed to decreasing efficiency.

This charge not only is related to the previous charge but is also the negative statement of the first research question, which will be discussed shortly. Examples in chapters 5 through 10 tend to refute this charge and at the same time to provide answers for the research questions. Many Coast Guard general managers have appeared to be highly aware of the stimuli for innovation and of how they have affected the development of the agency. In fact, they have displayed a keen sense of agency history.* In particular, they have been aware of certain threats to the existence of the Coast Guard, such as:

1. fiscal starvation, brought about in the budgetary process by the lack of capital, or operating funds, or both;
2. partial takeover, brought about by the acquisition of one or more Coast Guard programs or functions by another agency;
3. liquidation of the agency, brought about by the acquisition of all programs and functions and takeover of Coast Guard human and physical resources by another agency.

---

*Of many histories of the Coast Guard, the best was written by a Coast Guard officer who rose to the rank of rear admiral. See Stephen H. Evans, *The United States Coast Guard 1790–1915: A Definitive History* (Annapolis, Md.: United States Naval Institute, 1949).

Many early leaders of the Coast Guard undoubtedly heard the story of the birth and growth of their organization from their friends as well as learning its operating principles from painful experience. Evans and Captain Albert A. Lawrence made this learning process more formal in 1938 when they compiled a text, *The History and Organization of the United States Coast Guard,* for the use of cadets at the Coast Guard Academy. Their timing was fortunate, for the Coast Guard was about to expand at a rate unprecedented in its history.

Each of these threats has been experienced several times in the 190-year history of the Coast Guard. The threats to the flow of human and physical resources, the struggles to maintain programs that the Coast Guard could carry out better than anyone else, and the takeover threats from the navy provide rich examples of such a stimulus. The existence of these threats has provided strong motivation for the Coast Guard to adapt its operations and to change with the times, since credibility as a federal agency has been integral to its ability to deal effectively with them. To the extent that these threats are a stimulus for effectiveness, efficiency, and innovation, then this sixth charge is not valid, at least for the Coast Guard.

In examining the fifth and sixth categorical charges together, one soon realizes the subtle relationship between two views of the behavior of the managers of a federal agency—the bureaucrats, to use another term. If the managers see and respond to a threat, are they displaying effective, efficient, and innovative behavior? In the sense of the work discussed in chapter 1, are they displaying proactive behavior? Or are these bureaucrats simply creating dubious threats to justify retaining or expanding programs? Possibly the answer to these two views lies in the perceptions of the observer. At the very least, however, one realizes that one cannot have it both ways at the same time. One cannot urge the managers to be proactive, then term their behavior bureaucratic empire-building—or, even worse, tell them not to be aggressive, then chide them for not being proactive. Are such charges themselves credible?

When one considers these threats to a federal agency one may think, "This is true *but*...." In the next chapter, the part these threats play in making the Coast Guard a successful federal agency is discussed in the context of a theory of difference between public and private management. One may say, however, that at best we can apply such a theory only to the Coast Guard. And, since the Coast Guard is a successful federal agency, what does it matter?

Chapter 1 developed a rationale for presenting a detailed case study of one federal agency—the Coast Guard—with certain interesting implications. It is true that the arguments against the six categorical charges and for the theory of difference that are developed by the three research questions are more valid for successful agencies than for unsuccessful agencies. In great part this is because the existence of threats—the stimulus—has helped, or forced, the federal agency to be both proactive and innovative. Such behavior at least partially counters the threats and renders the agency successful. I submit that, on balance, the evidence presented so far disproves all six charges in regard to the Coast Guard.

ANSWERS TO THE THREE RESEARCH QUESTIONS

I stated earlier that the final charge against government organizations is really the inverse of the first research question. By now one should have a good idea of the answers to the three research questions posed in chapter 1. The first question asked, "Is there a mechanism analogous to the market that stimulates innovation in the public sector?" The evidence in part 3 strongly suggests that there is such an analogous stimulus in the Coast Guard—an effective threat to the existence of the agency. As such, any threat can serve as the motivating force in the simple models of figures 1 and 2. At the same time, a threat may appear in figure 6 as one of the environmental forces that is an input to agency structure.

A threat may appear on three distinct levels, each more severe than the preceding level in a hierarchy of threats. The nature of each form of threat has already been discussed, and a general theory of the role of the threats will be presented in the next chapter. The threats are, in order of increasing magnitude: the threat of fiscal starvation, the threat of partial takeover, and the threat of involuntary liquidation. The events described at the beginning of chapter 3 and listed in table 2 posed many threats to the Coast Guard. These events include the Senate Commerce Committee hearings of the 1840s, the 1847 disbanding of "headquarters," the pressures to "join" the navy in the late 1800s, the Cleveland commission hearings in 1912, the Roosevelt initiatives of 1920, and the House appropriations hearings of 1946 and 1957. The threats of each of these periods provide examples of motivation for the Coast Guard to be proactive and innovative.

These threats can also be observed in the case studies of part 3. How did Captain Lawrence Harding feel about the navy's taking over the loran system he developed in the early days of World War II? He integrated the system into the matrix of Coast Guard human, physical, and political resources and at the same time saw to it that superior services were provided to the users of loran.

How did Harding and Loren Brunner react to the cutback in skilled technicians and funding in 1946? They argued for extensive training at the RCA Institute for qualified enlisted men. A school of this nature was an innovation at the time and served not only to provide the necessary technicians but also to induce them to pursue careers with the Coast Guard after their initial enlistments were over.

Harding and Brunner also had to provide both "definition" and "impetus" for the postwar Radionavigation Aids program.* One requirement for doing this was winning a preponderant share of the capital funds the Coast Guard received during the difficult 1947 and 1948 budget requests. They worked with Captain Alfred Richmond, who later became commandant, to gain the funding needed for loran to survive the immediate postwar period.

How did Harding and Brunner react to the competition of Decca, which threatened to replace loran? They saw to it that loran service was made more extensive and more reliable for all its users. Both Harding and Brunner became

---

*The terms *definition* and *impetus* come from Joseph L. Bower, *Managing the Resource Allocation Process* (Boston: Division of Research, Harvard Business School, 1970), pp. 66–71, 321–22.

"champions" of loran, fending off a series of very real threats.* Brunner and Pearson followed this same pattern when they became champions during a new series of challenges to the loran system in the late 1950s and early 1960s.

Chapter 7 describes funding threats, followed by threats of partial takeover or involuntary liquidation of the loran system—perfect examples of the threats that affect a federal agency but quite different in form from the market mechanism and competition experienced in the private sector. Note that the *manner* in which these public-sector threats manifest themselves also differs from the way threats occur in the private sector.

For example, how did W. M. Benkert and Robert Price feel about public concern for the quality of the marine environment in the first years after the *Torrey Canyon* accident? How did the Coast Guard structure react to these concerns under the leadership of Commandant Willard Smith from 1966 to 1970 and Commandant Chester Bender from 1970 to 1974? Chapters 9 and 10 describe the interactions between external forces and forces within the Coast Guard structure during this period. A new program was necessary for the marine environment, and the question arose of what role government should take and what agency could best provide what programs.

Chapter 10 describes the threats and conflicts that arose after the *Argo Merchant* accident galvanized public concern over the threat of marine pollution. The actions of Rear Admiral Mike Benkert, Rear Admiral Sidney Wallace, and other interested individuals both inside and outside the Coast Guard demonstrate the workings of the agency's general management. The responses described in chapters 9 and 10 were shaped by the pressures of the external and internal environment in the manner shown in figure 6.

The answers these examples provide to the first research question are powerful evidence that the public sector does contain an analogue to the market mechanism of the private sector. That analogue is the three levels of threat to the continued existence of a government organization—a form of organizational Darwinism.

The second research question assumed that such a stimulus does exist for government organization and went on to explore the nature of the subsequent response: "If there is an analogue, what is the set of feasible responses, or options, available in the public situation?"

When simplified, the response of the Coast Guard in each of the threat situations just discussed has been to develop a strategy, and a structure to administer it, to build an organizational character and distinctive competence consistent with the strategy, and to accumulate a store of human, physical, and political resources for carrying out the strategy. The roles of the organization's

*The term *champion* comes from Donald A. Schon, "Champions for Radical New Inventions," *Harvard Business Review* 41, no. 2 (1963):77–86. See also Joel D. Goldhar, Louis K. Bragaw, and Jules J. Schwartz, "Information Flows, Management Styles, and Technological Innovation," *IEEE Transactions on Engineering Management* 23, no. 1 (1976):51–62.

leaders and the champions of various programs are an important part of the response in each example, as are the leaders' personal values. While some leaders have sought to improve organizational performance by internal diversification, others have adopted a strategy of acquisition. The response of each leader was shaped by the pressures of the environment that existed at the time.

For example, consider the specific actions taken by organizational leaders such as Alex Fraser in the 1840s, Leonard Shepard in the 1890s, Ellsworth Bertholf in the 1910s, Frederick Billard in the 1920s, Russell Waesche in the 1930s and 1940s, and Alfred Richmond in the early postwar years. These commandants all were men of their times, and each one helped shape responses that were effective in meeting the challenges he confronted.

These responses, although simplified in this description, constitute the same set of general management responses that are used in the private sector. For example, they include many integral steps such as the dual-role strategy and the multimission concept. Each was developed by itself, then tested and retested. Yet there are important differences. Each step by the Coast Guard is taken in a public environment and therefore is subject to the give-and-take of the public arena.

The third research question assumed that both an analogue and a set of feasible responses exist. It asked, "Given the existence of the stimulus, and given the set of feasible responses, what is the potential for transferring technique from the private to the public situation?" Parts 2 and 3 suggest many transferences of technique between applications made in the private and the public sectors. In both sectors general management revolves around several of the same central issues. They include:

1. How will the economic, social, political, and technological environments change?
2. How will goals and objectives change over the period under consideration?
3. What will the organization be able to do as well as or better than anyone else?
4. What external and internal demands from the present to the future will be closest to what the organization does well?
5. Will the organization be able to clearly define these demands? Will the private organization be able to segment the demands into markets, and the public organization into constituencies?
6. Since competition and the market mechanism are the stimulus for the strategic process in the private sector, it is important that the private organization identify the competition. By the same token, since threats to existence are the stimulus for the strategic process in the public sector, it is important that the public organization identify the threats. Can a public organization accomplish this by the same mechanisms as a private organization?
7. What risks will the organization have to assume?

Analyzing these questions leads one to conclude that the general management process, to be successful, must be anticipatory—both proactive and innovative.

Note also the differences between issues for public and private organizations; the differences involve the institutions and processes of the government environment that are reflected in figure 6.

The following is a summary of the operational elements of general management as defined in a business policy text. Notice how each element appears to be applicable to the management processes of the Coast Guard, particularly those described in chapters 3 and 4:

1. identifying relevant challenges, threats, and opportunities in the environment,
2. setting missions and broad objectives,
3. designing strategic action plans to fulfill these objectives,
4. developing and allocating the financial, human and physical resources to carry out the plans, and
5. monitoring ongoing performance to see that the desired ends are being accomplished and altering the mission, objectives and action plans as appropriate, and
6. structuring the interpersonal and intergroup relationships within the organizations to facilitate accomplishment of the desired future performance levels.[1]

In answer to the third research question, the general congruence of the key issues suggests that there is great potential for transferring technique from the private to the public situation. Many of the techniques I have described were used first in the private sector, then transferred to the government. Conversely, several originated with federal agencies and were transferred to industry, such as the management audit, organizational productivity measures, PPB systems, and procurement management techniques.[2]

My intent, however, is not to present a complete list of transferable techniques, but to assess the potential for such transfer by considering the similarities and differences in general management theory for the two sectors. The differences are far fewer than the similarities.

The important similarities occur in the areas of strategy and structure, management process, and, to some extent, the managerial processes developed by the structure to deal with the challenge of the environment. The important differences concern the environment itself. The environment in which a federal agency functions is far different from that surrounding a private organization.

THE AMBIENCE OF THE
GOVERNMENT ENVIRONMENT

The American democratic process creates a unique environment within which all federal agencies function, with an ambience all its own. Executive proposals or decisions not only must traverse the system of checks and balances but also must be implemented by a bureaucracy. Although this process and environment are well known, they are not well understood.

For example, the president may formulate a plan, and a subordinate may try to implement it, but the plan is still far from being an ultimate decision. This is so because the plan—or proposal, or order, or whatever form the plan may assume—remains just that if it cannot pass the review of the Congress and the judiciary. This same system of checks and balances applies no matter which branch initiates an action.

This description is not intended as an attack on American democracy. Yet, from an efficiency standpoint, the best government would be a benevolent dictatorship. There is no question about this; the trouble is that benevolent dictators do not remain benevolent. And the American government is based on many important values besides efficiency.* Possibly Winston Churchill summed this up best when he remarked that democracy is the worst of systems, except when compared to all the others.

In essence, a private organization is a dictatorship. This may be most easily understood by describing the roles the same man has played as a top executive in industry and in the federal government, then discussing the salient differences between them. For example, one might look at George Humphrey as president of a steel and shipping company. If executives of his company convince Humphrey that a new ore carrier of a certain capacity is necessary, the discussion quickly turns to financing. If either internal or debt financing is arranged, the ship is built and carries ore. If it makes a profit, the company benefits and all share to different extents in the gains. If the ship loses money, President Humphrey has many options, including firing those who advocated the expansion in ore-carrier capacity. Or, his board of directors has the option of firing him. The "bottom line" has an important value both as an objective and as a source of feedback on performance.

In government, the budgetary process for a federal agency is subject to intense scrutiny, but of a different type. The scrutiny comes from inside—much like that in a private organization—and also from outside, involving the executive and legislative branches—which has little similarity.

In the external budgetary process for the Coast Guard, the Department of Transportation, the Office of Management and Budget, and the Congress are all involved. All the constituents of the federal agency have the opportunity to participate formally in the external review stages. (The actions of both advocates and adversaries of the Loran-C system demonstrate this involvement; advocates and adversaries of Loran-C existed both inside and outside the Department of Transportation.)

When George Humphrey became secretary of the treasury in 1953, he found the government ambience quite different from what he had experienced in the private sector. If the Coast Guard convinced Humphrey that a new type of aircraft was necessary and he agreed, the aircraft remained a request—it became

---

*For a discussion of the "cult of efficiency" and why it does not apply to a federal agency, see Harold Seidman, *Politics, Position and Power: The Dynamics of Federal Organization,* 2d ed. (New York: Oxford University Press, 1975), pp. 3–37.

another budget claim sent on to the next level in the budgetary process. An obstreperous official at any stage of the process, or an unanticipated force such as macroeconomic policy, could effectively block the request. The government process and the private process that George Humphrey experienced in these two examples are entirely different. And the difference cuts to the heart of the general management process.

There are also differences in the way federal agencies handle inputs about what jobs they are to do. Often the input is in the form of a statute and takes a long time to change. The experiences of the Coast Guard with the Ebasco Report in 1948 and the Roles and Missions Study in 1962 are good examples.[3] The case study of the Marine Environmental Protection program also points up the long time sometimes involved in matching national needs and the means of the agency.

Yet there is another important dimension to the ambience of the government environment—the style of the leader and its effect on cooperation. Again, the tenure of Treasury Secretary George Humphrey offers an example. In his experience as chief executive of a large corporation, Humphrey would often tell subordinates they did not know what they were talking about. He would expect them to disprove this accusation by quickly supplying the information he wanted or be subject to dismissal. Supposedly the chief engineer at one plant, who was a favorite of Humphrey's, was often fired and rehired twice on the same day because he stood up to Humphrey. And subordinates who really did not know what they were talking about soon disappeared from the company.

Unfortunately, in government this style was not effective, particularly with the career civil service workers. That group's job security and tenure in the same geographic location fostered an attitude of "do what the boss says, and if he doesn't like it, what's the difference?" This approach did not breed the bold retorts from the Treasury Department staff that were needed to complement Humphrey's aggressive style.

With Coast Guard officers, however, the secretary had more leverage, such as the transfer. To the commandant he could threaten the health, and even the life, of the agency, thus bringing on the same aggressive retorts Humphrey had come to expect in the private sector.

On one occasion in 1954 Secretary Humphrey sent word that he wanted to see Vice Admiral Richmond, commandant of the Coast Guard, in one hour. When the commandant arrived he was informed that the secretary wanted to eliminate the Port Security program and the twenty-four-hour notification required of ships entering United States harbors. After a short conversation, Humphrey told Richmond that he did not understand the situation in United States ports. The following dialogue is an approximation of the rest of the conversation.

"Wait a minute, Mr. Secretary," Vice Admiral Richmond responded. "If I can show you a way I can destroy a port for one twenty-fifth the cost of transcontinental bombers, would you as a business executive be interested?"

"What would you do?" George Humphrey asked.

"If I was sitting on the other side, I would get a dozen broken-down liberty ships and have them secretly fitted with a false compartment in the corner of one hold. I would then install an atomic weapon in the compartment, which could be dropped out in a strategic part of any harbor—for example off Battery Park in New York or under the bridge areas in San Francisco Bay.

"I would then have a small group of fanatics, maybe two in each ship, who would know of this system and send them with sealed orders to the port areas I had preselected as targets.

"Have you ever tried to identify a ship from the air, Mr. Secretary? It is almost impossible to read the name and flag, even if they are properly displayed.

"Mr. Secretary, I feel that this system not only would be far cheaper than a fleet of bombers, it would also be more effective when implemented. In fact, I would urge my boss that it be combined with air power to provide redundancy to insure that the combined system is more effective than either when employed separately."

Secretary Humphrey sat quietly through the explanation, then called in his secretary from the outer office. While Richmond sat in the office, Humphrey dictated a memorandum to the national defense secretary within President Eisenhower's immediate White House staff, describing his new "Trojan horse theory" and telling how the Treasury Department through the Coast Guard was responding to this threat to national security. Humphrey told the national defense secretary he would continue the twenty-four-hour notification required of ships and would also authorize the construction of ninety-five-foot cutters to enhance harbor entrance patrol. Secretary Humphrey thanked Vice Admiral Richmond for his help and excused him.[4] Before deciding if Richmond in this 1954 incident was displaying proactive behavior or conjuring up dubious threats, let us consider more examples from the Coast Guard.

A COMPARISON OF TWO MODELS OF AGENCY MANAGEMENT

The description of government ambience draws attention to the inherent differences between the environments of the public and private sectors. The case studies of the development of the loran system and the Marine Environmental Protection program provide a detailed "history" of the growth of the strategy and structure of the Coast Guard that is rich in examples of the uniqueness of the ambience in the federal sector.

But the meeting between Humphrey and Richmond on port security provides material both to illustrate the workings of agency management and to help us judge the validity of figure 6 as a model of agency management. This encounter occurred while both men were new at their jobs. The Port Security program was not a new concept at the time, and the secretary's initial decision to end it and his final decision to strengthen it were just another increment in the long-run development of federal policy toward the port areas.

This example, moreover, provides a refreshing comparison. It appears that change in the United States government can occur a step at a time—by "muddling through." Change in a given area is often linked to that area's place in the "issue-attention cycle."[5] And, if one looks at the aggregate of the incremental decisions made over the long run in a particular area, it is apparent that many are good, some are mediocre, and a few are bad. Any judgment depends on an evaluation of events at the time. The instances of inefficient Coast Guard behavior discussed in chapter 3 further illustrate this.

One should avoid the idea that many Coast Guard decisions were made as part of a profound national policy. The evidence of the last eight chapters strongly indicates that decisions made at any one point in time are products of the forces at work at that moment. This seems to be true of a great many of the situations discussed earlier. For example, Vice Admiral Richmond might not have been able to convince Secretary Humphrey of the benefits of the Port Security program. After all, Richmond had only an hour's notice of his appointment with the secretary and no indication at all of the subject of the meeting. Yet the short-run direction of the Port Security program depended upon the outcome of this conversation, and the final result could have gone either way.

The development of loran as a radio-navigation technology progressed through a multitude of such decision points, stretching from the day in 1942 when Lieutenant Commander Lawrence Harding reported for a temporary assignment at the Navy Department to the day in 1974 when Commander William Mohin explained at a congressional hearing the rationale for expanding the Loran-C system to cover the area from Valdez to Puget Sound.

This is not to say that the concept of an incremental decision-making process is wrong. Quite the contrary—an idea may develop and progress until it becomes an element of national policy.[6] This development does not necessarily occur, however, because any group or committee plans it or says it will happen this way. It occurs through the definition, impetus, and context that result as a program champion fights for a new program or an important change in an existing program. And, of course, it occurs because of the structural context—the unique reward system that the federal agency provides for the program champion to motivate better performance.[7]

The general management model (fig. 6, repeated for convenience as fig. 33) for a federal agency matching national *needs* and technical *means* to deliver a mix of services to the public validly depicts the case of the Coast Guard, illustrating the constituents of the agency who advocate programs as national needs. The executive branch, the Congress, and the general public or special interests all act as advocates at one time or another. The model also portrays external and internal environmental forces as influencing the structure of the agency. The technical means—the distinctive competence the agency has acquired in the form of hu-

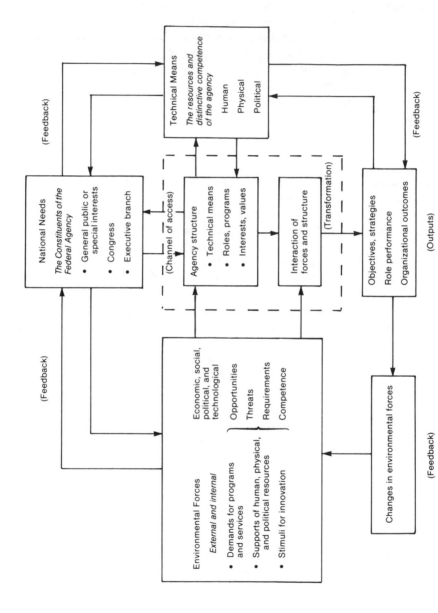

FIG. 33. A general management model for a federal agency matching national needs and technical means to deliver an optimal mix of services to the public. (This duplicates figure 6.)

man, physical, and political resources—are central as they affect the Coast Guard's ability to produce better and more cost-effective programs than anyone else. These means constitute the very character of the organization.[8] It is through the interplay of all these forces with the strategy and objectives of the agency that management takes place—at least in the case of the Coast Guard. Several studies of other federal agencies also support this finding.*

But the model of figure 33 does not convey fully the pluralism that exists within the government environment, nor does it convey the ad hoc nature of many of the decisions that are made day by day or month by month. In fact, the model of figure 33 implies a strong continuity of decisions by the feedback networks it portrays. Any model of agency management should consider pluralism and how it affects ad hoc decision-making.

Chapters 3 through 10 illustrate again that the Coast Guard—or the overall government of which it is one part—is not omniscient, though the adjective "federal" tends to convey such an image. Because there are so many people in government, it is even more fractionated than any private-sector organization.

The federal government is composed of individuals. Different people make day-to-day and month-to-month decisions in many diverse areas. In making these decisions, the leaders of agencies and the managers within the agencies who champion various programs interact in a complex way with a long list of actors, including the president and executive office groups as well as the departments, other agencies, the judiciary, the communications media, the career staff, the interest groups, the Congress, and the political parties.

Figure 34 shows a decision-making model for a federal agency developed by Walter Held from the early work of Wallace Sayre.† Comparing this model with the model of figure 33 reveals that Held's model is a better analogy to what really happens *at any one point in time* in the Coast Guard, whereas the model of figure 33 better represents what occurs over *a long time continuum*. Figure 34 has the important advantage of naming those who interact with agency leadership at any point in time. This model also shows more clearly than figure 33 the pressures the agency leader and the program champions feel while making any one decision.

To make a very broad—and therefore partially inaccurate—analogy with a

---

*See, for example, Philip Selznick, *TVA and the Grass Roots. A Study in the Sociology of Formal Organization* (Los Angeles: University of California Press, 1949). This study provides an institutional analysis to examine the interaction between a federal agency and its environment.

Other studies focusing on public policy as an outcome of bureaucratic political maneuvering are provided by Graham T. Allison, *Essence of Decision: Explaining the Cuban Missile Crisis* (Boston: Little, Brown, 1971), and Morton H. Halperin et al., *Bureaucratic Politics and Foreign Policy* (Washington, D.C.: Brookings Institution, 1974).

†Walter G. Held, director of the Advanced Study Program of the Brookings Institution, discussed this model in detail in a lecture at the Industrial College of the Armed Forces, Washington, D.C., on 21 July 1978. Held acknowledges the influence of the earlier work of Wallace S. Sayre in the development of this model.

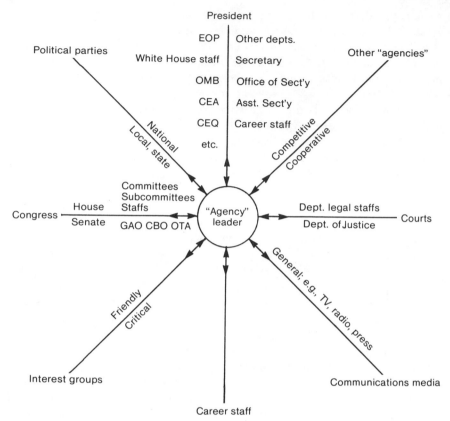

FIG. 34. A decision-making model for a federal agency. From a model developed by Walter G. Held, director of the Advanced Study Program of the Brookings Institution, based on the work of Wallace S. Sayre.

tool of business accounting, the model of figure 34 can be looked at as a balance sheet, reporting the status at the end of one decision increment. By comparison, the model of figure 33 can be looked at as an operating statement reporting the overall results of an extended period in the life of the agency. As such, the human, physical, and political resources are the assets that are stored after performances are tabulated for the extended period.

Indeed, the models of figures 33 and 34 are both conceptualizations of the process of managing a federal agency, as applied to the Coast Guard. The model of figure 34 provides a better framework for analysis of any one decision increment, while that of figure 33 is better suited for analysis of the long-run calculus of several increments. The main pitfall in figure 33 is that it may convey the impression that much of what happens results from intricate planning. As figure 34 shows, this is not always so.

In comparing the two models of agency management, one might conclude that figure 34 is *better* than figure 33. This value judgment is only partially true. Again, the model of figure 34 is far better for examining any particular decision faced by the Coast Guard at any one point in the development of the agency, and it has value for short-run analysis. The model of figure 33 is better suited for an analysis of the long-run development of the Coast Guard.

INCREMENTS OF UNPLANNED CHANGE

Incremental change for a federal agency often occurs without, and indeed in spite of, incremental planning. One of the earlier examples of this in Coast Guard history involves the events of the late 1930s. At that time Henry Morgenthau was new as secretary of treasury, and Russell Waesche was new as commandant of the Coast Guard. Shortly after becoming commandant in 1936, Rear Admiral Waesche developed a plan to acquire two other government agencies—the Lighthouse Service and the Bureau of Marine Inspection and Navigation. Although both agencies were then part of the Commerce Department, Waesche felt that their responsibilities and resources would meld well with those of the Coast Guard. But in 1936 neither agency was interested in this merger, and Waesche's plan was stymied.

The blockage was removed by an unexpected event. Secretary Morgenthau became very interested in the Coast Guard and its dynamic commandant. Whether his Treasury staff was subtly shifting Morgenthau's energies to issues less important to them, or whether Waesche had succeeded in winning the secretary's attention, the Coast Guard received more attention and support than it had enjoyed for ten years. Morgenthau's support provided far more political resources for the Coast Guard than would have been possible through its own strategic planning.

Secretary Morgenthau's extreme interest in the Coast Guard and in Rear Admiral Waesche is reflected in several budget increases the Coast Guard received in the late 1930s and in its ultimate acquisition of the Lighthouse Service and the Bureau of Marine Inspection and Navigation. Yet neither the increases nor the acquisitions came smoothly. In the public sector, the diffusion of power, the multiplicity of actors, and all the complications depicted by the model of figure 34 can come into play. Tracing the prewar budget increases and the acquisition of these two agencies through the 1946 reorganization plan provides a cornucopia of examples of unplanned change.

The preparations made during 1939–41 for what proved to be World War II may be one of the best examples of the shortcomings as well as the frustrations that can result from the planning process in a federal agency. Because of the successful job the Coast Guard had performed in convoy duty during World War I, and because of the Rum War experience of Coast Guardsmen in manning

United States Navy destroyers, the Treasury Department and Navy Department jointly decided during the 1930s that the Coast Guard should be prepared to use cutters and to man destroyers assigned to convoy duty. This is discussed, in chapter 3 as an instance of inefficient performance. In the hectic days of 1939–41 events moved faster than planning, and the plans for war quickly became irrelevant to actual needs, which would have presented great trauma to the Coast Guard had they not been associated with wartime. When President Roosevelt assigned every 255-foot cutter of the new *Lake* class to Great Britain, he removed more than half the newest and largest cutters from the Coast Guard inventory. In the "destroyer deal," the president assigned to England most of the remaining United States Navy ships the Coast Guard would have manned for convoy duty.

Still another increment of unplanned change was occurring at the time, however, which provided the Coast Guard an unforeseen mission that would overshadow convoy duty and replace the resources depleted by the departure of the cutters. The new mission was amphibious warfare. When the army and navy conducted joint water and land maneuvers in the Caribbean, they had trouble piloting small craft through the surf and landing them on the beaches. The Coast Guard was called on to provide the requisite seamanship. Many of those assigned to this duty were former surfmen from the Life Saving Service, experts without equal for the task.

Like these increments of unplanned change, many other events in the development of the strategy and structure of the Coast Guard were not the result of intricate planning. But one must consider these examples in relation to the environment in which they occurred and the causal factors present at the time. For example, although the agency's role in amphibious warfare was not planned, the distinctive competence available within the Coast Guard was pivotal in guiding the changes. This argument makes it easy to see that by interrelationships of the increments of change, *one step in the evolution of the organization tends to dictate the set of possible increments that may follow.*

With the drawdown of Coast Guardsmen for amphibious warfare, two more important Coast Guard programs received their beginnings. The first was loran, and the second was the Marine Environmental Protection program.

The beginning of loran sprang not only from the war-induced need for an all-weather, automated technique to obtain navigational positions quickly, but also from the technical and organizational skills of Lawrence Harding. Harding became a lieutenant commander in the Coast Guard only through the acquisition of the Lighthouse Service. Many of the important changes Harding was able to bring about as the innovation he named "loran" progressed were certainly incremental and were not in themselves part of any grand strategy.

Although the postwar commercial use of loran as a radio-navigation aid was planned by Lawrence Harding and later by Loren Brunner, the boost given the system by the advent of the Cold War and the Korean War was certainly not the result of planning. The sudden demand for Loran-C after Sputnik also was not planned, and the changeover to this system eventually led to the battle not only with the Omega system but with Loran-A as well. Despite the extent of his World War II and postwar experiences with Loran-A and Loran-C, Loren Brunner was constantly surprised by the influence of external events on both the rate and the direction of loran applications. These external events are an important part of the story of loran; yet much of their nature would have been hard to anticipate fully or correctly.

Chapter 7 describes the experiences of William Roland and William Mohin with Loran-C in the 1970s. All the elements of the model of figure 34 are involved; the executive branch, the Congress, interest groups, career staffs, and other agencies all come into play. Roland and Mohin experienced the same pressures as had Harding and Brunner before them. Change still came in increments.

Indeed, the demand for more widespread loran coverage, combined with the pressures of competing radio-navigation technology available from other agencies—and from Loran-A inside the Coast Guard—placed hard choices before the decision-makers within the Coast Guard. Neither Roland nor Mohin could have fully anticipated in 1974 the technical difficulties they encountered in switching to Loran-C as quickly as they did, or the acceleration in applications of Loran-C technology to areas once thought of as far removed from transport—or, for that matter, defense.

Note that when the agency switched to Loran-C on the West Coast chain, or provided updated timing equipment elsewhere, the funding did not go through the resource change proposal or the acquisition, construction, and improvement systems described in chapters 3 and 4. Instead, the priority generated by the demand for increased Loran-C services, as well as by the need elsewhere for the people who would be freed by the new timing equipment, led to internal reprogramming of funds to Loran-C. The demands for Loran-C were as potent as they were unexpected, and they brought about significant changes within the Coast Guard structure.

The Marine Environmental Protection program also provides good examples of the effects of unexpected events on strategic planning. Although the former cuttermen of the old Revenue Marine might have anticipated the environmental concerns of the nation from their experiences in Alaska and with John Muir, the Coast Guard's real beginning in this area dates to the port security efforts of World War II and the acquisition of the Bureau of Marine Inspection and Navigation. Without these two separate initiatives, the *Torrey Canyon* and *Argo Merchant* accidents would not have had the impact on the Coast Guard that was ultimately felt.

Because of the Coast Guard's involvement with shipping during World War II, Rear Admiral Russell Waesche's prewar design to integrate BMIN into the Coast Guard became a reality. The dual-role strategy and the multimission concept allowed the Coast Guard to augment its human resources in this area, and the key actors described in chapters 8, 9, and 10 had the chance to contribute to the development of marine environmental protection.

But despite the definition and impetus provided by W. M. Benkert, Robert Price, and Sidney Wallace, the context supplied by the *Torrey Canyon,* the Santa Barbara well blowout, the *Argo Merchant,* and other accidents described was vital to the development of MEP. None of these events or the incremental changes they brought could have been fully anticipated by strategic planning. In fact, these accidents may have played the most important part in the development of MEP, consistent with the impact on the Coast Guard of the earlier *Titanic* and *Morro Castle* incidents. On the other hand, the development of MEP by the Coast Guard after the *Torrey Canyon* and Santa Barbara Channel incidents would not have proceeded as it did without the skills and efforts of Benkert, Price, Wallace, and other Coast Guard leaders.

The importance of "structural context" is more obvious in the MEP case. Benkert, Price, and Wallace all were promoted from captain to rear admiral. Price later became a vice admiral. After he retired from the Coast Guard Benkert became president of the American Institute of Merchant Shipping. Of the loran champions—Harding, Brunner, and Pearson—only Pearson received the important promotion to rear admiral. Some say this was because Benkert, Price, and Wallace also held more "operational" assignments.

The task of the program champions, however, was far from easy. The structural context of the Coast Guard motivated them to follow Coast Guard strategy and attempt excellence. But from the vantage point of the champions themselves, their rewards of promotion to higher position were not always what they might have expected. A strong argument can be made that champions make enemies and arouse the jealousies of those less inclined to take similar risks or assume such active roles. Indeed, it appears that the jousting a program champion does in the process of alliance, bargain, and compromise—the ABC process of the American government implicit in the model of figure 34—leaves him with a good many enemies both within the structure and outside. Structural context may differ so greatly between the two sectors because of the ambience of the government environment.

In contrast to the workings of loran funding in the 1970s, the funding for MEP over the same years did come largely through the resource change proposal and the acquisition, construction, and improvement systems. The priority generated by the external demands for MEP may have been a result of unanticipated accidents, but the funding increases came in yearly steps.

The process through which these funds were obtained and the Marine Environmental Protection program was developed is a good example of the workings of the ABC process; yet it is consistent with the long-run goals of the Coast Guard produced within the general management model of figure 33.

THE ROLE OF STRATEGY AND STRUCTURE

Although there have been many increments of unplanned change in the evolution and development of the Coast Guard as a federal agency, there are central threads that weave them together. The two main threads are the dual-role strategy and the multimission concept. They also weave together the general management responses of the Coast Guard that, looked upon over time, become the very fabric of the agency as an institution.

The Coast Guard's responses to the challenge of the environment are on balance much the same as those made by a large private organization. As a federal agency, the Coast Guard developed a strategy, and a structure through which to implement it. In building a store of human, physical, and political resources, it developed a distinctive competence and character. And it acquired values and took on vitality as an organization and as a force in being.

Variations between the responses of a federal agency and those of a private organization, however, point out important differences in the application of general management theory in the two sectors, since the influences affecting them differ. For the Coast Guard these influences include many institutions: the executive branch—the Office of the President, the Office of Management and Budget, and the Department of Transportation; the Congress—the authorization and appropriations committees and subcommittees; the General Accounting Office; and the general public and special interest groups.

When any of these external influences tries to deflect the agency from a path pointed to by its strategy and structure, the pressure may be too strong for the agency to overcome. Indeed, in the short run the influences will probably override the agency's own initiatives.

Tensions may also occur when opposing interests advocate different ways to handle an issue. During the development of the Marine Environmental Protection program in the 1970s, the marine industry and marine environmentalists often took differing views. The compromises in programs and services that resulted from this clash of opposing interests are the very essence of the ABC process of the model of figure 34. All the influences and forces that affect the increments of change a federal agency deals with over a short period are represented in this model.

This clash of interests in the long run, however, is better represented by the model of figure 33. The same influences and forces are present, but over time the agency can develop its distinctive competence and character. It also develops vitality and a desire to perpetuate itself. It is this tendency to perpetuity that motivates it to struggle against the threats to its existence—the public-sector stimulus for an agency to be proactive and innovative and to adapt and change with the times.

THE ROLE OF LEADERSHIP

The long-run development of the Coast Guard affords many examples of the process of managing a federal agency. In analyzing these examples, the model of figure 33 becomes more useful. For instance, the choices that Rear Admiral Frederick Billard made and the values he held as he expanded the Coast Guard and its place within the federal government find much congruence in the model of figure 33. Billard opted to improve the human, physical, and political resources of the Coast Guard by advocating a new academy to educate officers, new cutters to provide services, and wider knowledge of the Coast Guard in the executive branch and the Congress to provide political strength. Billard was commandant of the Coast Guard for eight years. Again, one of the keys to the use of the model of figure 33 is the time span over which it is applied. The longer the period the better the comparisons.

The challenges Admiral Russell Waesche faced and the responses he made to them are also congruent with the model of figure 33. The ten years when Russell Waesche was commandant are without doubt the most important years in the development of the Coast Guard, for they spanned not only World War II but the final integration of the Life Saving Service and the acquisition of the Lighthouse Service and the Bureau of Marine Inspection and Navigation.

One can also examine the choices that Admiral Alfred Richmond made and the values he held in the eight years when he was organization strategist and builder and again see the applicability and usefulness of the model of figure 33. Indeed, the emphasis the Coast Guard placed on developing its distinctive competence and organizational vitality is evident in Richmond's career.

The decisions that Lawrence Harding, Loren Brunner, William Roland, and William Mohin made as advocates of loran and the leadership they displayed as program champions also demonstrate the applicability of the models of figure 34, for the short run, and figure 33, for the long run. The case study of loran provides great insight into how the program champions interacted with both the internal structure and the agency leader and with the external environment as well.

The roles that W. M. Benkert, Robert Price, and Sidney Wallace played in developing the Marine Environmental Protection program validate the models of figures 33 and 34 for the different time frames and provide even more insight into the interactions of the program champions with the structure and the surrounding environment.

The part that strategy, structure, and leadership played in the evolution of the Coast Guard is evident. In some instances the external environment was ready for change, and in other instances the internal environment was ready and eager. It is readily apparent, however, that the most important changes took place when *both external and internal environments* were ready for and receptive to change at the same time, and when a skillful leader was at the helm. The presence of skillful program champions was also important.

The examples in the historical development of the modern Coast Guard that best illustrate successful management occur under the leadership of Frederick Billard, Russell Waesche, and Alfred Richmond. All three admirals met serious threats to the Coast Guard and at the same time provided proactive and innovative leadership. Just because a federal agency meets threats to its existence does not mean that it necessarily is proactive or innovative; but Billard, Waesche, and Richmond all proved that both can be done.

A skillful leader is an important prerequisite to the proper use of the model of figure 33. The common qualities that Admirals Billard, Waesche, and Richmond displayed included not only complete knowledge of and dedication to the organization they had long served but also the desire and skill to use the privilege, status, and power that accompanied their top post to develop the agency's distinctive competence. To the extent that each commandant was successful as an organization strategist and builder, one can accept the model of figure 33. The better the leader one chooses as an example, the better the model will fit public management as demonstrated in the Coast Guard.

12 THE HIDDEN STIMULUS FOR A FEDERAL AGENCY

THREATS TO A FEDERAL AGENCY

The detailed case study of a federal agency—the Coast Guard—suggests that we can indeed identify an analogue to the market mechanism that stimulates innovation in the public sector. That analogue is the threat to the agency's survival, and it is often the hidden stimulus for improved performance. This is admittedly a primal and negative stimulus; nevertheless, it exerts a powerful effect on administrative behavior.

Such a threat can take several forms. In mild form it is manifested by fiscal starvation, brought about by the lack of capital funds, or operating funds, or both. Simply put, the agency's budget is cut or is held constant in an inflationary climate. In stronger form the threat is of partial takeover of one or more programs or functions of the agency by another agency. In its strongest form the threat extends to takeover or liquidation of the entire agency. This is usually effected by the acquisition of all its programs and functions and takeover of its human and physical resources by another agency. In the case of the Coast Guard all three varieties of threats have occurred on many occasions.

In examining the evolution and development of the Coast Guard as a federal agency, it is only natural to ask, "How can an organization whose duties have changed so often possibly have a real strategy?" Certainly the United States Navy, for example, can look at itself each year and know it has a mission of defense—as long as there is a federal government. For the Coast Guard, however, this has not always been so.

Consider the scramble of the Revenue Marine for roles after Thomas Jefferson became president in 1801; and again after the suggestions of Andrew Jackson in 1829; the question of dual roles raised anew by the Commerce committee attack in 1843; the pressure to become part of the navy in the 1880s, resolved by Senator John Sherman's advocacy of the "coast-guard" in 1890; the reorganization pressure brought by the Cleveland commission that threatened to dissolve

246

the Revenue Marine and ended instead in the acquisition of another agency—the Life Saving Service; the threat Franklin Roosevelt posed as assistant secretary of the navy in 1919; the fiscal threats posed by the budgetary process after World War II; and finally the threat posed by the creation of the Department of Transportation in 1967.* Often, however, these threats led directly to important new opportunities. The opportunities led in turn to more efficient, effective, and even innovative public service in accordance with the simple stimulus-response model discussed in chapter 1.

In most examples from the evolution and development of the Coast Guard, threats were not aimed directly at the survival of the agency. These indirect threats are far better thought of as external forces. In many instances it was not what the agency did to help itself that carried the day, but these indirect threats—or external forces—often far removed from the control, if not the foresight, of the agency, that became the stimulus for change.

These external forces can be categorized as economic, social, political, or technological. Wars are a salient example, and the Coast Guard or the Revenue Marine was involved in every one except expeditions against the Barbary States. Technological changes—such as in radio-navigation—are another, and the Coast Guard and its acquired organizations have been involved in all the mechanical, electrical, electronic, or energy-related changes in the marine environment. Natural disasters—such as those that endanger the quality of the marine environment—are a third, and the Coast Guard has felt the impact of hurricanes, floods and storms, and in particular of such catastrophes as the *Titanic, Morro Castle, Torrey Canyon,* and *Argo Merchant* accidents.

Despite all the threats and autonomous forces that have been described, the answer to the question, "Does the Coast Guard have a real strategy?" is a resounding yes. The dual-role strategy dates to the beginning of the nineteenth century and, as years passed, was expanded to a multimission concept. This not only includes the military-preparedness role inherent in the dual-role strategy but also provides for similar resource-sharing in peacetime missions. The presence and the guidance of the dual-role strategy and the multimission concept can be seen in both the loran and marine environmental protection cases.

If one assumes that the three specific threats to the vitality and even survival of a federal agency are in fact an effective stimulus for the agency to be proactive and innovative, then one must ask what feasible set of management activities can bring about responses that are favorable and desired by the agency. How can managerial responses remain clear of the charges of both the fifth and the sixth categorical charges?

General management approaches call for developing a strategy and a structure to administer it (for developing an organizational character and distinctive competence *consistent* with the strategy) and for building a store of human,

*For a description of these threats, see table 2 and Appendix 1.

physical, and political resources for the structure to use in carrying out the strategy. The vitality and character the agency develops during this process are among its most important assets.

The models of figure 33 and figure 34 help one visualize the general management process of the Coast Guard as a federal agency. Each of the two models takes a different perspective. The models do not, however, adequately portray the vital roles played by the agency leader and the champions—both external and internal—of various programs. These vital roles, shaped by the pressure of the external and internal environments the leader and the champions face, are important parts of the agency's general management responses.

The agency structure—the heart of the model of figure 33—consists of the technical means of the agency, the roles and programs it has acquired, and the interests and values it espouses. Just as the technical means of the agency form its *distinctive competence*—its human, physical, and political resources—so its structure determines its power as an organizational entity.

This structure is achieved, or accumulated, as a result of the general management responses of the agency over many years. The structure is much like a bank or repository for the accumulated competence of the agency, and as with a bank, both deposits and withdrawals can be made.

The structure can also be thought of as the institutional fabric woven together by the technical means of the agency; like a piece of cloth, it can either hold the agency together well or can unravel or be torn and thus be less effective in the future. Each decision that is made, each increment that is achieved, in its own way either strengthens the fabric, making it larger or more versatile, or diminishes it. In this light one can see how threats to the survival of the Coast Guard as a federal agency are the hidden stimulus for better performance by this agency, because the threats attack the very fabric of the agency as an institution. The hidden stimulus is a form of the survival instinct.

A DIFFERENCE IN GENERAL
MANAGEMENT THEORY

There are, however, limits to the comparisons we can make between the stimulus, public or private, and the feasible set of responses, public or private. There are points where the analogy between the market stimulus—competition for the private firm—and the hidden stimulus—threats to the federal agency— can be pressed no further because of major differences between the public and private sectors.

Chapter 2 discusses four broad differences between general management theory for the public sector and for the private sector. First, there are differences in the demand and support inputs of the two sectors. Second, there are differences in the nature of the motivations for proactivity and innovation. Third, there are differences in primary and secondary outputs in response to demands. Fourth, the transformation process of a large federal agency involves more group and institutional actors and different institutional and political processes than does the transformation process in a private firm.

Of these differences, the area least understood is the nature of motivations for proactivity and innovation. In both sectors there is a stimulus for self-preservation and self-perpetuation, but the *nature* of the stimulus is different in the two. A threat to self-preservation and self-perpetuation in the private firm is different from such a threat in the public organization, because in the public organization consumer sovereignty—or constituent interest—does not necessarily play a major part. In the public organization the major threat is not that competition will remove the consumer—or the constituent—but that either the executive branch or the legislative branch or the judicial branch will exercise its own sovereignty. This almost happened to the Coast Guard in 1974 in the Loran-C case. Ironically, this sovereignty may be exercised regardless of either the merits of the agency's performance or the relative power of its constituents.

In the private sector, if a firm does a good job—if consumers hold the firm in high regard and its products are in demand—then the firm is virtually invulnerable. For example, if a private firm has a state charter, has a good product line and is not in debt, does nothing illegal, and is sound, what can happen to it? Nothing, because the laws of the United States protect the private firm from illegal takeover, from blackmail or protection rackets, from stock takeover if the stock was set up correctly, and from foreclosure if the debt was correctly structured. The private firm is protected against *physical takeover* by the laws of property and business organizations. As long as the debt-equity ratio is watched, as long as the stock is held closely enough to prevent a stockholders' takeover, as long as the products maintain consumer acceptance, then the private firm is for practical purposes unassailable. Nobody can come in from outside and legally cut the firm's budget, or take away one of its products, or take over the entire firm, except by the workings of the market mechanism and competition. Bluntly, nobody can directly put a private firm out of business.

In the public sector, the payoff matrix is entirely different. A federal agency could do an excellent job and still be subjected by any of the three branches of the United States government to fiscal starvation, partial takeover, or involuntary liquidation. An agency must vigilantly tend to its sources of political support—the various constituents that are segments of its public, the overseeing department and other components of the executive branch, and the Congress and relevant committees. And it must constantly keep an eye to windward, or a raider may sail down and steal the wind, or come on board for piracy of part of the cargo, or even seize outright cargo, crew, and ship.

For example, the Department of Transportation might decide to limit or arbitrarily reduce the share of the department budget allocated to the Coast Guard. The Office of Management and Budget might make a similar decision or, for that matter, might "redline" any portion of the budget request that is not mandated by law and thus becomes an "uncontrollable" expenditure. Or, in the next level of threat, the navy may say it wants the Ice Operations program, or the air force may say it wants back the Search and Rescue program or, along with the navy, the Aids to Navigation program. Or the Environmental Protection Agency may say it wants the Marine Environmental Protection program, or the Maritime Administration may want the Commercial Vessel Safety program. At an even higher level of threat, either the navy or the National Oceanic and Atmospheric Administration may decide it wants to take over the entire Coast Guard. The navy has done just this in earlier days, and the Coast Guard itself managed takeovers of the Life Saving Service, the Lighthouse Service, and the Bureau of Marine Inspection and Navigation.

The security a private-sector organization has against threats outside the market mechanism and competition, to the extent that the security exists, is very different from the environment that confronts a public-sector organization. In the federal government, an Office of Equal Employment Opportunity or a Peace Corps, a Maritime Administration or a Coast Guard can be set up; its leader can do an excellent job of managing the organization and serving the intended constituents; and suddenly some element of the government may strike the agency so it either is wounded or ceases to exist in its former identity. This lack of any but product vulnerability in the private sector, as opposed to the categorical vulnerability of the public sector is an enormous difference in terms of the stimulus for innovation and the way a federal agency behaves.

TOWARD A GENERAL THEORY OF DIFFERENCE

In reexamining the model of figure 33 one notes among the external and internal environmental forces a general item marked "stimuli for innovation." Among the categorical vulnerabilities that continually confront a federal agency come the specific threats of involuntary fiscal starvation, takeover, and liquidation. These threats constitute a *hidden stimulus* that affects the administrative behavior of the agency and serves as a principal form of the "stimulus for innovation." This stimulus provides a very basic form of motivation for a federal agency.

Many discussions of differences between public and private management deal with what one may call the symptomatic—or even the superficial—differences in administrative behavior in the two sectors. For example, some discuss the differences between civil service regulations and private-sector personnel policies, or the differences between the tactics for the budgetary process in government and the tactics of the resource allocation process in a private firm, or even differences in values. But these discussions do not deal with a far more fundamental problem: Is there a fundamental difference in the stimulus for proactivity and innovation as it exists in the public sector and the private sector? If so, how does the difference affect the maximum feasible set of management options available to produce proactivity and innovation? Does the difference expand the set of options, contract it, or mutate it?

The case of the Coast Guard demonstrates that some mechanism analagous to the market and competition may operate in the public sector. Although the analogy does not hold at all points, the *hidden stimulus* is definitely analagous to the market and to competition in the way it influences the behavior of a federal agency. Threats to the Coast Guard have brought about responses no different from the behavior one would expect from an IBM, Sperry Rand, or Digital Equipment maneuvering around the same issue. The issue might be acquiring other organizations, diversifying internal operations, pushing this technology or that, or simply solving problems with existing programs, goods, or services.

One might protest, however, that this theory of difference applies only to the Coast Guard. It is true that a different stimulus-response paradigm has been proposed after detailed study of only one federal agency. Part of the rationale for selecting the Coast Guard as the one agency for scrutiny is that this close examination may reveal theoretical implications that are both realistic and worthy of further examination. In this respect the rationale has proved successful; the notion of a hidden stimulus as a public-sector motivator is certainly worth further study.

One might also argue that the hidden stimulus is present only because the Coast Guard is a successful federal agency and that one will not find this stimuli operating in unsuccessful agencies. This corollary may also be true and is itself worthy of further examination. But even if this second hypothesis is true, it does not detract from the modified hypothesis of a hidden stimulus for successful federal agencies. Indeed, the presence of a hidden stimulus in the case of any successful federal agency is a causal factor in the agency's success. It is the motivator of proactive and innovative behavior that brings about the appropriate general management responses.

The responses to the stimuli, whether the market mechanism in the private sector or the hidden stimulus in the public sector, are the familar general management options available to induce both proactive and innovative behavior in the organization. This hidden stimulus affords the government agency the chance to be effective and efficient and also to be innovative. And it belies the sixth categorical charge against government organizations.

But, even more important, the hidden stimulus can have a direct effect on the management options available to produce proactivity and innovation. Basically, three overall options have been available to agency leadership:

1. Install effective and efficient planning and policy-making processes.
2. Make adjustments in the centralization and decentralization of agency organization to allocate resources and implement policy.

3. Rearrange the organizational building blocks to make the agency more responsive to planning, policy-making, and resource allocation during the formulation and implementation phases of public policy.

The first two options are important to a federal agency, and the hidden stimulus gives agency leadership an impetus to pursue them.

The basic differences in general management applications between the private and the public sector become relevant when we consider the third option. When a "rearrangement of the organizational building blocks" is considered, a definite contraction or even mutation of the general management options occurs. Large-scale reorganization is not a viable option for a single agency because it requires simultaneous executive and legislative branch approvals that are difficult to obtain.

Reorganization may be considered to the extent that an agency can adopt a strategy of acquisition or diversification. The Coast Guard did this in the case of the three organizations it absorbed. But the construction of the public environment described by the models of figures 33 and 34 both influences and constrains this option. While great comparisons can be made in the first two options, comparisons in the third option are of limited application.

IMPLICATIONS FOR A THEORY OF DIFFERENCE

The theory of difference between management in the two sectors, when more widely understood, should assist those involved in managing a federal agency. The notion that a threat to the budget, to a program, or even to the very existence of the agency is analogous to the stimulus provided in the private sector by competition and the market mechanism has powerful implications. The hidden stimulus, if used properly by managers inside an agency or by outsiders interested in its performance, can bring about more effective and more efficient government service.

The passage of Proposition 13 in California in 1978 and the beginning of its implementation provided a stimulus to government organizations within that state. Similar referendums have been passed in other states and communities. Federal agencies and programs have also been threatened by increased calls for a balanced federal budget and by review of previously mandated programs. These calls are a new form of the hidden stimulus. "Sunset" laws calling for periodic open review of existing federal programs need not be an arbitrary death sentence for government services; they could provide the motivation for proactive and innovative behavior in the public sector. The case of the Coast Guard suggests that managers within federal agencies are stimulated by threats to their budgets and programs and are activated by challenges from their administrations and constituencies. What better way to fill the need of the nation for review of the size and composition of the federal budget and at the same time fill the perceived need for more proactive and innovative behavior by federal managers than to go ahead and apply the hidden stimulus to these managers and their agencies?*

Many people have said that not even Congress operates the federal government; it operates itself. It may even be the only organization in the United States where there is never an *overall* study of productivity or priority. Application of the hidden stimulus can bring a new control to the operation of the federal government and will certainly be a check on productivity and priority, as well as a partial cure for chronic inflation. After all, monetary policy cannot bear all the burden; fiscal policy must play some role.

Increased application of the hidden stimulus within the federal government will occur in the 1980s, and many federal agencies, programs, and services will be threatened. The concept of a hidden stimulus as the public-sector driving force will become less vague and will act as a more conscious motivator for proactivity and innovation by federal managers. The pressure of monetary and fiscal policy, the intertwining of the international economy, the increasing cost of energy and national defense, the inflation-unemployment dilemma, and public sentiment about how all these factors affect individual pocketbooks will ensure that this will happen. How then can the theory of difference this book proposes be of any practical value?

Those involved in the general management of federal agencies must realize anew the pressures that can be brought to bear. Civil service reform and calls for balanced budgets and even budget surpluses should help spread the reality. General managers in the federal government should anticipate these pressures and do their best to see that their agencies respond by being proactive and innovative—else they may see the threats materialize and the pressures upon their agencies increase until they either respond or cease to exist.

The most important implication of the hidden stimulus rests with those outside actors who take part in the year-to-year activities of a federal agency. These include not only the agency's constituents but also the cabinet secretaries, executive branch bodies such as the Office of Management and Budget, and the president. The Congress and its committees as well as the Congressional Budget Office and public interest groups also play a vital role. Indeed, these parties should demand better service. Conscious use of the hidden stimulus should become part of an integrated strategy designed to restore economic growth without inflation.

*A "summary agenda" enumerating several specific challenges and reforms along this line is suggested in William A. Niskanen, Jr., *Democracy and Representative Government* (Chicago: Aldine, Atherton, 1971), pp. 227–30. Among Niskanen's challenges are a requirement that all appropriations for an agency receive an approval vote by at least two-thirds of the legislators, the creation of competition among agencies to see who can best perform a given program, and better incentives for federal managers.

Students of management and public administration should also be concerned with the *hidden stimulus*. For this stimulus to be effective, it must be effectively applied. This case study of the Coast Guard has shown that general management in a federal agency is quite different from general management in the private sector—at least in the nature of an important stimulus to better performance.

APPENDIX 1

**SELECTED EVENTS
AFFECTING THE
COAST GUARD,
1790–1980**

Year	Event
1790	Alexander Hamilton develops fiscal plans and economic policies for the United States. On 4 August, Congress passes the Tariff Act, creating the United States Revenue Marine.
1791	First cutter built and first officer commissioned.
1797	United States relations with France deteriorate. While Congress argues over creation of the navy, it passes legislation authorizing the president to "increase the strength of several cutters." The Revenue Marine is kept a separate entity from the new navy.
1798	Congress establishes the Navy Department.
1798–99	Undeclared war with France. Cutters cooperate with navy but maintain their own identity.
1799	The dual-role strategy of the Coast Guard has its beginnings. Military status granted to Revenue Marine personnel by Congress. Congress mandates that "revenue cutters, when the President of the United States shall so direct, cooperate with the Navy . . . under the direction of the Secretary of the Navy." Revenue-collecting role retained under Treasury Department and local collector of customs in various port areas. Cutters diversified to a third role of enforcing laws and treaties.
1801	Loss of both Hamilton and Gallatin as secretaries of the treasury and the inauguration of Jefferson as president lead to a decentralized Revenue Marine. Cutter captains report to local collectors of customs.
1807	*Clermont*, equipped with Robert Fulton's steam-power equipment, sails from New York to Albany, initiating an era of rapid change in the technology of marine transportation. This change is punctuated by many marine casualties.
1912–14	Cutters participate in War of 1812.
1815	Cutters enforce piracy laws in Caribbean and Gulf of Mexico.
1829	In his first year as president, Andrew Jackson proposes that revenue cutters be built in navy yards and that midshipmen of the navy be appointed to fill officer vacancies aboard revenue cutters.

1836–37   Congress authorizes the Revenue Marine to diversify into offshore rescue work and "winter cruising" to search for and rescue vessels in distress. The dual-role strategy of performing both military and peacetime roles is later expanded to the multimission concept. The multiple peacetime missions include revenue collection, law enforcement, and search and rescue.

1838   Marine boiler and other casualties bring about marine safety legislation, leading to the creation of the Steamboat Inspection Service. At the same time, the combination of regional economic pressures in the United States and the Panic of 1837 lowers revenue collections. This sharply diminishes the original mission of the Revenue Marine and raises the question of liquidating or cutting back the organization.

1840   Senate Commerce Committee criticizes the decentralized operation of the cutters under the local collectors of customs. The Revenue Marine is threatened with takeover by the navy.

1843   Commerce committee examines the operation of the Revenue Marine in the Treasury Department and finds that "sound policy requires that the revenue service and the naval service should be kept distinct." The dual-role strategy is affirmed.

1843   John C. Spencer is appointed secretary of the treasury by President John Tyler. Spencer, former congressman and secretary of war, creates a centralized Revenue Marine Bureau in the Treasury. He appoints Captain Alex Fraser, a cutter captain, to head the bureau. A centralized Revenue Marine organization is established for the first time since 1790–1801.

1847–48   Offshore disasters create pressures in Congress that lead to the creation of the Life Saving Service.

1848   Cutters blockade Mexican coasts during Mexican War.

1849   Regionalism again becomes important in national politics. Congress creates a commissioner of customs in the Treasury Department. The centralized Revenue Marine is disbanded, and cutter captains again report to the local collectors of customs.

1861–65   Most cutters are on the side of the Union during the Civil War.

1867   After Alaskan purchase, cutters are sent to the new territory to patrol, to survey, and to provide medical and judicial aid to isolated communities.

1869   Secretary of the Treasury George Boutwell creates an interim bureau within the Treasury Department to include the Revenue Marine, the Steamboat Inspection Service, the Marine Hospital, and the Life Saving Service. Two committees within the Revenue Marine focus on the human and physical resources of the Revenue Marine and make important policy recommendations.

1876   On 31 July, Congress authorizes a school of instruction to train officers for the Revenue Marine.

1878   On 18 June, Congress authorizes the Life Saving Service as an autonomous organization within the Department of the Treasury. (It is operated separately until the act of 28 January 1915 merges the Revenue Marine and the Life Saving Service.)

1889   Leonard Shepard, a cutter captain, is ordered to Washington by the secretary of the treasury to serve as chief of the Revenue Marine Division. The process of institutionalizing an Office of the Commandant headed by a Revenue Marine career officer begins.

1894	Congress authorizes the Office of the Commandant, creating a legal as well as an administrative basis for the post.
1898	Cutters participate in Spanish-American War.
1911	Revenue Cutter Service, the new name for the Revenue Marine, is assigned patrol duties to enforce the North Pacific Sealing Convention.
1911	President Taft receives authority from Congress to appoint a Commission on Economy and Efficiency to study government reorganization.
1912	President recommends to Congress a reorganization of the Revenue Cutter Service. The reorganization threatens to liquidate the service. The plan calls for cutters and military personnel to be transferred to the navy and remaining resources to be transferred to various other federal agencies.
1912	*Titanic* strikes an iceberg and sinks in the north Atlantic.
1913	Two cutters begin the International Ice Patrol, designed to alert north Atlantic shipping to icebergs within the shipping lanes.
1915	Threat of liquidation is averted. Instead, an act of Congress adds the Life Saving Service to the Revenue Cutter Service. The expanded organization is named the Coast Guard, used as an informal name for the Revenue Cutter Service for more than fifteen years. Congress recognizes the dual-role strategy in the act as a vital part of the new Coast Guard.
1916	Congress authorizes Coast Guard aviation.
1917–18	Coast Guard is transferred as one organization to the Navy Department during World War I.
1919	Navy Department tries to retain the Coast Guard, but the Coast Guard is returned to the Treasury Department, affirming the dual-role strategy.
1920	Navy initiates congressional hearings as part of a continued yet unsuccessful attempt to take over the Coast Guard.
1920–33	Prohibition leads to the Rum War at sea.
1939	The United States Lighthouse Service is transferred from the Department of Commerce to the Coast Guard.
1941	World War II. Coast Guard is assigned to navy; performs varied functions in the United States and around the world.
1942	Bureau of Marine Inspection and Navigation, originally established in 1838 as the Steamboat Inspection Service under the Department of Commerce, is temporarily transferred to the Coast Guard.
1942	Coast Guard becomes involved with loran (a long-range electronic navigation aid).
1946	Coast Guard returns to the Department of the Treasury on 1 January. The temporary transfer of the Bureau of Marine Inspection and Navigation is made permanent.
1947	Committees on appropriations of the House and Senate order an independent study of the Coast Guard. Ebasco Services Incorporated of New York is selected to conduct the study.
1948	Ebasco Report makes wide recommendations to the Congress, the Treasury Department, and the Coast Guard on charting a postwar course for the Coast Guard.
1949	General reorganization and recodification of Title 14, United States Code, covering the laws governing the Coast Guard is prepared and passed by Congress.

1950–53   Coast Guard units serve in the Korean War. Port Security program is expanded.

1956–62   Aviation Board of 1956 leads to the Aviation Plan and then Cutter and Shore Unit Plans, which in turn lead to a more centralized planning system.

1961   Secretary of Treasury Dillon requests that a study of the roles and missions of the Coast Guard be conducted.

1962   Roles and Missions Study completed.

1965   Coast Guard operational units first serve in Vietnam.

1967   Coast Guard as one service becomes an operating agency within the new Department of Transportation.

1967   *Torrey Canyon* is grounded off England, heightening worldwide concern over the hazards of oil pollution.

1969   National Environmental Policy Act enhances domestic interest in the quality of the marine environment.

1972   Congress passes the Ports and Waterways Safety Act and important amendments to the Federal Water Pollution Control Act.

1974   Congress passes the Deepwater Port Act.

1976   *Argo Merchant* grounded near Nantucket.

1977   President and Congress express concern about tanker safety.

1977   United States establishes two-hundred-mile offshore fishing limit.

1980   General Accounting Office outlines Coast Guard problems.

APPENDIX 2

A CASE STUDY
FOR DISCUSSION

As he rode to his office on Wednesday morning, 15 January 1975, Admiral Owen Siler reviewed a draft of the "State of the Coast Guard" message he planned to present at a meeting scheduled for noon the next day. Siler reflected on the past six months, his first as commandant of the United States Coast Guard.

As Admiral Siler reviewed the challenges and opportunities covered in his address, he realized that since his return from the Pacific War Zone in 1945 the Coast Guard's missions had nearly doubled. The recent passage by the Senate of the Emergency Marine Fisheries Protection bill (SB 1988) by a 68 to 27 vote seemed to signal further growth. For good reason, he would predict the next day: "We have experienced considerable mission changes in recent years and the pace will likely quicken in the near future." He was particularly conscious that the pace of mission change had markedly accelerated over the past eight years, the time span of Coast Guard operation as a part of the Department of Transportation.

Admiral Siler glanced over his opening paragraphs:

As the CO or our ship of the Coast Guard during the next four years, I intend to follow the sound course that has been plotted by my predecessors. I wish to regroup and strengthen the Coast Guard and to build on what has been done before. This is not a stand-pat policy but one that will require us to respond quickly and enthusiastically to changing missions. . . . the Department of Transportation is pleased with the multi-mission functions of the Coast Guard. We are, in all modesty, its showcase in the increasingly important maritime world.

The Office of Management and Budget continually finds us to be a cost-effective service. It has vigorously challenged our budget requests and I am happy to report that we have justified them. For FY 1976, we are expecting to send our biggest dollar budget ever to the Congress. . . .

Due to budget constraints, we have been unable to reach the desired strength in marine environmental protection, enforcement of laws and treaties, port safety and security, and search and rescue programs. Although the quality of personnel working in these fields is excellent, we just don't have enough people on board to fulfill our missions performance standards.

While we are grappling with manpower restrictions in certain fields, we must also be concerned with our aging capital plant, which is becoming increasingly difficult to manage. Our ships, aircraft, and some shore stations are not being replaced at a satisfactory rate. They are becoming increasingly difficult and costly to maintain.

259

The commandant's eyes came to the part of his address dealing with SB 1988 and the "two-hundred-mile economic zone." For three years the chief of operations and his staff had done extensive staff work on fisheries and the two-hundred-mile economic zone. The chief counsel and his Law of the Sea group had been participating in international discussions on the pros and cons of extending the territorial waters of the United States. SB 1988, which had passed the Senate on 11 December 1974, emphasized American frustration at the failure of international negotiations and proposed, instead, a unilateral congressional extension of certain aspects of United States jurisdiction from the present twelve miles to two hundred miles offshore. The bill gave enforcement responsibility to the Coast Guard; it died when the House took no action on the bill by the end of the Ninety-third Congress.

With action on a new version of the Emergency Marine Fisheries Protection bill very probable in the Ninety-fourth Congress, Admiral Siler took these developments very seriously:

I fully expect action to be completed during the next 12 months on the establishment of a 200-mile limit for our fisheries—either by international agreement or unilaterally by the Congress. This zone will be equal to one-third the size of the continental United States or the size of the historic Louisiana Purchase. To implement this, we forecast the activation of six HEC's and ten HH-52's and procurement of six LRS aircraft and four additional MRS aircraft. This alone represents 1,700 personnel, operating funds of $47 million, and an initial investment of $63 million dollars. . . .*

Our old HEC's—High Endurance Cutters—and MEC's—Medium Endurance Cutters—must be replaced in the not too distant future. Six of the 327-footers were built in 1936 and, while they were more sturdily constructed than some later vessels, they do face replacement. We also have five 255's built in the Mid-40's that are now in reserve and would have to be replaced soon if required for patrolling the 200-mile economic zone.

The question of replacement becomes more significant if my expectation regarding the 200-mile economic zone is borne out during the next year. We will have to move quickly to activate the 255's and one of the older 327-foot vessels. They have been laid up for quite a while and we will experience problems when we bring them back into active service. . . .

When the 200-mile zone is created, more emphasis will be placed on the hot pursuit of violators. The Russians and Japanese have some speedy fishing vessels which can probably only be corralled by high speed vessels of at least 20 knots combined with helo operations from the ships.

During the next 12 to 36 months, we must launch a program of replacement for fixed wing aircraft. On 10 January the request for proposal for a medium range search, MRS, aircraft to replace the Albatross was distributed. We expect to start delivery of the first of 41 aircraft by the last half of 1977. Depending on the outcome of structural evaluations to be initiated soon, we may also have to replace the HH-52 short range helicopter and the HH-3 medium range rescue heliocopter.

Admiral Siler reflected on the challenges presented to the Coast Guard if the two-hundred-mile economic zone soon became a reality. An area "the size of the historic Louisiana Purchase" certainly stretched the concept of operations. Siler's thoughts returned to his "State of the Coast Guard Message":

In addition to considering the many problems related to our aging physical plant, . . . Program Directors must raise their planning horizon—become more involved in determining what the Coast Guard will need ten years from now. There must be a new effort to look at the needs we predict for the Coast Guard during the early part of the 1980's.

---

*High endurance cutters (HEC) are the largest Coast Guard cutters used for fishery law enforcement; some HEC's can launch shipboard helicopters (HH). Long and medium range search aircraft are designated as LRS and MRS, respectively.

As his car turned off Constitution Avenue away from a view of the Capitol and approached the Nassif Building, Siler's eyes fell upon one section of his address to which he planned to give particular emphasis:

Since we have had historically a "policy lag" averaging three years between the time of an incident and when remedial legislation is enacted, we must take steps to reduce this lag. Also, as the leader in the marine transportation field, we must take the lead in proposing and/or executing legislation in areas where new laws are needed.

As he walked from the elevator to his office in the Nassif Building, he reiterated to himself this desire to anticipate as well as react. Such concern convinced him to call for a review of the potential impacts of the two-hundred-mile economic zone on the Coast Guard.

At 0850, Rear Admiral Edward Scheiderer, chief of staff of the Coast Guard, came to the commandant's office with an agenda for the morning meeting of the office chiefs. Admiral Siler leaned back in his chair and said, "Ed, I have been giving considerable thought to the strategic decisions we face on the two-hundred-mile zone. They certainly will affect the long-term development of the Coast Guard. You remember the position paper Bob Scarborough presented for the Office of Operations; it developed a concept of operations for meeting increased fisheries activities. I am particularly concerned about both policy lag and budget lag."

"Well, Admiral," Scheiderer replied, "the two-hundred-mile zone certainly presents an important strategic problem. We must assess AC&I* and operating expense needs; we have done that, but we should look at how this new program best blends with our plans for other programs. We must also remember that the spring preview budget is due to the deputy undersecretary before 15 April."

"Ed, what do you think of polishing our alternatives on this, assessing costs, and then convening the Coordinating Board? But this time, in addition to the deputy chief of staff, the chiefs of Program, Budget, and Plans Evaluation, and the deputy office chiefs—the usual group—why not bring in the district chiefs of staff, the deputy area commanders, and the assistant superintendent of the academy?"

"By polishing our alternatives, Admiral, do you mean a meeting between Bob Scarborough, myself, and our staffs, preparing a position, with alternatives and questions that then could be presented to the expanded 'Coordinating Board?' "

"Exactly. When can you and Operations have the presentation to the expanded group ready for me to look over?"

"I will try to have a schedule set by Friday."

The Staff Study

Admiral Scheiderer turned first to a staff study that had been prepared and forwarded to the commandant on 31 October 1974, by the chief of the Office of Operations, Rear Admiral Bob Scarborough. This study was a position paper synthesizing previous studies and data gathered by the Coast Guard, and particularly by the program manager for Ocean Operations. Admiral Scarborough had defined the central problem as the need to develop

*Acquisition, construction, and improvement (AC&I) is the term used for capital budgets.

a concept of operations for meeting increased fisheries enforcement activities. His report made the following assumptions:

1. Within a year, as a result of unilateral action or the Law of the Sea Conference, the United States will claim jurisdiction over coastal fisheries to a distance of two hundred miles from United States coasts.
2. Control of anadromous species originating within the United States will be claimed to the full range of their migration except within the territorial waters or contiguous fisheries zone of any other nation.
3. Foreign vessels will be permitted to participate in United States coastal and anadromous fisheries in accordance with international agreements or licensing schemes yet to be developed.
4. Fisheries enforcement operations will provide a base for future enforcement operations dealing with nonliving resources.
5. This extension of jurisdiction will generate demands that some coverage be made of the entire zone.

These assumptions complemented the following facts that had been determined through several studies, summarized in supplement 1.

1. The active commercial fishing areas of the United States can be described both geographically and seasonally. Fishing fleet density and patterns can to some extent be predicted based upon several variables, including fish migration.
2. A two-hundred-mile zone contains 2,222,000 square nautical miles and has a perimeter of 8,700 nautical miles.
3. The total value of United States Fisheries landings within two hundred miles of United States shore was approximately $800 million.

These facts and assumptions had become the basis for further work and study by the Office of Operations. An extensive simulation model of fishery operations and patrols had been completed by the Operations Planning Staff a year earlier.

A Strategy Meeting

Early on Friday, 17 January 1975, Ed Scheiderer took the first step in fulfilling his promise to the commandant. He convened a meeting with Bob Scarborough and their respective Programs and Plans staffs to review Scarborough's proposals for meeting the responsibilities that would arise if a two-hundred-mile economic zone became a reality. Specifically, their agents called for "analysis of alternative methods for meeting increased fisheries law enforcement duties." It also called for preparing a presentation that would be given to the expanded Coordinating Board, as Admiral Siler had asked two days earlier. The chief of staff and operations had to determine what that presentation should be and when and how to present it to the commandant before its consideration by the expanded Coordinating Board.

Admiral Scheiderer began the meeting by asking Admiral Scarborough to summarize the general fishery enforcement situation. Admiral Scarborough began:

The Coast Guard will, in the long run, be more affected by any regulations actually imposed on foreign fishing vessels than by any extension of the contiguous fisheries zone. These regulations will probably change from time to time depending on such things as the status of fish stocks off our coasts, the availability of protein from other sources, and the harvesting capacity of the U.S. Coastal fishing fleet. Probability of violation will vary with such things as the status of fish stocks in other parts of the world, the attitude of other coastal nations towards foreign harvesting of their coastal stocks, and the degree of acceptance of the regulations by the nations whose vessels are fishing off our coasts. Composite plots of foreign fishing vessel sightings over a two year period give good indications where and for what species foreign fishermen are now fishing off U.S. coasts. Although the patterns change from time to time and new fisheries are developed, there is no reason to believe that the active fishing areas will expand dramatically following an extension of jurisdiction. Accordingly, the approaches that we will now consider reflect basically an active fisheries area approach.

He continued: "Basically, I see five separate alternatives for meeting increased fisheries law enforcement duties: As we discuss them, please be aware of our most current costs of acquiring new capital equipment and their annual operating expenses. You will have a copy of these costs" (see exhibit 1). He used a viewgraph projection to display the alternatives:

EXHIBIT 1
United States Coast Guard: Miscellaneous Coast Guard Cost Figures Associated with Fishery·
Enforcement Operations (costs in fiscal 1975 dollars)

Annual operating costs	
High endurance cutters (378′ HEC)	$2,800,000 each
(255′ WHEC)	2,000,000 each
Medium endurance cutters (MEC)	1,100,000 each
Long range search aircraft (LRS)—augmented	2,304,400 each
Medium range search aircraft (MRS)	600,000 each
Helicopter for shipboard use (at present HH-52A)	321,000 each

Acquisition costs

HEC(L)	$22,000,000 each	
MEC	10,600,000 each	
LRS	5,519,000 each	
MRS	$ 2,810,000 each	

Operate cutters without regard to fuel cost—$1,000,000 increase annually
Overload of cutter crews—$1,830,000 increase annually for 10 percent overload (increased costs are for operations in excess of 180 days)
Reactivation of 6 HECs—$6,800,000
Reactivation of HH-52 helicopter—for shipboard use—$100,000 each
Costs of coverage approaches (assuming that other Coast Guard mission loads permit use of cutters and aircraft for fisheries patrols at same rate as during fiscal year 1973 and 6 HECs and 17 helicopters are available in reserve)

1. Cutters 60 miles apart along 200-mile perimeter with aircraft coverage of zone twice weekly. Operate cutters and aircraft—$744 million annually.[a] Acquire or reactivate needed additional cutters and aircraft—$5.84 billion.
2. Cutters 400 miles apart along 200-mile perimeter with aircraft coverage of zone twice weekly. Operate cutters and aircraft—$202 million annually.[a] Acquire or reactivate needed additional cutters and aircraft—$1.4 billion.
3. Planned approach:

Acquire or reactivate needed cutters and aircraft	$52.2 million
One-time startup costs	11.0 million
Normal annual cost to operate annual cutters and aircrafts[b]	47.2 million
Total normal plus one-time costs	58.2 million

Source: Ocean Operations Division, 18 September 1974. These cost estimates may have to be revised as a result of unforeseen and rapidly rising costs of reactivating, acquiring, and operating the various equipment.
[a] Support costs not considered.
[b] Includes support costs.

Alternative I. The main thrust of this approach would provide various levels of coverage of known active fishing areas in direct proportion to the experienced intensity of foreign fishing activity, i.e., enforcement efforts would concentrate on those areas where and when the fishing will most likely be done. A mix of long and medium range aircraft would patrol the areas to monitor foreign fishing activity and provide fishing vessel locations to cutters on fisheries patrols. A mix of high and medium endurance cutters with helicopters embarked whenever possible would be used to monitor foreign fishing activity through examination from the helicopter and the cutter itself as well as through any boarding of the foreign vessels that may be permitted. The cutters would also make any seizures that might be required.

Admiral Scarborough stated that this part of the approach "is very similar to current efforts" under such provisions as:

1. 16 USC 986. National and international measures of control in connection with the International Convention for the Northwest Atlantic Fisheries. The convention covers the primary fishing areas off the East Coast and extends well beyond two hundred miles.

2. 16 USC 1083. Enforcement of the prohibition on foreign taking of continental shelf fishery resources. The area of enforcement of this provision extends beyond the two-hundred meter isobath as far as the depth of the superjacent water admits exploitation of the resources and the seabed and subsoil are adjacent to the United States. This area covers primary fishing areas off all coasts.

3. 16 USC 1027. National and international measures of control in connection with the International Convention for the High Seas Fisheries of the North Pacific Ocean. This convention applies to north Pacific Ocean and Bering Sea areas that are in some cases more than two hundred miles from the United States coast.

Scarborough went on to explain in more detail alternative I, which he obviously preferred:

In addition to the coverage of known active fishing areas, some coverage to the full range of 200-mile jurisdiction would be provided to: (1) determine if changes in patterns of fishing activity are occurring; (2) make Coast Guard's presence known throughout the area; and (3) facilitate apprehension. This additional coverage is basically the difference between the five-year plan assuming no extension of fisheries jurisdiction and a five-year plan with an extension of jurisdiction to 200 miles plus the range of anadromous species originating in the United States.

Implementation of this alternative will require an increase in operating facilities of six high endurance cutters (presently decomissioned in reserve), six long range search aircraft, four medium range search aircraft, and ten shipboard helicopters. To operate these facilities will require an increase in our annual operating funds of $47.2 million. The start up, acquisition and reactivation costs are estimated at $63.2 million. Both costs are estimated in 1975 fiscal dollars.

The chief of operations went on to detail the critical "concept of operations" needed to follow alternative 1. The capital cost of $63.2 million and annual operating expense of $47.2 million would provide coordinated air/surface operations in the form of regular coverage, and less extensive and periodic coverage. The regular coverage of the active fishing areas would include:

1. Surveillance patrols of each area; by long and medium range search aircraft at a frequency varying from monthly to three times a week depending on the season.

2. Patrols by high and medium endurance cutters with helicopters aboard cutters with flight decks, the number of vessels on patrol at any one time depending on the season.

3. Ship-helicopter teams and other cutters conduct coordinated surveillance, boarding and data-gathering activities in their own right and in response to information and reports from the surveillance aircraft.

The less extensive coverage of the entire two-hundred-mile zone to detect changes in fishing fleet operations would include:

1. Weekly surveillance patrols to the limits of jurisdiction by long and medium range search aircraft.

2. Periodic surface projections to the limit of jurisdiction by high and medium endurance helicopter-equipped cutters.

Admiral Scarborough then presented four additional alternatives, which he considered but seemed not to favor.

Alternative II. The approach is a variation of the planned approach we have just discussed. It omits coverage to the full range of the 200-mile jurisdiction.

To implement this approach would require increasing our operating facilities by four long range search aircraft, two medium range search aircraft and 10 helicopters. To operate these facilities will require an increase in our annual operating funds of $20.4 million. The start-up, acquisition, and reactivation cost are estimated at $32 million.

Alternative III. Picket line—vessel spacing 400 miles. This approach utilizes a mix of high and medium endurance cutters every 400 miles along the 200-mile perimeter and a mix of long and medium range aircraft patrolling the zone twice a week. This operates on the theory that most violators sighted by the twice weekly overflights could be boarded within 24 hours. Operating costs would be about $200 million annually and acquisition and reactivation costs would be about $1.4 billion.

Alternative IV. Picket line—vessel spacing 60 miles. This approach utilizes a mix of high and medium endurance cutters every 60 miles along the 200-mile perimeter and a mix of long and medium range aircraft patrolling the zone twice a week. Operating costs would be about $750 million annually and acquisition and reactivation costs would be about $6 billion.

Alternative V. Satellite and other monitoring. The use of satellites has been investigated in the recent Westinghouse study, "Application of Space Telecommunications Systems to Coast Guard Missions," which was limited to nonclassified systems. State of the art satellite systems can fix the position of surface vessels. This can be done very economically and accurately if the tracked vessels cooperate and carry some sort of transponder. The possibility is remote that potential violators would carry such equipment, and in any case cutters would still be required for apprehension. Further, information needs are greater than for mere tracking. Existing domestic laws and international agreements require knowledge of the mesh size of nets in use (requirements vary depending on material net is made of), proper record keeping, species being retained by size and quantity, type of gear being used and transfers being made between nested vessels. Unclassified state of the art satellite systems cannot provide this type of information. There are no other existing unclassified monitoring systems known which would be able to monitor and track foreign fishing vessels within a 200-mile zone.

Admiral Scarborough went on to discuss points that should be continually reexamined in the future.

Although Alternative V suggests that state of the art unclassified satellite systems do not afford us the necessary tools needed for fisheries law enforcement, it does not address classified systems. The various divisions of the Office of Operations are attempting to determine if there are DOD or NASA classified systems that may be of value. The information being sought will cover different types of surveillance/tracking systems not necessarily limited to satellites and will include underwater detection devices as well as high flying (U-2?) aircraft. The preliminary determination based on contracts with both DOD and NASA is that classified systems could do very little for fisheries law enforcement.

Additionally, inquiries should be made as to the availability/feasibility of lighter-than-air craft (blimps). They have some attractive aspects such as high visibility, durability, fuel economy, and an ability to hover. Unknown at this time is their availability and support requirements. Initial avenues of information will probably include DOD and the Goodyear Tire and Rubber Company.

Bob Scarborough summed up his presentation forcefully: "Gentlemen, after extensive examination of our studies and preliminary deliberations, I have concluded that:

1. Effective enforcement must provide for both surveillance and apprehension.

2. It is not feasible to provide 100 percent coverage of the entire zone at all times.

3. Augmentation of existing forces presents a reasonable interim 'state of the art' approach to meeting projected responsibilities. Therefore I recommend that we adopt alternative I as our initial concept of operations. At the same time we should continue to examine alternative intelligence and surveillance systems.''

After thanking the chief of operations for his presentation, Admiral Scheiderer asked the representatives of the Programs Division if they had any questions. Captain Jack Costello, chief of the Programs Division, questioned the costs:

"As I understand your cost estimates, you propose to reactivate six thirty-year-old cutters for $6.8 million and spend $4.8 million per year *each* to keep them in service. I hope that these estimates provide for all contingencies, but I'm not sure from the data

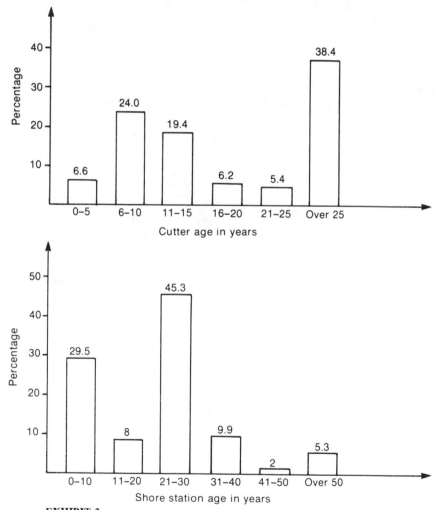

EXHIBIT 2
Distribution of United States Coast Guard cutters and shore stations by age, as of 1975

EXHIBIT 3

United States Coast Guard: AC & I Levels
Necessary to Replace the Coast Guard's 1975
Inventory of Cutters at Various Depreciation Rates

1975 cutter value	$1,812,325,000
Life 13.7 years	132,300,000
17 years	106,300,000
20.4 years	88,800,000

Note: Any valuation of existing cutters or pricing of
new cutters is of course complicated by rapidly rising prices and must be constantly updated and re-
evaluated.

before us. Also, does this proposal make sense given our cutter plan and our AC&I plans
for cutter replacement?''

"On that last point, Jack," Admiral Scarborough answered, "We are working with
the Office of Engineering in developing requirements and characteristics for a new cutter
uniquely designed for this duty, which we are referring to as a HEC/MEC. The reactivated
HECs will only fill the gap for necessary cutter days for fishery patrol in the interim.''

Costello responded, "I feel the age distributions of our cutters, aircraft, electronics,
and in some cases, the shore facilities, too, should be addressed. I feel we must examine
the AC&I capital flows necessary to replace older cutters, planes, and stations at a
satisfactory rate." (Exhibit 2 shows the distribution of cutters, planes and stations by age.
Exhibit 3 displays the capital budget necessary to replace cutters just to "stay even and not
catch up," at various depreciation rates. Exhibit 4 shows the capital needed just to retain
present age profiles for aircraft, electronics, and shore facilities.)

Bob Scarborough answered, "I feel that the strategy we develop to provide cutters to
respond to our fishery patrol duties is critical. But let's get back to you and your questions
on the other estimates.''

Costello responded, "You propose to go to the store and buy six new LRS and four
new MRS with a combined price tag of $44.2 million. I'm not sure just what this price tag
includes. For example, does it include the nonrecurring costs of recruiting and training
new pilots, air crews, and ground support personnel; or do we have enough people already

EXHIBIT 4
United States Coast Guard Capital Asset Profile Review

Asset Type	Percentage of Asset Type of Total	Asset Replacement Factor	Total CG Asset by Type (billions of dollars)	AC&I Required for Yearly "Stay even" (millions of dollars)
Shore plant	0.42	.057	1.814	100
Vessels	0.43	.055	1.812	100
Electronics	0.04	.089	0.151	13
Aircraft	0.11	.094	0.493	47
	1.00	.059	4.270	260

Note: 1975 review value of all Coast Guard physical assets was $4,270 billion.

on board to man and service these aircraft? Similarly, will any new facilities be required to house or service these aircraft, or can they be handled within existing capabilities? How confident are you in the $16.2 million annual cost operating cost estimate for these ten aircraft—particularly given rising costs of fuel, parts, and personnel?

"Just following along, you propose to spend $1.0 million to activate ten HH-52As, which will then cost us $1.9 million per year to fly. I have questions about pilots, crews, ground support, facilities, fuel and parts here, too.

"Finally, even if we feel confident in these estimates, the total price tag for alternative I is $110.4 million for 1976 and $47.2 million each year thereafter. I have some qualms about this, because my reading of SB 1988 suggests that only $13.0 million per year may be authorized for this program. What if that turns out to be the case?"

Admiral Scarborough wondered how to respond to Captain Costello and, more important, what he and Admiral Scheiderer would recommend to the commandant for consideration by the expanded Coordinating Board.

Supplement 1: A Bibliography Abstract of Available Studies—Ocean Operations Division

1. Composite plots of foreign fishing vessels off United States coasts. Four graphs covering the Atlantic, Gulf, West, and Alaskan coasts from July 1971 to the present.
2. Charts showing location of fish off United States coasts. Five charts showing location of fish types off Atlantic, Gulf, Pacific, and Alaskan coasts.
3. Charts showing surveillance areas off United States coasts by season. Six charts depicting surveillance areas off the New England, Midatlantic, Gulf, Pacific Northwest, and Alaskan coasts. The charts give the length of the tracks and time needed to fly them.
4. Charts showing additional planned coverage for a two-hundred-mile zone. Two charts depict the two-hundred-mile limit and search tracklines off all United States coasts.
5. Aircraft hour and ship requirements for active fishing areas approach. Gives the number of cutter and air patrol days and flight hours by month and locality for planned coverage of the active fishing areas.

EXHIBIT 5
Migratory Ranges: Coastal Living Resources off the Coast of the United States

---

Species by area

North Atlantic: cod, haddock, redfish, yellowtail flounder, silver hake, herring, alewife, mackerel, American lobster, deepsea prawn

West central Atlantic including Gulf of Mexico: snappers, drum and croaker, silver hake, menhaden, jacks, black mullet, anchovy, shrimp, royal red shrimp, spiny lobster, blue crab

East central Pacific: Pacific hake, north Pacific anchovy, sardines, crabs, shrimp

Northeast Pacific: Pacific Ocean perch, Pacific hake, sablefish, Alaska pollack, Pacific cod, Pacific halibut, arrowtooth flounder, yellowfin sole, rock sole, flathead sole, Dover sole, herring, squid, deepwater prawn, king crab, tanner crab, dungeness crab, shrimp

---

Source: *Atlas of the Living Resources of the Seas* (Rome: Food and Agriculture Organization of the United Nations, 1972).

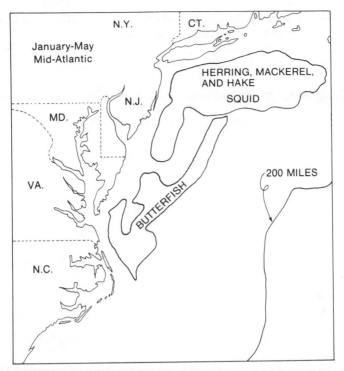

EXHIBIT 6
Locations of fishing grounds off the East Coast of the United States

6. Aircraft hour and ship day requirements for additional planning coverage. Gives the number of flights required to cover the entire jurisdiction of a two-hundred-mile regime over and above that required of the active fishing areas approach. Combining the two results in the planned approach.

7. Five-year resource requirements and operating costs for active fishing areas approach. Breakdown of procurement, reactivation, startup and operating expense costs through fiscal year 1979 to carry out the proposed active fishing areas approach.

8. Five-year resource requirements and operating costs for planned approach—two-hundred-mile jurisdiction. Breakdown of procurement, reactivation, startup and operating expense costs through fiscal year 1979 to carry out the proposed planned approach—two-hundred-mile jurisdiction.

9. Commandant letter of 23 August 1974 to Honorable John Murphy, chairman of the House subcommittee on Coast Guard and Navigation outlining Coast Guard plans for a two-hundred-mile zone.

10. Contingency plan to meet aviation requirements for enforcement of fisheries laws and agreements in a two-hundred-mile economic management zone. Explores the mix of different type aircraft suitable for the program. Includes interim leasing costs, procurement startup costs and availability of aircraft.

11. Enforcement of Fisheries Laws and Treaties study, Phase I, Plans Staff, Office of Operations, 10 September 1973. An aid in making informed judgments in determin-

ing resource requirements. Develops methods of quantitatively relating ELT program objectives to alternative resource allocation levels.

12. Westinghouse study: Applications of Space Telecommunications Systems to Coast Guard Missions.

13. G-000-4 Examination of November 1973.

14. G-CPE Study of December 1973.

NOTES

Chapter 1

1. Michael A. Murray, "Comparing Public and Private Management: An Exploratory Essay," *Public Administration Reveiw* 35, no. 4 (1975): 364.

2. See, for example, Edmund P. Learned, C. Roland Christensen, Kenneth R. Andrews, and William D. Guth, *Business Policy* (Homewood, Ill.: Richard D. Irwin, 1965); George A. Steiner, *Top Management Planning* (New York: Macmillan, 1969); Joseph L. Bower, *Managing the Resource Allocation Process* (Boston: Division of Research, Harvard Business School, 1970); and Kenneth R. Andrews, *The Concept of Corporate Strategy* (Homewood, Ill.: Dow Jones–Irwin, 1971).

3. Aaron Wildavsky, *The Politics of the Budgetary Process*, 2d ed. (Boston: Little, Brown, 1974). Also see Alan W. Steiss, *Public Budgeting and Management* (Lexington, Mass.: Lexington Books, 1972), and Bower, *Managing the Resource Allocation Process*.

4. Thomas Paine, *The Rights of Man*. See also Frank J. Goodnow, *Politics and Administration* (New York: Macmillan, 1914). This title contains the two words Woodrow Wilson applied to this dichotomy in 1887. For a further discussion of these points, see Steiss, *Public Budgeting and Management*, pp. 2, 45–52, 221.

5. Steiss, *Public Budgeting and Management*.

6. Ibid., p. 2.

7. Herbert A. Simon, *Administrative Behavior* (New York: Free Press, 1945).

8. Learned et al., *Business Policy*.

9. Charles E. Lindblom, *The Policy Making Process* (Englewood Cliffs, N.J.: Prentice-Hall, 1968). See also David Braybrooke and Charles E. Lindblom, *A Strategy of Decision* (New York: Free Press, 1963).

10. Bower, *Managing the Resource Allocation Process*.

11. Braybrooke and Lindblom, *A Strategy of Decision*. See Charles E. Lindblom, *Policymaking Process*, and his *The Intelligence of Democracy* (New York: Free Press, 1965). See also Charles E. Lindblom, "The Science of 'Muddling Through,'" *Public Administration Review* 19 (spring 1959): 79–88.

12. Lindblom, "The Science of 'Muddling Through.'"

13. Wildavsky, *Politics of the Budgetary Process*. See also Richard F. Fenno, Jr., *The Power of the Purse: Appropriations Politics in Congress* (Boston: Little, Brown, 1966), and Robert D. Lee, Jr., and Ronald W. Johnson, *Public Budgeting Systems*, 2d ed. (Baltimore: University Park Press, 1977).

14. Ibid., p. 205.

15. Allen Shick, *Budget Innovation in the United States* (Washington, D.C.: Brookings Institution, 1971), p. 104; idem, "The Road to PPB: The States of Budget Reform," *Public Administration Review*, vol. 26 (fall 1966). See also Wildavsky, *Politics of the Budgetary Process*, p. 200.

16. Robert N. Anthony and Regina E. Herzlinger, *Management Control in Nonprofit Organizations* (Homewood, Ill.: Richard D. Irwin, 1975). See David Novick, *Origin and History of Program Budgeting* (Santa Monica, Calif.: Rand Corporation, 1966); David Novick, ed., *Program Budgeting: Program Analysis and the Federal Budget* (Cambridge: Harvard University Press, 1965.) Hinrichs and Taylor have edited a collection of examples of the use of PPBS for both planning and evaluation of results of performance. See Harold H. Hinrichs and Graeme M. Taylor, eds., *Program Budgeting and Benefit-Cost Analysis* (Pacific Palisades, Calif.: Goodyear Publishing, 1969).

17. Thomas D. Lynch, *Policy Analysis in Public Policymaking* (Lexington, Mass.: Lexington Books, 1975), p. 49.

Chapter 2

1. See, for example, Edmund P. Learned, C. Roland Christensen, Kenneth R. Andrews, and William D. Guth, *Business Policy* (Homewood, Ill.: Richard D. Irwin, 1965); George A. Steiner, *Top Management Planning* (New York: Macmillan, 1969); Kenneth R. Andrews, *The Concept of Corporate Strategy* (Homewood, Ill.: Dow Jones-Irwin, 1971); Joseph L. Bower, *Managing the Resource Allocation Process* (Boston: Division of Research, Harvard Business School, 1970); or Alfred D. Chandler, Jr., *Strategy and Structure* (Cambridge: MIT Press, 1962).

2. Chandler, *Strategy and Structure,* p. 13.

3. Andrews, *Concept of Corporate Strategy,* p. 28.

4. See, for example, almost identical lists in Learned et al., *Business Policy,* pp. 25-28, and Andrews, *Concept of Corporate Strategy,* p. 28.

5. Philip Selznick, *Leadership in Administration: A Sociological Interpretation* (Evanston, Ill.: Row, Peterson, 1957), p. 42. See also Andrews, *Concept of Corporate Strategy,* pp. 38, 89-102.

6. Chandler, *Strategy and Structure.*

7. Hugo E. R. Uyterhoeven, Robert W. Ackerman, and John W. Rosenblum, *Strategy and Organization* (Homewood, Ill.: Richard D. Irwin, 1973), p. 71.

8. Andrews *Concept of Corporate Strategy,* pp. 26-41.

9. Uyterhoeven et al., *Strategy and Organization,* p. 12.

10. Peter Lorange and Richard F. Vancil, "How to Design a Strategic Planning System," *Harvard Business Review* 54, no. 3 (1976), pp. 75-81; and *Strategic Planning Systems* (Englewood Cliffs, N.J.: Prentice-Hall, 1977).

11. Richard F. Vancil and Peter Lorange, "Strategic Planning in Diversified Companies," *Harvard Business Review* 53, no. 1 (1975): 81.

12. Lorange and Vancil, "How to Design a Strategic Planning System," p. 81.

13. Robert A. Pitts, "Strategies and Structures for Diversification," *Academy of Management Journal* 20, no. 2, (1977): 197.

14. For a discussion of much of this research, see Pitts, "Strategies and Structures," pp. 197-208. Also see Chandler, *Strategy and Structure,* and R. P. Rumelt, *Strategy, Structure, and Economic Performance of the Fortune "500"* (Cambridge: Harvard University Press, 1974).

15. Henry Mintzberg, *The Nature of Managerial Work* (New York: Harper and Row, 1973).

16. Bower, *Managing the Resource Allocation Process.*

17. Ibid., p. 73.

18. Ibid., pp. 66-71, 321-22.

19. Ibid., pp. 66, 68, 321-22.

20. Ibid., pp. 66, 71-72, 267-77.

21. Charles Chester Burger, *Survival in the Executive Jungle* (New York: Macmillan, 1964), p. 190.

22. Russell L. Ackoff, "Toward a System of Systems Concepts," *Management Science* 17 (July 1971): 661.

23. Alan Walter Steiss, *Public Budgeting and Management* (Lexington, Mass.: Lexington Books, 1972), pp. 8-9. Steiss quotes Ludwig von Bertalanffy on the concept of open and closed systems. For a discussion of the openness of a system, see William A. Shrode and Dan Voich, Jr., *Organization and Management: Basic Systems Concepts* (Homewood, Ill.: Richard D. Irwin, 1974), pp. 127-28.

24. Frank T. Paine and William Naumes, *Strategy and Policy Formulation: An Integrative Approach* (Philadelphia: W. B. Saunders, 1974), pp. 47-54.

25. Ibid., p. 49.

26. Ibid., pp. 47–58.

27. Ibid., p. 50.

28. Frank T. Paine and William Naumes, *Organizational Strategy and Policy* (Philadelphia: W. B. Saunders, 1975), p. 99.

29. Michael A. Murray, "Comparing Public and Private Management: An Exploratory Essay," *Public Administration Review* 35, no. 4. (1975): 364–71. See Steiss, *Public Budgeting and Management*, Herbert A. Simon, *Administrative Behavior* (New York: Macmillan, 1949).

See also William A. Niskanen, Jr., *Bureaucracy and Representative Government* (Chicago: Aldine, Atherton, 1971).

30. For a similar list for the private sector, see Learned et al., *Business Policy*, pp. 25–28, and Andrews, *Concept of Corporate Strategy*, p. 28.

31. Charles E. Lindblom, *The Policy-making Process* (Englewood Cliffs, N.J.: Prentice-Hall, 1968), p. 29.

32. Herbert Emmerich, *Federal Organization and Administrative Management* (University: University of Alabama Press, 1971). See Michael P. Balzano, *Reorganizing the Federal Bureaucracy: The Rhetoric and the Reality* (Washington, D.C.: American Enterprise Institute for Public Policy Research, 1977). See also Niskanen, *Bureaucracy and Representative Government*.

33. Harold Seidman, *Politics, Position, and Power: The Dynamics of Federal Organization*, 2d ed. (New York: Oxford University Press, 1975), pp. 13–14.

34. James G. March and Herbert A. Simon, *Organizations* (New York: John Wiley, 1958). See also Richard M. Cyert and James G. March, *A Behavioral Theory of the Firm* (Englewood Cliffs, N.J.: Prentice-Hall, 1963).

35. Seidman, *Politics, Position, and Power*, p. 18.

36. Selznick, *Leadership in Administration*.

37. Francis E. Rourke, *Bureaucracy, Politics, and Public Policy*, 1st ed. (Boston: Little, Brown, 1969).

38. Ibid., p. 23.

39. Ibid.

40. Seidman, *Politics, Position, and Power*. See also Rourke, *Bureaucracy, Politics, and Public Policy*.

41. Richard F. Fenno, *The Power of the Purse: Appropriations Politics in Congress* (Boston: Little, Brown, 1966). See Aaron Wildavsky, *The Politics of the Budgetary Process*, 2d ed. (Boston, Little, Brown, 1974). See also Allen Schick, "The Appropriations Committees versus Congress," Paper presented to the 1976 annual meeting of the American Political Science Association, San Francisco, p. 1.

42. Richard E. Neustadt, *Presidential Power: The Politics of Leadership* (New York: John Wiley, 1960). See also Seidman, *Politics, Position, and Power*.

43. Anthony Downs, "Up and Down with Ecology: The 'Issue-Attention Cycle,'" *Public Interest*, no. 28 (summer 1972), pp. 38–50.

44. Ibid., pp. 39–41.

45. Ibid., pp. 48–50.

46. Francis E. Rourke, *Bureaucracy, Politics, and Public Policy*, 2d ed. (Boston: Little, Brown, 1976), p. 81.

47. Rourke, *Bureaucracy, Politics, and Public Policy*, 1st ed., p. 93.

48. Donald A. Schon, "Champions for Radical New Inventions," *Harvard Business Review* 41, no. 2 (1963): 84.

Chapter 3

1. Alfred D. Chandler, Jr., *Strategy and Structure* (Cambridge: MIT Press, 1962), p. 13.

2. Frank T. Paine and William Naumes, *Organizational Strategy and Policy*, 2d ed. (Philadelphia: W. B. Saunders, 1978), pp. 17–18.

3. Charles E. Lindblom, *The Policy-making Process* (Englewood Cliffs, N.J.: Prentice-Hall, 1968); *The Intelligence of Democracy* (New York: Free Press, 1965); and his "The Science of 'Muddling Through,'" *Public Administration Review* 19 (spring 1959): 79–88. See also Anthony

Downs, "Up and down with Ecology: 'The Issue-Attention Cycle,' " *Public Interest*, no. 28 (summer 1972), pp. 38-50.

4. William A. Niskanen, Jr., *Bureaucracy and Representative Government* (Chicago: Aldine, Atherton, 1971).

5. Ibid.

6. Hugo E. R. Uyterhoeven, Robert W. Ackerman, and John W. Rosenblum, *Strategy and Organization* (Homewood, Ill.: Richard D. Irwin, 1973), p. 13.

7. U.S. Coast Guard, *1976-1986 Plan Summaries,* 17 December 1973. This document has been updated yearly, but these basic objectives remain the same in 1980.

8. U.S. Coast Guard, Program Division, Office of the Chief of Staff, Interview, January 1979. Much of the material in this chapter was obtained in interviews at various offices at Coast Guard headquarters, May-July 1974, June-August 1975, January-December 1977. The material was updated in February 1979.

9. For a discussion of the concept of environmental constraints, see chapter 2. One of the primary references for the discussion there is Edmund P. Learned, C. Roland Christensen, Kenneth R. Andrews, and William D. Guth, *Business Policy* (Homewood, Ill.: Richard D. Irwin, 1965), or the 1978 revision.

10. U.S. Coast Guard, *U.S. Coast Guard Planning and Programming Manual* (CG-411), 21 July 1977, p. I-10.

11. Robert H. Scarborough, "Resource Allocation in the Coast Guard," an address given by the chief of staff of the coast guard to the corps of cadets at the United States Coast Guard Academy, 21 February 1976. In this talk, Rear Admiral Scarborough described the key actors, the roles, and the process itself.

12. See two student papers documenting early stages of this research. Daniel J. Elliott and Jeffery M. Garrett, "The Coast Guard Budget Process," a term project in the Department of Economics and Management at the U.S. Coast Guard Academy, 1974. See also Richard John Losea, "Planning, Programming, and Budgeting for Resource Allocation in the United States Coast Guard," an M.S. thesis in the Administrative Sciences Department at the Naval Post Graduate School, 1976. I was coadvisor for this thesis. The work of Dan Elliott and Jeff Garrett was helpful in the preparation of the thesis by Rich Losea and also of this chapter.

13. For one extensive discussion of the factors involved in introducing PPBS into the Defense Department, which created the background for its introduction into the Coast Guard, see Thomas D. Lynch, *Policy Analysis in Public Policymaking* (Lexington, Mass.: Lexington Books, 1975), pp. 1-6.

14. For a discussion of PPBS in the 1960s, see Robert D. Lee, Jr., and Ronald W. Johnson, *Public Budgeting Systems* (Baltimore: University Park Press, 1977), pp. 79-108. See also David Novick, "What Program Budgeting Is and Is Not," in *Current Practices in Program Budgeting (PPBS)* David Novick, ed. (New York: Crane, Russek, 1973).

15. U.S. Coast Guard, *Planning and Programming Manual,* p. I-2.

16. For general discussions of the roles and power of public role players, see either Francis E. Rourke, *Bureaucracy, Politics and Public Policy,* 2d ed. (Boston: Little, Brown, 1976), or Harold Seidman, *Politics, Position and Power,* 2d ed. (New York: Oxford University Press, 1975).

17. Scarborough, "Resource Allocation in the Coast Guard."

18. This is the familiar adversary process for making public budgets, well described in Aaron Wildavsky, *The Politics of the Budgetary Process,* 2d ed. (Boston: Little, Brown, 1974). Also see Novick, "What Program Budgeting Is and Is Not," and Lee and Johnson, *Public Budgeting Systems.*

19. Scarborough, "Resource Allocation in the Coast Guard."

20. U.S. Coast Guard, *The Long Range View,* Commandant Instruction 16014.1. See also the *Planning and Programming Manual,* pp. I-2, 3, 7, and III-1.

21. U.S. Coast Guard, *Planning and Programming Manual,* p. I-10, and appendix 1.

22. U.S. Coast Guard, *Plan Summaries.* For a detailed description of the process by which the plan summaries are prepared, see Losea, "Planning, Programming, and Budgeting," pp. 32-35.

23. U.S. Coast Guard, *Planning and Programming Manual,* pp. I-9; III-10, 11, 12; IV-2.

24. Ibid.

25. Scarborough, "Resource Allocation in the Coast Guard," p. 6.

26. U.S. Coast Guard, *Planning and Programming Manual,* p. III-3, and appendix I-2.

27. U.S. Coast Guard, *Planning and Programming Manual,* pp. I-5, III-7–15, IV-2, and appendixes D, J.

28. U.S. Coast Guard, *Shore Units Plan Report,* 6 March 1973, appendix I.

29. U.S. Coast Guard, *Planning and Programming Manual,* pp. I-6, III-4, IV-2.

Chapter 4

1. Rear Admiral Robert H. Scarborough, "Resource Allocation in the Coast Guard," an address given by the chief of staff of the Coast Guard to the corps of cadets at the United States Coast Guard Academy, 21 February 1976. In this talk Admiral Scarborough clearly differentiated between the "planning process for the ideal Coast Guard" and the "resource allocation process for the possible Coast Guard."

For a discussion of policy analysis in the Coast Guard, see Thomas D. Lynch, *Policy Analysis in Public Policymaking* (Lexington, Mass.: Lexington Books, 1975).

2. U.S. Coast Guard, *Planning and Programming Manual* (CG-411), 21 July 1977, p. III-4.

3. Scarborough, "Resource Allocation in the Coast Guard," pp. 8–9.

4. U.S. Coast Guard, *Planning and Programming Manual,* p. III-5.

5. U.S. Coast Guard, *Program Determinations for Fiscal Year 1976,* file 7110.2, 4 February 1974.

6. Ibid.

7. Daniel J. Elliott and Jeffery M. Garrett, "The Coast Guard Budget Process," a term project at the U.S. Coast Guard Academy, 1974, p. 24.

8. U.S. Coast Guard, *Planning and Programming Manual.*

9. U.S. Coast Guard, *Manual of Budgetary Administration CG-255,* pp. 2–3.

10. For general discussions of the budgetary process in Washington, see any standard text, such as Aaron Wildavsky, *The Politics of the Budgetary Process,* 2d ed. (Boston: Little, Brown, 1974); Richard F. Fenno, *The Power of the Purse: Appropriations Politics in Congress* (Boston: Little, Brown, 1966); or Robert D. Lee, Jr., and Ronald W. Johnson, *Public Budgeting Systems,* 2d ed. (Baltimore: University Park Press, 1977).

11. U.S. Department of Transportation, Instruction 5100.2.

12. U.S. Coast Guard, *Manual of Budgetary Administration,* pp. 2–8.

13. Ibid.

14. Scarborough, "Resource Allocation in the Coast Guard," p. 16.

15. Ibid.

16. Allen Schick, "The Appropriations Committees versus Congress," paper presented to annual meeting of American Political Science Association, San Francisco, 1976. See also Fenno, *Power of the Purse,* pp. 72, 114; and Wildavsky, *Politics of the Budgetary Process.*

17. See Schick, "Appropriations Committees," Wildavsky, *Politics of the Budgetary Process,* or Fenno, *Power of the Purse.* See also William A. Niskanen, Structural Reform of the Federal Budget Process (Washington, D.C.: American Enterprise Institute, 1973).

18. Scarborough, "Resource Allocation in the Coast Guard," p. 18.

19. Wildavsky, *Politics of the Budgetary Process,* p. 58.

20. Ibid., pp. 47–62, 89.

21. Scarborough, "Resource Allocation in the Coast Guard," p. 19.

22. Wildavsky, *Politics of the Budgetary Process,* pp. 61–62. See also Schick, "Appropriations Committees," and Fenno, *Power of the Purse.*

23. Scarborough, "Resource Allocation in the Coast Guard," pp. 19–20.

24. U.S. Coast Guard, *Manual of Budgetary Administration,* pp. 3–13.

25. U.S. Coast Guard, *Planning and Programming Manual,* p. I-8. "Format for submission by Program Managers is prescribed at the time the call for Planning Factors is made."

26. U.S. Coast Guard, *Manual of Budgetary Administration,* pp. 2–15.

Chapter 5

1. Warren G. Bennis and Phillip Slater, *The Temporary Society* (New York: Harper and Row, 1968), p. 56. For a discussion of the formative days of loran, see Gifford Hefley, *The Development*

of Loran-C Navigation and Timing (Washington, D.C.: U.S. Government Printing Office, 1972), pp. 5–7. See also J. A. Pierce, R. H. Woodward, and A. A. McKenzie, *Radiation Laboratory Series,* vol. 4 (New York: McGraw-Hill, 1948), for a thorough account of the days until 1946. A discussion of this period as well as of postwar development of the system appears in P. C. Sandretto, *Electronic Navigation Engineering* (New York: International Telephone and Telegraph Corporation, 1958).

2. Malcolm F. Willoughby, *U.S. Coast Guard in World War II* (Annapolis, Md.: United States Naval Institute, 1957), pp. 150–52. For a discussion of operational research teams developed for this purpose, and of "Blackett's Circus," see Stafford Beer, *Decision and Control* (New York: John Wiley, 1966), pp. 34–46.

3. Hefley, *Development of Loran-C*, p. 5. See also Willoughby, *U.S. Coast Guard in World War II*, p. 150.

4. Hefley, *Development of Loran-C*, p. 5. See Willoughby, *U.S. Coast Guard in World War II*, pp. 150–52. See also James L. Penick, Jr., et al., eds., *The Politics of American Science: 1939 to the Present* (Cambridge: MIT Press, 1972), pp. 57–77.

5. Willoughby, *U.S. Coast Guard in World War II*.

6. Ibid., p. 152.

7. Ibid., pp. 152–53.

8. For a good discussion of the role of the "champion," see Donald A. Schon, "Champions for Radical New Inventions," *Harvard Business Review* 41, no. 2 (1963): 77–86. For a discussion of the role of the project manager, see two articles by Edward B. Roberts: "Entrepreneurship and Technology," *Research Management* 11, no. 4 (1968): 249–66; and "Generating Effective Corporate Innovation," *Technology Review* 80, no. 1 (1977): 27–33. For a definition of the role of the "gatekeeper" in the process of technological innovation, see Thomas Allen, "The World. Your Company. A Gate of Information! Who Guards the Gate?" *Innovation*, no. 8 (1969), pp. 33–39. For a discussion of Commander Lawrence Harding's role, see Willoughby, *U.S. Coast Guard in World War II*, pp. 152–53. Harding was later promoted to captain.

9. Willoughby, *U.S. Coast Guard in World War II*, pp. 153–56.

10. Ibid., p. 156.

11. Richard A. Pasciuti, "The History of Detachment Mike," *Coast Guard Engineer's Digest* 19, no. 196 (1977): 2–11. See also Willoughby *U.S. Coast Guard in World War II*, p. 160.

12. Walter C. Capron, *U.S. Coast Guard* (New York: Franklin Watts, 1965), p. 181. See also Willoughby, *U.S. Coast Guard in World War II*, p. 161.

13. Capron, *U.S. Coast Guard*, p. 181. See also Willoughby, *U.S. Coast Guard in World War II*, p. 162.

14. Willoughby, *U.S. Coast Guard in World War II*, pp. 164–68.

15. Ibid., pp. 167–68. See also Capron, *U.S. Coast Guard*, pp. 181–82.

Chapter 6

1. U.S., Congress, House, Committee on Appropriations, *Hearings before the Subcommittee on the Coast Guard Appropriation Bill for 1947*, 79th Cong., 2d sess., 19, 20 March, 4 April 1946, p. 34.

2. Ibid., pp. 6, 14–15, 111–12.

3. Ebasco Services, Incorporated, *Study of United States Coast Guard* (New York: Ebasco Services, 1948), p. 1.

4. Walter C. Capron, U.S. Coast Guard (New York: Franklin Watts, 1965), p. 176.

5. Gifford Hefley, *The Development of Loran-C Navigation and Timing* (Washington, D.C.: U.S. Government Printing Office, 1972), p. xi.

6. Ebasco Services, *Study of United States Coast Guard*, pp. 5–6, 9–10, 189–92, 245–47, 255–60.

7. Capron, *U.S. Coast Guard*, pp. 179–84. See also H. R. Kaplan and James F. Hunt, *This Is the Coast Guard* (Cambridge, Md.: Cornell Maritime Press, 1972), pp. 75–76, 112–16.

8. Ibid., pp. 182–83.

9. Hefley, *Development of Loran-C Navigation and Timing*.

10. Ibid., pp. xi, xii, 1–4.

11. Ibid., pp. xi, 72.

12. Ibid., pp. 72–81.

13. U.S. Code, Title 14, section 81. See also Hefley, *Development of Loran-C Navigation and Timing,* pp. 83–86.

14. U.S., Congress, House, H.R. Doc. no. 93–30, *Hearings before the Subcommittee on Coast Guard and Navigation of the Committee on Merchant Marine and Fisheries on H.R. 13595;* 93d Cong., 2d sess., 26, 28 March, 25 April 1974, pp. 94–98.

15. Jansky and Bailey, Inc. "Engineering Evaluation of the Loran-C Navigation System," final report, September 1959 (Washington, D.C.: Contract no. Tcg-40547, 1959), p. 133.

16. Hefley, *Development of Loran-C Navigation and Timing,* pp. 94–98.

Chapter 7

1. U.S., Congress, House, H.R. Doc. no. 93-30, *Hearings before the Subcommittee on Coast Guard and Navitation of the Committee on Merchant Marine and Fisheries on H.R. 13595,* 93d Cong., 2d sess., 26, 28 March 25 April 1974, p. 266. The first quote came from a letter by Comptroller General Elmer B. Staats to Congressman John Murphy, subcommittee chairman, quoted in H.R. Doc. 93-30.

2. Polhemus Navigation Sciences, "Candidate Navigation Systems," May 1969. See also "Cost Benefit/User Requirement Analysis, Northwest Atlantic," October 1969, United States Coast Guard files. See also H.R. Doc. no. 93–30, p. 149.

3. H.R. Doc. no. 93–30, p. 99.

4. Ibid., p. 149.

5. Ibid.

6. Polhemus Navigation Sciences, "Radio Aids to Navigation—Coastal Confluence Region," interim report no. 1, March 1972; interim report no. 2, June 1972; final report, July 1972, United States Coast Guard files. See H.R. Doc. no. 93-30. See also Jansky and Bailey, Incorporated, "Engineering Evaluation of the Loran-C Navigation System," final report, September 1959, Washington, D.C.: Contract Tcg-40547, 1959.

7. Beukers Labs, "Differential Omega Monitoring and Analysis," vols. 1–3, May 1972, and addendum, June 1972, United States Coast Guard files.

8. Ports and Waterways Safety Act of 1972, 86 Stat. 424, P.L. 93-340, 33 U.S.C. 1221 et seq., 10 July 1972.

9. U.S. Department of Interior, *An Analysis of the Economic and Security Aspects of the Trans-Alaska Pipeline,* vol. 1 (Washington, D.C.: U.S. Government Printing Office, 1971).

10. H.R. Doc. no. 93-30, pp. 266–67. The quotes come from a letter written by Comptroller General Elmer B. Staats to Congressman John Murphy, subcommittee chairman, quoted in H.R. Doc. no. 93-30.

11. U.S. Department of Transportation, *National Plan for Navigation,* 1972. This plan was updated in July 1974, after the hearings before the Subcommittee on Coast Guard and Navigation in March 1974.

12. H.R. Doc. no. 93-30.

13. Ibid., pp. 104–6.

14. Ibid., pp. 223–26.

15. Ibid., p. 226.

16. Ibid., p. 1.

17. Ibid., p. 91.

18. Ibid., pp. 94–117.

19. Ibid., p. 118.

20. Ibid., pp. 119–20.

21. Ibid., pp. 121, 130–32.

22. Ibid., pp. 148–222.

23. Ibid., pp. 223–62.

24. Ibid., p. 264.

25. Ibid., p. 281.

26. Ibid., p. 285.

27. Ibid., p. 336. For further information on the Wild Goose Association, see *Radionavigation Journal 1976* (Acton, Mass.: Wild Goose Association, 1976).

28. Ibid., p. 301. Mr. Fraser's testimony appears on pp. 296–335.

29. Ibid., p. 516.

30. Ibid., pp. 514–19.

31. U.S. Department of Transportation, *National Plan for Navigation,* annex, July 1974, pp. 1–4.

32. *National Plan for Navigation,* 1972.

33. See Richard R. Nelson, Merton J. Peck, and Edward D. Kalachek, *Technology, Economic Growth, and Public Policy* (Washington, D.C. Brookings Institution, 1967); Joseph Schmookler, *Invention and Economic Growth* (Cambridge: Harvard University Press, 1966); Richard R. Nelson, *The Rate and Direction of Inventive Activity: Economic and Social Factors* (Princeton: Princeton University Press, 1962); William H. Gruber and Donald G. Marquis, eds., *Factors in the Transfer of Technology* (Cambridge: MIT Press, 1969); Brian Twiss, *Managing Technological Innovation* (London: Longman Group, 1974); and Robert R. Rothberg, ed., *Corporate Strategy and Product Innovation* (New York: Free Press, 1976).

34. Joel D. Goldhar, Louis K. Bragaw, and Jules J. Schwartz, "Information Flows, Management Styles, and Technological Innovation," *IEEE Transactions on Engineering Management* 23, no. 1 (1976): 51–62.

35. U.S. Department of Transportation, *Loran-C Conceptual Analysis,* report prepared for National Highway Traffic Safety Administration, July 1976, p. 56.

36. U.S., Congress, Senate, S. Doc. no. 2965, 94th Cong. 2d sess.; *Hearings before the Committee on Armed Services on Fiscal Year 1977 Authorization for Military Procurement, Research and Development, and Active Duty, Selected Reserve and Civilian Personnel Strengths* 15, 16, 17 March 1976, p. 5312.

Chapter 8

1. W. M. Benkert, "This Business of Tankers . . . ," Remarks to the Marine Transportation Board of the National Research Council, May 1977. Reprinted in *Bulletin* 39, no. 4. (1977): 20–24.

2. Morris A. Adelman, *The World Petroleum Market* (Baltimore: Johns Hopkins University Press, 1972), pp. 34–36, 85–88. See Melvin G. de Chazeau and Alfred E. Kahn, *Integration and Competition in the Petroleum Industry* (New Haven: Yale University Press, 1959, pp. 208, 212. See also Robert Stobaugh and Daniel Yergin, eds., *Energy Future,* (New York: Random House, 1979), pp. 16–26. See also *New York Times Magazine,* 10 March 1974, p. 25.

3. Adelman, *World Petroleum Market.* Also see Michael S. Macrakis, ed., *Energy: Demand, Conservation, and Institutional Problems* (Cambridge: MIT Press, 1974), and Zenon S. Zannetos, *The Theory of Oil Tankship Rates* (Cambridge: MIT Press, 1966). For a discussion of the power of the oil industry, see Robert Engler, *The Politics of Oil* (Chicago: University of Chicago Press, 1961).

4. Louis K. Bragaw et al., *The Challenge of Deepwater Terminals* (Lexington, Mass.: Lexington Books, 1975), pp. 1–2. See Energy Policy Project of the Ford Foundation, *A Time to Choose: America's Energy Future* (Cambridge, Mass.: Ballinger, 1974), pp. 1–6, 19–20. See also Stobaugh and Yergin, *Energy Future.*

5. Energy Policy Project, *A Time to Choose,* pp. 5–6.

6. Ibid., pp. 1–6. See also Bragaw et al., *Challenge of Deepwater Terminals,* pp. 3–4.

7. Committee on U.S. Energy Outlook of the National Petroleum Council, *U.S. Energy Outlook* (Washington, D.C.: National Petroleum Council, 1972), pp. 15–20. See Energy Policy Project, *A Time to Choose,* pp. 12–17. See also Stobaugh and Yergin, *Energy Future,* p. 232, and Macrakis, *Energy,* pp. 3–87.

8. Energy Policy Project, *A Time to Choose,* pp. 477–81. See also a preliminary report by the Energy Policy Project, *Exploring Energy Choices* (Washington, D.C.: Energy Policy Project, 1974), p. 74. A more detailed overview of this point is available in M. King Hubbert, "The Energy Resources of the Earth," *Scientific American,* vol. 224, no. 3 (1971).

9. Energy Policy Project, *A Time to Choose.* See also Bragaw et al., *Challenge of Deepwater Terminals,* pp. 1–14.

10. Bragaw et al., pp. 12–16.

11. Stephen H. Evans, *The United States Coast Guard 1790–1915: A Definitive History* (Annapolis, Md.: United States Naval Institute, 1949), p. 118.

12. Refuse Act of 1899, 30 Stat. 1152, 33 U.S.C. 407.

13. W. M. Benkert, "We Must All Go in the Same Direction . . . ," Address to the 1973

Conference on Prevention and Control of Oil Spills. Reprinted in *Bulletin* 35, no. 4, (1973): 49–50. Another account of activity in the control of pollution of the seas is contained in James E. Moss, "Petroleum: The Problem," in *Impingement of Man on the Oceans*, ed. Donald W. Hood (New York: John Wiley, 1971), pp. 391–419. Moss discusses international conferences on oil pollution going back to the 1926 conference held in Washington. See also Edward Cowan, *Oil and Water: The Torrey Canyon Disaster* (Philadelphia: J. B. Lippincott, 1968), pp. 215–16.

14. Kenneth E. Boulding, "The Economics of Spaceship Earth," in *Environmental Quality in a Growing Economy*, ed. Henry Jarrett (Baltimore: Johns Hopkins University Press, 1966). The problems of the cowboy economy are depicted in a parable related in Garrett Hardin, "The Tragedy of the Commons," in *Pollution, Resources, and the Environment*, ed. Alain C. Enthoven and A. Myrick Freeman, III, pp. 1–13 (New York: W. W. Norton, 1973).

15. Gerald Garvey, *Energy, Ecology, Economy: A Framework for Environmental Policy* (New York: W. W. Norton, 1972), pp. 33.

16. Cowan, *Oil and Water*.

17. W. M. Benkert and R. C. Hill, "Vessell Traffic Systems," *Bulletin*, vol. 34, no. 7 (1972). See also Garvey, *Energy, Ecology, Economy*, pp. 97–99, and Cowan, *Oil and Water*, pp. 217–18.

18. National Environmental Policy Act of 1969, P.L. 91-190, 83 Stat. 852, 42 U.S.C. 4321 et seq. See Anthony Downs, "Up and down with Ecology: The 'Issue-Attention Cycle,'" *Public Interest*, no. 28 (1972), pp. 38–50.

19. Federal Water Pollution Control Act Amendments of 1972, P.L. 92-500, 86 Stat. 816, 33 U.S.C. 1251 et seq; Ports and Waterways Safety Act of 1972, P.L. 92-340, 86 Stat. 424, 33 U.S.C. 1221 et seq. See *Environmental Quality*, Third Annual Report of the Council on Environmental Quality (Washington, D.C.: U.S. Government Printing Office, 1972). See also Henry S. Marcus et al., Federal Port Policy in the United States (Cambridge: MIT Press, 1976), pp. 73–86.

20. Noel Mostert, *Supership* (New York: Alfred A. Knopf, 1974).

21. Zannetos, *Theory of Oil Tankship Rates*, pp. 174–85. Material in this section is adapted from Bragaw et al., *Challenge of Deepwater Terminals*, pp. 14–24.

22. Adelman, *World Petroleum Market* pp. 102–6. See also Zannetos, *Theory of Oil Tankship Rates*.

23. Cowan, *Oil and Water*, pp. 1–8. See also Adelman *World Petroleum Market;* Zannetos, *Theory of Oil Tankship Rates;* and J. G. Hale and R. J. Dean, "Oil Transportation Studies," in Macrakis, *Energy*, pp. 417–24.

24. See Lewis Beman, "Betting $20 Billion in the Tanker Game," *Fortune* 80, no. 20 (1974): 14518. See also Christopher Hayman, "What to Do with All Those Tankers," *New York Sunday Times*, 14 April 1974, p. F-1, and "Heiress at the Helm," *Wall Street Journal*, 6 September 1977, pp. 1, 17.

25. Zenon S. Zannetos, "Some Problems and Prospects for Marine Transportation of Oil in the 1970s," in Macrakis, *Energy*, pp. 403–16.

26. For a discussion of required freight rate, see Harry Benford, "Measures of Merit in Ship Design," *Marine Technology* 7, no. 4 (1970): 465–76; see also Zannetos, *Theory of Oil Tankship Rates*, pp. 127–28. See also Joseph D. Porricelli and Virgil F. Keith, "Tankers and the U.S. Energy Situation: An Economic and Environmental Analysis," *Marine Technology*, vol. 11, no. 4 (1974).

27. Cowan, *Oil and Water*, pp. 8–11, 17–23.

28. Ibid., pp. 9–10.

29. Ibid., p. 22. An interesting account of other dealings of the president and managing director of Barracuda Tanker Corporation are contained in Morton Mintz and Jerry S. Cohen, *America, Inc.* (New York: Dell, 1971), pp. 234–35, 246–49.

30. Henry S. Marcus, "The U.S. Superport Controversy," *Technology Review* 75, no. 5 (1973): 49–57.

31. Fearnley and Egers, *World Bulk Fleet* (Oslo: Fearnley and Egers, 1974); idem, *Large Tankers* (Oslo: Fearnley and Egers, 1974).

32. Louis K. Bragaw, "Environmental Policy Formulation in Competitive Tanker Markets," *Decision Sciences Northeast Proceedings* 3 (1974): 31–34.

33. Samuel A. Lawrence, *International Sea Transport: The Years Ahead* (Lexington: Mass.: Lexington Books, 1972), pp. 34–35.

34. Ibid., pp. 34–36, 266n. See also Cowan, *Oil and Water*, pp. 204–6, and Moss, "Petroleum: The Problem."

35. Cowan, *Oil and Water*, p. 205. See also Lawrence, *International Sea Transport*, p. 266.

36. Cowan, *Oil and Water*, p. 204.

37. Ibid., p. 207.

38. Lawrence, *International Sea Transport*, p. 35. See also Cowan, *Oil and Water*.

39. Robert I. Price, "Anti-Pollution Measures: IMCO Subcommittee on Ship Design and Equipment," *Marine Technology* 8, no. 1 (1971): 1–7.

40. Battelle Memorial Institute, *Oil Spillage Study* (Washington, D.C.: U.S. Government Printing Office, 1967). See also Secretaries of the Departments of Interior and Transportation, *Oil Pollution* (Washington, D.C.: U.S. Government Printing Office, 1967). An analysis of statistics until 1971 are contained in Joseph D. Porricelli, Virgil F. Keith, and Richard Storch, "Tankers and the Ecology," *Transactions of the Society of Naval Architects and Marine Engineers* 79 (1971): 169–98. See also Moss, "Petroleum: The Problem," pp. 397, 404. For a discussion of the mood of the general public toward marine pollution in 1973, see Barry Newman, "Pollution of Oceans Is Enormous Threat, but Few People Care," *Wall Street Journal*, 2 October 1973, pp. 1, 16.

41. See U.S. Coast Guard, *Marine Environmental Protection Program: An Analysis of Mission Performance* (Springfield, Va: NTIS, report no. CG-WEP-1-76, August 1975), for an analysis of the meaning of the oil spill statistics.

42. Macrakis, *Energy*, pp. 1–87. Many of the models of supply and demand are proprietary. A good one that is not is contained in a U.S. Department of Transportation study, *Refinery–Deepwater Port Location Study* (Washington, D.C.: U.S. Department of Transportation, 1974).

43. Bragaw et al., *Challenge of Deepwater Terminals*. See also Stobaugh and Yergin, *Energy Future*, pp. 231–33.

Chapter 9

1. The Refuse Act of 1899, 30 Stat. 1152, 33 U.S.C. 407.

2. The Oil Pollution Act of 1924, 43 Stat. 604–6, 33 U.S.C. 431–37.

3. The Oil Pollution Act of 1961, P.L. 87–167, 75 Stat. 402, 33 U.S.C. 1001 et seq.

4. For a discussion of enforcement of pollution laws in Southern California in the late 1930s, see C. W. Thomas, "Water Pollution Enforcement—1940 Style," *Bulletin* 35, no. 1 (1973): 33–34. Thomas adapted this article from one he had originally published in *Hunting and Fishing* in 1940.

5. *Environmental Quality*, Third Annual Report of the Council on Environmental Quality (Washington, D.C.: U.S. Government Printing Office, 1972), p. 119.

6. The relative usefulness of these laws in pollution enforcement actions until 1970 is discussed in W. M. Benkert, "We Must All Go in the Same Direction . . . ," address to the 1973 Conference on Prevention and Control of Oil Spills, reprinted in *Bulletin* 35, no. 4 (1973): 49; S. A. Wallace, "To Fight to Save: The Environment," *Bulletin* 36, no. 1 (1974): 42; and Henry S. Marcus et al., *Federal Port Policy in the United States* (Cambridge: MIT Press, 1976), pp. 161–62.

7. Benkert, "We Must All Go in the Same Direction," pp. 48–49.

8. U.S. Coast Guard, *Planning and Programming Manual* (CG-411), p. V-55. See also Marcus et al., *Federal Port Policy*, pp. 162–63.

9. National Environmental Policy Act of 1969, P.L. 91-190, 83 Stat. 852, 42 U.S.C. 4321 et seq.

10. Water Quality Improvement Act of 1970, P.L. 91-224, 84 Stat. 91.

11. U.S. Coast Guard, *Ports and Waterways Administration and Management* (Washington, D.C.: U.S. Coast Guard, July 1971), p. 49. See also Marcus et al. *Federal Port Policy*, pp. 162–64.

12. Marcus et al., *Federal Port Policy*, p. 85. Also see United States Environmental Protection Agency, Office of Enforcement and General Counsel, *The National Water Permit Program* (Washington, D.C.: U.S. Government Printing Office, 1973), pp. 20–22; and U.S. Coast Guard, *Ports and Waterways Administration and Management*, p. 13-2-10. For the U.S. Code, see 33 U.S.C. 431, 33 U.S.C. 466.

13. Wallace, "To Fight to Save," p. 41. See also Marcus et al., *Federal Port Policy*, p. 143.

14. Wallace, "To Fight To Save," pp. 41–42.

15. U.S. Coast Guard, *Marine Environmental Protection Program: An Analysis of Mission Performance*, Report no. CG-WEP-1-76, (Springfield, Va.: NTIS, August 1975), p. ii. See also U.S. Coast Guard, *Vessel Traffic Systems Study: Final Report*, vol. 1, Executive Summary

(Washington, D.C.: U.S. Department of Transportation, 1973), pp. 1–3. See also Marcus et al., *Federal Port Policy,* p. 158.

16. W. M. Benkert and R. C. Hill, "Vessel Traffic Systems," *Bulletin* 34, no. 7 (1972): 44–45.

17. Ibid., p. 46.

18. Wallace, "To Fight to Save," p. 44.

19. Ibid., p. 42.

20. Benkert and Hill, "Vessel Traffic Systems," p. 42. See also Gerald Garvey, *Energy, Ecology, Economy* (New York: W. W. Norton, 1972).

21. *Environmental Quality,* p. 119.

22. U.S. Coast Guard, *Vessel Traffic Systems Study: Final Report,* vol. 1, Executive Summary, pp. 1–5.

23. Benkert and Hill, "Vessel Traffic Systems," pp. 52–53.

24. U.S. Coast Guard, *Vessel Traffic Systems Study,* Summary, pp. 8–9. See also Marcus et al., *Federal Port Policy,* p. 159.

25. Ports and Waterways Safety Act of 1972, P.L. 92–340, 86 Stat. 424, 33 U.S.C. 1221 et seq. See also U.S., Congress, Senate, *Doc. No. 92-55,* 92d Cong., 2d sess., 18 January 1972 to 18 October 1972, pp. 1130–36.

26. Federal Water Pollution Control Act Amendments of 1972, P.L. 92–500, 86 Stat. 816, 33 U.S.C. 1251 et seq.

27. Wallace, "To Fight to Save," p. 43.

28. Benkert, "We Must All Go in the Same Direction," p. 50.

29. Ibid.

30. Ibid., pp. 51–52.

31. Louis K. Bragaw, "Environmental Policy Formation in Competitive Tanker Markets," *Decision Sciences Northeast Proceedings* 3 (1974): 31–34.

32. U.S. Coast Guard, *Commandant's Bulletin,* 45-73 and 46-73 (November 1973).

33. Ibid.

34. Ibid.

35. W. M. Benkert, "This Business of Tankers . . . ,'" Remarks to the Marine Transportation Board of the National Research Council, May 1977. Reprinted in *Bulletin* 39, no. 4 (1977): 21.

36. U.S. Coast Guard, *Ports and Waterways Administration and Management,* pp. 10, 120.

37. Ibid., pp. 114–18. See also 33 CFR 6. For a discussion of the functions of the COTP and MIO organizations, see Marcus et al., *Federal Port Policy,* pp. 143–55.

38. U.S. Coast Guard, *Marine Safety Manual,* vol. 1, *Administration and Management* (CG-495), pp. 3-1–6.

39. Wallace, "To Fight to Save," pp. 43–44. See also L. H. Whittemore, "Men of the Coast Guard Strike Force: They Fight Oil Spills All over the World," *Parade,* 10 April 1977, pp. 10–12.

40. Ibid., p. 43.

41. Ibid., p. 42.

42. For a discussion of five stages of an issue, see Anthony Downs, "Up and down with Ecology: The 'Issue-Attention Cycle,'" *Public Interest,* no. 28 (summer 1972), pp. 38–50. For a discussion of bureau supply, see William A. Niskanen, Jr., *Bureaucracy and Representative Government* (Chicago: Aldine, Atherton, 1971), pp. 15–42.

43. U.S. Coast Guard, *Marine Environmental Protection Program: An Analysis of Mission Performance,* pp. 6–7. See also A. Baisuck, J. Harrald, J. Leotta, and W. A. Wallace, "The Implementation and International Applications of a National Information System on Marine Pollution," *Proceedings of the Inter-Governmental Maritime Consultative Organization Symposium on Prevention of Marine Pollution from Ships,* Acapulco, Mexico, 22–31 March 1976.

44. U.S. Coast Guard, *Marine Environmental Protection Program.* Also see A. Charnes, W. W. Cooper, J. Harrald, K. R. Karwan, and W. A. Wallace, "A Goal Interval Programming Model for Resource Allocation in a Marine Environmental Protection Program," *Journal of Environmental Economics and Management* 3 (1976): 347–62.

45. William E. Lehr, "Marine Oil Pollution Control," *Technology Review* 75, no. 4 (1973): 13–22. See also D. F. Boesch, C. H. Hershner, and J. H. Milgram, *Oil Spills and the Environment: A Report to the Ford Foundation* (Cambridge, Mass.: Ballinger, 1974).

46. Leo Jordan and Louis K. Bragaw, "U.S. Coast Guard Offshore Oil Pollution Control Systems," *Offshore Technology Conference Proceedings,* vol. 6., no. 1 (1974).

47. U.S. Coast Guard, *Commandant's Bulletin,* 36-77 (5 September 1977), pp. 6–7.

48. J. L. Robinson, "Marine Environment and Systems: An Exciting Career Pattern," *Bulletin* 35, no. 3 (1973): 43–44. See also Wallace, "To Fight to Save," pp. 46–47.

Chapter 10

1. Louis K. Bragaw, Henry S. Marcus, Gary C. Raffaele, and James R. Townley, *The Challenge of Deepwater Terminals* (Lexington, Mass.: Lexington Books, 1975).

2. U.S. Coast Guard, *Commandant's Bulletin;* 51-74 (23 December 1974), pp. 9–10. See also K. G. Wiman, "Deepwater Ports," *Bulletin* 37, no. 1 (1975): 44–49.

3. The Deepwater Port Act of 1974, 33 U.S.C. 1501, 3 January 1975. See also U.S., Congress, House, *Conference Report on H. R. 10701,* 16 December 1974, H.R. 12036 et seq. See also Wiman, "Deepwater Ports," p. 49.

4. Henry S. Marcus, James E. Short, John C. Kuypers, and Paul O. Roberts, *Federal Port Policy in the United States* (Cambridge: MIT Press, 1976), pp. 190–93.

5. Wiman, "Deepwater Ports." See also Bragaw et al., *Challenge of Deepwater Terminals,* and Marcus et al., *Federal Port Policy.*

6. Shirley Scheibla, "Seadock and LOOP: Industry Is Weighing a Crucial Decision on Deepwater Ports," *Barron's,* 4 April 1977, pp. 11–12, 14, 16.

7. Ibid., p. 11.

8. Ibid.

9. Ibid.

10. U.S. Coast Guard, *Commandant's Bulletin;* 33-77 (15 August 1977), p. 5.

11. Anthony J. Parisi, "A Supertanker Bonanza: Texas, Move Over," *New York Sunday Times,* 20 November 1977, p. F-1.

12. Ibid., p. F-11.

13. Ibid.

14. Ibid.

15. Ibid.

16. Don E. Kash et al., *Energy under the Oceans* (Norman: University of Oklahoma Press, 1973). See also G. Christian Hill, "Offshore Drilling Plan Stirs Heated Debate: Here Are the Facts," *Wall Street Journal,* 8 September 1975, p. 1. See also U.S. Department of Interior, *An Analysis of the Economic and Security Aspects of the Trans-Alaska Pipeline,* vol. 1 (Washington, D.C. U.S. Government Printing Office, 1971).

17. Outer Continental Shelf Lands Act of 1953, 43 U.S.C. 1331. See also Deepwater Port Act of 1974, 33 U.S.C. 1501, and Federal Water Pollution Control Act Amendments of 1972, 33 U.S.C. 1251.

18. U.S. Coast Guard files, *Outer Continental Shelf Scenario,* report of the chief of the Office of Merchant Marine Safety to the chief of staff, dated 10 January 1977.

19. See, for example, U.S., Congress, Senate, Committee on Commerce, "Oil and Gas Development and Coastal Zone Management," *Hearings before the National Ocean Policy Study;* 23, 24, 25 April, 2, 22 May 1974. serial 93-99, 93d Cong., 1st sess. See also U.S., Congress, Senate, Committee on Commerce, "The Oceans and National Economic Development," prepared at the request of Senator Warren G. Magnuson, 93d Cong., 1st sess. Also see Kash et al.,*Energy under the Oceans.*

20. Paul Langer, "Seeking the 'Why' of Argo," *Boston Sunday Globe,* 9 January 1977, pp. 1, 33. See also Stephen R. Katz, "Oil Spills: Who Can Collect?" *Boston Sunday Globe,* 9 January 1977, p. A3. And Daniel F. Gilmore, "*Argo* Just One of 874 Liberian Tankers," *Boston Sunday Globe,* 9 January 1977, p. A3. See also Russell Baker, "Is Nantucket Expendable?" *New York Times,* 29 December 1976.

21. U.S. Department of Transportation, *Report of the Marine Oil Transportation Task Force, 11 January 1977.*

22. *Presidential Documents: Jimmy Carter, 1977* (Washington, D.C.: U.S. Government Printing Office, 1977), p. 107.

23. Office of the White House Press Secretary, "Remarks of the President in an Address to the Nation," 2 February 1977, p. 3.

24. Memorandum for Members of the Interagency Task Force on Oil Pollution from the Director of the Office of Management and Budget, 3 February 1977.

25. Working Papers of the Interagency Task Force on Marine Oil Spill Pollution, 17 February 1977. Summary of DOT Response to Working Papers of the Interagency Task Force on Marine Spill Pollution, 22 February 1977. See also a letter from Secretary of Transportation Brock Adams to President Carter, 4 March 1977.

26. Summary of DOT Response. See also W. M. Benkert, "This Business of Tankers . . . ," Remarks to the Marine Transportation Board of the National Research Council, May 1977, reprinted in *Bulletin* 39, no. 4 (1977): 20–24.

27. U.S., Congress, Senate, Committee on Commerce, *Hearings on Recent Tanker Accidents, Part 1, serial no. 95-4,* 95th Cong., 1st sess., 11, 12 January 1977, pp. 1–9.

28. Ibid., pp. 9–96.

29. Ibid., p. 116.

30. Ibid., p. 117.

31. Ibid.

32. Ibid., p. 157.

33. Ibid, p. 167.

34. Mary Costello, "No End in Sight for Oil Tanker Accidents," *Editorial Research Reports,* 11 March 1977. See also Neil Ulman, "Navigation and Troubled Tankers," *Wall Street Journal,* 15 February 1977, p. 20. See also "Senate to Begin Investigation of Spills," *Boston Sunday Globe,* 9 January 1977, p. 32; Thomas Oliphant, "Two Sides to Tanker Regulations," *Boston Sunday Globe,* 20 March 1977, p. 18; and John D. Williams, "Oil-Tanker Fleets Seek to Increase Safety, but the Accident Rate Remains at Ten a Day," *Wall Street Journal,* 15 March 1977, p. 48.

35. Ibid.

36. U.S., Congress, House, Committee on Appropriations, *Hearings before the Subcommittee on the Department of Transportation and Related Agencies Appropriations for 1978,* 95th Cong., 1st sess., 21 February 1977, pp. 251–52.

37. Ibid., p. 255.

38. Ibid., p. 254.

39. "Tanker Group Urges Liberia to Tighten Its Safety Standards," *Wall Street Journal,* 3 March 1977, p. 23.

40. President Jimmy Carter, *A Message to the Congress of the United States on Marine Pollution,* 17 March 1977. See also White House Fact Sheet, Actions to Reduce Maritime Oil Pollution, 18 March 1977 (5 pp.).

41. White House Fact Sheet, p. 5.

42. See U.S., Congress, Senate, Report of the Senate Committee on Commerce, Science and Transportation on S.682, *The Tanker and Vessel Safety Act of 1977,* Report no. 95-176, 95th Cong., 1st sess., 16 May 1977. See also U.S. Congress, House, S.682, *An Act to Amend the Ports and Waterways Safety Act of 1972,* referred jointly to the Committee on Merchant Marine and Fisheries and International Relations, 1 June 1977.

43. United States Coast Guard, Programs Division, Coast Guard Resource Requirements to Implement President's Initiatives Contained in Message on Marine Pollution, 17 March 1977 (6 pp.).

44. For a discussion of some of the problems environmental regulations brought to the marine manager, see Louis K. Bragaw, William R. Allen, and Edward Roe, "The Impact of Environmental Regulations on the Marine Manager," *Proceedings of the American Institute of Decision Sciences,* vol. 8 (1974).

45. Benkert, "This Business of Tankers," pp. 21–22.

46. Ibid., pp. 20–21.

47. Ibid., pp. 21.

48. For a discussion of ways to handle large spills and a proposal of a spill cleanup system, see Jerome Milgram, "Being Prepared for Future *Argo Merchants,*" *Technology Review* 79, no. 8 (1977): 15–27.

49. James P. Sterba, "Tanker Set to Load First Alaska Crude," *New York Times,* 1 August 1977, p. 10. See also "Valdez: Soon to Be a Bustling Oil Terminal," *Seattle Sunday Times,* 10 July 1977, p. H-9.

50. "U.S. Agrees with Other Maritime Nations on New Rules Aimed at Halting Oil Spills," *Wall Street Journal*, 27 February 1978, p. 12.

Chapter 11

1. Frank T. Paine and William Naumes, *Strategy and Policy Formation: An Integrative Approach* (Philadelphia: W. B. Saunders, 1974), p. iii.

2. David S. Brown, ed., *Federal Contributions to Management* (New York: Praeger, 1971).

3. Ebasco Services, Incorporated, *Study of United States Coast Guard* (New York: Ebasco Services, 1948). See also U.S. Treasury Department, *Study of Roles and Missions of the United States Coast Guard* (Washington, D.C.: Treasury Department, 1962).

4. This conversation is reconstructed from one in a series of interviews I conducted with Admiral A. C. Richmond at his home in Claremont, California, on 26–28 July 1977.

5. Charles E. Lindblom, "The Science of 'Muddling Through,'" *Public Administration Review* 19 (spring 1959): 79–88. See also David Braybrooke and Charles E. Lindblom, *A Strategy of Decision* (New York: Free Press, 1963). See Anthony Downs, "Up and down with Ecology: The 'Issue-Attention Cycle,'" *Public Interest*, no. 28 (summer 1972), pp. 38–50.

6. Chalres E. Lindblom, *The Intelligence of Democracy* (New York: Free Press, 1965); and idem, *The Policy-making Process* (Englewood Cliffs, N.J.: Prentice-Hall, 1968).

7. Joseph L. Bower, *Managing the Resource Allocation Process* (Boston: Division of Research, Harvard Business School, 1970), pp. 66–72, 267–77, 321–22.

8. Philip Selznick, *Leadership in Administration: A Sociological Interpretation* (Evanston, Ill.: Row, Peterson, 1957), pp. 42–64.

SELECTED
BIBLIOGRAPHY

Books

Adelman, Morris A. *The World Petroleum Market*. Baltimore: Johns Hopkins University Press, 1972.

Allison, Graham T. *Essence of Decision: Explaining the Cuban Missile Crisis*. Boston: Little, Brown, 1971.

Andrews, Kenneth R. *The Concept of Corporate Strategy*. Homewood, Ill.: Dow Jones–Irwin, 1971.

Anthony, Robert N., and Herzlinger, Regina E. *Management Control in Nonprofit Organizations*. Homewood, Ill.: Richard D. Irwin, 1975.

Appelby, Paul H. *Policy and Administration*. University: University of Alabama Press, 1949.

Balzano, Michael P. *Reorganizing the Federal Bureaucracy: The Rhetoric and the Reality*. Washington, D.C.: American Enterprise Institute for Public Policy Research, 1977.

Barker, James R., and Brandwein, Robert. *The United States Merchant Marine in National Perspective*. Lexington, Mass.: Heath–Lexington Books, 1970.

Barnard, Chester I. *The Functions of the Executive*. Cambridge: Harvard University Press, 1942.

Baughman, James P. *Charles Morgan and the Development of Southern Transportation*. Nashville: Vanderbilt University Press, 1968.

Beer, Stafford. *Decision and Control*. New York: John Wiley, 1966.

Bell, Daniel, ed. *Toward the Year 2000*. Boston: Houghton Mifflin, 1968.

Bennis, Warren G., and Slater, Phillip. *The Temporary Society*. New York: Harper and Row, 1968.

Boesch, D. F.; Hershner, C. H.; and Milgram, J. H. *Oil Spills and the Environment: A Report to the Ford Foundation*. Cambridge, Mass.: Ballinger, 1974.

Bower, Joseph L. *Managing the Resource Allocation Process*. Boston: Division of Research, Harvard Business School, 1970.

Bragaw, Louis K.; Marcus, Henry S.; Raffaele, Gary C.; and Townley, James R. *The Challenge of Deepwater Terminals*. Lexington, Mass.: Lexington Books, 1975.

Braybrooke, David, and Lindblom, Charles E. *A Strategy of Decision*. New York: Free Press, 1963.

Burger, Charles Chester. *Survival in the Executive Jungle*. New York: Macmillan, 1964.

Burkhead, Jesse. *Government Budgeting*. New York: John Wiley, 1956.

Capron, Walter C. *U.S. Coast Guard*. New York: Franklin Watts, 1965.

Chandler, Alfred D., Jr. *Strategy and Structure*. Cambridge: MIT Press, 1962.

Cowan, Edward. *Oil and Water: The Torrey Canyon Disaster*. Philadelphia: J. B. Lippincott, 1968.

Crozier, Michel. *The Bureaucratic Phenomenon*. Chicago: University of Chicago Press, 1964.

Downs, Anthony. *Inside Bureaucracy*. Boston: Little, Brown, 1967.

Drucker, Peter F. *The Age of Discontinuity*. New York: Harper and Row, 1968.

Easton, David. *A Framework for Political Analysis*. Englewood Cliffs, N.J.: Prentice-Hall, 1965.

——————. *The Political System*. New York: Alfred A. Knopf, 1953.

Emmerich, Herbert. *Federal Organization and Administrative Management*. University: University of Alabama Press, 1971.

Engler, Robert. *The Politics of Oil*. Chicago: University of Chicago Press, 1961.

Evans, Stephen H. *The United States Coast Guard 1790–1915: A Definitive History*. Annapolis, Md.: United States Naval Institute, 1949.

Fayol, Henry. *General and Industrial Management*, Trans. Constance Storrs. London: Putnam, 1949.

Fenno, Richard F. *The Power of the Purse: Appropriations Politics in Congress*. Boston: Little, Brown, 1966.

Ford Foundation, Energy Policy Project. *A Time to Choose: America's Energy Future*. Cambridge, Mass.: Ballinger, 1974.

Furer, Julius Augustus. *Administration of the Navy Department in World War II*. Washington, D.C.: U.S. Government Printing Office, 1959.

Garvey, Gerald. *Energy, Ecology, Economy: A Framework for Environmental Policy*. New York: W. W. Norton, 1972.

Goodnow, Frank J. *Politics and Administration*. New York: Macmillan, 1914.

Gruber, William H., and Marquis, Donald G., eds. *Factors in the Transfer of Technology*. Cambridge: MIT Press, 1969.

Gulick, Luther H., and Urwick, L. F., eds. *Papers on the Science of Administration*. New York: Institute of Public Administration, Columbia University, 1937.

Halperin, Morton H., et al. *Bureaucratic Politics and Foreign Policy*. Washington, D.C.: Brookings Institution, 1974.

Hefley, Gifford. *The Development of Loran-C Navigation and Timing*. Washington, D.C.: U.S. Government Printing Office, 1972.

Hinrichs, Harley H., and Taylor, Graeme M., eds. *Program Budgeting and Benefit-Cost Analysis*. Pacific Palisades, Calif.: Goodyear Publishing, 1969.

Janowitz, Morris. *The Professional Soldier: A Social and Political Portrait*. New York: Free Press, 1960.

Jantscher, Gerald R. *Bread upon the Waters: Federal Aids to the Maritime Industries*. Washington, D.C.: Brookings Institution, 1975.

Johnson, Richard A.; Kast, Fremont E.; and Rosenzweig, James E. *The Theory and Management of Systems*. 3d ed. New York: McGraw-Hill, 1973.

Kaplan, H. R., and Hunt, James F. *This Is the Coast Guard*. Cambridge, Md.: Cornell Maritime Press, 1972.

Kash, Don E., et al. *Energy under the Oceans*. Norman: University of Oklahoma Press, 1973.

Katz, Daniel, and Kahn, Robert. *The Social Psychology of Organizations*. New York: John Wiley, 1966.

Kaufman, Herbert. *The Forest Ranger*. Baltimore: Johns Hopkins University Press, 1960.

Lawrence, Samuel A. *International Sea Transport: The Years Ahead*. Lexington, Mass.: Lexington Books, 1972.

————. *United States Merchant Shipping Policies and Politics*. Washington, D.C.: Brookings Institution, 1966.

Learned, Edmund P.; Christensen, C. Roland; Andrews, Kenneth R.; and Guth, William D. *Business Policy*. Homewood, Ill.: Richard D. Irwin, 1965; rev. ed., 1978.

Lee, Robert D., Jr., and Johnson, Ronald W. *Public Budgeting Systems*. 2d ed. Baltimore: University Park Press, 1977.

Likert, Rensis. *New Patterns of Management*. New York: McGraw-Hill, 1961.

Lindblom, Charles E. *The Intelligence of Democracy*. New York: Free Press, 1965.

————. *The Policy-making Process*. Englewood Cliffs, N.J.: Prentice-Hall, 1968.

Lorange, Peter, and Vancil, Richard F. *Strategic Planning Systems*. Englewood Cliffs, N.J.: Prentice-Hall, 1977.

Lynch, Thomas D. *Policy Analysis in Public Policymaking*. Lexington, Mass.: Lexington Books, 1975.

Macrakis, Michael S., ed. *Energy: Demand, Conservation, and Institutional Problems*. Cambridge: MIT Press, 1974.

Marcus, Henry S.; Short, James E.; Kuypers, John C.; and Roberts, Paul O. *Federal Port Policy in the United States*. Cambridge: MIT Press, 1976.

Merian, Lewis, and Schmeckebier, Lawrence F. *Reorganization of the National Government: What Does It Involve?* Washington, D.C.: Brookings Institution, 1939.

Mintz, Morton, and Cohen, Jerry S. *America, Inc.* New York: Dell, 1971.

Mintzberg, Henry. *The Nature of Managerial Work.* New York: Harper and Row, 1973.

Morrison, Elting E. *Men, Machines and Modern Times,* Cambridge: MIT Press, 1966.

Mostert, Noel. *Supership.* New York: Alfred A. Knopf, 1974.

National Petroleum Council, *U.S. Energy Outlook,* 1972.

Nelson, Richard R. *The Rate and Direction of Inventive Activity: Economic and Social Factors.* Princeton: Princeton University Press, 1962.

―――. *Technology, Economic Growth, and Public Policy.* Washington, D.C.: Brookings Institution, 1967.

Neustadt, Richard E. *Presidential Power: The Politics of Leadership.* New York: John Wiley, 1960.

Niskanen, William A., Jr. *Bureaucracy and Representative Government.* Chicago: Aldine, Atherton, 1971.

―――. *Structural Reform of the Federal Budget Process.* Washington, D.C.: American Enterprise Institute, 1973.

Novick, David. *Current Practices in Program Budgeting (PPBS).* New York: Crane, Russek, 1973.

―――. *Origin and History of Program Budgeting.* Santa Monica, Calif.: Rand Corporation, 1966.

―――, ed. *Program Budgeting: Program Analysis and the Federal Budget.* Cambridge: Harvard University Press, 1965.

Osgood, Robert E.; Hollick, Ann L.; Pearson, Charles S.; and Orr, James C. *Toward a National Ocean Policy: 1980 and Beyond.* Washington, D.C.: U.S. Government Printing Office, 1975.

Paine, Frank T., and Naumes, William. *Organizational Strategy and Policy.* 2d ed. Philadelphia: W. B. Saunders, 1978.

―――. *Strategy and Policy Formulation: An Integrative Approach.* Philadelphia: W. B. Saunders, 1974.

Pell, Claiborne, with Goodwin, Harold Leland. *Challenge of the Seven Seas.* New York: William Morrow, 1966.

Penick, James L., Jr., et al., eds. *The Politics of American Science: 1939 to the Present,* Cambridge: MIT Press, 1972.

Pierce, J. A.; Woodward, R. H.; and McKenzie, A. A. *Radiation Laboratory Series.* Vol. 4. New York: McGraw-Hill, 1948.

Pyhrr, Peter. *Zero-Base Budgeting.* New York: John Wiley, 1973.

Redman, Eric. *The Dance of Legislation.* New York: Touchstone Books, 1974.

Rourke, Francis E. *Bureaucracy, Politics, and Public Policy.* Boston: Little, Brown, 1969; 2d ed., 1976.

Rumelt, R. P. *Strategy, Structure, and Economic Performance of the Fortune "500."* Cambridge: Harvard University Press, 1974.

Sandretto, P. C. *Electronic Navigation Engineering.* New York: International Telephone and Telegraph Corporation, 1958.

Schendel, Dan E., and Hofer, Charles W., eds. *Strategic Management: A New View of Business Policy and Planning.* Boston: Little, Brown, 1979.

Schick, Allen, *Budget Innovation in the United States.* Washington, D.C.: Brookings Institution, 1971.

Schmookler, Joseph. *Invention and Economic Growth.* Cambridge: Harvard University Press, 1966.

Seidman, Harold. *Politics, Position, and Power: The Dynamics of Federal Organization.* 2d ed. New York: Oxford University Press, 1975.

Selznick, Philip. *Leadership in Administration: A Sociological Interpretation.* Evanston, Ill.: Row, Peterson, 1957.

―――. *TVA and the Grass Roots: A Study in the Sociology of Formal Organization.* Los Angeles: University of California Press, 1949.

Shrode, William A., and Voich, Dan, Jr. *Organization and Management: Basic Systems Concepts* Homewood, Ill.: Richard D. Irwin, 1974.

Simon, Herbert A. *Administrative Behavior.* New York: Macmillan, 1949.

Smith, Darrell H., and Powell, Fred W. *The Coast Guard: Its History, Activities and Organization.* Washington, D.C.: Brookings Institution, 1929.

Steiss, Alan Walter. *Public Budgeting and Management.* Lexington, Mass.: Lexington Books, 1972.

Stobaugh, Robert, and Yergin, Daniel. *Energy Future.* New York: Random House, 1979.

Twiss, Brian. *Managing Technological Innovation.* London: Longman Group, 1974.

Ulmer, S. S., ed. *Introductory Readings in Political Behavior.* Chicago: Rand McNally, 1961.

Uyterhoeven, Hugo E. R.; Ackerman, Robert W.; and Rosenblum, John W. *Strategy and Organization.* Homewood, Ill.: Richard D. Irwin, 1973.

Van Gigch, John P. *Applied General Systems Theory.* New York: Harper and Row, 1974.

Von Bertalanffy, Ludwig. *General Systems Theory.* New York: George Braziller, 1968.

Wenk, Edward, Jr. *The Politics of the Ocean.* Seattle: University of Washington Press, 1972.

Westin, Alan F., ed. *The Uses of Power: Seven Cases in American Politics.* New York: Harcourt, Brace and World, 1962.

White, Michael J. *Management Science in Federal Agencies.* Lexington, Mass.: Lexington Books, 1975.

Wildavsky, Aaron. *The Politics of the Budgetary Process.* 2d ed. Boston: Little, Brown, 1974.

Willoughby, Malcolm F. *U.S. Coast Guard in World War II.* Annapolis, Md.: United States Naval Institute, 1957.

Woll, Peter. *American Bureaucracy.* New York: W. W. Norton, 1963.

Zaleznik, Abraham. *Human Dilemmas of Leadership.* New York: Harper and Row, 1966.

Zaleznik, Abraham, and Kets de Vires, Manfred, F. R. *Power and the Corporate Mind.* Boston: Houghton Mifflin, 1975.

Zannetos, Zenon S. *The Theory of Oil Tankship Rates.* Cambridge: MIT Press, 1966.

Articles, Reports, and Other Publications

Ackoff, Russell L. "Toward a System of Systems Concepts." *Management Science,* vol. 17 (July 1971).

Adelman, M. A. "Is the Oil Shortage Real?" *Foreign Policy,* no. 9 (1972–73).

Aikins, James E. "The Oil Crisis: This Time the Wolf Is Here." *Foreign Affairs,* vol. 51, no. 3 (1973).

Allen, Thomas. "The World. Your Company. A Gate of Information! Who Guards the Gate?" *Innovation,* no. 8 (1969).

Baisuck, A.; Harrald, J.; Leotta, J.; and Wallace, W. A. "The Implementation and International Applications of a National Information System on Marine Pollution." *Proceedings of the Inter-Governmental Maritime Consultative Organization Symposium on Prevention of Marine Pollution from Ships,* Acapulco, Mexico, 22-31 March 1976.

Baker, Russell. "Is Nantucket Expendable?" *New York Times,* 29 December 1976.

Battelle Memorial Institute. "Oil Spillage Study." 1967.

Beman, Lewis. "Betting $20 Billion in the Tanker Game." *Fortune,* vol. 80, no. 20 (1974).

Benford, Harry. "Measures of Merit in Ship Design." *Marine Technology,* vol. 7, no. 4 (1970).

Benkert, W. M. "This Business of Tankers...." *Bulletin,* vol. 39, no. 4 (1977).

Benkert, W. M., and Hill, R. C. "Vessel Traffic Systems." *Bulletin,* vol. 34, no. 7 (1972).

————. "We Must All Go in the Same Direction...." *Bulletin,* vol. 35, no. 4 (1973).

Boulding, Kenneth. "General Systems Theory: The Skeleton of Science." *Management Science,* vol. 3 (April 1956).

Bragaw, Louis K. "Environmental Policy Formulation in Competitive Tanker Markets." *Decision Sciences Northeast Proceedings,* vol. 3 (1974).

Bragaw, Louis K.; Allen, William R.; and Roe, Edward. "The Impact of Environmental Regulation on the Marine Manager." *Proceedings of the American Institute of Decision Sciences,* vol. 8 (1974).

Carter, Jimmy. *A Message to the Congress of the United States on Marine Pollution,* 17 March 1977.

Charnes, A.; Cooper, W. W.; Harrald, J.; Karwan, K. R.; and Wallace, W. A. "A Goal Interval Programming Model for Resource Allocation in a Marine Environmental Program." *Journal of Environmental Economics and Management,* vol. 3 (1976).

Costello, Mary. "No End in Sight for Oil Tanker Accidents." *Editorial Research Reports,* 11 March 1977.

Downs, Anthony. "Up and down with Ecology: The 'Issue-Attention Cycle.'" *Public Interest,* no. 28 (summer 1972).

Ebasco Services, Incorporated. "Study of United States Coast Guard." 1948.

Gilmore, Daniel F. *"Argo* Just One of 874 Liberian Tankers." *Boston Sunday Globe,* 9 January 1977.

Goldhar, Joel D.; Bragaw, Louis K.; and Schwartz, Jules J. "Information Flows, Management Styles, and Technological Innovation." *IEEE Transactions on Engineering Management,* vol. 23, no. 1 (1976).

Hardin, Garrett. "The Tragedy of the Commons." In *Pollution, Resources, and the Environment.* New York: W. W. Norton, 1973.

Hayman, Christopher. "What to Do with All Those Tankers." *New York Sunday Times,* 14 April 1974.

Hill, G. Christian. "Offshore Drilling Plan Stirs Heated Debate: Here Are the Facts." *Wall Street Journal,* 8 September 1975.

Hubbert, M. King. "The Energy Resources of the Earth." *Scientific American,* vol. 224, no. 3 (1971).

Hunt, Raymond G. "Technology and Organization." *Academy of Management Journal,* vol. 13, no. 3 (1970).

Jordan, Leo, and Bragaw, Louis K. "U.S. Coast Guard Offshore Oil Pollution Control Systems." *Offshore Technology Conference Proceedings,* vol. 6, no. 1 (1974).

Lehr, William E. "Marine Oil Pollution Control." *Technology Review,* vol. 75, no. 4 (1973).

Lindblom, Charles E. "The Science of 'Muddling Through.'" *Public Administration Review,* vol. 19 (spring 1959).

Losea, Richard J. "Planning, Programming, and Budgeting for Resource Allocation in the United States Coast Guard." M.S. thesis, Naval Postgraduate School, 1976.

Marcus, Henry S. "The U.S. Superport Controversy." *Technology Review,* vol. 75, no. 5 (1973).

Milgram, Jerome. "Being Prepared for Future *Argo Merchants." Technology Review,* vol. 79, no. 8 (1977).

Moss, James E. "Petroleum: The Problem." In *Impingement of Man on the Oceans,* ed. Donald W. Hood. New York: John Wiley, 1971.

Murray, Michael A. "Comparing Public and Private Management: An Exploratory Essay." *Public Administration Review,* vol. 35, no. 4 (1975).

Newman, Barry. "Pollution of Oceans Is Enormous Threat, but Few People Care." *Wall Street Journal,* 2 October 1973.

Pascuiti, Richard A. "The History of Detachment Mike." *Coast Guard Engineer's Digest,* vol. 19, no. 196 (1977).

Pitts, Robert A. "Strategies and Structures for Diversification." *Academy of Management Journal,* vol. 20, no. 2 (1977).

Porricelli, Joseph D., and Keith, Virgil F. "Tankers and the U.S. Energy Situation: An Economic and Environmental Analysis." *Marine Technology,* vol. 11, no. 4 (1974).

Porricelli, Joseph D.; Keith, Virgil F.; and Storch, R. "Tankers and the Ecology." *Transactions of the Society of Naval Architects and Marine Engineers,* vol. 79 (1971).

Price, Robert I. "Anti-Pollution Measures: IMCO Subcommittee on Ship Design and Equipment." *Marine Technology,* vol. 8, no. 1 (1971).

Roberts, Edward B. "Entrepreneurship and Technology." *Research Management,* vol. 11, no. 4 (1968).

_____. "Generating Effective Corporate Innovation." *Technology Review,* vol. 80, no. 1 (1977).

Robinson, J. L. "Marine Environment and Systems: An Exciting Career Pattern." *Bulletin,* vol. 35, no. 3 (1973).

Rourke, Francis E. "The Politics of Administrative Organization: A Case History." *Journal of Politics,* vol. 19 (August 1957).

Russell, Gary. "The Coast Guard's Personality: A Product of Changing Roles and Missions." *United States Naval Institute Proceedings* 102, no. 3 (1976): 38–45.

Scarborough, Robert H. "Resource Allocation in the Coast Guard." Address given to corps of cadets at the U.S. Coast Guard Academy, 21 February 1976.

Scheibla, Shirley. "Seadock and LOOP: Industry Is Weighing a Crucial Decision on Deepwater Ports." *Barron's,* 4 April 1977.

Schick, Allen. "The Appropriations Committees versus Congress." Paper presented to annual meeting of American Political Science Association, San Francisco, 1976.

Schon, Donald A. "Champions for Radical New Inventions." *Harvard Business Review*, vol. 41, no. 2 (1963).

Thomas, C. W. "Water Pollution Enforcement—1940 Style." *Bulletin*, vol. 35, no. 1 (1973).

Ulman, Neil. "Navigation and the Troubled Tankers." *Wall Street Journal*, 15 February 1977.

Vancil, Richard F. "Strategy Formulation in Complex Organizations." *Sloan Management Review*, vol. 17, no. 2 (1976).

Vancil, Richard F., and Lorange, Peter. "How to Design a Strategic Planning System." *Harvard Business Review*, vol. 54, no. 3 (1976).

———. "Strategic Planning in Diversified Companies." *Harvard Business Review*, vol. 53, no. 1 (1975).

Wallace, S. A. "To Fight to Save: The Environment." *Bulletin*, vol. 36, no. 1 (1974).

Whittemore, L. H. "Men of the Coast Guard Strike Force: They Fight Oil Spills All Over the World." *Parade*, 10 April 1977.

Williams, John D. "Oil-Tanker Fleets Seek to Increase Safety, but the Accident Rate Remains at Ten a Day." *Wall Street Journal*, 15 March 1977.

Wiman, K. G. "Deepwater Ports." *Bulletin*, vol. 37, no. 1 (1975).

Zannetos, Zenon S. "Some Problems and Prospects for Marine Transportation of Oil in the 1970's." In *Energy: Demand Conservation and Institutional Problems*, ed. Michael S. Macrakis. Cambridge: MIT Press, 1974.

Selected Government Reports and Congressional Hearings

Annual Report of the United States Coast Guard, various years.

Cleveland Commission Report. H.R. Doc. no. 670, 62d Cong., 2d sess., 1912.

Third Annual Report of the Council on Environmental Quality. 1972.

U.S. Coast Guard. *Analysis of Budgetary Planning Procedures in Headquarters*. 1 August 1963.

———. *A Study of Cost, Benefits, and Effectiveness of the Merchant Marine Safety Program*. 5 November 1968.

———. *Coast Guard Capital Facilities Briefing*. 1975.

———. *Manual of Budgetary Administration, CG 255*.

———. *Marine Environmental Protection Program: An Analysis of Mission Performance*. Report no. CG-WEP-1-76. Springfield, Va., NTIS, August 1975.

———. *Pilot Study to Develop a Program Budget*. March 1964.

———. *Plan Summaries*. Yearly.

———. *Ports and Waterways Administration and Management*. Washington, D.C.: U.S. Coast Guard, July 1971.

———. *Program Determinations for Fiscal Year 1976*. 4 February 1974.

———. *Register of Commissioned and Warrant Officers and Cadets and Ships and Stations of the U.S. Coast Guard*. Various years.

———. *The Long Range View*. Commandant Note 16014.4. Yearly.

———. *U.S. Coast Guard Planning and Programming Manual* (CG-411). 21 July 1977.

———. *Vessel Traffic Systems Study: Final Report*. Vol. 1. Executive Summary. Washington, D.C.: U.S. Department of Transportation, 1973.

U.S. Congress. House. *Hearings before the Subcommittee on Appropriations on the Coast Guard Appropriation Bill for 1947*. 79th Cong., 2d sess., 19–20 March 1946.

———. *Hearings before the Subcommittee on Appropriations for Treasury and Post Office Departments on the Treasury Department Appropriations Bill for 1948*. 80th Cong., 1st sess., 3–4 February 1947.

———. *Hearings before the Subcommittee on Treasury–Post Office Departments Appropriations for 1958*. 85th Cong., 1st sess., 31 January, 1 February 1957.

———. *Hearings before the subcommittee on Treasury–Post Office Departments Appropriations for 1959*. 85th Cong., 1st sess., 22, 29 January 1958.

———. H.R. Doc. 93–30. *Hearings Before the Subcommittee on Coast Guard and Navigation of the Committee on Merchant Marine and Fisheries on H.R. 13595*. 93rd Cong., 2d sess., 26, 28 March, 25 April 1974.

———. *Hearings before a Subcommittee of the Committee on Appropriations, Department of*

Transportation and Related Agencies Appropriations for 1978. 95th Cong., 1st sess., 21 February 1977.

U.S. Congress. Senate. *Hearings before the Committee on Commerce on Recent Tanker Accidents.* 95th Cong., 1st sess., 11, 12 January 1977.

——. *Hearings before the National Ocean Policy Study, Oil and Gas Development and Coastal Zone Management,* 23, 24, 25 April, 2, 22 May 1974. Serial 93-99.

——. *Study of Roles and Missions of the United States Coast Guard: Report to the Secretary, U.S. Treasury Department.* Vol. 1, June 1962.

U.S. Department of the Interior. *An Analysis of the Economic and Security Aspects of the Trans-Alaska Pipeline.* Vol. 1. Washington, D.C.: U.S. Government Printing Office, 1971.

U.S. Department of Transportation. *Loran-C Conceptual Analysis.* July 1976. Report prepared for National Highway Traffic Safety Administration.

——. *National Plan for Navigation.* 1972.

——. *Refinery–Deepwater Port Location Study.* Washington, D.C.: U.S. Department of Transportation, 1974.

Files

United States Coast Guard files.

INDEX

The Johns Hopkins University Press

This book was composed in VIP Times Roman text and Helvetica Bold display type by The Composing Room of Michigan. It was printed on 50-lb. #66 Eggshell Offset Cream stock and bound by Universal Lithographers, Inc.